'Supriya Vani's book will educate people about gender equality and inspire women to rise up to their potential. It will inspire parents not to clip the wings of their daughters. All our girls are meant for stars, and they need equality and freedom to flourish.'

—**Nobel Peace laureate Malala Yousafzai and her father Ziauddin Yousafzai**

'Supriya Vani's stories of Nobel Peace laureates amount to much more than a sincere tribute to some of the world's most fearless women. By bringing us their voices, their vulnerabilities, their wisdom, she inspires us all to make a difference in the world by tapping into our better selves.'

—**Arianna Huffington, co-founder of The Huffington Post**

'Women have a fundamentally important role to play at the heart of our societies, communities and families. Women, as leaders, have a critical perspective to bring to the table in propelling our societies forward and in the fight against violence and conflict. This impressive book is not only a fitting honour to these sixteen women Nobel Peace laureates, who dedicated their lives, often at great peril and self-sacrifice, to make our world a more peaceful one, but also an inspiration for generations to come. The young girls of the world today and the women of the future are agents of change for a better world. Women cannot progress to greater heights if heinous crimes, as those under the jurisdiction of the International Criminal Court (ICC), are allowed to go unpunished. We must all recognize that violence against women is never allowed, is never normal and will never be tolerated, and that the shame, all too often placed on the victims, must be transferred to its rightful owners: the perpetrators. Until women and men can stand as full equals, our work is not done.'

—**Fatou Bensouda, chief prosecutor at the International Criminal Court**

'Women are underrepresented in public institutions and central decision-making bodies, and still to this present date hold only 25 per cent of positions of this nature. Supriya Vani's book pays tributes to some of the women that forged themselves a path through a patriarchal world, by confronting the social, cultural and political norms, to create a better world for future generations.'

—Najet Zammouri, vice president of Tunisian Human Rights League, which was awarded the Nobel Peace Prize in 2015

'Supriya Vani's book is for everyone across the globe. I am sure it will spur many souls to tread the path of humanitarian service, to choose a life of peace and love.'

—Nobel Peace laureate Tawakkol Karman

'This book will inspire and motivate young people to work for peace.'

—Cherie Blair, British barrister and spouse of former British prime minister Tony Blair

'I recommend this book to the youth. It can inspire them to reach their goals.'

—Nobel Peace laureate Shirin Ebadi

'Supriya Vani rightly highlights the fact that the world needs more women leaders, who are spiritually, mentally and emotionally equipped to bring peace to our planet.'

—Nobel Peace laureate Rigoberta Menchú Tum

'I hope those who read this book will feel inspired to work for disarmament and peace.'

—Nobel Peace laureate Mairead Maguire

'... This book celebrates diversity and will provide inspiration to readers in every continent. By recording the efforts of sixteen Nobel Peace laureates, it showcases their talent and illustrates the benefits societies enjoy when women are allowed to participate fully in them...'

—Rob Wainwright, director of Europol

BATTLING
INJUSTICE

SUPR
and
laurea
a men
The P

Praise for *Battling Injustice*

'Since 1999, Nobel Peace Prize laureates have been gathering to reaffirm their commitment to peaceful means of resolving the world's problems. I admire the contribution of women laureates, their energy and warmth. As shown in this book by Supriya Vani, they give their hearts to our common efforts and to the younger generations that will continue their great work.'

—Mikhail Gorbachev, former president of the Soviet Union and peace activist

'In February of 2017, at the XVI World Summit of Nobel Peace laureates held in Bogotá, I had the happy opportunity to meet with six of my fellow female laureates. They represent the values of courage, determination, generosity and solidarity shared by millions of women around the planet, who strive each day to make a better, freer and more peaceful world. That is why I welcome and cherish this book by Supriya Vani – the stories of all the sixteen women Nobel Peace laureates must be known. They are a source of inspiration for our youth and every one of us.'

—Juan Manuel Santos Calderón, president of Colombia and a Nobel peace laureate

'A monumental effort by a vivacious young woman on the human potential for goodness.'

—Sharon Stone, American actress and human rights activist

'The lives of the women Nobel Peace laureates detailed in this book by Supriya Vani are clear evidence of my belief that women are naturally more sensitive to others' needs and well-being. They have greater potential for expressing love and affection. Therefore, when, as now, compassionate leadership is required, women should take on a greater role in making this world a better place.'

—His Holiness the Dalai Lama

UNITED NATIONS NATIONS UNIES

'Empowered women are the best drivers of growth and the best hope for reconciliation. Today, there are more women who have attained access to education than ever before. More women are leading businesses, governments and global organizations. As women thrive, so will we all. If women are held back, the whole world feels the pain.'

— **UN Secretary General Ban Ki-moon at the opening session of the Commission on the Status of Women, 9 March 2015, New York**

BATTLING INJUSTICE

16 WOMEN NOBEL PEACE LAUREATES

SUPRIYA VANI

HarperCollins *Publishers* India

First published in India in 2017 by
HarperCollins *Publishers* India

Copyright © Supriya Vani 2017

P-ISBN: 978-93-5177-833-2
E-ISBN: 978-93-5177-834-9

2 4 6 8 10 9 7 5 3 1

HarperCollins *Publishers*
A-75, Sector 57, Noida, Uttar Pradesh 201301, India
1 London Bridge Street, London, SE1 9GF, United Kingdom
2 Bloor Street East, Toronto, Ontario M4W 1A8, Canada
Lvl 13, 201 Elizabeth Street (PO Box A565, NSW, 1235),
Sydney NSW 2000, Australia
195 Broadway, New York, NY 10007, USA

Typeset in 11/13.7 Arno Pro Regular at
Manipal Digital Systems, Manipal

Printed and bound at
Thomson Press (India) Ltd

To Nadia Murad, survivor of ISIS sexual slavery, whose courage and perseverance is our best hope against the worst of mankind

CONTENTS

CONTENTS

FOREWORD

O ur society owes its existence to women, for we all once lived
and breathed inside her.

It is my privilege to write this ode to the women who taught
this world the virtues of equity, democracy, peace, tolerance and
non-violence. Walking a road less travelled, these brave-hearts did
not once hesitate and surged ahead till they achieved their goal. I
salute their grit and courage.

However, in spite of the stellar progress made by these women,
gendered violence, inequity, illiteracy and social biases still stare at
the vulnerable. This compilation will give readers a deep dive into
the lives of these extraordinary women, whose lives are a ray of
hope in our battle for world peace. All of us have to come together
and challenge the wrong and stand up tall for the right.

Today the youth are at a crossroads, where they have two paths
to choose from. One is shorter but will come at the cost of human
ethics and values. Another, a longer one, will look less exciting
but will give solace, peace and happiness, not only to themselves
but also to everybody around. It is time the youth took the rein of
social change in their hands.

The adults, as custodians, should instil values in children,
adolescents and the youth that are the truest concoction for
achieving success and shared prosperity.

Through the pages of this book, I call upon everybody to assume their responsibilities with utmost agility and honesty of purpose, and work towards the creation of a world that is happier, safer and more peaceful.

Kailash Satyarthi

PREFACE

Lead us from the Unreal to the Real; lead us from Darkness to Light; lead us from Death to Immortality. Om peace, peace, peace.

These soulful urges from *Brihadaranyaka Upanishad* are not an invocation of the benediction of God but man's innate urge to conquer self and be part of the One, Pure Consciousness. While man strives to reach that state of bliss, he seeks his method from God – in all humility. Socrates says, 'All men's souls are immortal, but the souls of the righteous are immortal and divine.' However, they achieve divinity not through the prayers they make to God but by grooming their spirits with the magical stirrings of the Divine and by cleansing those around them with the Divine they possess.

They take in their warm clasp the low, the neglected, the abandoned, the orphaned. They are pained on finding others in pain. They are aggrieved on finding others in grief. Thus, through empathy and self-abnegation they achieve oneness with all existence – and, therefore, with God.

In this book, I script the sagas of sixteen women, who in their meeting with humanity found self-fulfilment through their unbound love and relentless struggle for peace and justice. Their stories, starting from humble origins, are awe-inspiring yet relatable. I believe we have much to learn about ourselves from these righteous souls; if not anything, how similar we are despite our many differences. Let us keep in mind that the bond of humanity we often invoke are our own shared vulnerabilities. Our salvation – spiritual and worldly – lie in knowing how to overcome them, and I hope the reader will find that *how* while reading the following pages, about some of the most exceptional human beings born of the wheel of time.

MALALA YOUSAFZAI

INCARNATION OF MALALAI OF MAIWAND

'When the whole world is silent
Even one voice becomes powerful.'

The twenty-first century has brought an awakening all over the world. Even in conservative and patriarchal societies which celebrate the birth of sons and lament that of daughters, there is an unmistakable shift in attitudes. Where girls were largely prevailed upon to marry early, bear children and remain confined within the four walls of their homes, there are signs of an increased focus on girls' education. Parents are beginning to recognize the benefits of women's empowerment; they see how through learning, their daughters and their families can prosper. We stand at the dawn of an era of universal education that is truly universal.

Thus, the developments in Swat Valley of Pakistan and parts of Afghanistan in recent years – where girls have been ordered by religious extremists to cease their schooling upon pain of violence or even death – have generated shock and disbelief. The world stands aghast at this regressive, even medieval regime and is rightfully horrified that it has been imposed in the name of piety. That militants in these regions have chosen to cloak their brutality with religious injunctions or fatwas only adds to the outrage across the globe.

At the tender age of fourteen, Malala Yousafzai, the brave child campaigner for girls' education, became internationally famous. Her defiance of the militants was brought to the world stage by a cowardly attempt on her life, which was made simply for her saying that she and her friends should be allowed to go to school. International furore gave way to righteous indignation and widespread concern for her welfare as she battled for life against terrible injuries.

It seems that only Malala's near-ultimate sacrifice has raised the issue of girls' struggle for education in the international consciousness. Previously, her cause had been limited to the odd column buried among more sensational news. While her defiance of the regime of fear of the Taliban had been public in her country for some time, Malala was thrust into the international spotlight in her convalescence. She has become a veritable poster child for girls' education since. Moreover, she has only become more determined since the craven attack against her to further her quest for women's self-empowerment.

Malala's advocacy for girls' education began at the age of eleven, when most had barely crystallized their dreams and rarely chosen their field of accomplishment, and much less had been an inspiration for others. Malala owes much to her father for this. Ziauddin Yousafzai, a poet and school owner, has been a tower of strength for her, and a role model as an educational activist. He encouraged his talented daughter's development and has been a leading proponent of women's empowerment in his own right. It is his groundwork that Malala has built on in taking the issue of women's education to the world.

It must be said that Malala's passion for learning is in her DNA. Her grandfather, Rohul Amin Yousafzai Ziauddin, was a school owner, and he passed his vocation and his vision of an educated youth to his son. The family founded a chain of schools under the name Khushal School; it was in one of these schools in Swat Valley of Pakistan that Malala had studied. She was in ninth standard, in 2012, when tensions with the Taliban culminated in the near-fatal attack on her.

Malala's family story is as much one of perseverance through courage as it is of a quest for the emancipation of women. The Taliban had constantly threatened violence against Malala's family for their public opposition to its edicts. After her father's friend Zahid Khan had been nearly killed by Taliban extremists, it became clear that Malala's father's life was in danger. He refused to change track though, and continued to campaign against the Taliban's push to destroy Swat's educational institutions. He had become somewhat accustomed to the militant's threats and was almost philosophical about the prospect of dying by a terrorist's bullet. Malala also understood that she might be a target for reprisals. But she and her family shrugged off the notion that the Taliban would harm a young girl, as this kind of atrocity was virtually unheard of in Pashtun culture and Islamic tradition. They also understood that, for any sane person of any culture, this conduct would be unthinkable.

However, the unthinkable would occur. On 9 October 2012, Malala was shot by two Taliban assassins in her school bus, as she was travelling home from school. Two of her schoolmates were also injured in the attack. Her injuries were horrific: she had been shot in the head at point-blank range – a clear indication of the Taliban's resolve to kill her. The numerous surgical procedures – and the substantial efforts coordinated across two countries to ensure her survival – do not diminish the miracle of her complete recovery.

The girls' injuries would not be in vain. While Malala's life would hang in the balance for days and her convalescence would last many months, the attention that her plight drew to her cause led to her meteoric rise as an activist and ambassador for universal education. In this regard, Malala's life fits William Shakespeare's aphorism: 'Some are born great, some achieve greatness and some have greatness thrust upon them.'

Malala was born on 12 July 1997 into a stiffly patriarchal society, where a girl's birth was commiserated and a boy's birth an occasion for jubilation. She was one of the few fortunate girls whose births were rejoiced by their fathers: Ziauddin Yousafzai had showered dry fruits, coins and sweets into her cradle, as was the tradition upon the arrival of a boy baby. Malala's father's celebrating Malala's birth in this manner astonished all in the family and even her father's friends. Ziauddin's cousin Jehan Sher Khan Yousafzai was the only one who came to felicitate her father, offering a handsome gift of money to Malala. He had brought with him a family tree beginning with her great-great-grandfather and ending with the name of her father, Ziauddin. Ziauddin wrote 'Malala' below his own name, thereby declaring Malala as the heir to the family's legacy. This is unheard of in conservative and patriarchal societies, particularly in the Pashtun community to which Malala belongs.

Ziauddin and Tor Pekai's young daughter was named after Malalai of Maiwand, the most revered heroine of Afghanistan. When Malala was an infant, her father used to sing a song penned by Rahmat Shah Sayel, the famous Pashtun poet. The expectations of Malala's father of her daughter were well articulated in the last verse of the song:

O Malalai of Maiwand,
Rise once more to make Pashtuns understand the song of honour,
Your poetic words turn worlds around,
I beg you, rise again.

Her father wished the same courageous spirit of Malalai of Maiwand to rise again in Malala, his daughter. He would often sing songs to her, and he cherished his young daughter's development. Something of a dissident in the increasingly narrow-minded society in which he found himself as his family grew, Ziauddin would write poems of secular import and tolerance. Swat Valley had seen a number of faiths: It had been a haven for Buddhism from the second century BC; it had been predominantly Hindu until the invasion of Sultan Mahmud of Ghazni early in the eleventh century, from which time Islam held sway. Malala's father, himself a devout Muslim, wrote the poem 'The Relics of Butkara' about the Butkara Ruins in the Valley, which was once a pilgrimage place for Buddhists. The poem alludes to inter-religious truths, a spiritual oneness throughout the ages in this ageless, picturesque land:

> When the voice of truth rises from minarets,
> The Buddha smiles,
> And the broken chain of history reconnects.

In Malala's father's youth, love marriages were taboo. Malala's father, though, never allowed himself to be bogged down by purposeless convention that restricted one's freedom. He appreciated well that in freedom lies the essence of life. While Malala's mother consented to marry him, the match was opposed by his parents and Tor Pekai's father. By the sheer force of his sincerity and perseverance, Ziauddin prevailed over his parents' reluctance, and his grandfather finally decided to send a barber to her mother's house with a proposal for Malala's mother's hand, as per the local custom. Tor Pekai's father, Malik Janser Khan, refused the proposal. But Ziauddin remained undeterred and continued to make overtures. After snubbing Malala's father for several months, Malik Janser Khan finally relented, and the delighted pair were married.

Malala, the eldest of three children, was thus born with a blessing: her supportive and enlightened – and evidently determined – father. Malala could never have become the confident, insightful and assertive young woman whom we know today without Ziauddin's encouragement and inspiration. He did not clip her wings, as is common in many traditional societies. He let her soar as high as she would, think as deep as she could and take in her grasp as much of the world as she could. Malala's rise from persecuted child human rights campaigner to the youngest, the first Pashtun – and indeed the first Pakistani – recipient of the Nobel Peace Prize evinces the boundless potential within young women. Malala has shown the world what may be achieved with a decent education.

That Malala is a remarkable young woman, of course, is an understatement. Her courage and determination is prodigious, and her passion for the emancipation of repressed women around the world is manifest. It infuses every word when she speaks about girls' education. Perhaps more significant, though, is that Malala has remained genuine and true to herself, to her family and culture, in spite of her horrific experience and her international exposure. Her authenticity, poise and forthrightness is evident to those who view her in the media.

Malala's remaining the very same young Muslim Pashtun woman from Swat Valley, who talks with conviction about people's right to freedom and education, has endeared her to the world. Many would have been broken or deeply scarred by the tribulations she has endured, and others would have spurned their people in the face of the injustice meted out to them. But Malala seems no different from the courageous teenager she was when she spoke with local media and posted blogs before the attack; only now, she is more of a woman than a child, with greater determination and focus.

Malala's unaffected manner and stillness was my first and lasting impression when I spoke with her. She exudes a calm strength, a quality innate of people aspiring to greatness. Her colourful headscarf frames a face that is at once compelling and attractive, and she holds eye contact naturally and in a way that is comforting rather than confronting. Malala talks about herself and her life disarmingly rather than with self-indulgence. She has quite pale skin, but says she would rather have inherited the white skin of her mother than the brownish complexion of her father, which is a closer hue to her own. Her mother, she says, is a white-skinned fairy whom her father seemed to cherish like a fragile china doll.

While she idolized her mother and admired her beauty and her femininity, Malala recognized that being a woman in Swat Valley under the Taliban meant living by strictures that impinged on everyday freedoms. Girls and women in her society could not go out without being accompanied by a male relative, for instance, even if he were only a small child. The expansive freedom she envisioned for herself, however, knew no horizon. She dreamt of scaling the mighty Mount Elum on the wings of support provided by her father, who always said about her, 'Malala will be free as a bird.'

It is ironic that her father wanted Malala to be as free as a bird, as he had been captivated by jihad when he was only twelve years old. A senior Taliban leader had come to his village during the Afghan war. The leader described jihad so gloriously that her father was entranced and he wanted to fight Russian 'infidels' who had occupied Afghanistan. He would pray every night to Allah to create war between Muslims and infidels so that he could die in His service and become a martyr. Her father's captivation by jihad and his later taking up cudgels against the Taliban in Swat Valley offers a study in contrasts. How could a person who himself wanted to be a jihadi later decide to counter the excesses of the jihadi Taliban in Swat Valley? Men such as Ziauddin lead one to suspect that most militants, other than mercenaries, are essentially pious souls who have been indoctrinated by religious fanatics. Malala's father was truly a case in point: He was a pious soul, but when he was indoctrinated by his theology teacher, he was prepared to achieve martyrdom in the cause of jihad.

Nevertheless, Ziauddin renounced violence, and he did so on the basis of scripture. The Quran sanctifies life and condemned the killing of innocents. Malala reminded everyone in her Nobel Prize speech that the Holy Quran says, 'If you kill one person it is as if you have killed the whole humanity.' Killing innocent human beings is, in fact, an act of blasphemy; it is against the will of Allah. And it may very well be that true jihad is opposing the Taliban's repressive campaign against education, for which militants have bombed more than 2,000 schools in Pakistan, including more than 400 in the Swat Valley alone. True jihad may be the striving for the sanctity of human life so that all will have the opportunity to flourish; it may be campaigning for girls' education and their freedom.

At any rate, banning education of girls under the threat of violence is not in consonance with the Holy Quran, which places importance on the acquiring of knowledge: There are several Hadiths where Prophet Muhammad (peace be upon him) enjoins his people to seek knowledge. Perhaps Malala and her father's efforts in championing education for young women are as much religious as secular; Malala and Ziauddin may thus be among the greatest and most courageous jihadists in Pakistan.

And their courage is paramount. Malala hasn't been the only student victim of extremist violence. The Taliban perpetrated among the worst atrocities in recent years when six Taliban fidayeen killed 132 school children and nine teachers of Army Public School in Peshawar on 16 December 2014. That this fiendish attack was carefully orchestrated exhibits the depravity of the organization and makes a mockery of their religious pretensions. Equally, it evinces the heroism of Malala and her father in continuing to stand publicly against them, unbowed by mortal threats.

There are numerous heroes in Malala's culture. Her father has always revered Khushal Khan Khattak, the legendary Pashtun poet who inspired the Pashtun's unity against Mughal domination in the seventeenth century. It was after him that he had named his son Khushal Khan and a school which he started. The war which

Ziauddin has waged, however, is not against any human enemy. His enemy is illiteracy and its progeny, ignorance, and his weapon is not a sword but a sharper and more effective weapon – the *kalam* (pen).

It is hard not to admire Ziauddin's indomitable will, redolent of the traditional Pashtun warrior ethos. His school was devastated some years ago by flash floods, and what was left of the school was entombed in thick, foul-smelling mud. He had already depleted his meagre resources in building the school; this was a veritable calamity for him. But Ziauddin refused to be defeated. His commitment to education and his vision would not be subdued by a mere natural disaster. With great effort, he supervised the rebuilding of his school. This same resolution in the face of adversity has been inherited by his famous daughter.

Adherence to principles is another of Ziauddin's strong suits that Malala has inherited. There is a ceremony called *woma* which is performed on the seventh day after a child's birth in a Pashtun family. Her father could not perform the ceremony for Malala, as he did not have enough money to buy a goat and rice to feed the guests; and Malala's grandfather did not help either. But when the woma celebration of her younger brothers was to be performed and her grandfather offered help, her father refused to accept it, saying her grandfather had not assisted with Malala's woma.

Ziauddin had shown since his youth that he was not one to go with the tide. When Indian-born British author Salman Rushdie was condemned all over the Muslim world for his novel *Satanic Verses*, Ayatollah Khomeini, the supreme leader of Iran, issued a fatwa calling for Rushdie's head. Ziauddin's college held a heated debate on the issue. Ziauddin suggested that the appropriate response to Rushdie's book would be to counter the blasphemy with their own book. 'Islam is not that weak that it can be threatened by a book,' he thundered.

With such an independent-thinking father, it is both unsurprising that Malala would be outspoken and that this would create difficulties for her. In a society in which some traditions patently deny a woman her worth, it is indeed a feat for Malala to have asserted her individuality. In Swat Valley, a woman may be given away as *swara*, a gift to one disaffected party to resolve a dispute with another. Once, a widower married a widow without the permission of her family. The issue was taken up by a jirga (a traditional assembly or court of local elders), which punished the widower's family by directing that their most beautiful girl be married to a boy with poor prospects from the widow's clan. Such outrageous, sexist edicts were common. Malala felt threatened, at times, by such bizarre persecution of women.

She was yet to know the worst. The Taliban under the leadership of Mullah Omar had taken control of Afghanistan and demolished and burnt girls' schools. Even US military intervention could not break their hold on parts of the country. They forced men to grow long beards and women to wear burqas. Malala saw the burqa as a cumbersome garment; it felt to her like an oven on hot days. The Taliban's fiats were devised to squeeze the life out of women. It banned laughing loudly, wearing white shoes and varnishing nails. Women were beaten up on any indication of defiance. It sent shivers down Malala's spine, but she felt comforted by the fact that in their country, girls could still go to school. Little did she know that the Taliban were about to assert their dominance over Swat Valley's women too. Nonetheless, she felt inspired by books like Leo Tolstoy's novel *Anna Karenina* and the novels of Jane Austen, and Malala banked upon her father's assurance: 'I will protect your freedom, Malala. Carry on with your dreams.'

Malala's father was not only a doting parent but also a guide. When Malala was a young child, she stole toy jewellery from her school friend Safina in retaliation for Safina's having stolen her toy mobile phone. But when she was caught she felt miserable; it was unbearable for her to fall in the estimation of her father. Her father, though, did not punish her unduly. He did not allow her self-esteem to be shattered by this childish error. He told Malala that great men had committed mistakes in their childhood, and quoted the revelatory words of Mahatma Gandhi: 'Freedom is not worth having if it does not include the freedom to make mistakes.' He hung a framed copy of a letter purportedly written by Abraham Lincoln to his son's teacher, asking the teacher to guide his son. The letter asks his son be shown that it is far more honourable to fail than cheat, but also entreats the teacher to spare him some time so he may ponder the eternal mysteries of nature.

Malala's enlightened father's expectations were not of the kind that crushes a child's individuality or will, but that would surely drive the young girl to extend herself. She would run errands for her elders whenever she was asked so that her father would not be disappointed in her that his daughter failed to help someone in need. Once she was asked by a neighbour to buy some maize. On the way, Malala was hit by a passing bicycle and her shoulder pained terribly. But she withheld her tears until she delivered the maize and cried only when she reached her home. Once, in a competition she was determined to win, she lost to her friend Moniba. But she took that in her stride, just as her father had instructed her.

As Malala grew, the Taliban's hold on Swat Valley became more overt, bolder. Prominent dissenters – or even those whose way of life was not to the liking of the Taliban's medieval vision – were increasingly targeted. It was perhaps inevitable that militants would train their sights on Ziauddin, and not merely on his school. Malala's father was not one to bend to dogmatic authority, however; this and his secular thinking only increased the Taliban's hostility towards him as he spoke openly against the Taliban's policies.

Ziauddin regretted so many things that prevailed in Pakistan at the time, and in his own way became an activist against the repression that he saw closing in on his people. He felt that the statement of Jinnah, the father of Pakistan, to the Constituent Assembly should have been adopted as a guiding principle of governance in the nation: 'You are free to go to your temples, you are free to go to your mosques or to any other place of worship in this State of Pakistan. You may belong to any religion or caste or creed – that has nothing to do with the business of the State.' To this day, Malala's father expresses his anguish over the persecution in the country of more than two million Christians and a similar number of Ahmadis, and the sharp divisions among the various sects and sub-denominations of Muslims. Ziauddin opines that the three wars fought against India since Pakistan's creation – and the endless waves of sectarian bloodletting within the country itself – have brought nothing but misery to the people.

It was in the middle of the last decade that extremists first made their presence felt in Swat Valley. Their arrival could not have been more ominous. The firebrand cleric Maulana Fazlullah's entry in Imam Deri, a small village near Mingora town, foretold no less a disaster than the earthquake that shook the Valley not long afterwards. Maulana Fazlullah, who would become the Pakistani Taliban leader in 2007, set up an unauthorized radio station in Mingora, which operated unchallenged by the government authorities.

The earthquake of 8 October 2005 caused widespread devastation, claiming 73,000 lives and rendering some 128,000 injured and about three million homeless. Initially, the extremists supported relief efforts after the disaster, helping the traumatized populace rebuild their lives. Maulana Fazlullah projected himself as an Islamic reformer, and his popularity among the uneducated, disaffected poor people of the Valley grew. He exhorted people to abandon bad practices and cultivate good habits. He asked men to grow beards and eschew smoking and taking heroin and hashish. He instructed people on how to perform their religious rituals, and he would cry while speaking of his faith, extravagantly expressing his love for Islam. But as with the Afghan Taliban, Maulana Fazlullah's dictatorial tendencies and repressive social agenda could not remain masked by his show of false piety.

Like most despots, Fazlullah wanted to establish his hold over the people of Swat Valley, and he would do so with the instrument of a narrow and sometimes patently false interpretation of Islam. Exploiting the people's ignorance, he interpreted the Quran in a manner that suited him and his ambitions. He declared that sinful acts were the cause of natural calamities like earthquakes. His men thus ordered people to stop listening to music, cease watching movies and shun dancing. Shortly thereafter, CD and DVD shops were forcibly closed, and Fazlullah's men collected televisions, DVDs and CDs from people and then burnt huge heaps of electronic gadgets on the streets. Initially, the Taliban paid shop owners due compensation, but later they simply bombed those music shops that dared to remain. All music except Taliban songs was declared haram.

The Maulana's growing dominance in Swat Valley – or rather, the effect his dominance was having on its people – greatly distressed Malala's father. Ziauddin knew that Fazlullah was a school dropout and was only fostering ignorance. In Fazlullah's popular radio show every evening, he would announce the names of the people who had eschewed smoking or hashish and would congratulate them on having ceased being sinful. He would say that such people would have their reward in the life hereafter. Maulana would also criticize the Pakistani government for having failed to introduce shariat law. He was opposed to the feudal system and would declare that Khans would face retribution. Fazlullah's broadcasts, however, were particularly focused on women, whom he advised to stay veiled and remain confined to their homes. His men would display the fancy clothes of women they looted from the homes of notables.

Several women made offerings of gold jewellery and money in the hope that it would please Allah. With the support of the people, Fazlullah began constructing his headquarters, a large, two-storey madrasa in Imam Deri village. Fazlullah's growing influence would soon be felt by Malala's father. His Urdu teacher Roshan Ali once demanded leave for constructing Fazlullah's buildings. Fazlullah issued a call for girls to withdraw from schools, and many responded. In his evening radio show, the names of girls who had quit schools were announced, and they were congratulated for doing so.

Ziauddin was deeply aggrieved by this turn of events. Fazlullah issued fresh edicts virtually every day. There were few voices of protest in the valley apart from those of Ziauddin and a few of his friends. Beauty parlours were ordered closed and men were asked to abjure shaving. Fazlullah's men even started a campaign against polio drops, declaring that shariat does not approve of curing a disease before it besets anyone. Their diktat was followed religiously, and not a single child took the vaccine in the areas where Fazlullah had established his dominance.

But merely dictating the lifestyles for the residents of Swat was not enough for Maulana Fazlullah. The religious fanatics' holy grail is presiding over their own justice system, with which they can dispense their bigotry with a semblance of legitimacy. Fazlullah's men thus started holding *shura*, a local court without the approval of state law – in simple terms, a kangaroo court run by extremists. Quick decisions were pronounced. Some decisions were well received, but soon they resorted to imposing corporal punishment, and sinners were publicly whipped. With a trademark sense of drama, Fazlullah, with his long locks and chin curtain beard, would sometimes appear astride a white horse at these public floggings.

Wherever religious hardliners have imposed shariat – be it in Saudi Arabia, Iran, Afghanistan or Pakistan – a morality police is formed to enforce decrees on matters ranging from personal conduct to dress codes and more serious matters. The Taliban morality police in Swat Valley was called the Falcon Commandos, and they operated with impunity. The provincial government in Swat was largely run by parties sympathetic to the extremists, who in any case dared not criticize anyone who committed atrocities in the name of Islam. It was certain that they would ask Malala's father to close his school.

One morning, the Taliban pasted a letter on the gate of Ziauddin's school, which read, 'Mr Principal, the school you are running is Western and infidel. You teach girls and have a uniform that is un-Islamic. Stop this, or you will be in trouble, and your children will weep and cry for you – Fedayeen of Islam.' Ziauddin, encouraged by his friend Hidayatullah, disseminated an open letter to the Fedayeen of Islam in the *Daily Azadi*, a local newspaper, in which he wrote: 'Please don't harm my children, because the God you believe in is the same God they pray to every day. You can take my life, but please don't kill my schoolchildren.' The newspaper published Malala's father's name and also the name of his school, which made Ziauddin somewhat jittery, but he received immense support from some quarters. Many came to congratulate him for having bravely engaged with the Taliban, and declared that they too would pluck up the courage to speak.

Around this time, there were a number of other groups that were persecuting people in the name of shariat. Taliban leaders eventually formed a united front under the name Tehrik-i-Taliban–Pakistan, or the Pakistani Taliban, and chose Baitullah Mehsud as their leader. Fazlullah was given charge of Swat Valley. The Pakistani Taliban started indiscriminately targeting whomsoever they thought had violated Islamic norms, e.g., women without purdah or men shaving or wearing shalwar-kameez (traditional dress) in inappropriate dimensions. It was in this uneasy time that Benazir Bhutto, former prime minister of Pakistan, was assassinated. Fear stalked ordinary people throughout the country.

The zeitgeist of oppressive conservatism and the haunting spectre of violence in Pakistan was bound to affect the impressionable minds of the nation's young children. Malala was no exception. While some of her classmates wanted to be doctors, she thought of being an inventor who would devise an anti-Taliban machine that could destroy the Taliban's arsenal. But the Taliban held sway over the entire Swat Valley and acted as a de facto government. They started blasting the region's schools at night, razing them to rubble. These attacks became more frequent each day. The situation had degenerated to such a state of lawlessness that in February 2008, a deputy superintendent of police, Javid Iqbal, was killed in a suicide bombing along with three constables. His funeral was similarly attacked hours later, killing more than fifty-five mourners, including the officer's young son. Ten of Malala's friend Moniba's family members were either killed or seriously injured.

Swat Valley's moderate citizens were outraged by the Taliban's actions but were numbed by fear of the Taliban. Ziauddin, his friends and a few notables of Swat, however, created a Qaumi Jirga (local private body) with a view to challenging Fazlullah. A few eminent people of Swat joined the Qaumi Jirga, and since Malala's father was neither an elderly person nor a Khan, he was chosen as the spokesperson of the Jirga. He was respected for his wisdom and had demonstrated his courage on several occasions earlier, and had garnered much respect for confronting Fazlullah in the local newspaper. He was also well versed in Urdu and English and could communicate effectively. Malala's father said that those who want peace must swear by truth and speak nothing but the truth, as it is truth alone that can demolish fear.

That Malala had inherited her father's fearlessness was for all to see when she made a public stand for girl's education. Ziauddin's friend Abdul Hai Kakar, a BBC radio correspondent, telephoned him and asked him to suggest a female teacher or a schoolgirl for writing a diary for a blog on life under the Taliban in Swat. Abdul Hai Kakar envisaged a diary in the tradition of that of Anne Frank, an ill-fated Jewish girl who had kept a diary about her life under the shadow of death during World War II. No teacher was prepared to risk his welfare for this. One brave tenth-standard girl Aysha volunteered and made one entry, but the following day her father informed Ziauddin that his daughter would not continue this perilous task. The duty of representing the oppressed girls of Swat Valley thus fell to Malala, who was now just eleven years of age.

With a view to hiding her identity from the Taliban, Malala was given the pseudonym Gul Makai, and she began writing the BBC blog. The first entry she made in her diary was dated 3 January 2009 under the title 'I Am Afraid'. She recorded her personal feelings and everyday life under the terror of the Taliban. She lamented that the girls had to wear plain clothes instead of the erstwhile royal blue school uniform and that they had to hide school books, wrapping them in shawls. One diary note was written, under the title 'Do Not Wear Colourful Clothes'. In this note, she recorded that she was about to wear her uniform when she remembered the advice of her principal and decided instead to wear her favourite pink dress. On another occasion, the diary note discussed the burqa. Malala was overjoyed to see her words on the website.

At her school, the pupils started talking about the diary. The desire to be identified as the author was overpowering her, but Malala could ill afford to ignore the BBC correspondent's advice to stay incognito. The diary was being widely read. Extracts of the diary were printed by some newspapers. The BBC had even made a recording in the voice of another girl. Malala felt satisfied that the words which came from her pen could vanquish the whole of the Taliban's arsenal.

Malala had faith that Allah would help her in her campaign for girls' education, and her faith bolstered her resolve. She began to give interviews to the media. She appeared on local and national television, including Geo TV, one of the most popular news channels in Pakistan. Upon finding that she was so forthright and articulate in her answers on the rights of girls, many people came forward to support her, including local journalists who had not dared to voice their opinions in public. Journalists gave her a powerful forum to issue counters to the Pakistani Taliban's propaganda.

Once, she appeared with her father on a BBC Urdu talk show which was hosted by the well-known columnist Wasatullah Khan. Malala and Ziauddin were to counter an arch-conservative's pre-recorded pronouncements on the issue of women's rights. With her characteristically outspoken manner, Malala immediately asserted, 'How dare the Taliban take away my basic right to education?' There could be no response from her opposite, and it is doubtful if he could have mounted a successful defence had he been in the studio, anyway. Such a bold question instantly demolished the perception that the Taliban's authority was unassailable: here was a young girl, a devout Muslim, bluntly admonishing the extremists for their conduct.

The interview emboldened some to confront the Taliban, at least verbally. Malala was congratulated by many people. Nonetheless, Malala would not be swayed by the jubilant mood in the aftermath of her interview, as she and her father understood the magnitude of the struggle ahead. In any event, the Taliban did not stop blowing up schools. On the night of 7 October 2008, Sangota Convent School and the Excelsior College for boys were razed down by improvised explosive device (IED) attacks. Malala's father was mortified, but perhaps more crushing was the looting of the broken furniture, the books and the computers that remained after the blasts.

The reasons the Taliban proffered for their grand acts of depraved vandalism were that Sangota Convent School was a school for the propagation of Christianity and that Excelsior College was co-educational. Her father denounced the Taliban's claims the very next day in a live interview on the Voice of America. He pointed out that since Sangota School's establishment in 1962 there had been no reported case of conversion; and Excelsior College had co-education classes only at the primary levels. Malala's father passionately campaigned for the reconstruction of both the institutes. At times, he would be almost overcome with emotion on the issue of girls' education. Once, he lifted a girl from an audience he was addressing and implored, 'This girl is our future. Do we want her to be ignorant?' The crowd responded, rising up in defiance and declaring that they would sacrifice themselves for the sake of their daughters' education.

But all this public remonstration did little to sway the Taliban. Indeed, their bitter obduracy hardened and their campaign against girls' education intensified with the public opposition. They announced a deadline: No girl, they declared, should go to school after 15 January 2009. Malala's response was: 'How can they stop us from going to school? They say they will destroy the mountain but they can't even control the road.' Many other girls were less confident. They felt that none had been able to stop the Taliban's destroying schools – around 400 schools had already been bombed and reduced to rubble by the Taliban – and only by risking life and limb could one defy the extremists' fiat.

Shortly before the deadline expired, the Taliban made their presence felt with a brutal murder. Shabana was a traditional dancer and singer and taught young dancers her skills. She had defied the Taliban's ban on dancing and teaching and had ignored their warnings to her. On 2 January 2009, militants knocked at her door in Banr Bazaar at around 9 p.m. They demanded that she dance for them. She went to her room to change into her dancing costume. When she returned, they threatened to slit her throat. She begged for her life. Despite her heart-rending plea to spare her as a woman and Muslim and her desperate assurances that she would never dance again in her life, the assailants dragged her at gunpoint to Green Chowk and shot her dead. They strewed money, photographs and CDs of her performances over her bullet-ridden body. The Chowk came to be known as Bloody Square, as the bodies of many such victims of the Taliban's savagery would be dumped there, as a warning to all who would defy them.

Some days after Shabana's murder, a teacher was shot dead after refusing to pull his shalwar above his ankles in the manner of the Taliban. His cogent argument that nowhere in Islamic texts is it stated that the wearing of a shalwar above the ankles is required perhaps sealed his fate. While all these disturbing events were straining the nerve of Malala and her father, the worst was still in store for them. After some days, one Shah Douran announced on Mullah FM that Ziauddin was on the Taliban's hit list.

There was no saviour in sight. The government appeared to have abrogated its responsibility for protecting people from the Taliban's depraved violence. The local administration – and even the army – was behaving as if it were unaware of the Taliban's murderous activities. The deputy commissioner of Mingora, Syed Javid, had begun to attend Taliban meetings and even, at times, to lead them. He refused to meet those who would come to seek his help against the Taliban's threats. Once, Malala's father dared to question the deputy commissioner as to whose order he would obey – Fazlullah's or that of the government. People had lost their hope. Moreover, they seemed to have abandoned their Pashtun values and the qualities which Islam had imbued in them. Malala, and her father Ziauddin, and a few of his friends stood in glorious isolation; but they were determined not to capitulate.

With the deadline of 15 January 2009 approaching fast, Malala and her father resolved to keep Khushal School's bell ringing – even if it remained the only school functioning on the last day before the deadline. Malala spoke on radio and television as many times as she could to protest against the Taliban's farman. She declared, 'They can stop us going to school, but they can't stop us learning.' She posed very pertinent questions to the Taliban. She asked if girls are not to go to school, from where will they find lady doctors? When they ordain that women should only be treated by lady doctors, how can there be lady teachers for girls aspiring to be doctors if there were to be no schools for girls?

Malala became more and more impassioned in her attacks on the Taliban. She questioned why the Taliban had destroyed five more schools after the deadline when no school was open for girls. She did not spare even the Pakistani army, which she felt was least interested in controlling the Taliban's lawlessness. Even more than the civil and military establishment's abrogation of their responsibility to the people of Swat, she regretted the people's thronging to witness the floggings announced on Mullah FM.

On 16 February 2009, the government reached an agreement with the Taliban, whereby the government agreed to impose shariat law in the whole of Swat Valley in return for the militants ceasing hostilities. From the government perspective, the truce had two purposes: first, to bring peace to Swat Valley; and second, to expose the Taliban's demand for peaceful shariat law. Malala and her father welcomed this development, as girls were permitted to go to school – albeit well veiled.

The Taliban, however, could not be so easily contained, and the agreement proved a disappointment for anyone who saw in it any hope of the return of peace and normalcy in the Valley. Militants captured the nearby Buner district only 100 kilometres away from the country's capital, Islamabad. The federal government dithered and appeared to deny the gravity of the situation until Hillary Clinton, the US Secretary of State, said, 'I think the Pakistani government is abdicating to the Taliban and the extremists.' The Taliban had become bolder; the agreement had only conferred upon it a form of recognition, bolstering its morale.

Needless to say that the Taliban had usurped the role of the state at gunpoint. Each night, they embarked on a flag march on the roads with guns and sticks, as if the task of maintaining law and order were thrust upon them. Many pinned their hopes on a meeting which was to be addressed by Sufi Mohammad on 20 April 2009. A crowd of about 40,000 people assembled to hear him; many were common citizens and others Taliban supporters. Some of the latter sang jihadi songs. Sufi Mohammad's speech confirmed the worst fears of the moderate and progressive Muslim citizens of Pakistan. He called for the stamping out of democracy in the country and claimed that Western democracy had been imposed upon Pakistan by the infidels. He stunned everyone when he announced, 'Now wait, we are coming to Islamabad.'

The fear that stalked Swat Valley now loomed large all over Pakistan, especially Islamabad, the nation's capital. That Pakistan's former prime minister Benazir Bhutto had been brazenly assassinated in Islamabad less than two years earlier only heightened the fear that extremists could take control at the nation's centre. It was only when America threatened to withhold billions of dollars in aid and issued thinly veiled warnings of drone attacks that the government decided to act. It announced the launching of Operation Rah-e-Rast (true path) to eliminate the Taliban in Swat.

The military operation brought upheaval rarely seen in countries ostensibly at peace, and Malala's family were affected as much as anyone. The authorities announced over megaphones that all residents of Mingora should leave. Her father resisted, until her mother issued the ultimatum that she would leave with their children should he decide to remain in Swat. She knew her husband would not let her leave unprotected, and Ziauddin thus had to capitulate. On 5 May 2009, this courageous family joined the ranks of internally displaced persons (IDPs), which Malala felt sounded like some infectious disease. The streets were jammed with people in their cars, rickshaws, mule carts and trucks, stuffed with their belongings, rushing out of Swat before the impending firefight.

This marked the biggest exodus of Pashtuns from their own land, with some two million fleeing their homes. There was some element of farce in the process, as people encountered both government and Taliban checkpoints as they left the Valley. It appeared that the military were still barely taking cognizance of the Taliban's presence, mere days before launching a concerted assault on the Taliban.

Malala's family finally reached Mardan city from Mingora, leaving Swat behind. The journey is a little more than 100 kilometres, but with roads choked with refugees, this distance was a major trek. In Mardan, massive camps of tents had been established to accommodate those who had fled Swat. Staying in those hastily arranged and unsanitary tent cities, though, was fraught with the danger of outbreaks of diseases like cholera. It was here that the renowned hospitality of the Pashtun people shined. Somewhere in the order of three quarters of the IDPs were accommodated by the residents of the districts of Mardan, Swabi, Nowshera, Charsada and Peshawar – in their homes. In Pashtun culture, women do not mix with men who are not related, and with a view to ensuring the sanctity of this tradition, most of the men of the host households slept away from their own homes. They became voluntary IDPs, thus demonstrating a glorious example of voluntary sacrifice in a time of need.

Malala's family had no relative in Mardan and planned to travel to Shangla, their family village. Despite Tor Pekai's insistence, her father did not accompany them to Shangla, as he wanted to inform the people of Peshawar and Islamabad about the terrible conditions in the camps and the military's neglect of its responsibilities. Malala and her family stayed at Karshat, her mother's village, and after a few days they became settled there. Malala enjoyed there the company of Sumbul, her cousin, who is one year her senior. Sumbul was studying in class seven, and Malala was admitted to class seven so that they could study together.

One day, there was a prize-giving ceremony in the school. The boys made speeches in the main hall, while the girls were allowed to speak from a microphone in their classroom, with their voices relayed to the main hall. Malala was by this time given to public speaking, so she chose to speak in the hall itself as the boys did. She recited a poem penned in praise of Prophet Muhammad (peace be upon him). She also read a poem that emphasized the importance of hard work in achieving the heart's desire: 'A diamond must be cut many times before it yields even a tiny jewel.' She then spoke of her namesake Malalai of Maiwand whose oratory had fired the spirit of her countrymen to defeat the British forces in battle in 1880.

While still not yet a teenager, Malala was uniformly impressive, and her speech mesmerized the audience; but some were more than a little concerned that she was not wearing a veil. She was unruffled by such matters though. Her maturity and poise in conversing with those in power belied her age. Ambassador Richard Holbrooke, the American envoy to Pakistan and Afghanistan, was in a meeting in Serena Hotel discussing the plight of IDPs and the Taliban's expulsion from Swat. Delegations from Swat and FATA (Federally Administered Tribal Areas) visited the hotel to meet with him, and Malala and her father were among them. Holbrooke was a man of hope and had been credited with bringing peace to Bosnia in the late 1990s. Malala sat close to the ambassador. Taken by her keenness, he asked her how old she was. 'I am twelve,' she replied, and added, 'I request you, please help us girls to get an education.' He laughed and informed Malala that America was doing much for Pakistan, but Pakistan had many problems which he suggested were of its own making.

The army eventually announced that Swat Valley was free of the Taliban, but the fate of Fazlullah was not known. The army asked the IDPs to return to their homes. Many, however, were sceptical that there would be abiding peace, as they thought Fazlullah would soon return and again take over the Valley. Nonetheless, people returned, and on 1 August 2009, the school bell at the

Khushal Public School rang again. Malala was overjoyed. Her joy was short-lived though. There were unmistakable signs that the Taliban had not really surrendered Swat; much of their forces had simply melted over the Afghan border, allowing them to return when the fighting ceased. Two more schools were attacked. Three members of a Christian group were kidnapped and murdered when they returned to their base in Mingora, and the Taliban were still openly operating in districts adjacent to Swat. The most compelling proof of their presence in the region came when two Taliban militants burst into the office of Dr Mohammad Farooq, the vice chancellor of Swat University, and viciously murdered him. Dr Farooq had earlier issued a fatwa against suicide bombing and was a well-known critic of the Taliban.

This event convinced Malala and her family that neither the army nor the politicians were sincere about keeping Swat Valley free of the Taliban. President Asif Ali Zardari fiddled while Rome burnt: as Pakistan was descending into chaos he found time for a holiday at his château in France. Malala resolved that she had to be a politician herself one day to lift the country from the morass into which its political leadership and army had plunged it.

While the Taliban were still active in the Valley, Pakistan's military was making tall claims of heroism in its operation. A prime-time television soap opera carried stories of the military's valour while fighting the Taliban in Swat under the title: 'Beyond the Call of Duty'. The show featured real-life stories of soldiers fighting militants in Swat. Doubtless, the army had blunted the Taliban's vigour, but the ground situation was still very grim. Hundreds of men had been reported missing, and inquiries about their whereabouts were being answered by no one. Malala's house was frequented by many people seeking to know the fate or whereabouts of their loved ones, as her father was the spokesman for the Swat Qaumi Jirga and had been liaising with the army.

Another scourge that remained was the Blasphemy Ordinance, which had been enacted under General Zia, Pakistan's military ruler from 1977 to 1988. The world was shaken when in November 2010, a Christian woman called Asiya Bibi was sentenced to death by hanging for purported blasphemy. Asiya Bibi was a farm labourer working in a predominantly Muslim workforce and was subjected to continual efforts to convert her to Islam. She brought water for her fellow workers after they had harvested berries one day in June 2009, but some refused to accept the water because it was offered by a Christian, which they maintained rendered it unclean. This led to an argument, during which she was castigated for her beliefs by her co-workers. She retorted that Christ had sacrificed himself on the Cross for the sins of Christians and asked what Prophet Muhammad (peace be upon him) had done for Muslims. This statement was the basis of charges of blasphemy against her.

The matter made its way to the court and she was sentenced to death under the blasphemy law. The sentence sparked worldwide outrage, in contrast to the relative silence of saner voices within Pakistan. Extremists, however, were vociferous in the demand for Asiya to be executed. Indeed, the fate of those who criticized the proceedings against Asiya Bibi served as a grisly warning to others holding similar views. The governor of Punjab, Salmaan Taseer, who had petitioned President Zardari to pardon her and publicly described the blasphemy law as a 'black law', was gunned down by his own bodyguard on 4 January 2011. His fanatical assailant, smirking conspicuously, was led away from the scene of his crime in handcuffs by the police. He claimed to have committed this cold-blooded murder for Allah. Minority Affairs Minister Shahbaz Bhatti, who had also lent his support to Asiya Bibi, was slain by gunmen in an ambush on his car less than two months later, on 2 March 2011.

For Malala and her father and others of their ilk, the response of extremist elements to these killings was almost as distressing as the brutal assassinations themselves. Salmaan Taseer's killer was lionized. When he was presented before a court in Islamabad, he was showered with rose petals and cheered by a crowd of thousands, including lawyers from Islamabad and Rawalpindi. Moreover, the local imam refused to recite Salmaan Taseer's funeral prayers, and the country's president was conspicuously absent from the governor's funeral. It seemed the country itself was hostage to extremism. And the Pakistani government seemed loathe to confront its home-grown terrorists; moderate, law-abiding citizens lived in fear, while militants were open and unabashed in their lawlessness.

A rude awakening for Pakistan's authorities came in the form of a brief American incursion into Pakistan a few months after the killings. In a well-planned and daringly executed commando raid on 2 May 2011, US Navy Seals killed Osama Bin Laden at his residence in Abbottabad, less than a kilometre from Pakistan's military academy. This audacious operation stunned Pakistan. Malala's father described it a shameful day. Indignation at this breach of the country's territorial sovereignty gave way to intense humiliation for Pakistan's leadership, particularly that of the military. The unabashed American military operation – conducted without prior knowledge, much less approval of senior Pakistani authorities – exemplified US willingness to tackle terrorism within Pakistan.

The Pakistani establishment would change track, at least publicly, in the wake of the US raid in Abbottabad. Perhaps as part of a face-saving exercise, government figures decided to honour Malala and her father for the fortitude with which they had opposed the Taliban. The chief minister of Punjab Shehbaz Sharif invited Malala to speak in Lahore at an event organized to promote education. A cheque for half a million rupees was presented to her there for her work in campaigning for girls' rights and their education. She spoke of how she and her father had defied the Taliban's edicts and carried on their campaign for girls' education.

Pakistan's first Malala National Youth Peace Prize was also conferred on Malala. This award was instituted with a view to honouring her in perpetuity, and the ceremony took place at the prime minister's official residence. She began to collect considerable sums of money. Five hundred thousand rupees each from the prime minister, the chief minister of Punjab, the chief minister of Sind and also from the chief minister of her own province, Khyber Pakhtunkhwa; but this enrichment did not cause her to lose sight of her goals. She presented the prime minister with a list of requests for furthering girls' education, which included the rebuilding of schools that had been destroyed by the Taliban and the establishment of a women's university in Swat.

The Taliban began to make its presence felt in Swat Valley again; and militants marked their resurgence with threats and murder. In June 2012, a Pakistan Muslim League–Nawaz (PML–N) activist in Swat Valley and owner of the Swat Continental Hotel, Afzal Khan, was killed in an ambush as he left his home. Afzal Khan had stood up to Fazlullah in previous years, and he paid with his life for his courage. Malala and her family were rocked when Zahid Khan, Malala's father's close friend, was shot at point-blank range, in the face, as he went for the last prayers of the day at a mosque near his home.

Both Zahid Khan and Malala's father were on the Taliban's hit list, and no one knew which of them would be the first to fall victim to an extremist attack. Malala's family begged Ziauddin not to visit the hospital where Zahid Khan had been admitted, as they suspected that the Taliban may be waiting in ambush, but he said that it would be cowardly not to go. He went to the hospital and stayed there until quite late in the night, despite the grave threat to his life and everyone's exhorting him to leave. He returned home only after Zahid Khan had been shifted to Peshawar for an operation. His friend Hidayatullah impressed upon Ziauddin the real threat he faced when he told him that the Taliban was killing members of the Qaumi Jirga one by one and he, being the spokesman of the Jirga, could not be spared by the Taliban.

It became clear to Malala's father that the Taliban would hunt him down and kill him, but still he chose to refuse security from the police. His motive was pragmatic, if not heroic. He reasoned that if he was protected by security, the Taliban would attack him with Kalashnikovs or suicide bombers – significant force which would perhaps kill many other people – and if he refused security, he alone would be killed. But little did her father know that it was Malala who was fated to be attacked by the Taliban.

Evidently, the family underestimated the dangers Malala faced. She had received threats in the form of Facebook messages and notes slid under the front door of the family home. But Ziauddin saw these more as bluster, attempts to intimidate than statements of intent. In hindsight, it is easy to see his error. But Ziauddin figured that he was much more likely to suffer the Taliban's violence. After all, why would a devout Muslim consider murdering a child? Malala's family had made some changes in her routine for her safety, however. While she enjoyed walking home, her mother had told her she should take the bus, as it would be safer for her.

The school bus is a rudimentary vehicle, with two laterally facing steel benches for seats, and is boarded from the rear. On

9 October 2012, Malala and her friends spilled from the school gates in their usual high spirits and into the bus for their trip home from school. Malala had just completed a Pakistan studies exam, and she felt the exam had gone very well. The bus turned in the direction of Malala's home, slowing to negotiate a bend on a deserted stretch of the road.

Two young men who were unknown to the schoolgirls – and who were perhaps still students themselves – signalled to the driver to stop. As the minibus came to a halt, one of them approached the rear of the vehicle and shouted: 'Which one of you is Malala?' Though none of the girls accompanying Malala spoke a word, their reflexive glances towards her betrayed her identity to the assailant. The young man aimed at Malala and fired three rounds from his pistol. One bullet hit Malala above the socket of her left eye and became embedded in the base of her skull, near her spine. Malala slumped on Moniba, her best friend's lap, critically wounded. Her friends Shazia and Kainat were hit by the other two rounds. The driver of the school bus, Usman Bhai Jan, immediately sped off, rushing the injured girls to Swat Central Hospital. Malala was bleeding from her head and ear as Moniba nursed her. The whole passenger compartment of the bus seemed to be awash with the blood of these innocents.

Ziauddin was addressing a gathering of 400 school principals from all schools of Swat Valley when he heard the news that Malala had been shot and was critically injured. He immediately rushed to be by her side. The hospital was crowded with photographers and television cameras, and Ziauddin had to jostle his way through to Malala, who was lying on a trolley. Malala's father's whole world lay in Malala and Malala's world lay in her father's. The duo were a formidable combination; that the Taliban would resort to such a cowardly act as killing a young girl was testimony to their effectiveness in countering the Taliban's power. The Taliban had the measure of the civil administration, the political class and even managed to evade military reprisal; but this schoolgirl and her father had seemed beyond their reach. Now, with the Taliban's latest atrocity Malala's father's worst fears were realized; and he didn't know if his beloved daughter would emerge from her ordeal.

At the hospital, Ziauddin was informed by the doctors that Malala was safe, as the bullet had not touched her brain. Her other two friends were injured, but their lives were not in danger: Shazia had been hit in the collarbone and Kainat in her right arm. The chief minister of Khyber Pakhtunkhwa province was the first to call Malala's father. He informed him that Malala would be shifted to Lady Reading Hospital. The army, however, took the lead, and Malala was lifted by helicopter to Combined Military Hospital (CMH) in Peshawar. Malala's father felt quite perturbed at this turn of events, as he had invested his hope in Dr Mumtaz, a renowned neurosurgeon of Lady Reading Hospital, tending to Malala's injuries.

A young neurosurgeon in CMH, Colonel Junaid Khan, examined Malala. Ziauddin was immediately fearful that Dr Junaid was too young and inexperienced to offer Malala the treatment she required. Dr Junaid hurriedly ordered a CT scan to gauge the scope of Malala's injuries, and it revealed cause for far greater concern. From the initial CT scan performed at Swat Central Hospital, the doctor there had concluded that the bullet had not touched Malala's brain. But after the CT scan at CMH, Dr Junaid informed Malala's father that her brain's membrane had been damaged by some particles of bone, which had fragmented when she had been shot. Further, Dr Junaid's diagnosis of Malala's condition was sobering. He informed Ziauddin that her condition was critical, and she required urgent surgery.

One of Ziauddin's friends advised him to shift Malala from the army hospital. But concerns about Dr Junaid's experience, at least, proved unfounded. Dr Junaid told Malala's father that Malala's vomiting of blood was not abating and that this indicated that her brain was swelling and her condition deteriorating. He told Ziauddin that a part of her skull had to be removed to relieve intracranial pressure, or the pressure of the swelling brain against the skull – a procedure called decompressive craniotomy. Malala's situation was dire, and her father was placed in the nightmarish situation of having to consent to an operation that could just as easily end his daughter's life as save it. But the thoughtful manner in which Dr Junaid explained the situation to Ziauddin – along with the news that Dr Mumtaz would join Dr Junaid in the operating theatre – reassured Ziauddin; at least as much as was possible under the circumstances. He consented to the operation, though he trembled when he read on the consent papers the words 'The patient may die'.

On the following morning, some top surgeons came to examine Malala, and they applauded Colonel Junaid and Dr Mumtaz for their excellent surgery. Malala's life still hung in the balance though. While she was fighting for her life, the Taliban claimed responsibility for shooting her. It did not state that it had shot Malala for her campaigning for girls' education. It asserted that Malala had been shot for speaking against the Taliban, for preaching secularism, promoting Western culture in Swat and declaring President Obama her idol.

The Taliban's pronouncements in the wake of their craven attack only added fuel to the conflagration of outrage in Pakistan and around the world. While the Taliban were quite inured to international condemnation – indeed, they seemed, at times, to relish it – the dismay from virtually all quarters at this attempt to kill a young Muslim schoolgirl did nothing to help their cause. Fear and loathing from their enemies and the West were their mainstay; it gave power to their movement and silenced dissenters.

But in this botched attempt to assassinate a child, in which two further innocent children had been injured, the Taliban earned the disgust of all and sundry – including many of its supporters. In the day following the attempt on Malala's life, an outpouring of sympathy spilled over in public protests in a number of Pakistan's cities. Perhaps more significantly, a group of fifty Islamic clerics in Pakistan issued a fatwa against the gunmen who had attacked Malala and her friends and pointedly denounced attempts by the Taliban to justify the attack.

While Malala was in the hospital, there was a rush of the country's who's who to the hospital. Generally, a family's stature is raised when high dignitaries visit, but Malala's father was not at all enthused by their attention. He felt them no less culpable for creating the environment that gave rise to the attack on his daughter than the Taliban itself. Among the litany of luminaries who visited Malala in hospital was Rehman Malik, the interior minister. He had brought with him a passport for Malala. This courtesy of the minister actually upset her father. While handing over the passport to Tor Pekai, Ziauddin remarked, 'This is Malala's passport, but I don't know whether it's to go abroad or to the heavens.'

Crucial, though, was the personal intervention of General Ashfaq Parvez Kayani, chief of the armed forces of Pakistan, and one of the most powerful men in the country. General Kayani had met Malala when he came to Swat after the campaign against the Taliban. Malala had applauded him for his efforts in ousting the militants but had reminded him that he had yet to catch hold of Fazlullah. The taciturn general was evidently impressed with Malala, and his regard for her and his determination that she be saved was to be a critical factor in her survival.

General Kayani had initially ordered that Malala be airlifted to the CMH, and in the days following her surgery, he took a personal interest in her condition. General Kayani had received conflicting reports about Malala's prognosis following Dr Junaid's operation. He promptly arranged for two visiting English consultant physicians, Dr Javid Kayani and Dr Fiona Reynolds, to fly by military helicopter to Peshawar to evaluate Malala's condition. They arrived on Wednesday, 10 October, a little more than twenty-four hours after Malala had been shot. Whereas the surgery that Dr Junaid had performed had surely saved her life, the dearth of up-to-date facilities in the intensive care unit at the hospital left her life hanging by a thread. Dr Kayani and Dr Reynolds strongly urged that experts from Rawalpindi be immediately sent to oversee Malala's care, and that she be transferred to Army Hospital in Rawalpindi for care at its state-of-the-art facility.

By Thursday morning, Malala's state was dire; her body and face had swollen, and her kidneys and lungs were not adequately functioning. Dr Kayani and Dr Reynolds had her flown to Rawalpindi, so that every effort could be made to stabilize her deteriorating condition. At this point, Ziauddin began to contemplate preparations for Malala's funeral. The team at Army Hospital, though, went to work, administering different antibiotics, stabilizing her blood pressure and averting the need for dialysis. In desperation, Ziauddin asked Dr Reynolds if there was any hope for Malala. She replied that the only reason she was there was because there was hope. In an unusual gesture for a devout Muslim man, he kissed Dr Reynolds's hand. By Friday, however, this hope was materializing; Malala's condition had stabilized. When Dr Reynolds told Ziauddin that his beloved daughter would survive, he burst into tears.

But the threats against Malala were not merely medical. The Taliban had amply demonstrated that no place in Pakistan was beyond their reach. A detail of soldiers guarding Malala was stationed around the hospital to deter any further Taliban attack. Purportedly also for security reasons, family members' mobile phones were confiscated. This could just as well have been for the purpose of preventing Malala's father from talking to television channels.

Unable to communicate through his usual channels, Ziauddin apprehended the outside world through the media. He learnt from newspapers of the international outrage at the ghastly attempt on his girl's life. President Obama had described the shooting as 'reprehensible, disgusting and tragic'. Ban Ki-moon, the UN Secretary General, termed it 'a heinous and cowardly act'. In Pakistan, both President Asif Ali Zardari and Prime Minister Raja Pervaiz Ashraf condemned the attack, as did legislators from many political parties in the National Assembly. The story was headline news on most television channels, in which prominent media personalities expressed anger at the Taliban's heinous crime. Several newspapers hailed Malala as a peace icon.

Some Urdu publications, however, carried conspiracy theories. The adverse propaganda was unleashed by Raheela Qazi, a female member of parliament from the Islamist Jamaat-e-Islami party, who called Malala an American stooge. Raheela Qazi exhibited a photograph of Malala in which she was sitting with American ambassador Richard Holbrooke and cited this as proof of Malala's being in league with the US military.

Thankfully, given the immense pressure that Malala's family was enduring, General Kayani's patronage continued. Besides his apparently genuine humane concern for Malala, perhaps he wished to galvanize a political consensus and prepare the political leadership for engagement in further military action against the Taliban. At General Kayani's insistence, arrangements were made for Malala to be shifted to Queen Elizabeth Hospital in Birmingham, UK. The royal family of United Arab Emirates volunteered the use of a suitably equipped aeroplane for the purpose.

Before her departure, Ziauddin expressed his grave fears for his wife's and sons' safety, should they remain without him in Pakistan. He insisted that the whole family accompany Malala; but this was impracticable, as their passports were not ready. Dr. Javid told her father, 'It is my belief God sends the solution first and the problem later.' He suggested a feasible solution, whereby Dr Fiona Reynolds would act as Malala's guardian during her treatment in the UK, and Ziauddin would remain in Pakistan with the rest of his family. Ziauddin relented, and Malala was flown out of Pakistan on the morning of 15 October 2009, arriving in the UK later the same day.

Back in Pakistan – and with all his hopes pinned on Dr Reynolds' care – her father repeatedly chanted a verse of the Holy Quran. The verse related to the story of Prophet Yunus, who had been swallowed by a whale; the verse was recited by Yunus when he was in the belly of the whale. It is believed that if we keep faith and chant this verse, even the worst adversity can be vanquished. Ziauddin's prayers were answered.

On 16 October, Malala began to regain consciousness, and the first thoughts she remembers were those of thanking Allah profusely that she was not dead. She realized that she was out of Pakistan; but in which country and hospital she was, she had no knowledge. She registered a mild recovery. Her benefactor and guardian Dr Fiona came and brought her a white teddy bear and asked Malala to call the teddy bear Junaid, after the army surgeon whose actions had saved her life. Not knowing who Junaid was, Malala named the bear Lily.

Malala was still disorientated, and everything appeared hazy to her in this alien land. She asked where her father was. Dr Fiona informed her that her father was back in Pakistan. Malala was greatly upset upon hearing this. It was only when Rehanna, a Muslim chaplain, arrived and prayed with her that she calmed, and she uttered 'Amin'. She only felt assured about the safety of her father when Dr Fiona showed her a Pakistani newspaper featuring a photograph of her father talking to General Kayani. Malala also identified her mother's feet in the photograph.

After some time, Dr Javid brought Malala a mobile phone so that she could speak to her parents. Before allowing her to talk with them, he asked for her assurance that she would neither sob nor shed tears, as it could affect her health. Only then did he dial her father's number and hand Malala the phone. That brief call was a life-giver for both father and daughter. Malala was still contemplating the reasons for her father's staying back in Pakistan. She thought that her father must be selling their home and the school and begging loans from rich people to pay for her expensive treatment. She could not know, at this stage, that her father had stayed back in Pakistan to ensure the safety of her mother and brothers.

The final word of solace reached her father from Major General Ghulam Qamar, who told him, 'There is good news coming from the UK. We are very happy our daughter has survived.' Ziauddin was touched by the use of the word 'our', as by now virtually the whole of Pakistan had taken Malala as its daughter. Her father, who had been quite overwhelmed by events and in a state of suspended animation, was given another jolt by Major General Ghulam Qamar. He informed Ziauddin that Malala's eyesight had been impaired by her injuries. Ziauddin was anguished by this news. He pondered giving Malala one of his eyes, but feared that at his age of forty-three, his eyes may not be of much value to a young girl of just fifteen. He could not sleep that night.

On the following morning, he contacted Col. Junaid so that he could inquire about Malala's condition. Dr Junaid rubbished the news as nonsense and told her father that upon regaining consciousness, she had first inquired about him in writing. How could she write if she were suffering from some serious eye problem? He cautioned Ziauddin, though, that Malala had not yet regained full consciousness. Further, he said that she did not remember who had shot her; and when told by Dr Fiona that two of her friends had also sustained injuries, she did not remember their names. Malala's recovery would take time, and there would be many hurdles ahead for her.

The swiftness of her progress, though, surprised nearly everyone. And it was clear as she gained in strength that her determination to campaign for girls' education was still firm. Indeed, her commitment to her principles seemed at least as strong as it was before the attempt on her life. Malala said that her only regret about the attack was that she could not talk to her attackers before they shot her. She said she wished she could have informed them that whatever she had been doing was in accordance with Islam, as Islam gives equal rights of education to men and women, and that she would have implored them to renounce the path they had been following. She never harboured any feeling of ill will, however, against those who had tried to kill her. She had inherited an enduring moral code that even the worst kind of wrong could not shake.

Her father was a great source of Malala's character, and it is for all to see. The public was accustomed to the father–daughter duo, and their resolve for their cause was well recognized. What was perhaps overlooked was Malala's mother's contribution to her make-up. Tor Pekai had remained in the background over the years and had been content to support her more gregarious daughter and husband. In the days following the attempt on her daughter's life, she would show her mettle.

With no arrangement being made for her family's flight to Birmingham to accompany Malala, and her family stuck in the army hospital in Rawalpindi for a week, Tor Pekai issued an ultimatum. She declared that she would go on a hunger strike if there was no news about their flight to Birmingham by the following day. The army major in charge of dealing with Malala's family became jittery at the prospect of Tor Pekai going on a hunger strike. Within ten minutes, Malala's family were informed that they would be soon flown. Ziauddin was astonished by this development. He said to Tor Pekai, 'All along I thought Malala and I were the campaigners, but you really know how to protest!'

After Malala had begun to speak again, scores of journalists from different countries flocked to cover her story. Fiona Alexander, the head of the hospital press office, briefed the journalists about Malala's health. Several dignitaries from different countries – ministers, diplomats and politicians – came to see Malala. Rehanna, the hospital chaplain, informed Malala that millions of people across the globe had prayed for her. Some people had volunteered to adopt her, presuming that she was an orphan. There was even a marriage proposal. Fiona Alexander brought Malala a huge bag of cards, toys and pictures which had been sent by children across the globe, wishing her a speedy recovery. More than 8,000 cards had been received. Several packets containing chocolates and teddy bears were among them.

The packet which Malala most valued, though, was that sent by the late Benazir Bhutto's son and daughter, Bilawal and Bakhtawar. It contained two shawls which were owned by Benazir, Malala's idol. Malala sank her face deep into the shawls, inhaling and familiarizing herself with Benazir Bhutto's fragrance. Malala had received messages from several celebrities too. The one which she relished the most came from her favourite actress and social activist, Angelina Jolie. She keenly wished to share Angelina Jolie's message with her close friend Moniba, but she did not know when she was destined to be back in Swat again to meet her.

Malala felt thrilled to receive good wishes from people across the globe and was treated affectionately by the nurses and doctors. Their support was invaluable, for she had to undergo trying procedures. Part of her skull was even grafted in her belly to be later implanted, repairing the aperture left in her skull by Dr Junaid's emergency surgery. Though she silently bore the physical pain, the emotional pain is something altogether different. When her parents arrived at the hospital and the door of her room was opened and she heard the voice 'jani' and 'pisho', she burst into tears. She embraced her parents and wept inconsolably. Her parents too wept like children. After this outpouring, Malala felt as if she had been relieved of a huge burden of pain. Her parents were dismayed, though, to see that Malala could not offer a smile: her left eye bulged, and her mouth tilted downward. But she did not mind having lost her smile, as she said she was very much the same Malala.

Later Malala underwent a marathon eight-and-a-half-hour operation which would correct this symptom, performed by the prominent surgeon Richard Irving. Finally, the much-awaited smile began to reappear on her beautiful face. Each day that passed saw more of her trademark engaging expressions, and she looked just as she had before the attack. The operation was an impressive accomplishment for Dr Irving, who later remarked that Malala's facial nerve surgery was his life's greatest feat. The procedure not only restored Malala's looks but also caused her incessant headache to lift, and she could start reading again.

Malala's parents, remaining concern was her memory. She could not remember anything about the shooting, nor could she recollect names of her friends. Her father asked Malala if she could recite some Pashto *tapa*, a two-line verse containing a message. Malala sang a tapa written by Darvesh Durrani which meant:

When you start your journey from the end of a snake's tail,
You will end up on its head in an ocean of poison.

Malala's urge for reciting tapas grew, and she told her father that she wanted to recite a tapa which she had rewritten. Her father was surprised, because tapas are centuries-old pearls of wisdom; they are not usually altered by those of the present generation. But on his request, Malala sang the tapa she had rewritten – one which inspires women to a higher level of consciousness and confirms their pre-eminent role in the world. The original tapa reads thus:

> If the men cannot win the battle, oh my country,
> Then the women will come forth and win you honour.

The rewritten tapa reads:

> Whether the men are winning or losing the battle, Oh my country,
> The women are coming and the women will win you honour.

My motivation for writing this book is to inspire women, particularly young women and girls, for in their future lies the future of the world. It is from women that all of humanity owes its creation; it is only with women of the world at the centre of all human affairs that the safety and happiness of humanity may be secure. Malala's rewritten tapa echoes such sentiments, which may provide mankind with ultimate hope.

Malala beckons us all in memorable words in her Nobel Peace Prize speech, given on 10 December 2014, to do our duty:

> Dear sisters and brothers, dear fellow children, we must work. Not wait. Not just the politicians and the world leaders – we all need to contribute. Me. You. We. It is our duty.
>
> Let us become the first generation to decide to be the last to see empty classrooms, lost childhoods and wasted potential.
>
> Let this be the last time a girl is forced into early child marriage.

Let this be the last time a child loses life in war.

Let this be the last time we see a child out of school.

Let this end with us.

Let's begin this ending. Together. Today. Right here, right now.

Yes. Every one of us must come forward. Women must come forward first. They do not belong to a country, to a caste, to a creed, to a clan – but to the whole of humanity. We urgently need many more women like Malala to emancipate the whole world. It is my turn or your turn to emulate Malala's spirit and make this world free of hatred, free of killings and animosity of any kind. Every girl child must be educated and freed from all societal bondage.

This chapter on Malala would remain incomplete if I fail to clearly enunciate Malala's deepest urge – to feel her pulse, as it were. Having spoken with her, I can say with conviction that Malala's heart goes out to every orphan and underprivileged child; and especially every girl child. She is firmly committed to transforming the lives of millions of such hapless children around the world – that they all experience the empowerment of a proper education and the uplift that will bring them.

When I think about Malala, I am reminded of Bill Clinton's remarks about the Taj Mahal. Upon seeing the Taj Mahal during his visit to Agra in 2000, he had remarked, 'There are two kinds of people in the world. Those who have seen the Taj Mahal and those who have not seen the Taj Mahal.' Bill Clinton prides himself for being fortunate enough of being among the former. In a similar sense, there are two kinds of people with regard to Malala: those who support Malala Yousafzai and her father in their quest for girls' freedom and education and those who would rather have the world languish in ignorance.

This divide is not peculiar to Pakistan. The issue has been particularly bitterly fought there, though, and one may only hope that Malala and her father's efforts may bear fruit in the coming generation. One may also hope that Pakistan may bring its daughter Malala, who is currently living in the United Kingdom, back to her native land. There, she may be at home with her nation, her culture and her glorious task of educating every girl child in Swat Valley; the task which she vowed in her speech at the Nobel Prize ceremony in Oslo to undertake with unremitting zeal.

Since her recovery, Malala has been good to her word: she has continued to campaign for universal education, an aspiration that encompasses humanity far beyond Swat. Malala and Ziauddin, with the support of the highly regarded Vital Voices Global Partnership founded by Hillary Clinton, have founded the Malala Fund. This non-profit foundation is dedicated to helping girls receive twelve years of safe and proper education and training. It has made numerous carefully targeted grants to this end since, in Africa, the war zones of the Middle East – and in Malala's home valley.

Malala knows there is much work ahead of her – particularly in her own country. The barbarous attack on Army Public School in Peshawar on 16 December 2014, in which 132 innocent schoolchildren and nine of their teachers were slain, has shown just how great the challenges are that face Pakistan and its people. With proper leadership, this could prove a defining moment in Pakistan's nationhood. It remains to be seen whether its leadership grasps this opportunity. Needless to say, former US secretary of state Hillary Rodham Clinton's blunt admonition to Pakistan is pertinent here. She said, 'You can't keep snakes in your backyard and expect them only to bite your neighbours. Eventually those snakes are going to turn on whoever has them in the backyard.'

In any event, for all the pain of Malala's ordeal and the sacrifices she has made in her quest for girls' education, Malala has had the satisfaction of seeing that the Taliban's murderous acts towards her not only earned worldwide condemnation but also ultimately elevated her campaign for girls' education beyond her wildest imaginings. The Taliban's attack on Malala has, in the final analysis, only bolstered the case for girls' education and their rights. And it afforded Malala an audience infinitely larger than that of Pakistan radio and television she reached prior to the attempt on her life. Her sacrifice immediately captured the imagination of people across the globe, and she has remained in the limelight since. No other person in recent times has influenced world opinion on the rights of girls so profoundly as Malala. May her quest continue.

Long live Malala Yousafzai of Swat!

ELLEN JOHNSON SIRLEAF

AFRICA'S FIRST WOMAN HEAD OF STATE

'I was ahead of my time, but I am no longer alone.'

SCENE I: A girl is born in Monrovia, Liberia, on 29 October 1938. When she is a few days old, an elderly man visits her parents to bestow his blessings on her. Her mother leads the old man into the room, where on the bed, the infant is cheerfully cycling her legs and cooing. The old man looks at the mother in utter astonishment and predicts spontaneously that her child will one day be a great woman, that she is destined to lead others.

SCENE II: A young woman is married even before crossing her teens, and burdened with the responsibility of rearing her sons. She toils in lowly jobs to feed her family and has to contend with an abusive and drunken husband.

Can these two scenes be reconciled? A woman in her early twenties with four sons and an abusive husband seems hopelessly mired by her circumstances, and is most unlikely to ever distinguish herself in public life. Thus, the old man's prophecy could barely be about the girl mentioned in SCENE II. Nonetheless, these two contrasting scenes do converge in one life, giving the world the wonder known as Ellen Eugenia Johnson Sirleaf, the current president of Liberia and one of the three proud recipients of the Nobel Peace Prize for the year 2011.

Whether she was fated to become a great leader of the masses as the old man prophesied or whether she achieved greatness by sheer dint of her own determined efforts is something even Ellen admits that she still ponders. The Norwegian Nobel Committee, however, does not confer the Nobel Peace Prize lightly; it undertakes a rigorous process examining the achievements of candidates over many months, including shortlisting and reviewing before finally voting for the recipients. The immense accomplishments in bringing peace to Liberia and the region that merited the award for Ellen Johnson Sirleaf could barely be ascribed to good fortune.

The year 2011 marked a watershed in the history of the Nobel Peace Prize because, in that year, three women were chosen for this prize. Besides Ellen Johnson Sirleaf, the other two recipients were Leymah Gbowee of Liberia and Tawakkol Karman of Yemen, which raised the number of women winners of this prize from twelve to fifteen.

Ellen Johnson Sirleaf was born of a Gola father and a mother of Kru and German ancestry. Her paternal grandfather, Jahmale, was a Gola chief of some repute from Bomi County. He used to travel for many months far from his home, through the verdant jungles of coastal Liberia. On the way, he learnt to speak many languages and dialects and soon started acting as a mediator when indigenous people quarrelled among themselves. This way, he garnered considerable popularity and respect. On one occasion, Hilary Wright Johnson, Liberia's eleventh president, visited him, an encounter that was to influence the family's future, and confer on Jahmale and his descendants a new name.

President Hilary Wright Johnson advised Jahmale to send Ellen's father to the city as a ward. Her father was taken in by an Americo-Liberian family named McCritty and given the last name of Johnson. After westernizing his first name from Karnley to Carney, he was known as Carney Johnson. The McCritty family treated him well and gave him a solid primary education he would not have received in his village. He could not afford to study law because there was no law school in Liberia, but he chose another route to becoming a lawyer: apprenticing with a practising attorney. After some time, he qualified to practise law and soon gained a reputation for being a poor man's advocate.

Ellen's mother's story is similarly colourful. Ellen's maternal grandmother, Juah Sarwee, was a native of Greenville, Sinoe County, who had been courted and married by a German trader. Ellen's mother, Martha, was born with her father's fair skin, and, because of her colour, many settler families were eager to take her into their homes.

It was just as well. Circumstances were against Juah Sarwee and Martha, and they had little choice but to rely on others' largesse. Martha's father fled the country after Liberia declared war on Germany in World War I, leaving his wife and daughter behind, and Juah Sarwee was destitute. Martha had to be given up for adoption in Monrovia. Ellen still refers to the 'unimaginable indignities and humiliation' her mother first suffered, before she was finally adopted by Cecilia Dunbar, a childless lady belonging to a prominent Americo-Liberian family. Cecilia treated Martha as her own daughter, and Martha enjoyed a decent education and home life thereafter.

Martha grew into an attractive young lady, and Ellen's father spotted her in Mrs Dunbar's house while passing by their street. Martha was not enthused with her suitor's declaration, 'Oh, I like you.' He, however, was not one to give in so easily. Some years later, Carney Johnson divorced his wife and came to Ellen's grandmother Cecilia to ask for Martha's hand in marriage. By now, Martha had grown up and was quickly enamoured of him. Neither Cecilia nor her daughter could resist Carney: He was tall, smart and stylish in appearance; he was a man of great self-confidence. This is how Ellen's mother, Martha, and her father, Carney Johnson, were married.

Ellen's parents owned a house on Benson Street, one of Monrovia's busy thoroughfares. First, Ellen's brother Charles was born and then her sister, Jennie. Ellen was the third child of the family, followed by her brother Carney. Ellen's father's wanderings made her mother feel lonely back at home, so she opened a school, which Ellen attended throughout her primary years. Her mother became an itinerant minister in the Presbyterian Church, which enjoined her to travel throughout the countryside preaching the word of God. On one such trip, her mother took Ellen and her sister, Jennie, along. One Sunday, Ellen was chosen to give the recitation. She had spent the whole Saturday night in learning the recitation by rote, but when the occasion arose, she simply froze. She could not remember a word and dropped back into her seat, deluged in a torrent of tears, despite her doting mother's ministrations.

As is true of every person destined to achieve greatness, however, Ellen turned her failure into her strength, her invincible forte. At the age of eight, she vowed she would never again fail at public speaking. It is no wonder that she is today credited with having given numerous memorable speeches. And for a major part of her early life, she remained a student, despite personal circumstances which were anything but conducive to learning. She started her studies in 1948, and in 1971 obtained a master's in public administration from Harvard's John F. Kennedy School of Government.

The apparently dichotomous **SCENES I** and **II** were reconciled much later, after Ellen surmounted all odds with her incredible grit and determination. The first tribulation she had to face was her father's crippling stroke when he was in his early forties. This tragedy dramatically changed everything for Ellen. Her father, who had enjoyed an active law practice, who had been the first indigenous man elected to the Liberian House of Representatives – and who had aspired to becoming the first Speaker of the House – was abandoned by all his friends and legislature colleagues. Besides suffering social deprivation, the family also had to face a greatly reduced income, so much so that Ellen's mother had to make and sell baked foods to keep the family afloat. Ellen's sister, Jennie, went to England to work as a nurse so that the family's dwindling finances could be supplemented.

Ellen was studying in high school at the College of West Africa, one of the oldest and most prestigious European schools in Liberia, at the time of her father's stroke. Only the children of privileged and well-connected parents could manage admission. Ellen had obtained admission to the school on the strength of her father's status as a legislator. After her father's stroke, her position in the school might have been precarious, but Ellen found sufficient refuge in her doting teachers and caring classmates.

Falling in grace in society usually engenders immense pain – especially for children. Falling and then rising again affords immense satisfaction. Rising when her family had fallen abysmally from its earlier position of eminence and privilege, however, required that Ellen suffer countless stings of public humiliation. Yet Ellen's grand vision – with her inexhaustible store of resilience, grit and determination, and relentless efforts – surmounted all impediments on the path leading to regaining the lost family glory. In the process, Ellen left many awestruck.

Her mettle first showed itself on the sports field. She was, after all, a tomboy. There were hardly any boys' games she did not play, and she often led her school teams to victory. She also absorbed life's vicissitudes with aplomb. When all her affluent friends had gone off to colleges in Nigeria or London or the United States because their families continued to enjoy positions of privilege and position, she had to stay back in Monrovia.

Although her mother's nurturing preserved some semblance of normalcy in her children's lives, Ellen encountered more grief after marrying James 'Doc' Sirleaf. Doc had recently returned from attending college at Alabama's Tuskegee Institute. He emanated an aura of charm, courtliness and culture; he was highly articulate and sure of himself, and possessed a military bearing. These qualities combined to make him irresistible for Ellen, who started dating him. He was very possessive, though, and prevailed upon Ellen not to maintain even innocent friendships with other men. Ellen conceded whatever he wished from her, because she was hopelessly infatuated.

Her mother, however, did not take to Doc's influence kindly. She warned Ellen against any temptation and made it abundantly clear that she expected Doc to appreciate that she had reared her daughter on the path of righteousness. Finding herself deeply in love with Doc, Ellen entreated her mother to agree to their marriage, and Martha capitulated despite her reservations. The couple was wed in 1956, when Ellen was just seventeen years old. Her brother walked her down the aisle because her father could not. Soon her eldest son, James, known as Jes, was born on 11 January 1957, and her second son, Charles, arrived in the final hours of the same year on 31 December. Two more sons, Robert and Adamah, followed.

The family spent their initial days with Doc's mother, while Doc and Ellen sought employment. Ellen had acquired typing skills in high school and was soon able to get a job as a secretary in Stanley Engineering Company. She later shifted to Elias Brothers' garage, where she worked as a junior accountant. This opened up a career in accounting, though she had wanted to be an English teacher. She could never have imagined that this humble position would lead her to a career that would earn her eminence and prosperity, and restore her to the privileged position she had lost after her father's illness.

Meanwhile, Doc became a teacher at the Booker Washington Institute, a vocational high school. By this time Ellen's friends, who had gone abroad for higher studies, had begun returning, sophisticated and professional. Ellen endured the pain of failure: she had been left behind to produce sons and rear them, and she felt that her future was bleak indeed. Doc, though, received a scholarship for a master's in agriculture in the US, and this fired Ellen's imagination. She too wanted to go abroad for further studies, but securing a scholarship was a significant hurdle: she no longer enjoyed the benefit of her father's connections, which had been instrumental in securing a scholarship for her elder sister. She frantically entreated everyone and lobbied everywhere she could for a scholarship; and fortunately, she succeeded.

The young couple flew to Madison, Wisconsin, leaving behind two sons with Doc's mother and two sons with Ellen's mother. It hardly bears mentioning that Ellen's separation from her children was painful, yet she was excited to be in the country of her dreams. However, her excitement was short-lived. Doc's possessiveness worsened, and her misery was heightened by Doc's drinking, which would invariably be accompanied by his launching cruel tirades against her. The verbal abuse soon spiralled into the physical kind. He once struck Ellen's head with the butt of his gun. Her 'failing' was that she had overstayed at a dinner that day with some of her friends who were visiting from Liberia. Just as innumerable women have done before, and almost as many since, Ellen endured her abusive marriage far beyond the dictates of reason.

After one year Doc's study was over, and he returned to Liberia. Ellen stayed for another year to complete her studies. Upon returning from Madison, Doc took a job at the Agricultural Ministry, while Ellen became a division head in the Treasury Department, where she quickly carved a niche for herself. This job brought Ellen back to herself and inspired her to pursue her ambitions. Driven to enhance her career, she became a workaholic and would regularly bring home work. The more she progressed in her career, however, the more Doc became jealous and unhappy, which would manifest with ever-increasing demonstrations of violence. Though as yet the marriage had not broken, the wife–husband bond had irreparably strained, and Doc began to engage in extramarital relationships. Eventually, Ellen also found other companionship, and this sounded the death knell for the marriage. A court later granted Ellen's divorce petition, because Doc simply did not contest it.

As in Dr Shirin Ebadi's Iran, custody rights in Liberia fell to the father. Ellen and Doc's elder two sons had gone to a mission school. Her youngest son, Adamah, had been left with Doc's father's brother, and her third son, Rob, demanded to stay with Ellen. One day, Doc dropped Rob off at Ellen's home. Not long afterward, Doc died, and Ellen delivered the eulogy at his funeral. Thus, Rob was there with Ellen on her journey forward.

Until her job in the Treasury Department, and even for some time subsequently, Ellen's life was characterized by struggle and determination to overcome adversity. While her contemporaries had enjoyed sojourns of study overseas supported by their parents, in Madison, Ellen had to resort to menial work to earn her living. Perhaps hardship wrought in her an even greater determination, which was essential to survive the later upheaval she would suffer along with her compatriots. Although she toiled at the Treasury Department, her assurance of her own capacities – which she had been nurturing within and which no amount of adversity could subdue – convinced her that it would be only a matter of time before she would fulfil her ambitions.

Her challenges had not just been economic and personal; they were also ethnic. Ellen had inherited her mother's pale complexion. In school, she was teased because of her fair skin. Children taunted her with the nickname 'red pumpkin', which caused her considerable distress. The hurt was not simply on account of her colour, but because it signified that Ellen was not an ethnic Liberian. Indeed, to this day, Ellen is assumed by many to be Americo-Liberian – part of the nation's economic and social elite – or at least is considered by many to be culturally Americo-Liberian. The effect on the young Ellen being derided as not ethnic Liberian was profound – she would pray to God at bedtime that she awoke black.

As with her issues regarding ethnic identity, Ellen's tribulations during her marriage would be mirrored in the horrific challenges of her country in later years. Once when she took Doc's car to run some errands, the car broke down far from home. Ellen called to ask for Doc's help, but instead of helping her, he berated her and demanded that she return his car. She was amazed at his irrational cruelty, but she accepted living with Doc as a challenge to strengthen her will. Rather than feeling disheartened and dismayed, she felt emboldened by her experience to encounter life head on. Ellen says she learnt a valuable lesson from this incident with the broken-down car. 'When push comes to shove and at the end of the day, depend on yourself. No one else is guaranteed to be there – no one.' This is how great people use every adversity as a stepping stone to rise beyond their apparent limitations.

It is hard to imagine that a president of a sovereign country has risen to her station from performing humble jobs such as cleaning floors, just to put bread on the table. While in Madison, Ellen took up work of cleaning, and was quite happy to do so to earn an honest living. Once while she was at work, Doc visited her and, upon seeing her sweeping the floor, yelled at her, took the broom from her hands and tossed it away. He ordered Ellen to stop her job, which, he declared, did not befit the status of the wife of a man of his standing. Doc created quite a ruckus. Ellen did not wish to aggravate matters. She accompanied Doc home; but she returned to her cleaning job the very next day. This incident evinces Ellen's courage as much as it does her pragmatism, strengths that have been her mainstay throughout a sometimes harrowing political career. The incident also shows that extraordinary people such as Ellen always embrace the ordinary in their lives, whereas those who try to dissemble being extraordinary only betray their ordinariness.

At any rate, Ellen's courage would sometimes extend to outright audacity. Once, at the insistence of Harvard's Gustav Papanek, a noted economist and professor, President Tubman organized a conference on Liberia's economic future. Though President Tubman and others in power did not believe so, it was clear to any dispassionate observer that the country's economy was in the doldrums. Papanek had invited Ellen to speak. The occasion demanded that someone tell the authorities to act and act firmly before it was too late. Ellen decided to run the gauntlet herself. The central theme of her speech was that people must believe their government to be honest, efficient, as well as willing and able to utilize resources for the common good. She opined, 'I think the deliberation of this conference, if it is to be meaningful, while endorsing the achievements in economic development in recent years, must correspondingly recognize the failures which may have led to relative economic stagnation.' She made a most stinging observation: 'With little regard for this situation, we still indulge in obvious public wastes such as innumerable foreign embassies, a constantly swelling civil service and other abuses of meagre public funds such as payroll padding and outright stealing of public monies.'

She bluntly suggested in her speech that the decline in her country's economic fortunes was due in no small measure to government corruption. The inference was clear that the country's leaders presided over a kleptocracy. Her speech created ripples in the conference hall. After the conference, Papanek applauded Ellen for her speech and confessed that he had not expected such an address from a junior female deputy in an African government. He feared government reprisals against her, however, and advised Ellen to leave Liberia. To facilitate her escape, he promised her a fellowship to Harvard University for a programme that entailed a year of study and the chance to earn a degree in public administration. Ellen was overjoyed at the prospect of studying at one of the most prestigious universities of the world and immediately accepted this offer.

One can only marvel at Ellen's almost reckless courage in giving a very public condemnation of her country's most senior officials. It would not be the last time that she risked her own welfare to speak her mind for the welfare of her nation either. Many great souls such as Ellen Johnson Sirleaf, when they take bold stands for the greater good, remain naive about the risks involved or even seem careless of their personal welfare. For the sake of a principle in which they believe, they steer themselves towards the worst consequences to confront the status quo; and it is often little more than good fortune that saves them.

Ellen displayed a similar lack of concern for her health at times. While studying at Harvard, she was given to late-night studies and began smoking, much to her elder sister Jennie's dismay. When Jennie's insistence that Ellen eschew smoking went beyond her capacity to withstand it, she told Jennie that the cigarette she was smoking then would be the last cigarette of her life. After inhaling a hard last puff, Ellen exhibited rare willpower and never smoked again.

Ellen was sailing towards home on 23 July 1971 when one of the stewards broke the news of the death of President Tubman, who had died due to a complication during a prostate cancer surgery. Back home, she was offered the responsibility of a deputy ministership and called upon to look after fiscal and banking policies under Finance Minister Stephen Tolbert. The mantle of presidency fell to former vice president William R. Tolbert, her new boss Stephen Tolbert's brother. William R. Tolbert relayed his pious intentions even before assuming office when he went to West Point, the worst slum of Monrovia at that time, and spent an evening with the people living there. He said, 'If you are poor, I identify myself with your poverty, and together we should work to better our conditions.' He asked them to share his vision of mat to mattresses, which would literally uplift them from sleeping on the floor to sleeping on mattresses. He was a well-meaning president but was surrounded by several self-seeking individuals, among whom were his own kith and kin.

With Ellen's newly elevated status, her alma mater, the College of West Africa, invited her to deliver the graduation address in November 1972. She wanted to use this opportunity to let the people of Liberia know where their beloved country was heading, and how there was a telling lack of urgency on the part of the powers that be to embrace change. The title of her speech was 'Some Fundamental Constraints to a Liberian Society of Involved Individuals'. The address marked an important turning point in Ellen's life. She had come into public reckoning and was on the threshold of achieving great things. While addressing the students, she called upon them to compare the sacred rights embodied in Liberia's constitution with actual practices. She declared that only then would they know how those sacred rights had been muzzled. They would then, she said, hold in contempt those who swear by the rights guaranteed in the constitution but are, in fact, ruthlessly denying these rights to the common people. Ellen touched the hearts of the students when she expressed her deep concern for their well-being and for Liberia.

What she told the Liberian students is of universal significance. She could just as easily have been addressing an audience of Indian students. Social tensions were straining the fabric of Indian society no less than in Liberia at the time of Ellen's speech. Her words were at once profound and touching:

> When we learn to avoid, in the subconscious, making distinctions between one another on the basis of last or first name, when all of you graduating today can compete for higher

education scholarships and be assured that the yardsticks for measuring who will receive such a reward will be based solely on merit, when every youth of the land is exposed to equal opportunities in school, housing and employment, when we learn to respect character over family name and moral achievements over material accumulation, then, and only then, will the walls of social constraints come tumbling down.

Such sentiments emanate only from the heart of a person blessed with an enlightened soul such as Ellen's. She ended her speech with a note of caution, advising the students to shun materialism for the sake of their nation and their personal good. She warned that widening economic disparities would create tensions and bring Liberia to the verge of a precipice. She cautioned that if economic disparities were not mitigated before it was too late, her generation might face serious consequences, and posterity would suffer accordingly. She expressed her wish that God would save them.

Ellen was conscious that her speech would ruffle many feathers in government, and so it did. Her speech was banned from being reported in the media. Some members of cabinet labelled her a saboteur and all rallied around the view that they could not allow one woman to criticize the government. They did not realize, however, that she was not 'one woman' but an institution unto herself. Soon they had realized that it was not in their interests to make a martyr out of Ellen and decided to dismiss the idea of any retribution. She was sidelined, though, and it became increasingly clear to her that she needed to quit the political scene. With the help of a World Bank official, she managed to secure a position at the bank as a loan officer. When Ellen tendered her resignation from the post as deputy finance minister, Stephen Tolbert personally came to her home and arranged a rousing farewell party for her. This was perhaps not as much a mark of his esteem for Ellen but a celebration of her leaving Liberia. For her part, Ellen viewed leaving Liberia for a World Bank job as a tactical retreat; she always knew that she would return.

People who studiously guard their childhood innocence, groom themselves in simplicity, refuse to learn chicanery and prefer to be duped than dupe, either possess an innate sublimity or their souls become sublimated in the pursuit of such values. Such souls alone have the courage of conviction and face the challenges of life with fortitude, unmindful of consequences. Ellen is an illustrious embodiment of such sublimity; and time and again she would unflinchingly take on the mighty, heedless of the consequences. In doing so, she exhibited a rare gift for maintaining the esteem – or at least the grudging respect – of her adversaries.

On 29 April 1975, Stephen Tolbert tragically died when his twin-engine Cessna crashed into the Atlantic a few minutes after lifting off from Greenville Airport. After mourning his brother, President William R. Tolbert appointed James T. Philips to the post of Minister of Finance, and Ellen took up a position in the Treasury Department.

President Tolbert decided Liberia should host the 1979 Organization of African Unity's annual conference. Critics were sceptical about the purported benefits of hosting the annual conference. Nonetheless, President Tolbert went ahead with his plan. For Ellen, it was a highly misconceived idea: Liberia's economy was languishing and could ill afford such an extravagance. In addition to overspending on the arrangements for the event, contractors were submitting highly inflated and sometimes blatantly fraudulent bills. One such bill came to Ellen's desk. A British contractor had approached President

Tolbert, claiming that his company had not been paid properly. The president referred the complaint to Finance Minister Philips, which eventually percolated to Ellen for her comment.

Ellen discovered that the bill was simply outrageous. She had in her office a rubber stamp which read BULLSHIT that she had bought from a small souvenir shop in the United States. Ellen thought the bill's claim could not be more appropriately described, and, never one to pull her punches, she stamped the bill accordingly and returned it to the contractor. The issue was leaked to the press. The day the story appeared in the *Financial Times*, Finance Minister Philips called Ellen to his office and ordered her to hand over the stamp. He admonished her for using the stamp. His concern was only for the domestic and international ridicule the government suffered as a result of Ellen's action. He seemed least worried for the sentiments that had moved Ellen to take a stand against the bill, or for the dubious merits of the contractor's claim.

Ellen evidently took her job seriously – more so, it would seem, than her superiors. She tried several times to impress upon President Tolbert the need to take action to stimulate the economy, but he could not apprehend that though the country seemed calm on the surface, beneath simmered a volcano that could erupt any time. The volcano erupted when the agriculture minister proposed raising the price of subsidized rice from $22 to $27 per 100-pound bag. This led to the Rice Riots on 14 April 1979. In the violence, around 140 people were killed and hundreds injured, and around 160 stores were ransacked, causing property damage worth around $35 million. The rioters had gathered at the headquarters of the Progressive Alliance of Liberia (PAL), headed by Gabriel Bacchus Matthews, which was later formally registered as the political party the Progressive People's Party (PPP). Tolbert ordered Matthews's arrest, and he was imprisoned along with some thirty other radicals. He also fired several of his ministers, including his finance minister, James T. Philips.

After the OAU summit, in August 1979, President Tolbert summoned Ellen and told her that he had decided to make her the finance minister. Ellen immediately got to work, implementing austerity measures to prevent the economy from derailing. Little did she know that her stint as finance minister would not last long. On 12 April 1980, seventeen soldiers led by Samuel Kanyon Doe, an indigenous Liberian master sergeant, brutally assassinated President Tolbert in his bed and took his wife, Victoria, prisoner in a bloody coup. The soldiers freed the PPP leaders, who joined them at the Executive Mansion. Doe had become the new executive head of the nation overnight. He offered predictable justifications for his actions, saying that 'rampant corruption and continuous failure by the government to effectively handle the affairs of the Liberian people left enlisted men no alternative'. Despite the ensuing chaos, the government and the media issued assurances that the situation was under control. Many senior members of the Tolbert government were ordered to report to the Executive Mansion in Monrovia, including Ellen. Most were subsequently arrested.

Aware of the mayhem on the streets and that she would be targeted as a member of the elite settler class because of her fair complexion, Ellen resolved not to go to the Executive Mansion without protection. Only when a friend offered to escort her did she venture out and present herself at the Mansion as Samuel Doe had demanded. Doe ordered Ellen to explain the budget to persons whom he wanted to look after finance under his new dispensation. Having done that, she was allowed to return home. The next day, Doe announced on radio the formation of his new fifteen-member cabinet, which included Gabriel Bacchus Matthews as the new foreign minister. Ellen was questioned on budget matters. She did not know what her fate would be after they decided that they had no further use for her.

The violence in the streets sent chills down Ellen's spine. There were cries of 'kill all the Congo people, they have stolen the money, they have stolen the land'. Drunken soldiers roamed about in cars threatening, harassing, and beating whomsoever they thought deserving of such treatment. Some from the poor and oppressed classes seized the opportunity in this lawless chaos to settle scores with their erstwhile masters. They incited soldiers to ransack the very houses where they had worked as servants just days earlier, and even urged them to imprison or brutally murder their employers. Though the affluent Americo-Liberian minority bore the brunt of the violence, even rich indigenous Liberians were not spared. Ellen could only bear the trauma of these days – losing friends and colleagues to this mindless violence – with her inner reserves, her utmost fortitude.

Ellen admits that had she not enjoyed a flawless reputation, she too would have been lost. Despite her reservations, she chose to extend her cooperation to the perpetrators of the assassination of the legitimate president of Liberia. It struck her that the interests of the nation lay in her assisting the new government, or else the situation could deteriorate beyond redemption. Two days after the coup, Doe addressed the nation on television and spoke in conciliatory tones, promising to eliminate differences on account of descent and class and calling upon people to think collectively: 'What can you do?' The soldiers who had plundered stores and intimidated people were executed.

Two days later, trials of the arrested ministers and others began. Former minister Chesson and several associates were charged with treason and corruption. They were barely allowed a semblance of due process, denied counsel to defend themselves; they were summarily pronounced guilty and sentenced to death. In those tumultuous days, the most chilling situation Ellen had to confront was accompanying Samuel Doe in his car to the Barclay Training Center (BTC), a military base, only to find her own brother Carney incarcerated there. She was horrified to see him among other men without their shoes and shirts, under armed guard. Her fears for her brother's welfare notwithstanding, she was concerned about being perceived as a supporter of Doe, who had by now assumed the rank of general. Had she refused to accompany Doe in his car to the BTC, though, she may have faced an even more dire fate than her brother. Ellen later learnt that Carney had found his place at the BTC for having laughed at the new minister of justice, Chea Cheapoo, for losing his seat in the legislature.

Ten days after the coup, on 22 April, nine former members of Tolbert's administration were executed in a macabre demonstration of the new regime's violence, and the whole sordid episode was filmed for posterity, as if its architects were proud of their actions. The executions foreshadowed the barbarousness that would overtake the country in coming decades. The former officials were stripped of their shirts, led to nine massive wooden posts buried in the sand, tied without blindfolds facing away from the sea and roundly taunted and jeered by the surrounding multitude of soldiers. They were then massacred with several haphazard volleys fired by a line of gunmen in uniform. Their bodies were cut down and left at the foot of the posts. Besides these nine men, four more men were also executed. The thirteen men so executed were all prominent members of Tolbert's administration. Only four ministers from the Tolbert government, including Ellen, were spared.

Doe later told the nation why Ellen escaped the purge. He recounted that once he and his men had gone to some area and Ellen's mother happened to be there. They were thirsty, and she had provided them water to drink. Doe claimed it was owing to his gratitude to Ellen's mother, for her kindness, that Ellen was granted a reprieve – otherwise she would perhaps have been the fourteenth person to be executed on the beach. Her mother could not confirm Doe's story. The tenor of his explanation, though – that Ellen's mother was altruistic and caring to give water to Doe and his thirsty men – was true to her character and was not denied. The executions, at any rate, prompted worldwide condemnation of Doe and his governing council. International opprobrium seemed to have had its effect; there were no further summary executions.

Doe occupied the Executive Mansion, suspended the country's 133-year-old constitution and imposed martial law. Ellen was summoned daily to answer questions, and finally Doe asked her if she would serve as president of the Liberian Bank for Development and Investment. She accepted the post, thereby putting herself in an invidious position: those who remained associated with Tolbert and Tubman's successors accused her of betrayal; those in control of the new dispensation distrusted her. Ellen had altogether different concerns however. She was deeply concerned about the state of the nation's economy.

The situation was grim. The country's economy groaned under the $700 million foreign debt. Massive outflows of capital had been taking place almost daily. Foreign investment had dried up after the coup and skilled workers with any means had fled the country. It was in the face of such a dismal scenario that Ellen decided to suffer accusations of betrayal for the sake of saving the country from financial ruin. She soon discovered, however, that the new regime was less focused on building the economy than increasing their hold over the country. Doe proved as greedy as the men surrounding him; the government coffers were being emptied at an alarming rate for the benefit of a new kleptocracy, and Liberia's people suffered.

The situation was saved by American patronage; the US did not want Liberia to slip into the USSR's pocket, and a steady flow of American aid propped up the nation and Doe's administration. President Ronald Reagan's government in the 1980s pursued an aggressive foreign policy, whereby it exerted pressure on communist countries to keep the USSR in check, while offering all manner of assistance to friendly nations. Perhaps unsurprisingly, Doe aligned himself firmly with the US against the communist USSR. Doe expelled the Soviet ambassador, berated Libya and established ties with Israel. All the while, though, the Doe government acted in a manner that harmed the country's interests, and the country's debt ballooned.

In this period, where values were eroded and self-interest reigned supreme, Ellen stuck to her principles. She had not lost her mettle and her rare willingness to openly challenge the mighty. Once again she was granted an opportunity to express her views publicly, at another address to a graduation ceremony. This time it was at the Booker Washington Institute, in November 1980. In her address, she criticized the happenings in Liberia. She told the story of a farmer who was worried about a rat that was stealing his rice. He laid a rat trap, but the rat always dodged the trap. One day, his wife injured herself when she accidently put her foot on the rat trap. Her foot developed gangrene and to cure her of the gangrene, the farmer killed his chicken to make soup for her so that she might be saved. When she did not survive, the farmer had to kill his cow for her funeral. The story was a metaphor for the coup and Doe's maladministration of Liberia. Ellen declared that the coup leaders were running the economy with the same recklessness as the farmer and were putting the country's welfare at stake.

The news of Ellen's speech reached the Executive Mansion, and Ellen was told in fairly stark terms that her oratory had not been appreciated. Fearing reprisal, Ellen thought it was time to beat a tactical retreat again and so decided to leave Liberia. She asked her seniors at the World Bank to call her back to her Washington post, and they secured her release because Doe could barely oppose their request. He was attempting at that time to project himself positively on the world stage, and he could hardly afford to face accusations of thuggery of the kind that had marked his rise to power. Ellen hastily packed and flew to Washington. It was eight months after the coup, and she left with hardly any hope of returning to Liberia.

Amazingly, Ellen had managed to evade the rat trap of these turbulent times in Liberia with deftness and audacity, all the while maintaining her integrity. She could easily have collaborated with Doe's government, as some may have suspected, but she was throughout acting in the interests of the nation. In any event, her fearlessness in speaking frankly of the ills that plagued Liberia earned for her the lasting and unreserved respect of the nation's people. Ellen stayed with the World Bank for some months and then accepted an appointment as a vice president of Citibank. She was posted to Citibank's African regional office in Nairobi. The main task assigned to her at Nairobi was to market Citibank financial products in new markets. Her duties required that she tour extensively; she would visit countries such as Uganda, Rwanda and Ethiopia. Ellen enjoyed a comfortable stay in Nairobi and also her stint at Citibank. She found that the ambience in the bank facilitated learning and enhanced her marketing skills and analytical abilities. Ellen, despite being busy in her demanding job, kept herself abreast of developments back home in Liberia during her sojourn in Nairobi. Amazingly, she also continued her contact with Doe and paid him courtesy calls from time to time. True to her character, she once chided General Doe: 'You promised the people so many things, and you are not keeping those promises.' Doe retorted, 'I did not promise them shit.' In one desultory sentence, General Doe laid bare the contempt of a despot for his people.

As every coup leader is apt to do under international pressure, General Doe announced action for the restoration of democracy in Liberia. He confirmed that elections would be held in January 1985, and a new constitution was adopted after being overwhelmingly approved by voters in a national referendum. The constitution raised the minimum age for president to thirty-five – the youthful Doe added two years to his age. He launched his own political party, the National Democratic Party of Liberia (NDPL). Many political parties sprang up. While the NDPL was granted registration easily, others encountered many hurdles. Ellen began receiving calls from friends in Liberia to return to form a political party. Ellen, always eager to be at the forefront of Liberian affairs, was soon in Monrovia to launch the Liberian Action Party (LAP). In the party, a popular politician, Jackson F. Doe, was slated to stand for president and Ellen for vice president. It was clear from the bureaucratic chicanery, though, that Doe never intended to grant registration to political parties other than his own.

Meanwhile, Ellen received an invitation from a group called the Union of Liberian Associations in the Americas, where she was to deliver the keynote address. As was her wont, she delivered a blistering speech, which quickly reached Doe's ears. Ellen returned to Monrovia to visit her mother and assess the political situation there. Soon President Doe sent for her. The soldiers who came with his message also demanded Ellen's passport. With little choice but to comply, she reported before Doe at the Executive Mansion. He ordered his foreign affairs minister Eastman to read Ellen's speech. When he reached the line in the speech, 'All the nicest words and the biggest promises written by someone trained in the use of the pen and read by someone trained in the use of the gun are taken for what they are

– words.' At this Doe yelled, 'They think I am stupid!' The worst was still to come when Eastman read the line in which Ellen said that the country was being run by idiots. 'Oh, you think we are idiots,' yelled Doe again.

By now, Ellen knew that she was in serious trouble. The chorus of yelling was intimidating, but Ellen decided to wield the weapon of equanimity to deter the raw and angry men. General Doe, says Ellen, seemed to wonder why she never squirmed before him. General Doe then put her under house arrest, under strict observation. Even her mother living next door, who was a great support to Ellen, was not permitted to meet her. Ellen's bravery, at any rate, seems to have come to her through her mother, who never counselled Ellen to take the easy path or the path of submission. Her mother perhaps firmly believed the prophecy of the old man that Ellen would one day be great and that no one could interfere in the divine design.

While under house arrest, Ellen resumed her political activities by surreptitiously sending messages to the outside world. One of the messages was intercepted, and said, 'To the people: Stand firm! Don't give in! Our course is right and we will win.' Soon she was put in a military prison where some university students had already been detained. Doe turned Ellen's case into a cause célèbre when he put her on trial before a military court. It instantly made Ellen a hero, because her trial invited international attention. Her colleagues in the World Bank and her employer at Citibank demanded her release, but Doe pressed ahead and charged her with sedition. The US Congress called upon the American government to secure her freedom and block all aid to Liberia if Ellen was not released. For the first time in the history of Liberia, the country's women formed groups. These were led by Ellen's friend Clave, who collected more than ten thousand signatures demanding that she be freed.

The military tribunal met at the Temple of Justice on Capitol Hill to decide her case. Every day, Ellen was escorted on foot to the tribunal and returned to the prison in the same manner. She was accorded the aura of a folk hero when the people lined the streets as she walked by, surrounded by policemen. The whole case hinged not on sedition but on the use of the word idiots with reference to the government. Before the tribunal, her stance was neither apologetic nor defiant. Nonetheless, she was found guilty, sentenced to ten years of hard labour and incarcerated in the infamous Belle Yalla prison in the remote north of the country, which was notorious for its routine torturing of political prisoners.

Doe's heavy-handedness proved to be a blessing in disguise. Doe, in awarding such harsh punishment, inflicted injury on his reputation; and he found himself under intense internal and external pressure to release Ellen. Ellen says during the whole tribulation, whenever in low moments, a biblical injunction her mother used to recite would come to her aid: 'Be still and know that I am God.' Then, in that stillness, when everything seemed to be lost, a miracle happened. Doe granted Ellen and the students clemency. Ellen was released, but Doe had not given in. He sent for senior members of her party, the Liberian Action Party, and asked them to make a choice: Either deny Ellen's nomination for vice president or see the party lose its registration. He wanted the party to expel Ellen. The party leadership did not possess Ellen's grit – it did a volte-face and condemned Ellen's 'seditious' activities. Immediately, the party's registration was granted and Ellen was left disenfranchised.

Ellen's courage could barely be questioned, but the pain of being abandoned by her own party may only have been devastating. Nevertheless, at the insistence of a few of her supporters, Ellen decided to run for senator and launched her campaign immediately. A few days after her release, Doe again sent for her and told her point-blank to leave the country quietly. In return, he assured her, he would file no more charges. Ellen, however, knew that Doe had already done his worst and could do little more against her under the circumstances. She firmly declined his offer and again launched her campaign.

Elections were held on 15 October 1985, but election results were declared only on 29 October. Although the vote count proceeded in secret – and at a glacial pace – no questions were entertained about the process. There were reports of ballots being stolen and burnt. A *New York Times* editorial claimed that the elections were neither free nor fair. The result of the rigged elections was bound to be in favour of Doe, who was declared elected with 50.9 per cent of the vote. The margin of victory seems to have been kept deliberately to a minimum to inspire international faith in the free and fair conduct of the elections; but it was set just high enough to avoid a run-off.

It was later revealed that the counting of the ballot was conducted in secret by staff handpicked by Samuel Doe for this very purpose. Indeed, Doe's party won twenty-one of the twenty-six Senate seats and fifty-one of sixty-four seats in the House of Representatives. Ellen too was elected senator, with the highest number of votes, for the Montserrado County Senate seat. Complaints were lodged with the Special Elections Commission and it was decided to boycott the seats which others had won in the legislature. With the reins of power firmly in his hands, the self-appointed General Doe, in any case, became president-elect Samuel Doe.

Ellen refused to act legislatively in protest at Doe's hijacking the presidential election. Considerable pressure was brought to bear on her to accept the legislative position. Even the US prevailed upon her to assume her senatorial duties. But it was too well known that Ellen would not work as a senator under the dispensation of a president she openly referred to as 'an idiot', and further she felt that accepting the senatorial seat would lend legitimacy to the rigged elections. In hindsight, Ellen regretted her decision. She finally realized that her being the focus of peoples' distrust and disaffection against President Doe undermined Liberia's political stability. It is little wonder, though, given the furore over the election result, that another coup attempt took place shortly thereafter. Thomas Quiwonkpa turned out to be a second Doe. On 12 November 1985, gunfire again erupted on the streets of Monrovia. Again a voice on the radio proclaimed that patriotic forces – this time led by General Quiwonkpa – had taken control of the radio station, surrounded the Executive Mansion and overthrown the regime.

During his years of rule, Doe had thoroughly discredited himself – locally and abroad. Stealing the election was a continuation of a litany of illegitimate assumptions of power. When Quiwonkpa took over, people danced in the streets. But the celebration proved to be premature. The coup failed; Doe and his supporters blamed Jackson Doe and Ellen for the debacle. President Doe's men took Ellen prisoner, bundling her into a jeep and ordering her to take them to Jackson Doe's house. She deliberately misdirected them, and soon found herself being terrorized. One soldier held a burning match near her hair, saying, 'I am going to burn your hair off.' Another soldier ripped her gold ring from her finger. Yet another roared, 'We are going to take you there and bury you alive.' Ellen kept looking into their eyes, engaging them in conversation and calming them. This seems to have had its effect, for they turned the jeep, took Ellen to a building, shoved her into a cell and immediately slammed the cell door. Some men were huddled in the next cell. They were taken out and shot.

Ellen was scheduled to meet the same fate. A soldier came to her cell around midnight with the intention of raping her, but the moment he unlocked the cell door, a voice from behind him commanded him to retreat. The soldier locked the door and went away. Thus, Ellen was saved from one of the worst fates for a woman. Then, around 2 a.m., a naked Gio woman of about twenty years of age, crying hysterically, was pushed into her cell. Upon Ellen's petitioning the soldiers, a wrapped skirt was brought for the young woman to cover her body, and both she and Ellen spent the night sitting together on the floor of the cell, fearing every moment for their lives.

In the morning, Ellen was taken away and produced before General Moses Wright, who asked her, 'Why are you causing all this trouble?' He ordered her to accept her seat in the legislature and assured her she would then be spared further harassment. Ellen said, 'I'm sorry but I can't do that.' After failing to be persuaded to change her decision, Ellen was ordered back to the cell she shared with the young woman. The pair was ordered to cook meals for the soldiers. Before Ellen could engage herself in meal preparation, however, she was ordered to be taken again to the Executive Mansion to appear before President Doe. Ellen admits that though throughout the ordeal she had inwardly maintained some semblance of equanimity, this time she was completely overcome by terror. She was convinced that her execution was only a few minutes away.

Again, however, fate intervened. One Colonel Smith ordered her to be taken to Barclay Training Center rather than to the Executive Mansion. Quiwonkpa, though, was brutally dispatched. His body was put on display at the Barclay Training Center and his mutilated remains paraded through the streets of Monrovia and publicly exhibited on the grounds of the Executive Mansion, heightening the reign of terror that Doe now unleashed on his opponents. Thousands were slaughtered in Doe's subsequent ethnic purging.

On 6 January 1986, Samuel K. Doe was sworn in as Liberia's president. In his inaugural speech, he talked of reconciliation across the land. Though he released many prisoners after the coup, Ellen remained incarcerated. She and Jackson Doe, who had been located without Ellen's assistance, were charged with sedition, a capital offence. Once again international pressure was brought to bear on Samuel Doe, and Jackson Doe and several others were released. Ellen, however, was not released until further international pressure was exerted. Ellen was eventually freed in the name of national reconciliation and promotion of peace and stability. She was granted amnesty along with several others. After she was released, she was asked to board a truck and sit on the front seat, while several men rode in the open back of the truck. Ellen refused to sit on the front seat and went to the back of the truck with the men. As the truck passed through the streets, crowds lined the pavements, and once again Ellen became a folk hero. Ellen alighted and mounted a table in the street, addressing the crowd with her fist raised in a power salute.

'Freedom!' she cried out.

'Freedom!' the crowd roared back.

'We will overcome! Tyranny will not prevail!'

'Aluta continual!' (the struggle continues), the crowd echoed.

Nonetheless, Ellen's challenges seemed unending. Again Doe summoned her to the Executive Mansion. He told her that she should accept the seat in the legislature, which again she politely but firmly declined. She was asked to relent because some other legislators of her own party, including Chairman Michael Wreh, had already taken the seats and withdrawn their complaints regarding electoral fraud. In the party's executive meeting, Wreh and others were asked to reconsider their decision, but they did not oblige and left the party. Ellen, however, still held firm; she refused to accept the seat, regardless of Doe's reaction. She instead told Doe that it was not too late for him to make amends. Doe demanded that she write out what he should do. Ellen sent her suggestions, but they were never taken seriously. She learnt later that he ignored her letter because she had not addressed him as President Doe.

Ellen represented one of the few serious challenges to Doe's rule at that juncture and it became clear that she faced elimination. How, where and under what circumstances were perhaps the only matters of conjecture. She was hounded wherever she went. She travelled incognito whenever she could, and ultimately – on the strength of an old passport – she managed to flee Liberia by air from Buchanan Airport, about ninety miles from Monrovia. She left on the day of her son's wedding, because no one suspected that she would be absent from this important event. She reached Abidjan and flew from there to New York.

Back in America, she became vice president and director of Equator Bank, while in Liberia, Doe thwarted yet another coup attempt, this time led by J. Nicholas Podier, in July 1988. The saga of oppression and suppression, hounding opposition leaders and killing innocent civilians replayed. There was yet another coup attempt, led by Charles Taylor, on 24 December 1989. Another rebel force led by Prince Yormie Johnson, who had split from Taylor, also revolted. The rival forces closed in on the streets of Monrovia. The people of the city were greatly terrorized, and some 500,000 sought shelter in neighbouring countries. Due to looting, there was an acute scarcity of food, and people survived on edible plants, swamp weeds, wild cassava, bush rats, frogs and snails. A resident of the city told a reporter for the *Boston Globe* that 'the dogs ate the dead and we ate the dogs'.

In the midst of fierce fighting, some 2,000 people took shelter in St Peter's Lutheran Church in the Sinkor section of Monrovia, which had been designated a Red Cross shelter. A few hours after dusk on 29 July 1990, about fifty government soldiers entered the church and began shooting indiscriminately. They then hacked the injured civilians to death with machetes. Around 600 people, including women and children, were slaughtered. Ellen was horrified. She blasted Doe and his soldiers and said they were no better than beasts. On 9 September 1990, Doe's regime came to an end when Prince Johnson and his troops captured him at the ECOMOG (The Economic Community of West African States Monitoring Group) headquarters, where Doe had come to seek safe passage out of Liberia. Doe was taken to Johnson's headquarters, where he was tortured brutally, his ears cut off, and killed.

Doe's homicidal regime and the terror it unleashed on Liberia's population is difficult to comprehend for those who have lived only in times of peace and democracy. Suffice it to say that Ellen stared death in the face numerous times; yet she did not capitulate to the demands of tyranny. With almost preternatural courage, she adhered to her ideals and steadfastly refused to participate in a system that she believed to be hopelessly corrupt and riven with fraud. In doing so, she demonstrated her unerring integrity; she placed her concern for her country and its people above not just her personal comfort, but her safety. Her stand against her country's dictators could easily have cost her her life, and her people would remember her bravery.

Back in America, in 1992, Ellen joined the United Nations Development Programme's (UNDP) Regional Bureau for Africa as assistant Secretary General of the United Nations. It was a cooling period for Ellen, away from Liberia's politics, though she kept herself abreast of developments back home. While at the UNDP, she acquired a much broader perspective on Africa when working with Boutros Boutros-Ghali and later with Kofi Annan. With Kofi Annan at the helm, she was afforded greater responsibility. In this role, she interacted closely with several heads of state in Africa, including Julius Nyerere and Nelson Mandela, who were instrumental in shaping and enriching her understanding of statesmanship. Violence continued to rage in Liberia, but she maintained her political neutrality.

When elections were declared for May 1997 in Liberia, Ellen started receiving calls from home urging her to return, because many considered that only she could mount a meaningful challenge to Charles Taylor's election. Her initial reaction was lukewarm. Soon afterwards, however, she decided to contest the poll against Taylor. Not one family member supported her decision: they thought she was comfortable and well ensconced at the United Nations; she had a promising career, so why come back and become embroiled in the country's political machinations? She stood a good chance of one day becoming the UNDP associate administrator. Ellen's loved ones called her decision to run against Taylor crazy and stupid. Ellen says no one could appreciate why she was ready to sacrifice all her comforts and promising career at the United Nations and instead choose to invite trouble. Nonetheless, serious canvassing began, and though there were twelve other contestants in the fray, the real fight was between Charles Taylor and Ellen. Wherever she went, the people cheered her, regardless of the fear Taylor inspired.

The election received international attention, not the least because former US president Jimmy Carter was present as an observer. Strangely, President Carter appeared to hold Charles Taylor in some esteem, despite Taylor's involvement in heinous war crimes that would later merit a fifty-year sentence imposed by the special court at The Hague. Along with his wife, Rosalynn, President Carter visited Ellen at her house in Monrovia. He also cautioned Ellen that Taylor was going to win, and asked her what she would do once Taylor was elected. Ellen told President

Carter that she was determined to give Charles Taylor a run for his money.

Ellen was fighting the election, banking upon herself and the people's support, but Charles Taylor had several critical advantages. He had money to bribe, power to intimidate, a twelve-seat helicopter to reach rural electorates; and last but not least, he banked on a pervasive fear in the minds of Liberians that if they did not elect Taylor he would govern the country by brutal dictatorship anyway. Thus, a war-weary populace felt that electing him would bring some peace and stability to the country. A bizarre electoral slogan for the Taylor campaign seemed to sum up the electorate's quandary: 'He killed my Ma, he killed my Pa, but I will vote for him.'

On the day of voting, 19 July 1997, reports of rigging poured in from all sides. Charles Taylor was declared the winner, polling more than 75 per cent of the ballot, with Ellen trailing with a miserable 9.5 per cent. Jimmy Carter stamped his seal of approval on the polls, certifying that the elections were conducted fairly and freely, and hailed Liberia's functioning democracy 'almost a miracle'. Ellen, however, again displayed her hallmark audacity in declaring that the elections were conducted in a fraudulent manner.

Charles Taylor called Ellen after his victory but she declined to meet him. President Carter went again to meet Ellen and asked that she work with Charles Taylor. Ellen retorted indignantly that on account of all the death and destruction Taylor had caused, she could never work with him. She told Carter that she believed that the elections were rigged, notwithstanding his stamp of approval. Ellen admonished Carter that he should speak against the fraud in the elections rather than upbraid her for not joining Taylor's government. Carter left for America dissatisfied; he deprecated Ellen's stance and charged her with being unreasonable. Ellen regretted that President Carter misread her, and that he appeared to have taken her response personally.

After his victory, Taylor sent a messenger, Blamoh Nelson, asking Ellen if she would join the government and lead the social security agency. Ellen bluntly retorted: 'Great – he wants me to take care of the people while he steals the money?' It seems that gaol, intimidation and the ever-present prospect of an extrajudicial death had immunized Ellen against fear.

Ellen knew Taylor's government would soon fall due to several innate contradictions. Taylor was, after all, a warlord attempting to run a democratically elected administration. In order to better monitor the situation back home, Ellen settled in Abidjan, where she had set up a consultancy firm. True to his track record of reactionary violence, Taylor brooked no criticism from any quarter. He ordered the closure of radio stations and newspapers. He arrested journalists, some of whom were beaten and their houses ransacked and destroyed, and all key posts were given to his henchmen or his former soldiers. Taylor's cronies began destroying the country's economy. Seeing the dismal state of affairs in the nation, Ellen periodically visited Liberia and made public statements criticizing Taylor. It became clear to all and sundry that Ellen and Taylor were on a collision course. Ellen continued to receive death threats, which for the most part she ignored. Ellen admits that she could, without fear, face threats and intimidation. She could do so, she says, because of her belief in predestination. She always thought that if the moment of her death arrives, let it come, and if it has not come, there is no need to fear.

It was not long before Taylor resorted to political assassinations, which were orchestrated by his chief bodyguard, General Benjamin Yeaten. Samuel Dokie, a former colleague of Taylor and who had run for senator, was abducted and brutally murdered in November 1997, along with his wife and two other relatives.

Their mutilated, charred bodies were found in their burnt-out car. Widespread demonstrations were held in Monrovia against these killings. One Norwai Flomo, a fierce critic of Taylor, was also done to death after he was dragged out from his home. Taylor was quickly dissipating the people's trust and blatantly reneging on his commitment to work for their welfare.

Taylor sowed the seeds of his own downfall when after substantially looting his own country, he trained his sights on the rich resources of neighbouring countries. In Sierra Leone, Taylor had supported a small group known as the Revolutionary United Front (RUF) since 1991, and his involvement continued from the Executive Mansion in Monrovia. The RUF has gained control over much of the country's diamond mines as Sierra Leone spiralled into chaos, fuelling a civil war notable for the depravity of its combatants. Taylor was a master in the game of enlisting the support of child soldiers, though other rival factions also indulged in this practice. His commanders gave the child recruits drugs – opium, marijuana and amphetamines – to heighten their ferocity and fearlessness. The RUF, borrowing a leaf from Taylor's book, recruited child soldiers by forcing them to rape or kill their own mothers and sisters before they swore allegiance to the RUF's leader, Fodoy Sankoh. Sankoh knew that children who could rape and kill their own parents could stoop to any level of bestial behaviour.

The RUF's war in Sierra Leone claimed tens of thousands of lives, with a similar number brutally maimed; and some two million people were displaced by fighting. It was later learnt that Taylor went as far as to personally direct RUF operations in Sierra Leone. Taylor's atrocities and support of the RUF could no longer be ignored by the international community. Even the forbearant Jimmy Carter had grown weary of him. In November 2000, President Carter closed down his Carter Center in Monrovia and made known his anguish and disappointment in a public letter to Taylor. In this letter, Carter admitted that Taylor had left no space for meaningful political debate and that Liberia's role in the conflicts of the region had been destructive. Ellen's stand against Taylor and his regime stood vindicated. Carter, meanwhile, may only have repented his earlier support for Taylor's government.

Taylor's murderous days in power were numbered, however. A group calling itself Liberians United for Reconciliation and Democracy (LURD), a loose coalition of dissident groups, began an armed campaign against Taylor's government, attacking Taylor's forces in Lofa County and surging towards Monrovia. Taylor linked Ellen with LURD and vowed to personally arrest her if she set foot in Liberia. Ellen denounced the charge of her alignment with LURD. She publicly challenged Taylor to substantiate his allegation. Otherwise, she said, he would prove himself a pathological liar, as he had been characterized by Liberian cleric Archbishop Michael K. Francis.

Eventually, the people's suffering in the region spurred action in the UN Security Council, which imposed restrictions on Liberia in May 2001. Taylor, among other senior Liberian officials, was subject to travel restrictions, and the export of Liberian diamonds was banned. In 2001 Taylor further revealed himself when he was invited to a conciliatory conference held in Ouagadougou and organized by Blaise Compaoré, the president of Burkina Faso. Instead of attending, Taylor sent a message which read, 'I have God and I have guns. I don't need anybody else.'

The worst for Taylor and the country's civilians was yet to come, though. In July 2003, Monrovia was subject to a medieval-style siege. LURD, attacking from the north and west, trapped the city's residents in the nation's capital. Doe sympathizers of the Krahn tribe, under a group called Movement for Democracy in Liberia (MODEL), moved in from the east. Taylor, meanwhile, found himself in the centre with supplies of food, water and medicines cut off. Widespread devastation took place in Liberia's capital.

In June, President George Bush had asked Taylor to resign for the sake of peace; he spoke more forcefully in July when he said, 'Mr Taylor has got to go.' Ellen was elated beyond measure upon hearing President Bush's warning. Secretary General Kofi Annan appointed Jacques Klein as special representative of the Secretary General and coordinator of United Nations Operations in Liberia. Taylor proved a tough man to deal with; Klein described him as a 'psychopathic killer'. Although he was hardened by years of guerrilla warfare and had no intention of capitulating, Taylor could ultimately do little else when international troops reached Liberia. Monrovia became infamous. The international press labelled the city the 'world's most dangerous place'. Under immense pressure from all sides – African leaders, the United States and the growing chaos within the country as rebels maintained a stranglehold on Monrovia – Taylor resigned on 11 August 2003. With his resignation, a gory, nightmarish fourteen years of mass murders, rapes and barbarism came to an end. Taylor boarded a plane and flew to Nigeria to live in exile. An hour after his departure, three US helicopters appeared in the sky above Monrovia, and the people cheered.

In choosing his successor, rival parties led by LURD, MODEL and Taylor's representatives made claims and counter-claims. A rumour was floated that Taylor would accept anyone other than Ellen as head of the transitional government. Nonetheless, the mantle fell to Gyude Bryant, who would serve as the chairman of the Transitional Government of Liberia from 14 October 2003 to 16 January 2006. Ellen was appointed head of the Governance Reform Commission. The charge of this Commission was promotion and support of good governance in Liberia. In the final analysis, the Commission turned out to be only a policymaking body with hardly any enforcement power. The interim government was to be substituted by a duly elected government. Elections in Liberia were announced for 11 October 2005.

Several factors were stacked against Ellen's becoming president. Of these, a few appeared insurmountable: She was a woman in a male-dominated society; she was a light-skinned, erudite scholar; and at sixty-seven years of age, she seemed too mature to inspire the country's youth at that critical time. In view of her perceived dismal prospects for election, media reports projected football star George Weah as the sure winner of the polls. US intelligence and diplomatic reports concurred. The US ambassador to Liberia, John Blaney, also made known his preference for Weah, and was unashamedly forthcoming in asking Ellen to make way for the youthful Weah. She discounted his assessment to his face.

She resigned from the Governance Reform Commission in early 2005 and plunged headlong into the electoral battle. The scene was clear of any warlord who could threaten peace, and with the largest United Nations Mission in the world at the time to guarantee stability and a peaceful election, Ellen would at last enjoy a fair opportunity for election to the highest office of the land. Ellen's family and all her friends lent their support. She immediately organized the Unity Party and started the campaign, working full steam ahead, day and night.

Ellen led a vigorous campaign apprising the people of her vision and agenda for the Unity Party. She declared that it was time to turn the current adversity into an opportunity for national reconstruction and renewal. She successfully enlisted the support of several of her friends, prominent among them Harry Greaves. Greaves in turn recruited Larry Gibson, an American attorney and professor of law at the University of Maryland, who was instrumental in the successful conduct of the election campaign of Bill Clinton in the 1992 US presidential election. Both of them provided critical support to Ellen.

One of the unconventional ideas that Larry Gibson floated was regarding the freedom to wear African or Western clothes. Ellen, he said, should exercise the same prerogatives as men. So she shed her head wrap and flooded the country with her photographs. Larry secured campaign materials: posters, stickers, banners and a large number of T-shirts. Amara Konneh, an information specialist, formed a group called Liberians for Ellen and created a website to mobilize support.

Weah declined to take part in a live public debate with Ellen in Monrovia. He also suggested that there would be trouble if he failed to win. To vitiate the atmosphere further, he declared that the only way he could lose was by fraud. Final voting took place on 8 November. On the following day, news of Ellen's commanding lead came, showing her ahead by 40 to 60 per cent. In the final round, she was declared the winner of the election, polling 60 per cent of the vote. Weah alleged fraud and also ballot tampering, but failed to produce any evidence to substantiate his claim. On 23 November 2005, the National Elections Commission declared Ellen the twenty-third president of Liberia. Ellen accepted her victory with profound gratitude to the Liberian people who had elected her – more so on account of her being a woman.

Jubilant crowds welcomed her electoral success, and it was after decades that the streets of Monrovia again witnessed people dancing freely, assured that their streets would now be free of murder, mayhem, rape and fear. Euphoria spread throughout the country. The day 16 January 2006 was one of rare elation for all Liberians, particularly women, who saw in Ellen's election hope of a better tomorrow – a tomorrow where none of them would be subject to the savagery, humiliation, rape and naked parading that had stained the years of dictatorship. The Capitol Building wore a festive look as never before. Ellen being administered the oath of office of the president of Liberia was witnessed by the heads of state of Nigeria, South Africa, Niger, Ghana, Sierra Leone, Burkina Faso, Mali and Togo, as well as a host of other dignitaries from China, France and Finland. Special guests in attendance were the US first lady Laura Bush and Secretary of State Condoleezza Rice. George Weah and the other presidential candidates occupied the first row. Chief Justice Henry Reed Cooper of the Supreme Court administered the oath of office.

Ellen's inaugural speech was tremendously inspiring and ennobling, and when she touched upon the role and future of women in Liberia, those assembled for the function could not contain their enthusiasm. It seemed that women had been rescued from barbarism: murder, rape, public humiliation and – most abominably – sons being recruited as Charles Taylor's child soldiers committing atrocities against their own families.

Upon witnessing the ecstatic reaction of the audience at the inauguration, Condoleezza Rice remarked that she had not seen such a moving event in her life.

After being sworn in as president, Ellen's challenge was to heal the bruised psyche of the nation, to bring it back to life from numbness, back to action from ennui, back to hope from despair, back on the path of development from destruction. This was a time for consecrating the whole nation and securing for Liberia a place of dignity and honour in the comity of nations, especially those of the African continent. After taking over as president, Ellen immediately engaged in national reconstruction. The first task of importance was rehabilitating orphaned, deserted and neglected children and providing them food, housing and education. A task of greater importance still was to heal the perverted psyches of child soldiers whom Charles Taylor had drugged and mesmerized to the extent that they would follow him to the end of the earth. They had known complete freedom to loot, kill and rape. For Ellen, guiding these desperado children back to normality was a daunting task. She considered their education paramount for their rehabilitation, and to this end instituted a revised, compulsory education programme. Under this programme, tuition fees for primary classes were abolished and fees for higher classes were reduced and standardized.

The second important task was to revive the moribund economy. This proved especially challenging, because most Liberian businessmen and entrepreneurs had long fled the country. Nevertheless, she achieved spectacular success, due in no small degree to her years of training and employment in the fiscal sector. Her most prominent achievement was securing – with the assistance of a host of countries – significant reduction in the national debt, which stood at US $4.9 billion in 2006. The US waived $391 million, and G-8 countries headed by Chancellor Angela Merkel of Germany, in appreciation of Ellen's pursuing macroeconomic policies, provided assistance of $324.5 million for paying 60 per cent of Liberia's IMF loan. Many other forums, such as the World Bank, the IMF and the Paris Club also came forward to provide some relief to Liberia. These measures, and the stability that Ellen inspired in the nation, finally succeeded in restricting the national debt to 3 per cent of Liberia's GDP. Ellen also adopted a host of welfare measures to give succour to the country's long-suffering underclass.

In the international arena, where Liberia had long been considered the epitome of a failed state, with its macabre human rights violations making regular lurid copy in the world's press, the nation's image faced redemption. Whereas its citizens abroad had earlier been ashamed to call themselves Liberians, they were now proud to announce their nationality and were welcomed for this. Because of President Sirleaf, Liberia had become a paragon for people across the globe struggling against unjust systems. Liberia had begun to regain its lost glory.

Ellen ran for a second term in 2010 as a nominee of her Unity Party and was pitted against Winston Tubman of the Congress for Democratic Change. Just four days before the elections, she was awarded the Nobel Peace Prize, which Tubman termed 'undeserved' and characterized as external interference in Liberia's politics. Ellen did not trumpet her prize, though, and called its conferment at that time mere coincidence. She secured 43.9 per cent of the votes in the first round, and because her vote share was less than 50 per cent in the first round, she had to run for the second round also. Tubman, however, did not contest the second round, alleging fraud in the first round. Thus, Ellen was declared president for a second term. She took the oath of presidency for the second time on 16 January 2012. After her re-election, she started a national dialogue to integrate the country, and created a national peace and reconciliation initiative under the leadership of her co-recipient of the Nobel Peace Prize, Leymah Gbowee.

Ellen's has been a life of self-fulfilment and service in equal measure, and she has barely any regrets. Her family have undoubtedly suffered greatly from her engagement in fierce struggles for survival: survival not just in mundane terms but in terms of her values, her vision and her hope for a vibrant, progressive Liberia as it is today under her able stewardship. She does not regret not remarrying; perhaps remaining single has allowed her greater latitude to determine her life's course and commit her energies to her country. There are few people who can say, as Ellen says, 'There is nothing I would have done differently. Everything I did, every action I took, matched the circumstances of the times. If I could live my life again, I would live it exactly the same way.' To say that Ellen Johnson Sirleaf is charismatic would perhaps understate her personal magnetism. She is relaxed in her demeanour, and her presence is palpable to those in her company. She chooses her words carefully, enunciating her thoughts in clear and attractive English, which along with its unmistakably African tones, has a slight southern American lilt. Ellen was characteristically forthcoming in her interview with me, and her responses to my questions show her to be a self-aware, thoughtful woman, whose humility and firm but considered approach to her duties can serve as inspiration for women of the world.

Supriya Vani: *Your parents had humble beginnings. They had borne the brunt of poverty at a very young age. But your father rose to a position of eminence when he became the first Liberian from his indigenous ethnic group to be in the country's legislature. Clearly, this must have provided you with a quantum leap in the social and political reckoning and must have gone a long way in shaping and moulding your life's ambitions. Is it so? Or did you achieve success by your sheer grit and determination?*

Ellen Johnson Sirleaf: Yes, we come from a very humble background. My father became a member of the legislature (parliament), and we obtained some social standing, but it didn't last long. My father suffered a severe stroke and became totally dependent on us for everything; from a young age, we had to cater to his every need. So, what we got from our parents was not really a cakewalk into life. From them we gained a firm understanding of hard work, integrity, a deep sense of family and strong religious belief. And that guided me and my three siblings throughout our lives.

In my particular case, by the time I was twenty-two, I was stranded in an abusive marriage, with four sons. I only had a high school diploma and was working in a car parts store. However, that bad marriage took me to America, gave me an opportunity to go to school and earn a degree, and become more assertive and independent. When I returned home and started to work, things moved quickly, maybe too quickly at times. Did I achieve things by my sheer grit and determination? I strongly believe in the core values my parents embedded in me, but I also met many good people who believed in the same things I believed in, and they helped me achieve my goals.

SV: The rebel in you first got noticed publicly when you, as an assistant minister of finance under the William R. Tolbert government, delivered a bombshell speech to the Liberian Chamber of Commerce, where you said that the country's corporations were harming the economy of the nation by hoarding or sending their profits overseas. How do you reflect today on that incident and the reaction of the corporates at that time?

EJS: Looking back, I believe that was a turning point in my political awakening. As a Liberian official, I thought I was saying the right thing, defending our national interest and questioning the bad practices at the time. It was not something that our people in government were used to hearing. One had to simply accept a job, climb the social and economic ladder and enjoy life. But I couldn't do that, and it didn't sit well with many of my colleagues.

SV: How do you reflect today on your having accepted the presidency of the Liberia Bank for Development and Investment (LBDI) under the military regime of Samuel K. Doe, and then having shunned him and fled the country? Do you regret having joined the dispensation of a military dictator?

EJS: I don't regret having taken the presidency of the LBDI. I didn't see it as working for Samuel Doe, but rather working to help the people of my country who needed access to loans and other services. I believed that no matter the violent nature of the change, it had happened, but we couldn't abandon our country. You also have to consider the historical context: This was Africa in the 1980s, when there was a military coup every day somewhere. One could choose to run away, or stay home and work for change. Many of us gave Samuel Doe the benefit of the doubt; we thought that he would take advantage of that goodwill and put the country on a new path. But that did not happen, and I ended up in exile, like most of the growing Liberian middle class.

SV: As a proud recipient of the Nobel Peace Prize and so many other coveted peace prizes, don't you think as an international peace activist and also as a head of a nation's government, that no military dictator should ever be recognized by the people of the world and also the governments of the world? Will not such non-cooperation by the people and the nations discourage men in uniform from indulging in military coups?

EJS: I agree with you and I think Africa is also moving in that direction. Now, people who take up arms and overthrow governments are the exceptions on the continent, and they are not welcomed in the African Union. The military coups very negatively affected Africa's growth and undermined its stability. Many of the difficulties that our countries face today happened as a result of bad governance under military dictators, especially during the cold war.

SV: You never hesitated to resign from eminent positions to acquire political space. You resigned from Citibank in 1985 to participate in the 1985 elections in Liberia. Later, you resigned your position in UNDP's Regional Bureau for Africa to run for the Liberian presidency; and today you are happily saddled on the president's chair. Are you really settled now, or do you have yet to go miles and miles before the ultimate full stop? To put it precisely, what are your further ambitions as an individual?

EJS: As long as I can live at home, do what I want to do, be with my family and my friends, I am settled. I always came back, leaving high-paying jobs, because I have never wanted to leave home and go anywhere else. Circumstances pushed me into exile, and I always longed to return home. So, every time there was talk about elections, I thought we were emerging from the tunnel. Finally, in 2003, the conditions for peace were present, and I moved back and worked on the Good Governance Commission until I was elected president. My ambition for the future? Upon leaving the presidency, I plan to spend lots of time with my grandchildren, and see Liberia grow and prosper.

SV: *You had occasions to study the effect of wars and conflicts on women, and must have formulated a vision of what should be the role of women in peacemaking. Kindly elaborate how women can be helpful in building world peace?*

EJS: I have seen the effects of war on women and also their tenacity, their drive and their dedication when they started to fight for peace, both in Liberia and elsewhere in the world. I think women have a special approach to life in general – maybe it comes from motherhood, or because women spend so much time caring for children – so they see life differently and their preoccupations are different.

I believe that women are helping to build world peace. There are many women today who are involved in peacemaking; they are in leadership positions and they take actions and say words that have an impact on world peace. They are finding their own voices, working together and ensuring that the gains we made are not rolled back.

SV: *You and Leymah Gbowee led forceful campaigns against Charles Taylor and succeeded in banishing the tyrant. Both of you concertedly scripted a saga of valour in Liberia. Both of you are shining examples of how women alone can beat a tyrant or how women alone can lead a nation. I believe the trio of you, Leymah Gbowee, and Tawakkol Karman can fire the imagination of women the world over by joint travels worldwide. All living Nobel Peace laureates have an obligation to work for world peace, to fight against all kinds of injustice jointly and severally, and make world peace a palpable reality. Am I right, madam?*

EJS: We are already doing that. We are still engaged in the advocacy work we started long ago, and that brought us the Nobel Peace Prize. We didn't start our struggles because we were aiming at the Nobel Peace Prize or to gain any recognition. We believed in what we did, and we continue to do that work, speaking for things we believe in, and standing against injustices, violence and bad governance. For example, Tawakkol Karman and I were members of the high-level panel set up by the UN Secretary General Ban Ki-moon to prepare a global approach post-2015, when the Millennium Development Goals expire. Leymah Gbowee has an NGO in Liberia, where she works with the young people, especially girls, and she travels around the world. So, we are all engaged in the struggle.

SV: *Now when the controversy regarding the recommendations of the Truth and Reconciliation Commission was resolved by the Supreme Court in January 2011, in the famous case of* Williams *vs* Tah, *do you regret having supported Charles Taylor initially? Do you now* *hold that no military dictator should be lent any support by people and governments?*

EJS: I've said many times that I regret the harms caused by the war, and I regret my name being associated with that of Taylor, as if there were a collaboration between us. I was a member of a pressure group that was trying to put pressure on Samuel Doe to make him turn to democracy, and we were getting nowhere. Then, the war started, and our group, the Association for Constitutional Democracy in Liberia (ACDL), raised $10,000 that I delivered to Taylor for the victims of the war. I am against any form of dictatorship, be it military or civilian. This is why I spent so much time fighting.

SV: What is your vision of world peace? How do you think we can attain it?

EJS: I believe that we can attain world peace. To do so, we must ensure that freedom and dignity for every human being is respected everywhere. We must fight to end violence between countries and against women and children. We must end inequalities by eradicating poverty in all its forms, and we must ensure that every child grows up healthy, has access to quality education and is prepared for a productive future.

SV: What is your message for the youth of the world?

EJS: Go to school, learn and prepare yourself for the future. Do not sit and expect others to do things for you. Don't be afraid to dream big, have ambitions, and work with honesty, integrity and respect for others.

SV: Last, but not the least, will you tell me who are the people who have influenced your personality.

EJS: First, I will say my parents and my family. Then, a whole lot of people that I met, in school, at work and around the world. I think it's always hard to say this person or that person had the greatest influence on one's life. It all depends on circumstances. There are a great many people that I admire; I read their work and am inspired by their thoughts.

~~~

Ellen has elevated womanhood on the African continent to its true place of honour and dignity. When asked whether she would have achieved the same success if she were a man, she emphatically replies,

> I would have accomplished far, far less. I would have been, really, just another man. I think as a woman I was an exception and being an exception gave me both the visibility and the drive to succeed. I was ahead of my time, but I am no longer alone. We are breaking barriers daily; in another decade there will be hundreds of women in real positions of leadership all over Africa and all over the world.

Now it is my turn and your turn to be one of those hundreds and raise this number by a million more. If humanity is to survive, women have to be at the centre stage of all human activity: to save and nourish humanity; to knit humanity into one family, transcending all man-made barriers of national boundaries – of colour, of caste, of high and low and of ethnicity – and to prove the following Sanskrit aphorism true:

<div align="center">

वसुधैव कुटुम्बकम् (Vasudhaiva kutumbakam)
The world is one family.

</div>

LEYMAH GBOWEE

THE MASTER STRIKER

'You can never leave footprints that last if
you are always walking on tiptoes.'

Leymah Roberta Gbowee, one of the three proud recipients of the Nobel Peace Prize for the year 2011, is quite an enigma. Perhaps she has remained so even to herself: Her life's journey from abysmal lows to the zenith of human endeavour is, to say the very least, astounding. But the question remains: What uncommon trait does she possess in such uncommon measure that she was able to overcome adversity to become an iconic figure for her nation and a paragon of women's empowerment for the world? And all the while, nurture her family and rebuild her self-worth from the ruins of an abusive relationship?

Though it was the sudden eruption of civil war in Liberia that tore her life apart, the reason for her experiencing the deepest lows of her life was her children, and the motivation for her rising beyond them was also her children. She was able to withstand the widespread devastation and hunger inflicted on Liberia's people by the war, but she endured an abusive relationship because she wanted a father's protection for her children. She could never invoke the courage to rear her children without a father's presence in those war-ravaged years. Her thoughts for her children's welfare may have caused her to tolerate situations of immense suffering, but they also provided impetus for her to tackle her country's issues. She felt that she simply could not allow herself to seem wanting when she would be later asked by her children, 'Mama, what was your role during the crisis?'

Leymah' life journey, like that of most of her compatriots, has seen many peaks and valleys. At seventeen, she felt that not even the sky was the limit, for she had received visions of a wonderful future. On New Year's Eve 1989, outside St Peter's Lutheran Church, Leymah Gbowee and several of her friends wrote their hopes for the new year on pieces of white paper and placed the papers in a steel drum. The priest ignited them with a match, and their burning sent smoke curls rising to the sky as Leymah and her friends sang songs of praise to God. Beholding the smoke ascending to the heavens, the hopeful teenage Leymah felt sure that God had heard all her prayers.

A month later, upon her high school graduation, Leymah's father threw a party – the biggest party in their Monrovia neighbourhood – for Leymah and her sisters. Leymah was elated. Everyone was dressed beautifully: her mother wearing a traditional African *lappa* (colourful traditional African wrapper garment, worn with a blouse and headscarf) embroidered with gold, and Leymah attired in a trouser suit and adorned with glittering gold earrings, bracelet, chain and ring. Leymah's family lived in a good house with all the modern amenities except an air conditioner. Her father felt it was a great day for the family: two of his daughters had graduated from school. Neighbours brought expensive gifts. Her father told Leymah in the presence of the gathering that he was proud of her. She profusely thanked her parents and their guests. The party was long remembered in the neighbourhood for its rich food and drinks, and the celebration marked the happiest time of Leymah's life.

Leymah was emerging from her adolescence – confident, sure of her beauty. She dreamt of being a doctor, marrying, having children and someday owning a huge air-conditioned mansion on Payne Avenue in Monrovia. Little did she know that her country and her life would be shrouded for years in the darkness of civil strife that would lay waste to her fortunes along with those of the nation. She would live during these years from moment to moment. Hungry for days on end, she would find herself lured into a tempestuous relationship with an eminently unsuitable partner who would become the father of her children. And after his abuse, she would find it nigh on impossible to regain her lost self-esteem. She would also suffer the deep emotional wounds of her father shunning her and describing the very daughter he had earlier praised as a 'damned baby machine'.

Nevertheless, even after falling to a personal nadir, Leymah retained the essence of her self and astounded the world with a daring campaign that helped to secure Charles Taylor's exit from Liberia and brought peace to her beloved country.

Her story of personal redemption and service to her people is an elixir for all who have fallen on hard times. It inspires confidence; it shows that periods in one's life which seem to be swallowed by darkness are transitory; the challenge is surely a matter of persevering, sustaining oneself until dawn inevitably appears.

Leymah finished high school as President Samuel Doe's repressive regime was beginning to falter. Doe had thoroughly discredited himself. He had alternately bestowed benefits on some and persecuted others, largely on the basis of their tribal identity, with the intention of staving off attempts to oust him from the government. His own Krahn tribe was preferred for positions of power, and Doe had systematically hounded the Gio and Mano tribes, which he considered disloyal and a threat to his rule. By late 1989, he had quelled two coup attempts – one in November 1985 and the other in July 1988, both orchestrated by former comrades – and was now facing more organized and determined adversaries. Charles Taylor, a brutal warlord, was heading towards Monrovia with a group of armed rebels from northern Liberia, and his rival Prince Johnson was vying with him for control of the nation's capital. Their missions were to overthrow Samuel Doe.

Leymah first witnessed killings at the impressionable age of seventeen, when soldiers shot at two fleeing boys wearing red T-shirts, a rebel uniform. One of the boys fell to the ground, dead. The other, dodging the pursuing soldiers, escaped. Leymah was horrified to see the murder in cold blood. The thought of death had barely crossed her mind at this age, and she became angry at God for failing to respond to her prayers. Losing one's faith in God may be a rite of passage for some, but once one loses faith in oneself, everything is lost. The manifestation of faith in one's self is betrayed in one's anger. The core of her anger, Leymah says, derived from witnessing children dying of malnutrition or simply being slaughtered. With time, and as she grew and strengthened from her own personal tribulations, she decided to do something about the nation's plight. She says she did not hope for someone to come and change the situation. This was the crux of her transformation from poverty-stricken and half-starved mother to enlightened peace activist. She plunged headlong into the maelstrom of ruthless violence and savagery around her because she could not bear to remain a passive observer while her people suffered.

Besides the deadly engagements of hostile forces, random, mindless killing became the order of the day during the civil war. A soldier had killed a boy only because he wanted to have his shoes. In another incident, a woman had encountered an emaciated man with hunger etched on his features, searching through a heap of garbage for something to eat. 'What are you looking for?' the woman had asked. 'Palm kernels,' the man had replied. The woman knew well his searching was futile. She asked him to wait, brought a few cups of rice in a plastic bag and threw the bag towards him. Moments after the poor man retrieved the bag, some soldiers ordered him to stop and asked him what he was carrying. 'Rice,' the man replied. The soldiers immediately seized the rice and shot him dead, believing that whoever carried rice did so to distribute it for winning support against the government. The woman began wailing, because it was she who had given him the rice and made him suspect in the eyes of the soldiers. The woman was Leymah's mother.

Leymah had a close shave with death at the hands of Samuel Doe's soldiers when they came to loot her home. They surrounded the house and ordered everyone outside. The children, frightened, ran down the staircase crying, 'Jesus! Jesus! Satan, we rebuke you!' They had been taught to pray in such moments, but it made Leymah angry because she had come to believe that God does not help. One woman kept repeating this prayer and the soldiers took hold of her. The woman's sister came to her aid, but a soldier slapped her. She slapped the soldier in return and then she was shot dead. The soldiers started whipping other older women with their belts and hitting them with their rifles.

When Leymah saw soldiers hitting her mother and understood that she faced imminent death, she was almost numb with fear. One of Leymah's uncles arrived and saved her mother and other family members. When a commander learnt from him in Mende language that he belonged to the Mende tribe, the commander allowed her uncle to take Leymah and the others away – ordering them never to come back. Soon thereafter, her sister Geneva, her mother, her cousin and all the children huddled in a room to spend the night. The city seemed totally deserted, and in the middle of the night a deathly silence was suddenly broken. Loud screams were heard, pleading for help. President Doe's Krahn-dominated army had begun targeting members of the Gio and Mano tribes.

In the hope that Doe's soldiers would not enter a place of God, the Liberian Council of Churches offered asylum to some thousand Gio and Mano people in danger, many of them women and children, at St Peter's Lutheran Church, where Leymah and her friends had offered their prayers for the future little more than a year earlier. Doe's soldiers paid no heed to religious sentiment; they barged into the church at around 3 a.m. and indulged in a spree of rape, mayhem and slaughter, shooting and hacking to death those who had sought refuge inside. In a futile bid to save themselves, many came running outside but were cut down by gunfire from soldiers outside the church. Later the bodies of men, women and children were found littering the streets. Leymah trembled when she saw pregnant women among the dead. She also saw a dead man lying on the street with his dead child in his arms – a bottle of milk still in the child's hand. Leymah's mother outside heard that Leymah and her sister had been killed inside the church and she had come there to identify their bodies. Leymah found her collapsed, weeping at the sight of the carnage.

In contrasting tribal fortunes, in Lofa County and the coastal city of Buchanan, south of Monrovia – but with similar, depraved violence – Charles Taylor's troops were massacring members of the Krahn and Mandingo tribes and pushing towards the capital. Prince Johnson's men were also closing in on Monrovia, and as they gained ground they cut water lines, telephone lines and electricity and blocked the escape route to Sierra Leone.

Leymah and others crossed Gabriel Tucker Bridge to Bushrod Island in the hope of finding some food. The children were crying with hunger. This was Prince Johnson's territory. His soldiers, upon spotting Leymah and others, asked them to identify their tribe. Upon learning that they belonged to Kpelle tribe, a soldier asked her to speak some words in Kpelle. Her mother said, '*Ba ngun, ku me ni na?*' ('Hello, what news is there?') The soldier allowed Leymah and others to proceed. On the way ahead, Leymah found the body of a dead woman. A hungry dog was pulling on one of her legs. Soon she discovered that it was not the only sight of a dog eating a human corpse. Then Leymah and others took refuge in the Logan Town slum. After a week, Leymah's sister Josephine arrived and informed Leymah that their father was at the US embassy – he was convinced that all his family members were dead.

They made their way to the US embassy, where they stayed for three weeks and were then evacuated in a Ghanaian Cargo ship. In the midst of the Tano river, they encountered thousands of people. Leymah became so seasick that she almost wished she were dead. After three torturous days, the ship reached land. It was not Sierra Leone, as Leymah had hoped, but Ghana. They found shelter in Buduburam refugee camp. Life in the camp was no less miserable than what they had fled, but there was no threat of physical elimination or rape. Each evening they would glue themselves to the radio to listen to the latest reports from Liberia. On 9 September 1990, they learnt that Prince Johnson had captured President Doe and tortured him to death. In 1991, when a new interim government was formed in Liberia, Leymah returned to Monrovia, which she deeply regretted: She found the city a vandalized, burnt-out shell of its former glory. Death and destruction were widespread. There was no civic amenity left in the city. Her father was still in the US embassy. Others began returning to Liberia to rebuild their lives. Leymah went to Paynesville, where the family owned a house, but everything was in total ruin there too.

Leymah found that everyone in Paynesville had fled and that while leaving, had grabbed anything of value that had been left behind. Leymah discovered that one of her neighbours was wearing her Dexter boots, which she had received as a gift at her graduation party. She wailed in grief: Her home was gone. The people she loved had left or had been killed. She could never have imagined while dancing at her graduation party just two years earlier that total catastrophe would so quickly overtake her world. The grief Leymah experienced is expressed starkly in her poignant words: 'When you move so quickly from innocence to a world of fear, pain and loss, it's as if the flesh of your heart and mind gets cut away, piece by piece, like slices taken off a ham. Finally, there is nothing left but bone.'

Liberia's history of these years is chilling, and Leymah's story of her late teen experience is alien and sobering to those whose lives have been filled with relative peace and comfort. Her life, along with those of most compatriots, was a fight for survival: financial insecurity and scarcity haunted her every day. Food is an almost irresistible bait to a hungry person. It led her into the arms of a philanderer who would alternately love her and torment her.

While she was in Buduburam refugee camp in Ghana with her family, Daniel lived next to them with his wife and a two-year-old son. There, he set his eyes on Leymah. Daniel's wife had fallen seriously ill while at Buduburam, and a woman had offered her help. Daniel developed a relationship with that woman and abandoned his wife. When he returned to Monrovia in July 1991, Daniel sought out and pursued Leymah.

She knew that he was trouble and she should not encourage him. Daniel, however, knew well how to inveigle himself into a woman's heart, and was persistent with his courtship. One day, when Leymah returned home, she found her roommates feasting on sandwiches. They told her that Daniel had delivered a huge bag of sandwiches for her, which they were now relishing themselves. For a long time, Leymah had not seen food in such quantities that she could eat to satisfaction. Daniel continued his advances and made Leymah agree to visit restaurants with him, where he would order her decent meals. Touched by his care for her, she allowed herself to be drawn into an intimate relationship, though she instinctively knew Daniel was not a suitable partner. As much as anything, she was unable to withstand his subtle ways of intruding into her life in these desperate times.

Once, when Leymah had contracted malaria, and was suffering a high fever and unbearable headache, her friends took her to a local doctor; but she had no money to pay for her treatment. She asked her friends to approach her father for money. She was later surprised to discover that Daniel instead had footed the bill. Daniel was employed as a logistics officer at the American embassy complex and spent money lavishly on her, buying her gifts of jewellery, perfume and other costly things. He feasted with her at his favourite restaurant, Angel's. All these favours, though, were recompense for an abusive relationship.

If there had been no war, Leymah would have been in college, living with her parents; but the war had completely devastated her entire country when she was at a critical stage of her development. Unable to keep herself afloat amidst widespread hunger, she succumbed to Daniel's overtures, which she knew were only for her body and not for her as his life's companion. By the time she became aware of the morass in which she had landed herself with Daniel, it was too late. She had deluded herself that she was barren like one of her aunts, but this veil of self-deception was torn one day when she discovered that she was pregnant. Leymah now felt that she had little option: She had to rely on Daniel for support. Little did she comprehend at this time that in giving herself to Daniel, she had bartered away her freedom.

This she learnt before long when she went in search of him late one evening. She knew he would probably be in a small rented room that he had kept before they were together. Upon reaching the room, she found that he had a woman with him. He smirked at her and was quite unabashed in declaring that he was doing no wrong. He was, he said, only heeding the advice of the president that every Liberian should help as many displaced people as possible – and he was simply giving that poor girl a home for the night. On another occasion, Daniel brought a girl to their home and slept with her. His lust new no bounds. If Leymah ever showed any disinclination for having sex, he would react violently. Becoming pregnant to Daniel had rendered her hopelessly trapped.

Leymah gave birth to her son, Joshua Mensah, whom she called Nuku, and when she was confined with her second child, her parents relented and allowed her to live with Daniel at the Old Road house. In April 1994 her daughter Amber was born. Daniel by this time had lost his job, because he was caught accepting a bribe for recommending visas without investigation. This prompted Leymah to start taking charge of her destiny. She began making cakes and pastries and selling them.

Shortly thereafter the civil strife began to subside. Leymah joined a UNICEF programme that trained social workers to help those traumatized by war to lead normal lives. Leymah herself needed to be comforted. She had allowed herself to be sexually exploited and had become trapped in a dysfunctional relationship for the security of her children. In the training programme, she felt as if she were receiving treatment for herself as much as learning to treat others. She was assigned to work in an orphanage, but she could not withstand the misery of the suffering children and was unable to bear their trauma. She opted to work instead with twenty women refugees from Sierra Leone. All these women had been raped. Part of Leymah's job was to make them aware of sexually transmitted diseases and HIV prevention.

She began asserting her independence; and Daniel began withdrawing from the relationship. Yet there seemed no end to her travails. One night, Daniel came home very late and started a fierce fight with Leymah and forced himself upon her. Soon thereafter, she discovered that she was pregnant once more. This broke her spirit to rise on her own. War again erupted in April 1996; sounds of rockets flying overhead and automatic rifle fire were only somewhat less terrifying than bullets hitting their house. It was again time to flee. In her nightgown and slippers, carrying her children and medicines and nothing more, Leymah ran from her home as bullets whizzed in the air around her. The city was burning again, falling victim to a now familiar madness of war.

Daniel wanted to go to Accra, to his mother, and Leymah could easily have let him go and been free of him forever. But she was still not sure of herself and was woefully lacking in the self-confidence needed to rear her children away from their father's care. Further, she felt she could turn to no one, because her parents were scornful of her abusive relationship with Daniel. So she decided to accompany Daniel to Accra, Ghana's capital, despite her reservations.

But she found that she was not welcome in his mother's house. His mother told her that she was in a sinful relationship with her son, and she was taking her into her home simply out of Christian compassion. She never addressed her as Leymah, but always as 'You'. She thought Leymah had performed *juju* (magic) on her son to compel him to take care of not his, but her children. Sadly, it seemed that Daniel shared his mother's belief. Soon, she was burdened with the responsibility of rearing her third child. Arthur was born in June 1996, in a hospital where Daniel had taken and then abandoned Leymah. The hospital administration would not let her leave without paying for her treatment; but neither would they provide her proper care. She lay in the hospital's hallway, where she remained on the floor in the cold night with her shivering newborn child, providing him warmth with her skin only and covering him simply with her lappa. She stayed in the hallway for a week. After a week, Daniel came but vanished without paying a penny, while Leymah was still bleeding.

For seven days, in the hallway of a hospital, this intelligent, promising young woman found herself reduced to helplessness and privation; and worse, this was the world into which she had brought her third child. She was in such a terrible state that passers-by took her for a beggar and tossed coins and loaves of bread before her. She was comforted by a lady who took her to her private room, provided her with a clean blanket and gave her diapers. Leymah cried. But her benefactor was quick to admonish her, telling her that she was young and educated and competent to rear her children independently and educate them. A doctor she had consulted earlier for being badly anaemic came forward to foot her hospital bill. The doctor had earlier advised Leymah to leave Daniel, because he did not deserve her. It appears that Daniel had deserted her at the hospital as he was engaged in a fierce court battle for divorce.

In spite of her abandonment, Leymah returned to Daniel. Leymah started going to church, where mothers would look for helpers to braid their daughters' hair. She braided girls' hair and would get a dollar in return, with which she would buy her morning breakfast. Still it did not provide her enough to feed her children. Sometimes, she would try to satiate her hunger by eating the crust left in the pot after she had cooked. Once she braided a woman's hair, and it took her longer than usual because the woman's hair was dishevelled. It was late in the evening, and the woman did not know the way to the main road. Leymah escorted her to the main road, and when she returned, Daniel gave her a hard slap and cursed her.

The constant refrain of his tirades was calling her stupid, and he seemed to regard her with contempt. Indeed, Leymah was treated more like a slave than a servant. Once when she cooked rice, others ate it, leaving nothing for her. At the time, her sister-in-law was visiting, along with some guests. Leymah brought some yams from the market, boiled them and served her visitors. Everyone was enjoying a hearty laugh while eating the delicious yams. Her sister-in-law had, however, not shared even one piece of yam with Leymah. After eating, her sister-in-law left the bowl near the kitchen and departed. Leymah entered the kitchen and surreptitiously devoured the leftovers in the bowl. She then hurriedly cleaned it so that no one could see that she had eaten their leftovers.

As time passed, Daniel began a relationship with a neighbour, and by this time Leymah had become completely disabused of any notion that she and her children were unable to live without him. Daniel left home, and Leymah decided to go back to Paynesville by bus. The bus driver allowed her to travel on credit because she had not even a cent to pay for her fare. She brought the three children to Liberia and was expecting her fourth. Leymah found a Liberia exhausted to its core, just as she herself felt. The worst spectacle was children crying: 'He killed my Ma, he killed my Pa, but I will vote for him.' Charles Taylor had perverted a sizeable portion of Liberia's young. He had given children Kalashnikovs to kill those who were opposed to him, and allowed them to rape and plunder at will. In the elections of July 1997, Taylor won through fraud abetted by widespread intimidation.

Leymah surrendered herself and the children to her parents' mercy. Her father rhetorically inquired of her plans for the future, and expressed his utter contempt for her at her failure to reply. She had fallen into such a personal abyss that she had been living without any aspiration, any dream for the future. When her mother asked her the same question, Leymah admitted that she had no plans. Her mother promised her she would do everything for her, but Leymah was far from enthused. She had lost all hope, burdened with the duty of rearing four children without any stable source of income. She believed that if she died, people would take better care of her children. A verse of the celebrated Urdu poet Mirza Ghalib is worth recalling here: 'It is the desire of every drop of water to get merged into the ocean, and when the cup of woes gets filled, it acts as an antidote for such woes.'

When Leymah found herself at this low ebb, a new awakening was bound to occur for her. One day her son would not rise from his bed, even as the day wore on. When Leymah's mother went to wake him, he asked her where he was. When his grandmother told him that they were in Liberia, he said he had dreamed they were still in Ghana, and so he did not want to get up. This proved to be a turning point in Leymah's life. She cursed herself for having been resigned to the circumstances she encountered. She regretted having blamed her parents for her predicament; she regretted having given herself to Daniel and for not plucking up the courage to rear her children independently. And above all, she regretted not having given her youngsters the childhood they deserved.

What she needed most was a job. The very thought of a job reminded her of Tunde, a thoughtful, pleasant man whom she had met while working with the women refugees from Sierra Leone. She made arrangements to meet Tunde in his office, and when she arrived, he welcomed Leymah with a warm hug. When Tunde learnt that Leymah had left Daniel, he began to show a romantic interest in her. Leymah discovered that he was an amiable and decent person; someone she could share her feelings with. She found him to be the gentlest person she had met. Upon learning that Leymah had given birth to a daughter, Tunde rushed to her side in defiance of the curfew in place at the time, bringing with him several gifts. His caring nature impressed Leymah, and she concluded that he was the man she could love. He began to find a place in her life and her heart. Her father did not approve of her affair with Tunde, though, because he feared she was simply rushing into another abusive relationship. Her mother was but supportive of them.

Upon Tunde's insistence, and with his assuring her of her competence, Leymah decided to pursue a degree. Her mother was the head of the church's women's division and facilitated Leymah's admission to Mother Patern College of Health

Sciences, which offered an associate of arts degree programme. She knew the pastor in charge, Reverend Bartholomew Bioh Colley, whom everyone called BB. Leymah impressed BB when he entrusted her with counselling traumatized women from Lofa County. BB recommended her for accompanying a study group from Manchester. She received a stipend of two hundred British pounds, which gave her a degree of security, though she had to suffer the pangs of separation from her newborn daughter, Nicole (nicknamed Pudu). BB told Leymah that each one of them was a victim, and after one has overcome one's own victimization, one has to help others overcome theirs. BB's words proved enlightening. Leymah secured good grades, and Tunde was impressed. Her self-confidence, long repressed during the tumultuous years of war and from abuse at the hands of her previous partner, was returning.

BB charged her with the task of healing disabled former child soldiers at the Trauma Healing and Reconciliation Programme (THRP). The children had acquired a truly fiendish mindset. They could kill anyone without the least concern, and commit atrocities with abandon. There were tens of thousands of them, and among them some were as young as eight years of age. Many were so small they could hardly lift an AK-47; but they had been merciless killers nonetheless. They had been corrupted by sinister mentors, who had administered them alcohol, marijuana and other drugs. Leymah's job was to reintegrate them into Liberian society.

They had grown into veritable monsters, however, and resisted her efforts. When Leymah addressed them, one of them shouted back at her, 'Fuck you. What do you know? They want to destroy Taylor. So we kill them.' Leymah remained calm and gazed straight into his eyes. The boy realized that she was a woman who could not be cowed down and declared, 'This is a general!' Soon she became known as general among the children. Leymah learnt that each of them had a unique story of recruitment and macabre initiation.

There were many who had lost a leg or an arm, and most were addicted to drugs. There were female fighters among them too, who had joined the rebels to save themselves from being raped.

Although the vast majority of people in Monrovia cursed the child soldiers, Leymah had good reason to sympathize with them. She felt that just as her sheer hunger during wartime had caused her to submit to an abusive relationship, the child soldiers had been exploited by Charles Taylor. They, like Leymah, had been led into a situation from which there seemed no escape. If anyone deserved hatred, Leymah opined, it was men like Charles Taylor, Prince Johnson, Roosevelt Johnson and Alhaji Kromah, whose greed for power had resulted in war and ruined the lives of an entire generation.

Leymah's time at the THRP was rewarding for her. She encountered people from different walks of life who told varied stories of suffering, and she garnered a deeper understanding of the impact of war. She also became convinced of the need for forgiveness to heal its psychic wounds. Leymah dedicated herself to mending broken lives and communities. She was convinced that it was this work that she wanted to do. She became influenced by the teachings of Hizkias Assefa, a highly regarded Ethiopian conflict mediator whose concept of reconciliation appealed to her. Assefa postulated four dimensions required for true reconciliation: You must be reconciled with God, with yourself, with your environment and, finally, with the person who has done wrong to you. In her own way, Leymah articulated Assefa's message in the following words:

> You are in the valley of misery, a place of anger, depression and hurt. The person who hurt you, who raped you or killed your family, is also here. If you are still angry at that person, if you haven't been able to forgive, you are chained to him. Above you

is the mountain of peace and prosperity where we all want to go. But when you try to climb that hill, the person you haven't forgiven weighs you down. It's a personal choice whether or not to let go. Nobody can tell you how long to mourn a death or rage over a rape. But you can't move forward until you break that chain.

Through her work in redeeming the lives of others, Leymah found her own redemption. Impressed by her commitment, Leymah's family rallied for her cause. Geneva, her sister, came to live with her and took care of her children. She became the manager of Leymah's household for the following seven years. Gradually, Leymah's confidence grew, and she began to realize that she was still an attractive woman. It was a time of rediscovery for her, both personally and in her worldly destiny. In 1999, her mother was encountering difficulty in finding someone agreeable to chair the committee for planning that year's Women's Day celebrations. Leymah stepped into the breach. With the help of some of her friends, she collected thousands of US dollars and was eventually elected president of the women's association.

Around this time Leymah met Daniel again, and took no time to tell him that she had forgiven him. She used forgiveness as a benign weapon to heal wounded psyches at the THRP. She urged the women to talk openly so that they might feel relieved of the burdens they had carried in silence. This was groundbreaking. Talking openly of sex was considered taboo in Liberian society. Leymah told women at the healing centre that they are the sponges of society. Women soak up the pain around them and must squeeze out rage. In October 2000, Leymah was at the West Africa Network for Peacebuilding (WANEP) conference in Ghana, where the focus of discussion was non-violence. There she saw the film *Gandhi*. Leymah says she had doubts about non-violence as a strategy, for she had seen the power of guns. She realized after watching the film that non-violence is ultimately far more effective than violence. She understood that people could look up to Charles Taylor for perhaps ten years, but they would always look up to Gandhi, Nelson Mandela and the Dalai Lama.

Liberia, Leymah concluded, needed people inspired by these great leaders: It craved peace with vision and strength. She knew BB, Sam Doe and Tornolah Varpilah, who served on WANEP's board, to be humble but fearless and committed to the cause of peace. They spoke truth to those in power and were the saviours of their country. Leymah aspired to becoming like them.

By now, Leymah had laid the groundwork for her aspirations. She graduated from Mother Patern with an arts degree. A lavish ceremony to celebrate her achievement was attended by all her friends, her mother, her sisters and her father. This ceremony contrasted with the party which her father had hosted when Leymah and her sister had completed high school. Earlier, her father had felt proud of her, but had since rarely passed up an opportunity to denigrate her for her abusive relationship with Daniel – though he had himself fathered five children outside wedlock. At the ceremony, she addressed her father: 'I thank you for your insults. If you hadn't insulted me the way you did, I might not have made the changes I was supposed to make.' Her father was thoroughly embarrassed and just as remorseful. This moment made Leymah feel proud; that she had ultimately triumphed.

Just after receiving her degree, the THRP office appointed her to a full-time position and doubled her monthly salary to $200. Right at this time, she received a message from Thelma Ekiyor, her close friend, that WANEP had given a grant to her to start her women's network and that she was invited to launch a conference in Accra. At the conference, while others spoke of their qualifications or exalted positions, Leymah spoke of her miserable days when she was lying on the hospital floor with her newborn son Arthur and revealed that she was simply a holder of an associate of arts degree. Leymah says it helped her purge herself of shame and she felt as if a wound within had healed. After the conference, Leymah realized that trauma cannot be cured when violence is ongoing. She became convinced that the primary thrust of efforts to rehabilitate afflicted societies and individuals has to be on peace. If peace prevails, this will in itself greatly relieve people's trauma.

The primary focus of her activity was improving the lot of women as a means of building peace. She found inspiration from an account she had read in a Christian magazine, of enlightened women cooperating in the midst of the Bosnian war. The magazine told the story of two groups of women, one Serbian and the other Muslim, on opposite sides of Sarajevo city. One group had water and the other had electricity. The women with water carried buckets to those who had electricity and they used their washing machine to wash their clothes together. They talked about their menfolk, who while engaged in fierce civil conflict had left their families behind, wounded and broken. The women organized a sisterhood that transcended the power of the gun.

Buoyed by Thelma – who loved Leymah for her honesty, simplicity and desire to work hard – Leymah felt inspired to bring change to Liberia. Thelma took Leymah to every conference or peacebuilding training she attended in Ghana, Nigeria, Senegal and Sierra Leone. Thelma announced the launch of the Women in Peacebuilding Network (WIPNET) – an initiative of WANEP – in Liberia and Leymah's selection as its coordinator. Leymah's appointment was not well received. Everyone seemed to question, 'Who the hell is this Leymah?' Leymah's eyes welled with tears. Her nomination was resented, but Thelma stood by her decision. Etweda 'Sugars' Cooper, a senior activist and the host for the evening, chastised Leymah for weeping and ordered her, 'Dry your eyes and stop that shit. If those women smell fear on you, they will use you for the rest of your life.' Sugars was a fiercely radical feminist and had Leymah's best interests at heart.

Regardless of others' disapproval, Leymah forged ahead in her new position. As coordinator of WIPNET, Leymah used Thelma's training manual, which prescribed exercises that transformed women. Each woman was asked to relate to others what being a woman meant to her. This lent them confidence; they were urged to cherish and reinvigorate their strengths. Leymah acknowledges that she still relies at times on Thelma's training manual.

Some of the deeply reflective questions that Thelma wanted women within the programmes of WIPNET to ask herself are worth every woman pondering: 'As a woman, what is your crown? What are your thorns?' The women's replies converged in almost identical answers. Each one of them answered that her thorn was her inability to care for her children and the crown was also her children. Some other questions were so poignant that each woman would ultimately discover that she was at once a homemaker, an activist, a provider and a peacemaker. This led each woman to realize her inherent strength and thus the importance of her roles as a woman for her family and society.

Leymah continued to perform her regular work at the THRP. But she had not yet dealt with her own guilt of having given herself to drink and maintained a physical relationship with a man who was not her husband. On one spring morning when she was sleeping, she had a dream. It was totally dark all around, but she heard a voice, and the voice commanded Leymah, 'Gather the women to pray for peace.' When she woke up she was still hearing its echoes. It seemed to her that it was the voice of God, but she could scarce believe that God would speak to her. She thought God would never visit her because she was a fallen woman, given to drinking and recovering from an abusive relationship. Nonetheless, she shared her dream with her friend Vaiba. Esther Musah, a female evangelist from the church, overheard the conversation. Esther immediately asked all women to kneel down and pray to God. 'Dear God, thank you for sending us this vision. Jesus, help us. You are the true Prince of Peace, the only one who can grant us peace.'

Around this time, Leymah formally launched the Liberian chapter of WIPNET. She had mobilized: Vaiba, representing THRP; Asatu from the Female Law Enforcement Association; Cerue and Cecelia Danuwali from WIPNET; Janet Johnson, president of the Female Journalists Association; Mariama Brown, an NGO leader, and thirteen others. They all went to St Peter's to lend support to the women of the Christian Women's Peace Initiative (CWI) during their meeting with the World Council of Churches delegation. While addressing the gathering, Leymah declared that the women of Liberia were tired. It was high time for them to stand up and be counted, and they wanted other Christian churches to join them to make their voice louder. A Muslim woman joined them at church, which emboldened Leymah; her reaching out to her Christian sisters was the inspiration for future concerted efforts of Christian and Muslim women. The Muslim woman Asatu's proposal for an alliance of this kind stunned everyone.

There was another landmark proposal floated at the meeting, which brought into being the Peace Outreach Project. It was founded on the premise that across Liberia, it had been men's business to negotiate peace treaties. Now, the initiative should be wrested by women activists.

Leymah was transfixed by this idea. She had already realized the limited effectiveness of her work at the THRP and also concluded that she had been investing her hope in false leaders.

Leymah understood that the real task ahead of them was to wrest the country from the tentacles of Charles Taylor's organization, which served only to amass wealth and firm up his hold on power. His word – in parts of the country, at least – was almost absolute. He had ordered the closure of radio and television stations except those that ran under his control. He even banned music that was not to his liking. Once a singer released a song which had the first line, 'What kind of life is this?'. Charles Taylor's reaction to the song exhibited his bizarre approach and iron-fisted stance to his people. He went on the radio to announce that he had heard the song, which the people liked. He informed people that no one would receive salaries and no one would have money for batteries to listen to the song. The finance minister did not pay salaries to the government employees that Christmas. The singer was so frustrated he went into exile.

Leymah appreciated the futility of passive activism. Charles Taylor, whose actions had shown him to be a depraved and somewhat unhinged warlord, had presented himself as a devout Christian who could 'pray the devil out of hell'. It was time, Leymah resolved, for direct action to send the devil, Charles Taylor, back to hell. She mobilized women, and they decided to travel in pairs to the mosques on Fridays at afternoon prayers, and to the markets and to churches on Sundays. The message to all Liberian women was the same: Liberian women, awaken for peace. Leaflets the women distributed read like this:

> Hello, sister, I'm Leymah from WIPNET and I'd like to tell you about a campaign we have just started. This war has been going on a long, long time, and all of us have been suffering. People have tried to end it and there have been some big meetings, but we think the answer lies with women. We need to step forward and get involved.

The women the activists engaged were informed that there seemed to be no end to the war, and it was the women only who could help retrieve the situation and save themselves and their children. All that the women needed was to step forward and get involved. Leymah's efforts to raise the awareness of Liberia's women quickly yielded results. A significant proportion of the country's women had been raped, the husbands of some had been killed, and many children had been forcibly recruited into the army. The women came to realize that while they had remained passive their children had been taken from them and their families had been destroyed. They joined Leymah's movement en masse, because they saw it as the country's only hope; and they understood that it was left to them to bring the nation to its senses. Pamphlets were distributed to women carrying the following message: 'We are tired! We are tired of our children being killed! We are tired of being raped! Women, wake up – you have a voice in the peace process!'

For the women who could not read, a boy was hired to draw colourful pictures that explained their mission. The pamphlets inspired the women from all walks of life, and more and more joined the movement. Thus, the movement gained momentum quietly, without media coverage. A new workshop was convened with a view to bringing about a Christian and Muslim women's synergy and enhancing the movement's cohesion. Leymah asked the women to write their titles or occupations on a sheet of paper – lawyer, doctor, mother, market woman – and put the paper in a box. The box was locked, and Leymah informed them that they were not lawyers, activists or wives there. They were not Christians or Muslims; they were not Kpelle, Loma, Krahn or Mandingo. They were not indigenous or elite. They were only women. It was decided that Christian and Muslim women would have their own leadership, but they would work together on one overriding issue – the need for peace.

In December 2002, the Peace Outreach Project was closed and the Christian–Muslim alliance was formed. Monrovia's people were astonished when 200 Christian and Muslim women marched down Tubman Boulevard to City Hall. Christians were wearing their lappas and Muslims their headscarves. As the women walked, they sang alternately a Muslim song and a Christian hymn. The multitudes gathered to watch them. The press covered the event during which the following document was read: 'We envision peace. A peaceful coexistence that fosters equality, collective ownership and full participation of particularly women in all decision-making processes for conflict prevention, promotion-making processes for conflict prevention, promotion for human security and socio-economic development.'

Leymah was not sure which direction the collective leadership of Christians and Muslims would take. But as more and more women gathered, the fear, depression and loneliness of thirteen long years were fast disappearing as she began to fulfil her destiny.

The presidential elections were slated to take place in Liberia in 2003, but President Charles Taylor was under attack from LURD and MODEL; and neither side relented, even under pressure from the United States. President Taylor postured that he was the democratically elected president and could not negotiate with terrorists. His refusal led the LURD leadership to shun negotiation. The intense fighting resulted in 360,000 people being driven from their homes and forced to live in filthy tent camps in five neighbouring countries. All the while, the fight inched closer to the capital Monrovia.

The Christian and Muslim women activists, totally distraught with the latest developments, met at the WIPNET office on 2 April 2003. They decided they needed to ramp up the pressure on the government because the men had failed. They broadcast a message on Radio Veritas, which was under the control of the

Catholic Church rather than the government. People heard the statement and also an invitation to future WIPNET meetings. The response was overwhelming. Each night meetings were held. On finding that the WIPNET office was not sufficient to accommodate the number of women participants, it was decided to hold a gathering at Monrovia City Hall on 11 April.

Charles Taylor banned street marches. 'Nobody will get into the street to embarrass my administration,' he had warned. In defiance, Janet's radio show broadcast a message that if the people wanted peace they should make it their duty to come to the Monrovia City Hall at 8 a.m., wearing only white. Charles Taylor was also invited. On 11 April, there was a sea of white at City Hall. Different women had suffered on different counts, but all of them had a common interest in securing peace. Only peace could save them from further rape and the country from devastation. Leymah wanted an immediate and unconditional ceasefire. She declared, 'In the past, we were silent. But after being killed, raped, dehumanized and infected with diseases and watching our children and families destroyed, war has taught us that the future lies in saying no to violence and yes to peace! We will not relent until peace prevails!' The women echoed, 'Peace! Peace!'

They gave Charles Taylor three days to respond to their demands and in the event of his failure to respond, they decided that all the women would stage a sit-in. The protest was non-partisan, focused on peace and not politics, with everyone wearing white T-shirts to signify peace. All women were to dress simply. The focus was on one target, with one spokesperson and one public face: Leymah. Charles Taylor's threat was real, and his army – which by now was little more than a well-armed personal militia – could easily target any one of them. There were stories of girls being raped in prison cells behind the Executive Mansion, but the women had grown tired of fear. There were only two options left: surrendering or fighting back – as a united force. And the women were in no mood to surrender.

The three-day ultimatum given to Taylor expired. When Leymah received no response from the government, she led women in a sit-in demonstration outside parliament. Charles Taylor, however, did not acknowledge their presence. The women then met each morning, with both Christian and Muslim prayers:

> The Lord is my shepherd; I shall not want...
> In the name of Allah, the Beneficent, the Merciful.
> Praise be to Allah, Lord of the worlds...

After three more days had elapsed, the women laid siege to the parliament and blocked the parking area so that no one could go in or come out. It was raining, but not one woman moved from her place. The Speaker of the parliament came out and questioned Leymah, asking her why she was using people for her personal interests. Leymah retorted in rage that it was he and the president and others in the government who had been using the people of Liberia for their own selfish gains. She declared that the women would continue to sit in the sun and in the rain until they heard from the president. More and more women joined the movement, christened as Women of Liberia Mass Action for Peace. From dawn to dusk the women would gather daily. They would dance. They would chant the slogan, 'We want peace, no more war.' This chant turned into a song:

> We want peace, no more war.
> Our children are dying – we want peace.
> We are tired of suffering – we want peace.
> We are tired of running – we want peace.

After a week, the Speaker again appeared and invited them to come on 23 April to meet President Taylor. The women were excited but wary; they feared anything could happen. Only the date had been given and no time had been indicated. Leymah, with 2,000 activists, reached there at 6 a.m. All were filled with anxiety. Some began to panic, because they knew that they were going to meet a monster. Leymah's prepared text conveyed that the women wanted an unconditional ceasefire, a dialogue between the government and the rebels and intervention by an international force. She felt an impulsive urge to go beyond her text and told the president that the women of Liberia were tired of begging for bulgar wheat. They were tired of their children being drugged and raped. They were protesting to secure the future for their children.

The wily Taylor told the women that he was sick and no group of people could make him get out of his bed except the women of Liberia, whom he considered to be his mothers. He told the women that he was ready to engage in peace talks if the rebels were also ready for this. Thereafter, Taylor sent them a contribution of $5,000 dollars. Although the women knew that the president had tried to buy their fidelity by bringing them under obligation, it was culturally improper to refuse the contribution. Taylor was playing politics. Soon, at any rate, it was announced that LURD's leaders had agreed to come to the negotiating table with President Taylor for peace talks. The only remaining issue was where to meet.

A deputation of women activists – Grace, Sugars and Asatu – decided to meet the LURD leaders in Sierra Leone. When the LURD leaders arrived to meet representatives from the Liberian Council of Churches, Grace literally rebuked them. She told them, 'We've born you! We are tired! We want you to go to Ghana for peace talks! People are dying and you must listen to us!' One of the LURD leaders had been Asatu's schoolmate. Asatu admonished him for deaths occurring daily because of the war. Sugars appealed to their egos, saying that peace in Liberia was dependent on them. They were such important men. They could save Liberia. The deputation of three ladies succeeded in persuading the LURD leadership to agree to peace talks. The men told Asatu, Grace and Sugars, 'Our mothers came all the way from Liberia to talk to us. Well, mothers, because of you, we will go.' The women's peace movement was largely one of the indigenous poor, with the exception of a few such as Sugars, who had cast aside her social standing once she had become allied with the movement.

Inevitably, the movement would encounter its own internecine conflicts. A number of women indulged in accusations and counter-accusations, with some charging others with being Taylor's spies. Leymah was not spared. Because Tunde had not yet divorced, it was whispered that Leymah pretended to be working for good, but was in fact evil and immoral. Incensed at such accusations, Leymah offered to resign, but Sugars advised her to wear such stories like a loose garment. Leymah's remorse over having involved herself in extramarital relationships with both Daniel and Tunde was becoming more pronounced, however. And she was smarting at accusations that she was trying to be the star of the movement. Such suggestions deeply vexed Leymah, for she had no life any more away from her activism.

One day, a new weapon revealed itself to the activists. It was one that had found its place in other African and European conflicts throughout history, and it was an ultimate tactic in asymmetrical warfare. Asatu was talking to a journalist and she joked with him that the women would force men to go along with them and that until they did so they would deny them sex. Soon this notion caught the fancy of women, particularly among the rural communities, where the strike took a religious turn. They said they would not have sex with men until they saw God's face for peace. It made men fearful. They thought that if they forced their women to have sex, it might invite the wrath of God. Some of the women, however, gave in to the men and some were beaten by their husbands for refusing sex. Nonetheless, the movement lasted for a few months.

It may be difficult to assess the effectiveness of the sex strike in forcing Liberia's men towards peace. Leymah herself doubts that the sex strike in itself had any tangible effect for the cause, but maintains that the massive publicity it garnered was invaluable in highlighting the issue of peace in Liberia.

Leymah adopted an orphan girl, Lucia, and now had five children, but she continued to remain immersed in the struggle for peace. With the tremendous increase in women's participation, women wore WIPNET identity cards. The movement attracted peoples' support such that bus drivers would not charge WIPNET volunteers. Some powerful figures lent their tacit support to the women. Leymah savoured her own personal victory, before her campaign for peace had prevailed over the warlords' violence, when her father once again expressed his pride in her. He acknowledged his daughter's competence and courage in leading Liberia's peace movement, unmindful of the consequences.

The women's efforts seemed to be having their effect. News broke that talks would be held in Ghana on 4 June 2003. Everyone started singing and dancing. The Christian women sang Muslim songs and the Muslim women sang Christian hymns. The talks were to be mediated by General Abdulsalami A. Abubakar, a former president of Nigeria. The WIPNET activists were not invited. Nonetheless, Leymah, Sugars and Vaiba went to Ghana. The Buduburam refugee camp where Leymah had lived earlier was still crowded with tens of thousands of Liberians. Leymah lobbied the women there to join in the protests at the conference centre where the talks were to be held. It proved a Herculean task. Some women feigning commitment to peace were secretly working for Charles Taylor. Some dubbed the activists 'Congo people' – elites. By the time the conference had begun, however, 500 women were with them: camp dwellers, refugees living in Accra and WIPNET members from northern Ghana. The war in Liberia – which had initially been given little attention throughout the world – was now recognized for its potential to flare up and consume the entire region.

The presidents of South Africa, Nigeria, the Ivory Coast and Sierra Leone, along with a US delegation, arrived at the three-star Lake Volta Hotel in Akosombo, where representatives of LURD were also present. Taylor portrayed himself as a peace lover and offered to remove himself from the post of president of Liberia if that could bring an end to the war. He granted amnesty to prisoners who had been arrested while fighting his government. Then came shocking news. The UN-backed Special Court for Sierra Leone (SCSL) issued a sealed indictment against Taylor for his involvement in war crimes – murder, mutilation and rape – that the Foday Sankoh–led RUF rebels had committed. The indictment was unsealed, and the court asked Ghana to execute a warrant for Taylor's arrest. Taylor, however, fled by plane to Liberia, leaving behind his delegation to negotiate.

Total chaos prevailed in Monrovia. Taylor's goons roamed the streets in jeeps broadcasting that if the president was arrested they would kill everyone and burn everything and Liberia would cease to exist. The talks had to be postponed. The LURD forces reached the outskirts of Monrovia. More than 100,000 people had fallen under the control of the rebel forces. The population of the countryside had swiftly migrated to Monrovia, fleeing the steady advance of rebel forces. Peace talks back in Ghana were not making any headway; LURD men predictably demanded that Taylor step down as president because he had been indicted as a war criminal. Taylor's representative, however, ridiculed the demand, saying that an elected president could not be asked to abdicate. Leymah and her associates continued to sit and chant 'we want peace'.

One morning, General Abubakar passed by them and asked Leymah if they were the same women who had been there throughout. When Leymah replied in the affirmative, he smiled and said, 'Keep up the good work.' Days passed, but there was no progress in the peace talks. The only words the men at the negotiating table had with Leymah was, 'Would you like to have a drink?' Leymah had the audacity to tell them that she did not drink with killers. On 17 June, a ceasefire was signed between two rebel groups and Taylor. The agreement envisaged a transitional government without Charles Taylor. It created instant euphoria, and there was dancing in the streets of Monrovia.

The euphoria, however, was short-lived. Taylor withdrew his support for the agreement, on account of its requirement for him to leave office. The ceasefire agreement was torn apart, and the LURD forces launched a horrific offensive against Monrovia. They indulged in rape and killing with impunity. Bombardment caused widespread devastation. Every place was looted and smashed. Taylor was no less obdurate, declaring, 'We will never desert the city. We will fight street to street, house to house.' The women's patience was exhausted and their prayers were becoming bitter and vengeful. They invoked Isaiah 49:25, where it is written, 'Yes. Captives will be taken from warriors and plunder retrieved from the fierce; I will contend with those who contend with you. I will make your oppressors eat their own flesh. They will be drunk on their own blood as with wine.'

The WIPNET women could barely contain their frustration and grief. On 21 July, artillery shells hit the US embassy's diplomatic compound in Monrovia, where 10,000 people had taken shelter from the fighting. Dozens were killed, including women and children. Two little boys had been brushing their teeth outdoors when the shells hit, and all that was left of them was their slippers. The incident made Leymah cry. She damned herself for being so stupid as to believe that a handful of women could stop a war. She delivered an anguished protest to heaven: 'You fooled me, God.' Grace comforted Leymah, telling her that they could not let them win. Leymah's desperation now lent her courage, and she knew she must act.

When the negotiating hall was filled with representatives from LURD, MODEL and Taylor, and also activists of political parties and civil society groups, Leymah led her women in the hallway and began to disrobe in front of the glass doors at the main entrance to the meeting room. The hall was crowded with some 200 women holding black-lettered signs that read, BUTCHERS AND MURDERERS OF THE LIBERIAN PEOPLE: STOP!

Leymah delivered a note to General Abubakar: 'We are holding these delegates, especially the Liberians, hostage. They will feel the pain of what our people are feeling at home.'

General Abubakar immediately took to the public address system and declared, with more than a hint of levity, 'Distinguished ladies and gentlemen, the peace hall has been seized by General Leymah and her troops.' Immediately security guards rushed towards the women. One of them inquired who the leader was. Leymah thundered, 'Here I am.' He told Leymah that she was obstructing justice and that he was going to arrest her. She was so desperate and beside herself that she took off her hair tie and pulled off her lappa, exposing the tights underneath. Sugars did the same.

Leymah's thought was that if they wanted to humiliate her by arresting her, she would eclipse their move with the magnitude of her own self-humiliation. Moreover, her threat to strip herself alarmed the guards and those at the negotiating table, because in

Africa, it is believed that if an old or married woman strips herself in the presence of a man, it brings a terrible curse on him. If an old or married woman strips before a man, it signifies that, as he is born through a woman's vagina, she intends to take back his life. For the men at the peace conference, Leymah's attempt to strip herself amounted, at least psychically, to a serious threat. For the battle-hardened men at the negotiating table this was no small matter: Many of the combatants in Liberia's war had resorted to such bizarre and depraved rituals as human sacrifice – or wore women's clothing and appeared naked in battle – in the hope they would be protected from bullets and enjoy victory. When it appeared that Leymah and others would bare their bodies before all, General Abubakar promptly stepped forward to stop them. 'Madam, no!' he said. 'Leymah, do not do this.'

Both Sugars and Leymah stopped, and in rage and frustration, Leymah burst into tears. General Abubakar asked Leymah to take the women out, but they protested vociferously, declaring they would continue to lay siege to them and would not let any one of them come out and have food. They declared that many of their families had died and others were still facing death due to hunger, and they would not let the men depart until they gave them peace. It was decided that the peace talks would move on, that all of the participants would attend sessions regularly, and that they would pass by the women without ever insulting them.

Although the Liberian war still raged, that day marked the beginning of the end of this most horrific period in the nation's history. The dramatic turn in the women's protest had its impact – the mood at the conference became more sombre, and it seemed that the peace talks were thenceforth held in earnest. Finally, when it was agreed that Charles Taylor would resign the presidency and live in exile in Nigeria, it seemed that peace was imminent. The activists of Mass Action gathered at Leymah's house to watch his departure on television. Everyone felt hope and trepidation in equal measure. They feared that terrible fighting could break out just after Taylor's departure and that death would spread when his plane lifted off. The women – and indeed, all of Liberia's people – heaved a collective sigh of relief when Monrovia remained calm.

On 14 August 2003, the rebels lifted their siege of Monrovia and American troops landed to support the African peacekeepers, bringing order to a ravaged country. Leaders of LURD and MODEL and representatives of forces loyal to Taylor signed the Accra Comprehensive Peace Agreement. Gyude Bryant, a businessman without any political affiliation, would head the interim Liberian government. The agreement had been reached much earlier than expected and Leymah, along with Sugars, attended a meeting of West African women leaders in Côte d'Ivoire. Interim president Bryant told Leymah, 'Something great happened, and we can say it happened because of you all.'

Leymah and Sugars returned to Liberia, where a huge crowd of women wearing WIPNET T-shirts greeted them singing, 'We want peace. No more war.' When they and other women were passing through airport security, the security men congratulated them: 'These were the peace women. These were the women who did great work. Thank you, mothers. Thank you.'

In this bitter conflict that had raged for fourteen years and was later referred to as the Second Liberian Civil War, somewhere in the order of 250,000 lives had been extinguished. A quarter of theses were children. Every third person had been displaced. One million people were highly vulnerable to malnutrition and diseases such as diarrhoea, measles and cholera, because of contaminated water. About 75 per cent of the nation's infrastructure had been reduced to rubble: hospitals, school buildings and roads. The worst damage, however, had been to the collective psyche of the nation. An entire generation of young men had no idea what to do without a Kalashnikov in their hands. Many women had been widowed and raped and many had witnessed their daughters and mothers being raped. Some were cursed to see their own sons killing and raping at the bidding of Charles Taylor. The real challenge was still ahead. It was the challenge of rehabilitation and bringing life back to normality.

Leymah had personally seen hunger and faced extreme desperation. One can barely imagine Leymah's despair as she lay, abandoned and bleeding on the floor of a hospital with her newborn child. She had suffered her share of the country's agony during the war, but she did not allow her personal suffering to shroud her heart; the horrors that she witnessed would not impair her natural gift of compassion. Once, Leymah met a young woman who had married an old man and was pregnant with their fourth child. Her husband had been killed in front of her, her in-laws had abandoned her, and she was almost bereft of hope. But still she wanted to salvage her life and planned to buy dry goods to sell to support her children. She was penniless, though; doing business was simply impossible. Leymah gave her $500 that she may begin her work. Another woman Leymah met had been viciously beaten by her husband and was left with scars on her face. She had four children. Leymah gave money to her also.

Undoubtedly, Leymah helped these women because she acknowledged that they were in need; but her motivation to ameliorate their suffering was born of her innate empathy; and in dealing with their suffering, she encountered her own. The moment she saw such women, with pain writ large on their faces, a whirling sensation overtook her, and she felt that she would black out.

After the war, the Truth and Reconciliation Commission (TRC) was formed, and Leymah was named a commissioner-designate. Her appointment was politicized, and she tendered her resignation. She had risen from being a coordinator of WIPNET to a position where there wasn't a consultation on the future of Liberia that did not include her. Her horizons even broadened beyond Liberia. She gave presentations on women's roles in contributing to Liberia's recovery. Leymah was invited to Switzerland. She had achieved something great in Liberia, and other countries were keen to hear how she had led the nation's peace movement; how she had brought forces to the negotiating table to banish a tyrant and secure peace.

Leymah felt ill-equipped to apply her solutions to conflicts in other countries, though. She began studying books on conflict resolution theory, such as *The Journey Towards Reconciliation* and *The Little Book of Conflict Transformation*, by Jean Paul Lederach. In 2004, she attended Eastern Mennonite University's four-week annual Summer Peacebuilding Institute in Harrisonburg, Virginia, USA. There, she studied with Hizkias Assefa, whose teachings had earlier helped Leymah to overcome her anger towards Daniel, and Howard Zehr, an American criminologist and pioneer of the concept of restorative justice.

In the context of healing communities wracked by conflict, restorative justice entails addressing the victims' harms and needs and holding offenders accountable to put right those harms. The process involves victims, offenders and communities, with the view that victims and offenders will eventually become contributing members of society. It is a most powerful healing method, and it relies on forgiveness: If a community is to be made whole after a war, especially a civil war, perpetrators need to make amends and victims must forgive. Leymah was now bolstering her practical skills in dealing with conflict with sound academic theory, and it was a transformative experience for her.

In 2005, elections were declared in Liberia, and Leymah was thrilled to learn that one of the candidates for the presidential election was a woman: Ellen Johnson Sirleaf. She was not so enthused over her candidature in some respects, though, because Ellen Sirleaf had supported Charles Taylor in his initial days. Leymah declared that she had never forgiven her for her comments, 'Level the Mansion, we will rebuild it.' Nonetheless, Leymah saw in the election an opportunity for women's empowerment. Women's views had been barely represented in Liberia before the 2005 election. Women would not seek registration to vote and so were turned away at the polling booths.

Leymah took up the issue of women's registration with the officials of the United Nations Development Programme, which was supervising the elections to ensure their fair conduct. The official response was at first uninspiring. Yet five days before the elections, a call came from a UNDP official, 'Come in! Hurry! We need to talk!' Soon thereafter Leymah dispatched ten teams of twenty women each to work for registering women voters. Before the close of the time limit for registration, the registration touched 51 per cent, in contrast to the pitiful 15 per cent when the drive started.

The presidential contest was ultimately between George Weah, a football player regarded as one of the greatest African players of all time and an icon of Liberian youth, and Ellen Johnson Sirleaf, who had earlier been a minister and would later share a Nobel Peace Prize with Leymah. George Weah surged ahead of Ellen in the first round of voting and seemed sure to dominate the second round as well. Leymah was undecided in her preference. Some friends from the community and church approached her to support Ellen Johnson Sirleaf. Leymah agreed to lend her voice to the Sirleaf campaign at the urging of Joseph Boakai, who was to serve as Ellen's vice president. He had funded Women of Liberia Mass Action and had publicly advocated for women's rights. Leymah received a pledge that the Sirleaf government would respect women's rights. She was told, 'Leymah, if it gets to the point where the rights we had been fighting for are threatened, I will join you in the street.'

For Leymah, though, the most effective advocacy for Ellen Sirleaf's candidature was from her son Nuku, who told her that George Weah was a school dropout and could not lead the country properly. Leymah had long inculcated in her children the value of education, and she herself had shown her commitment to bettering her life through learning, having graduated from college in the face of overwhelmingly adverse circumstances. Leymah says she realized that her personal reservations about Ellen Johnson Sirleaf should not come in the way of her making a selection from the two candidates. No actual canvassing for Ellen Sirleaf could be done from the forum of WIPNET, but Leymah emphasized the need for a woman president who would best represent women's interests.

The results of the second round run-off ballot held on 8 November 2005 evinced quite a dramatic reversal of fortunes for Ellen Sirleaf, who won with 59 per cent of the vote to George Weah's 41 per cent. History was made in Liberia: Ellen Johnson Sirleaf became the country's first woman president. Moreover, she was the first native woman African head of state since Empress Zewditu, who reigned in Ethiopia from 1916 to 1930. Upon being elected, Sirleaf profusely thanked her sisters, whose votes she claimed had significantly contributed to her victory. Ellen Sirleaf made a special mention of Mano River Women in Peace Network (MARWOPNET), but made no mention of either WIPNET or Women of Liberia Mass Action.

This omission outraged several of Leymah's friends, but Leymah held that whatever they had contributed was not for winning any glory or any prize. Whatever they had done, they had done for the country, and more so they had done as ordained by God. It was now time for disbanding Mass Action. In the annual conference of WIPNET held at Monrovia's City Hall in December 2005, Leymah thanked everyone, including the participating women's husbands, partners and their families. Leymah announced that she was leaving and that day's event would be her last as WIPNET coordinator.

President Sirleaf was present on this occasion and told Leymah that she wanted to have lunch with her. Leymah told the president that she would call her, but she never did. She did not perceive any future for herself under Sirleaf's dispensation. She thought she could only excel in peacemaking. Leymah now decided to expand her focus from Liberia to the whole of the African continent, where women had been suffering under corrupt regimes and with the devastation of terrible civil wars. It was a bold decision, but she felt that she was given divine encouragement when she randomly opened the Bible to Isaiah 54:4: 'Don't be afraid. You will not suffer shame. Do not fear disgrace, you will not be humiliated.'

Early in 2006, she began mobilizing donations, and the first support she received came from Tunde, who contributed $600. Abigail Disney, an American documentary film maker, feminist and activist and the grand-niece of Walt Disney, helped to raise the sum of $50,000 from New York philanthropists for the foundation of a new organization. It would be named the Women in Peace and Security Network–Africa (WIPSEN–Africa). Leymah and her colleagues Thelma Ekiyor and Ecoma Alaga rented a small, one-room office in Accra for WIPSEN.

In order to enhance her earning capacity, Leymah decided she would pursue a relevant postgraduate degree that would further her academic understanding of the sphere of activity to which she had now dedicated her life. She undertook in 2006–07 a full-time master's programme in 'conflict transformation and peacebuilding' at the Center for Justice and Peacebuilding in Eastern Mennonite University (EMU), where she had earlier attended a summer course. Armed with this qualification, Leymah would finally be able to stand confidently alongside those in exalted posts or holding seats of power. She could now give a formal name, 'strategic peacebuilding', to the work that she had performed by instinct in the midst of Liberia's civil strife. And she could now fulfil her promise that had long been deprived the opportunity by civil war and personal setbacks.

This new period of Leymah's life was not one of unalloyed success, though. Her time in Virginia and her growing fame strained her relationship with Tunde, and she bore yet more personal pain when her beloved sister Geneva, who had run her household and cared for her children, died tragically. Geneva passed away because she had been denied medical treatment; doctors in the hospitals were on strike at the time of her illness. Hers was an unthinkable loss for Leymah. She had relied heavily on Geneva's help to care for her children: her household had almost been entirely Geneva's domain while Leymah led Liberia's peace movement and prepared herself for a greater role in peacemaking in the region.

Other difficulties dogged her as she rose in stature. The peace movement that Leymah had been instrumental in building in Liberia would, ironically, be a source of painful conflict for her. In September 2006, Leymah went to New York to address the United Nations. It was the fifth anniversary of the passage of Resolution 1325, which had called for bringing more women into UN peace and security efforts. While she was there in a hotel, she received a call from Abigail Disney, who along with film-maker Gini Reticker, came to see her. They wanted to hear the story of Liberia's struggle, directly from Leymah. After a week, the two ladies asked Leymah if they could meet her in Liberia.

When Leymah went to the WIPNET office with them, everything changed for her. The other WIPNET women thought that Leymah was taking all the credit for their movement. One by one, the women whom Leymah had thought to be her friends or allies attacked her, accusing her of undermining them and being power-hungry. They even alleged that she had stolen money. Leymah realized that it was all humbug.

Unsurprisingly, Leymah was crestfallen. She had never thought of securing power for her own advantage. If her intention had been to secure power, she would have joined Gyude Bryant's interim government when he asked her to work with him; or she would have supported George Weah, who had asked her to run on his ticket for vice president. She had rejected overtures from both these men only because she wanted a stable Liberia for her children. She declared to the women that she never had any secret bank account in her life. She told them when they came to WIPNET, she had held their hands in hers, and now when they were making malicious, false allegations against her, she regretted having laid eyes upon them. Leymah could barely have imagined that those women, whom she valued so much, would be so cruel to her merely through jealousy. If only she could open her heart so that they would see that she had always considered them her sisters. At any rate, Abigail and Gini were impressed enough with Leymah that they decided to make a documentary about her story.

She finished her course at EMU in April 2007 and had the choice of either submitting her thesis or undertaking a practical project. Her natural choice was a project on WIPSEN's development. Leymah was to undertake a different course shortly. Two women from Sierra Leone, whom Leymah knew from the days of WIPNET, approached her expressing their grave apprehensions of violence in their country in the ensuing elections. Images of Sierra Leone's civil war were horrifying in the extreme – child soldiers, civilian massacres, gang rapes and amputated hands of children. Leymah took a team of twenty-two women to Sierra Leone and launched a women's campaign for violence-free elections. To manage awareness drives for free elections, Sierra Leone was divided into four regions. The women gave radio interviews and sometimes radio hosts would jokingly remark, 'Beware! Liberian women have come to Sierra Leone to elect a woman president.' The elections in Sierra Leone were conducted peacefully, and the president-elect, Ernest Bai Koroma, gave due credit to Leymah and her friends for this.

After she completed her master's degree, Leymah's relationship with Tunde began to falter. Feeling that she had outgrown him, he once remarked to her, 'I guess you're too high-class for me now.' Leymah was heartbroken. It was Tunde who had inspired her to do the master's degree, and Leymah felt eternally obliged to him. He had been her mainstay and a father figure for her children for nigh on a decade, and despite their difficulties she would have continued her relationship with Tunde but for one telephone conversation. A mysterious caller informed her that Tunde was involved with another woman. Leymah confronted him. He initially denied the affair but later confessed to her, and their relationship ended.

With all the upheaval in Leymah's life, and with its dumbfounding trajectory, it is little wonder that her health and personal life suffered. For years she had juggled competing demands on her time – a familiar predicament for most women. And she had come to depend on alcohol as a means to cope with stress over the years. Leymah realized early in 2008 that her drinking had become excessive, to the point that her health was in serious jeopardy. After she collapsed following her eldest daughter Amber's fourteenth birthday party and seeing the concern of her children that she may die, she resolved there and then that she would cease drinking and begin to take greater care of herself. Her children had been through too much: they had been estranged from their father, lost their beloved aunt Geneva and become distanced from Tunde. Leymah knew she must be there for them, that they could not bear her loss.

In 2008, Leymah went to Abigail's apartment for a private screening of the documentary film *Pray the Devil Back to Hell*, which she had narrated and in which she was the central character. She found the experience of viewing her story on screen overwhelming. While she was in the thick of the peace campaign, Leymah had not realized the scope of her influence, nor had she appreciated the magnitude of the struggle she had been engaged in. She invited Tunde several times to the screening of *Pray the Devil Back to Hell*, but on each occasion, he failed to attend. Nothing could detract from her achievement, however, in praying the devil – personified by Charles Taylor – back to hell. In the wake of the end of the war, and with the successful transition to democratic government, Leymah's success seemed preordained. Leymah, though, had earlier received divine comfort that she would triumph when she opened the Bible to Isaiah 54:11: 'Oh thou afflicted, tossed with tempest and not comforted, behold I will lay thy stones with fair colours and lay thy foundations with sapphires.'

Great persons envision greatness. After having brought peace to Liberia and elected a woman as its president, Leymah had one more unique idea: ensuring the welfare of the Liberian women under President Ellen Johnson Sirleaf. She organized a review meeting with President Sirleaf in which some women's rights activists gave their thoughts on the president's efforts to ameliorate the lot of Liberian women. The meeting, a first of its kind, lasted for seven hours. President Sirleaf listened to the women. Subsequently, the government included women in its planning process and recognized the work that women did. President Sirleaf immediately accepted Leymah's idea of a review and persuaded her to lead the session. All the leading women of Liberia's struggle were present: Sugars, Vaiba, Asatu, Varbah Gayflor, Lindora Beatrice Sherman and Ophelia Hoff.

At this time, Charles Taylor's trial in The Hague for war crimes – murder, rape, sexual slavery, terrorism and enlisting child soldiers into the armed forces – was coming to a close. The women were waiting for the outcome of the trial with bated breath; they wanted to see Taylor given a fitting sentence. Leymah, however, could not forgive Charles Taylor, howsoever severe punishment might be meted out to him, because he had destroyed the lives of an entire generation of Liberian people.

Her own family had borne its share of the destruction wrought by Taylor and his ilk. Leymah regretted that she had five children but could not be available for them. All the time she had been engaged in struggles. She says she always had the feeling that she would have another child born in peacetime, for whom she would prove to be a doting mother. She became involved with James, a Liberian information technology expert living in America. She gave birth to James's daughter in June 2009, in New York City, and named her Jaydyn Thelma Abigail (nicknamed Nehcopee, which in Loma language means 'my own'). Jaydyn bears the names of Leymah's staunch supporters Thelma and Abigail in her gratitude.

Her family aside, nothing has given Leymah more happiness than Liberia. Liberia is her deepest dream, she says. She sleeps, eats and breathes Liberia, and the very thought of her country is of happiness. Leymah's story is the story of a woman's love for her country – a love all-consuming such that it overwhelmed her personal pain, her trials and tribulations: her family tragedies; her poverty; her exploitation and abandonment by her partner; her father's condemnation; her disaffected colleagues' wrangling, and the horrors of a brutal civil war that tore a region asunder. Leymah appears to be fundamentally unaffected by all that she has endured. She maintains an optimistic but pragmatic outlook, and her demeanour is at once cheerful and engaging. Neither has she abandoned her faith – in God and in the sublime qualities of humanity which she never fails to recognize and serve.

Once Leymah accompanied some women to meet a rebel leader to ask for peace. When they arrived, he held out his hand to one of the women accompanying her, but the woman refused to shake it. When Leymah was attending a workshop in another city, she related the story of that woman's valour to the women there. One of the women who was sitting there raised her hand and said, 'That was me.' Leymah maintains that if women like this come forward, tyranny will vanish and goodness will always prevail over evil. Her own remarkable story invokes optimism: If you have unshakeable faith in yourself, in your sisters – and in the possibility of change – you can do almost anything. Leymah responds to the call of the older Liberian lady's voice, 'Don't ever stop.' Leymah's answer to her was, 'I never will.'

Each of us has been blessed by God with an almost inexhaustible store of resilience and an ability to reach far beyond apparent limitations. Rare indeed, though, is one such as Leymah, who has had to rely not simply on her inner reserves of resilience, but all the while move beyond the limitations of her circumstances. I asked her a difficult question: 'Did it not ever worry you as to what would have happened to your children had you died braving the guns of a tyrant ruler?' Leymah gave an answer that was as philosophical as it was enlightened. She told me that one thing she knew for sure was that if she had lost her life in the fight for peace, for which she was sincerely struggling, it would have finally brought peace and her children's lives would have been better for it.

She told me that when she stepped forward to lead the peace movement in Liberia, she did so not because she wanted to guarantee a tomorrow for herself. She was fighting to guarantee a tomorrow for her children and other children of Liberia. When I asked Leymah what role she expects India to play in the comity of nations, she rightly identified India's vulnerability and declared that India needs to abolish its caste system. She told me that her faith has taught her that all are equal under the sun and that no one is superior or inferior in the eyes of God.

Leymah has emerged from the debris of civil war a philosopher of divine wisdom. It is often noted that people focus on differences, which gives rise to dissension and conflict. But Leymah, like a saint, seems to focus only on commonalities. She told me that when they started cooperative efforts for peace with Christian and Muslim women, their motto was to reinforce their similarities. She told me that they stood up, shouted and sang songs to look into what was common in them, which was the death of poor children, their miseries and their goal to defy the devil.

Leymah's achievements are the achievements of a common woman. She claims no superiority of intellect or of upbringing; neither does she give any indication that she is possessed of any unusual quality of head or heart. She told me that there were many low times in her life when it was really hard for her to pray. She says that she would be lying if she says that she remained in good spirits even in her low times. Once, as she was feeling particularly downcast when her son Nuku was only three years old, he comforted her saying, 'Mama, I am going to pray for you.' He further told her that whoever would do any evil to her, God would reply to them. When she laughed at his words, Nuku said, 'Mama, God loves you.' Leymah told me that even now, after winning the Nobel Peace Prize, she has seen several low moments. She cries at times and becomes angry, but she still goes to God in prayer, to ask for His guidance.

This is how she acknowledges her being a simple, ordinary woman. It is in her ordinariness that her extraordinariness lies. Extraordinariness is within every ordinary woman; but only a few women such as Leymah succeed in realizing it. The opportunity to do so, however, is there for me, for you and for every other woman across the globe. Our quest must be to recognize, acknowledge and develop our extraordinary skills and characteristics – that are often given little attention in the humdrum of daily life – just as Leymah has. Rightly does she remind us, 'You can never leave footprints that last if you are always walking on tiptoes.'

TAWAKKOL KARMAN

MOTHER OF THE REVOLUTION

'I am a universal citizen. The earth is my homeland
and humanity is my nation.'

Tawakkol Karman, the Yemeni journalist, human rights activist, politician and senior member of the Al-Islah political party, was awarded the Nobel Peace Prize in the year 2011, sharing this honour with Ellen Johnson Sirleaf and Leymah Gbowee. She is the second Muslim woman to have received the Nobel Peace Prize; Shirin Ebadi of Iran, who was awarded the prize in 2003, was the first. At the age of thirty-two, Tawakkol became the youngest woman recipient of the Nobel Peace Prize at the time. Malala Yousafzai has since earned this distinction, receiving the award at the tender age of seventeen in 2014. The two most youthful Nobel Peace laureates have another feature in common: an adamant fearlessness that has seen both brave mortal threats, seemingly oblivious of their personal welfare. Indeed, the Norwegian Nobel Committee noted that Tawakkol 'is a courageous lady who has never heeded threats to her own safety'. In her defiance of the veil, in putting herself in harm's way for freedom and in her protests against tyranny, Tawakkol has doubtless personified courage.

Tawakkol has also stayed true to her faith and maintained her cultural identity; her colourful hijab has become something of a trademark. Yet she seems to take the whole world in her sisterly embrace. Her declaration to an audience at the University of Michigan, 'I am a universal citizen. The earth is my homeland and humanity is my nation,' gives voice to an ethos that is the very essence of peace. In her interview with the independent news programme Democracy Now! in 2011, she expanded on these sentiments when she said, 'We are one world. We are one nation. And therefore, what is common between us, what should be common among us, is love and peace.'

In a volatile region with shifting alliances and fortunes, Tawakkol has forged a reputation as a woman guided by her conscience. When distancing herself from her Al-Islah party line and setting out on an independent path for herself, she made yet another laudable assertion: 'I do not represent the Al-Islah party, and I am not tied to its positions. My position is determined by my beliefs, and I do not ask anyone's permission.'

Her personal beliefs may sometimes have been at odds with her colleagues in her own party, but she has garnered respect for her advocacy of women's rights in a country not at all noted for feminism. She told the *Yemen Times* in 2010, in a clarion call to women to defy their marginalization, that

> Women should stop being or feeling that they are part of the problem and become part of the solution. We have been marginalized for a long time, and now is the time for women to stand up and become active without needing to ask for permission or acceptance. This is the only way we will give back to our society and allow for Yemen to reach the great potential it has.

Thus, she proved herself to be not only a leading proponent of liberty and freedom in her region but also a woman dedicated to the emancipation of her sisters, knowing that this would serve her people's greater aspirations. Tawakkol well deserves the epithet Mother of the Revolution. She shines as an example for women of the Middle East by adhering to conventional standards and spiritual values in the pursuit of empowerment. She is a wife, mother and practising Muslim; she is also among the most prominent activists in the Arab world.

Tawakkol Abdel-Salam Karman was born on 7 February 1979, in Mekhlaf, Taiz Governorate, Yemen. She grew up near Taiz, the third largest city of Yemen, a picturesque metropolis surrounded by mountains in the Yemeni highlands. Taiz has historically maintained its stature as the cultural centre of Yemen, but more recently has seen military confrontation and a crippling siege.

Tawakkol has nine siblings: six sisters and three brothers, some of whom enjoy a public profile. Her brother Tariq Karman is a poet, and her sister Safa Karman works as a journalist for Al Jazeera. Abdel-Salam Karman, her father, was a renowned lawyer and was, at one time, Yemen's minister for legal and parliamentary affairs.

Tawakkol earned her undergraduate degree in commerce from the University of Science and Technology and later her graduate degree in political science from Sana'a University. At the age of seventeen, she accepted a marriage proposal on the condition that her fiancé allow her to continue her studies and consent to her taking an active part in public affairs. Her husband, Mohammed al-Nehmi, proved to be more than just the model of a supportive husband: he has been her true alter ego, taking part in public activities with her with equal enthusiasm. Tawakkol and Mohammed have been blessed with three children.

As an activist, Tawakkol's first bold step was in 2004. She removed her niqab, a black veil that covers the face except the eyes. In its place, she began wearing a colourful hijab (headscarf), which she still wears, and for which she is now instantly recognizable. She declared that nowhere in Islamic texts is it stated that women must wear a niqab; it is only a tradition, one to which she does not subscribe, because it inhibits one's freedom. She further elucidated her stance by saying that as an activist she could not hide her face from the public behind a veil. When journalists commented that her hijab did not go well with her intellect and education, though, she replied,

> Man in the early times was almost naked and as his intellect evolved he started wearing clothes. What I am today and what I am wearing represents the highest level of thought and civilization that man has achieved and is not regressive. It is the removal of clothes that is regressive.

Besides her repudiation of the niqab as mandatory Islamic observance, she took firm stands against the prejudices to which women of her country were subject. She alleged that many Yemeni girls were victims of discrimination in their own homes, where they suffered malnutrition because boys were invariably fed lavishly at their expense. She advocated a law that prescribed a minimum age of seventeen for girls' marriage. This set alarm bells ringing in Yemen's conservative Muslim society. She told Human Rights Watch that Yemen's revolution did not happen just to solve political problems but also to address societal problems – the most important being child marriage. While several of her party members held divergent views on child marriage, she claimed that her party is the front runner in espousing the cause of women. She said, 'Our party needs the youth, but the youth also need the parties to help them organize. Neither will succeed in overthrowing the regime without the other. We don't want the international community to label our revolution an Islamic one.'

In 2005, she came into direct confrontation with the government. Along with several other women, she formed a group called Female Journalists Without Borders, which was later renamed Women Journalists Without Chains. They sought a licence from the government for a newspaper and radio station, and also for a news service which would issue bulletins via the mobile phone network. The name 'Women Journalists Without Chains' is clearly indicative of Tawakkol's passion for freedom. When the Ministry of Information failed to grant the licence they had applied for, Tawakkol held weekly protests against the government. Despite her movement gaining momentum, the government did not respond with any urgency. Soon, besides issues concerning freedom of the press, the group also began raising human rights issues. The group received financial support from the US National Endowment for Democracy.

This brought Tawakkol under intense scrutiny, and she subsequently endured bitter allegations that she was an instrument in the hands of foreign powers. She remained unruffled, however, and declared that she was against both President Ali Abdullah Saleh and the US, which supported his government and had secured his assistance in its fight against Al-Qaeda. She declared that her revolution was two pronged: one against Saleh's authoritarian regime and the other against customs and traditions that seek to restrict women's freedom. It is little wonder, therefore, that her protests have encompassed freedom of the press, freedom of women, protection of human rights and protests against the government.

The 'Jasmine Revolution', which saw the ousting of long time president Zine El Abidine Ben Ali and the fall of his government in Tunisia in January 2011, was a shot in the arm for the Yemeni protest movement. Tawakkol was elated and resolved to capitalize on this watershed event. Her hopes for Yemenis soared, because she felt that Saleh's government would likewise be unable to withstand mass demonstrations for long. She surmised that the government would collapse under its own weight, if only due to its flagrant corruption and unpopularity. She called on her people to celebrate the Tunisian revolution on 16 January, and student and youth activists mobilized to her call.

Thousands of youths responded to Tawakkol's celebration call. She was arrested, but released under intense public pressure. Defiant, she responded to her arrest by organizing more protests and demonstrations. She named her movement in Yemen the 'Second Jasmine Revolution', and a Supreme Council for the Youth Revolution was formed. Tawakkol started living in a tent outside the gates of Sana'a University, and in turn, a tent city sprang up outside the university, which was dubbed Change Square.

The government did not take kindly to Tawakkol's leadership of the protest. On 22 January 2011, she and her husband were stopped by three policemen in plain clothes when she was driving, and they were taken to prison, where she was detained and shackled. Tawakkol was only released on parole after thirty-six hours behind bars, when thousands of people poured on to the streets of Sana'a in her support. In an editorial that appeared in the *Guardian*, she wrote about her ordeal:

> After a week of protests I was detained by the security forces in the middle of the night. This was to become a defining moment in the Yemeni Revolution: media outlets reported my detention and demonstrations erupted in most provinces of the country; they were organized by students, civil society activists and politicians. The pressure on the government was intense, and I was released after thirty-six hours in a women's prison where I was kept in chains.

Reportedly, Tawakkol's brother Tariq received a telephone call at this time from President Saleh himself, warning him to 'keep his sister under control' and hinting at dire consequences if she continued her protests. Tawakkol seems to have taken this threat in her stride. She continued to crusade relentlessly against Saleh's regime, declaring 3 February 2011 a Day of Rage, in kinship with the Egyptian Day of Revolt on 25 January 2011. The Egyptian revolution had, like Yemen's protests, been inspired by the Tunisian revolution a year earlier. Tawakkol was rearrested on 17 March, but she was not deterred. She declared that, 'We will continue until the fall of Ali Abdullah Saleh's regime. We have the Southern Movement in the south, the Houthi rebels in the north and the opposition in the parliament. But what is most important now is the Second Jasmine Revolution.'

Explaining the popularity of her demonstrations, she said, 'The combination of a dictatorship, corruption, poverty and unemployment has created this revolution. It is like a volcano. Injustice and corruption are exploding while opportunities for a good life are coming to an end.' She led the movement, however, on the principle of non-violence, which was almost unthinkable in a country where violence was widespread: Guns in Yemen numbered somewhere in the order of three times its population. The goal of the Second Jasmine Revolution in Yemen was not only to bring down Saleh's government but also to establish democratic values and a democratic government.

Yemen is a conservative Muslim country, and young male activists formed the mainstay of Tawakkol's support. Women, however, joined the movement in surprising numbers, and were active to the extent that President Saleh denigrated them for participating in the protests. He drew the women's ire by saying that their mingling with men during demonstrations was forbidden under shariat law. It appears that Tawakkol had started a social revolution within the political revolution, and women taking to the streets deeply unsettled the government.

Although Tawakkol strictly advocated non-violent protest – she later credited Mahatma Gandhi for inspiring her – the movement could not escape the wounds of the government's armed reprisals. Demonstrations were marred by violence, injuries and deaths. The worst violence took place on 18 March 2011, when as many as fifty-three souls perished under the guns of President Saleh's forces and loyalists. In May, Tawakkol staged a demonstration with more than 2,000 participants at the Presidential Palace. The army responded with a ruthless crackdown that resulted in the deaths of ten demonstrators.

At this critical time, Tawakkol received vital support. The Norwegian Nobel Committee announced that Tawakkol would be conferred the Nobel Peace Prize, along with two other women leaders from Liberia: Ellen Johnson Sirleaf and Leymah Gbowee. This lent Tawakkol a larger-than-life stature and international celebrity status – particularly being the youngest ever recipient of the Nobel Peace Prize at that time. The Saleh government was most perturbed that this honour was being conferred on Tawakkol, not least because the prize was largely awarded for her spearheading a sustained campaign against it.

In any event, the expanse of Tawakkol's activities began to spread beyond Yemen. Tawakkol criticized all Arab governments' ministers for their blatant selfishness, accumulating wealth and holding on to power by suppressing human rights and undermining democratic values. She was sure that the sovereignty of the people and their indomitable will would ultimately prevail.

Tawakkol used her eminence as a Nobel Peace laureate to further the cause of women. In her speeches, she emphasized women's role and women's legal status in new Arab governments: Tunisia, Egypt, Libya and also Yemen. In none of these countries did women enjoy an equal status with men. Tawakkol also later joined the Advisory Council of Transparency International, where she championed the United Nations Security Council's Resolution 1325, which called upon women's participation in all conflict-resolution and peace-related discussions; a resolution that was being implemented only selectively. Meanwhile, she upped the ante in her attacks on the Saleh government's rampant corruption.

The Mother of the Revolution has often been charged of being hand in glove with foreign powers, which she has stoutly refuted, declaring that she has never succumbed to any foreign influence. Tawakkol has acknowledged her strategic ties with American organizations acting as watchdogs of human rights and also with American ambassadors and other officials of the United States. She also acknowledges her ties with activists in most of the European Union and Arab countries. She asserts, however, that her ties are maintained on equal terms.

In a stance that is quite at odds with allegations that she is an agent of Western powers, Tawakkol is vehemently critical of US drone attacks in Yemen. Denouncing them as utterly unacceptable, she charges that they violate human rights as well as international laws, and describes the US drone campaign in Yemen as 'worse than the terrorist activities of individuals and groups'. Moreover, she has repeatedly claimed that they do more harm than good, and has highlighted the numerous cases in Yemen where civilians have needlessly perished from drones' rocket strikes. In 2013, she further condemned America's drone attacks on grounds that they undermined Yemen's sovereignty and contributed to the upsurge in Al-Qaeda's recruitment efforts.

In May 2011, she faced opposition from her own sympathizers when she urged them to march to the Presidential Palace to lodge their protests against the government's killing of thirteen protesters. Tawakkol's bravery was not called into question, though. She seemed more than willing to stand firm in the face of tear gas, rubber bullets and live fire; not to mention government inducements and outright threats to her life.

In June 2011, Tawakkol wrote an article for the *New York Times* entitled 'Yemen's Unfinished Revolution', which assailed the United States and Saudi Arabia for being supporters of the corrupt government of President Saleh. She stated that America was unconcerned about human rights abuses and the evolution of the democratic movement in Yemen. In an interview with the news programme Democracy Now!, she declared, 'In our weekly protests in front of the cabinet, we called on the government to allow people to have freedom of speech and for people to be able to own online newspapers. We knew and know that freedom of speech is the door to democracy and justice.' She expressed regret that each time she and her colleagues had stood up for freedom, the government had responded with violence.

She also declared that despite their repression by Saleh's regime, Yemeni women would not hide behind veils or behind walls; they would remain on the forefront of their struggle for their rights, for their freedoms and for ousting Saleh's corrupt government. She wanted President Saleh to be brought to justice. She implored the UN Security Council and the United States not to enter into any deal with Saleh to pardon him, and that instead he be prosecuted and his assets be frozen. Due largely to Tawakkol's lobbying, the UN Security Council on 21 October 2011 passed Resolution 2014 that condemned Saleh's government for its violent suppression of protests. But Tawakkol expressed her gravest concern at proposals to grant Saleh immunity against prosecution in the event of his resignation. She wanted Saleh to be tried at the International Criminal Court, and roundly criticized the Gulf Cooperation Council's support for these proposals.

Tawakkol expressed her displeasure to US Secretary of State Hillary Clinton, who told Tawakkol that the United States supports a democratic transition in Yemen and rights of the people of Yemen to choose their own leaders and futures. Tawakkol responded to Ms Clinton's comment in the Yemeni press saying, 'In Yemen, it has been nine months since people have been camping in the squares. Until now we did not see Obama come to value the sacrifice of the Yemeni people. Instead the American administration is giving guarantees to Saleh.' Tawakkol secured a partial victory when President Saleh signed the Gulf Cooperation Council's plan in Riyadh on 23 November 2011. Under the plan, President Saleh would transfer power to Vice President Abd Rabbuh Mansur Hadi to start a political transition towards democratic government. On

22 January 2012, the Yemeni parliament passed a law that granted Saleh immunity from prosecution. Saleh stepped down and formally ceded power to his deputy, Abd Rabbuh Mansur Hadi, at the Presidential Palace on 27 February 2012.

The Yemeni people had prevailed in their asymmetrical war with the government. War, Tawakkol declares, does not just encompass conflicts between states. The wars that despotic leaders wage against their own people in oppressing them are far bitterer. People first entrust their lives and destinies to their rulers, but the rulers turn despotic and betray the trust placed in them. And though people entrust their security to despots, the weapons of security are ultimately directed against them. She exhorted young men and women to tread the noble path, armed not with weapons in retaliation but with faith in their right to freedom and dignity. Their peaceful demonstrations should embody the beauty of the human spirit of sacrifice and the aspiration to freedom and life. Their war should seek to eliminate all the ugliest forms of selfishness, injustice and the desire to grasp power and wealth. Such wars are still being waged by people of the Arab states. Tawakkol tells activists that their revolutions have to pass through four stages for establishing a vibrant democracy:

STAGE 1: Toppling the dictator and his family.
STAGE 2: Toppling his security and military services and his nepotism networks.
STAGE 3: Establishing the institutions of the transitional state.
STAGE 4: Moving towards constitutional legitimacy and establishing the modern civil and democratic state.

In her Nobel Lecture, she expressed her optimism that the youth would take revolutions of the Arab Spring through each of the four stages progressively and stated that the civilized world should start detaining the leaders of the regime and its security and military officials and freeze their assets.

Underpinning all of Tawakkol's political activity is an unwavering commitment to freedom of thought and expression. Evincing the depth of her commitment to freedom, Tawakkol advocates its cause even when Western freedom of expression deeply offends her religious sensibilities. In 2005, the Muslim world was scandalized by the publication of cartoons depicting Prophet Muhammad (peace be upon him) in the Danish newspaper *Jyllands-Posten,* and the Middle East erupted in protest. In a statement years later, she takes a broader view of the power of freedom of expression:

> We are not to call for tyranny and bans on freedom. It is obvious that we cannot stop publication of what we view as indecent in our sacred faith … failing to make use of Western freedom of press and other technologies to show the West the values of Islam is intellectual failure and a guilt that should not be linked to Islam.

Much of Tawakkol's refreshing blend of intellectual rigour and piety can be credited to her upbringing. After all, the seeds of greatness are most often sown by one's parents. Her parents, though conservative, combined their love of Islam with a deep regard for a progressive education. When Tawakkol was young, her father joined President Saleh's government as minister for legal and parliamentary affairs. He later resigned from the government, charging it with indulging in corrupt practices, and joined hands with Al-Islah, an Islamist opposition reform party founded in 1990, which is supportive of the Muslim Brotherhood and Salafists (ultra-orthodox Sunni reformists). Tawakkol also became a member of the party and spurned offers of jobs in the establishment to silence her, just as her father had left his ministerial post in the government.

Although Al-Islah is aligned with the Muslim Brotherhood, Tawakkol has remained moderate in her approach. Tawakkol's credentials as a moderate leader have come under scrutiny because she is a member of a conservative party in which Abdul Majeed al-Zindani, president of the Yemini Muslim Brotherhood, is also a member. He is presently the head of the Salafi wing of the party, which is highly resistant to reform of the rights and freedoms of women and marriage laws.

Tawakkol's campaign for laws curtailing childhood marriage, though, would not be fettered by her membership of Al-Islah. She has managed to chart her own course in the most turbulent times; her compass has been only her conscience.

Rough seas elicit good seamanship. If the sailing is tough, someone must emerge to navigate, to show others their way. Tawakkol is one such shining figure, who shows the women of the world how they can assert their identity, have their freedom and enjoy their rights – even under the most tempestuous conditions.

The rough seas Tawakkol Karman faced and continues to face, is ongoing civil strife in her country – north against south, Sunni against Shia – and a proxy war of Saudi Arabia against Iran. The strife began as a fight between South Yemen and North Yemen, which first decided to merge in 1990, and later, in 1994, engaged in internecine war. The North's prevailing over the South would not bring lasting peace to this troubled land, and its people are still suffering the ravages of a protracted civil war fuelled by religion, ideology and the geopolitical aspirations of this small nation's neighbours and world powers.

Throughout the shifting alliances and alternate brutality of a repressive regime and civil war, Tawakkol has done her utmost for the cause of freedom, the rule of law and representative government. And all the while, she has espoused women's emancipation and actively sought to eradicate discriminatory practices. Elucidating its reasons for awarding her the Nobel Peace Prize, the Norwegian Nobel Committee said, 'In the most trying circumstances, both before and during the Arab Spring, Tawakkol Karman played a leading part in the struggle for women's rights and for democracy and peace in Yemen.'

Referring to the UN Security Council's Resolution 1325 – which states that women and children suffer great harm from war and political instability and that women must have a larger influence and role in peacemaking activities – the committee called on all actors involved when negotiating and implementing peace agreements to include a gender perspective. While announcing the Nobel Peace Prize, Thorbjørn Jagland, the chairman of the Norwegian Nobel Committee said, 'We cannot achieve democracy and lasting peace in the world unless women obtain the same opportunities as men to influence developments at all levels of society.' He also elaborated that in selecting Tawakkol Karman for the prize, the committee wanted to send an important message to women all over the world.

Tawakkol was taken aback by the honour. She described the conferment a victory of Arabs around the world, a victory for Arab women and a victory of her peaceful revolution. She said, 'I am so happy and give this award to the youth and the women across the Arab world. We cannot build our country or any country in the world without peace.' She declared that the fight for a democratic Yemen would continue. She dedicated the award to all the martyrs and the wounded of the Arab Spring in Tunisia, Egypt, Yemen, Libya, and Syria and to all the free people fighting for their rights and freedoms. She especially mentioned Yemenis, who preferred to make their revolution peaceful, thereby underscoring the importance of non-violent struggle for establishing a democratic government and restoring human rights. She was named first in the list of *Foreign Policy's* Top 100 Global Thinkers of 2011.

Tawakkol had emerged as an icon of the Arab world, and she was determined to employ her renown for the greater good. She saw a pressing need to foster the nascent free media in Yemen, and set about establishing a television and radio station for the purposes of educating Yemeni reporters and promoting female journalists. In the weeks following the announcement of the Nobel Peace Prize, she went to Qatar and met with Sheikh Tamim bin Hamad Al Thani to ask for the Sheikh's assistance in his capacity as chairman of the Doha Centre for Media Freedom (DCMF). The Sheikh and DCMF obliged, and the media station Bilquis, named in honour of the Queen of Sheba, was launched.

It is unthinkable for Tawakkol to rest on her laurels. She has remained engaged in political life in the Middle East, and stayed true to her commitment to the values of democracy and freedom since. Tawakkol supported the mass countrywide demonstrations on 30 June 2013 demanding Egyptian president Mohamed Morsi's resignation. But she was harshly critical of the military's subsequent iron-fistedness. She denounced its ousting Morsi, suspending Egypt's constitution and restricting freedom of the press – and its banning the Muslim Brotherhood to prevent the movement from participating in Egyptian politics. She declared that the military had no role in a democratic polity and that undermining democratic values directly results in thriving extremist groups.

Tawakkol even travelled by air to Egypt early in August 2013 with the intention of joining protests against the coup; but Egypt's military barred her entry to the country for 'security reasons', and she was deported back to Sana'a on the same plane in which she had arrived. The military's decision was condemned by Egypt's

Anti-Coup Coalition, Pro-Democracy National Alliance, which described the deportation as conduct reminiscent of a police state. Tawakkol flayed the military's arbitrary arrests of high officials of the Muslim Brotherhood and their deadly violence against protestors at sites occupied by Morsi's supporters.

As the situation in her own country has descended into further civil war, Tawakkol has been astute in her analysis and fearless in stating her views. She has been particularly outspoken in her criticism of world and regional powers for their part in Yemen's strife. In January 2015, she highlighted the role of Iran in fomenting the nation's conflict, saying, 'It's a coup orchestrated by [former president] Ali Abdullah Saleh. He's manipulating Iranian-backed Houthi armed militias. Iran is trying to create divisions and extend its power in the region.' Subsequent recordings of telephone conversations broadcast by Al Jazeera appeared to validate her assertions.

In addition to her prominent role in Yemen's affairs – and her lectures at numerous educational institutions throughout the world – Tawakkol takes an active role in Bilquis and in other progressive organizations. Tawakkol is a member of the advisory board of the MBI Al Jaber Media Institute in Yemen, which imparts training in journalism. She has awarded scholarships to promising students from Yemen to study at Istanbul Aydin University, at both undergraduate and postgraduate levels, in collaboration with the MBI Al Jaber Foundation. She also figured prominently in Yemeni film-maker Khadija al-Salami's film *The Scream* in 2012, which carried her interview. The film, as the title connotes, is about women vociferously demanding equality with men in a traditional, patriarchal society.

I visit Tawakkol Karman in Turkey at the Bilquis media office, where we enjoy a perfect Turkish coffee and a tour of the station. When we meet, I am immediately struck by her radiant countenance, framed by a hijab of rich purple, and her winning, uncomplicated smile. Then, her warm greeting embrace. Her gaze is direct but reassuring, and she possesses an unusually sweet voice which is, it seems, as much an instrument for her quick wit as it is for her activism. I am immediately put at ease. As we take the rounds of the office, I note its cheerful but industrious ambience. Like many great people, Tawakkol evidently nurtures an ascetic spirit: her office is merely a room with a table and two chairs. It is difficult to imagine that she oversees her many activities from these spartan surrounds; but I recall that her earlier office was a tent in a city square. As we chat over coffee, she describes the deteriorating conditions in Yemen, and her aching for her country's plight is palpable.

I am most curious to learn from Tawakkol how she could assert and acquire space for herself in a traditional Muslim social milieu. A woman in Yemen is not generally welcome to participate in public affairs, but is expected to remain confined within the four walls of her home. Tawakkol admits that it is difficult to convince the people of Yemen to adopt peaceful means of gaining their rights, and it is also especially difficult to present herself as a leader because she is a woman. She tells me that at times, she walked with just two of her female assistants among thousands of men. She says the men would question how she could mingle with them; they would even raise their voice in her presence. With time, however, they became convinced that she, along with her group, was working for the good of the country. They became convinced that she was working for the sovereignty of Yemen. And once convinced, the men became the foundation of her activism, because women still did not have the courage to emerge from the status quo.

It was with her male comrades, Tawakkol says, that she carried the campaign to the streets, with microphones and raised voices, calling to the people of Yemen, 'Wake up. Wake up. People,

Wake up. We don't want dictatorship in this country.' Tawakkol confesses that it was dangerous to undertake street marches, and for that she had to face attacks many times. Nonetheless, the people believed her – and in her. She was the first female political figure to be arrested time and again by the regime. The people started declaring, 'Tawakkol Karman is the queen of the Yemeni Revolution.'

Tawakkol explains to me that Islam, like other religions, respects women, and no practice that undermines the status of women is attributable to Islam. She adds, though, that some clerics have a flawed understanding of their religion, and many politicians are afraid of women's empowerment. She holds that such people do not want women to enjoy lives beyond the walls of their homes and play any significant role in public life, because they know that things will then change. She stresses that Islam is not against democracy; indeed, she says, no religion is against democracy. Only dictators are against democracy.

She further maintains that they have convinced the criminals to admit their crimes, to regret their deeds and also to ask forgiveness from the people. This, she assures me, is like a revolution in itself. She asserts that it is only due to women's non-participation in politics that dictatorships and corruption thrive, and it is high time that women come forward to contribute for a better, peaceful world.

I find myself drawn into Tawakkol's orbit, as if I have established a familial relationship with her in our short time together. Perhaps this quality of hers has much to do with her appeal and success in galvanizing her nation to demand freedom. But though her obvious charisma and resolve may have brought her to prominence, unshakeable idealism and a formidable mind sustain Tawakkol's role as a leader. In her Nobel Lecture, Tawakkol evinced the fecundity of her thoughts, her lucid expression more penetrating than erudite. Her practical understanding of non-violence is manifest in her words: 'I have always believed that resistance against repression and violence is possible without relying on similar repression and violence.' The lecture imparted wisdom that transcends cultural and national boundaries:

> ... human civilization is the fruit of the effort of both women and men. So, when women are treated unjustly and are deprived of their natural right in this process, all social deficiencies and cultural illnesses will be unfolded, and in the end the whole community, men and women, will suffer. The solution to women's issues can only be achieved in a free and democratic society in which human energy is liberated, the energy of both women and men together. Our civilization is called human civilization and is not attributed only to men or women.

One may only wish that Tawakkol's vision becomes an article of faith for the entire world, but the developments in Yemen – and regrettably, throughout the whole Middle East since her pronouncement – suggest it may remain a distant dream. Until a woman becomes self-sufficient and self-reliant, she will always be deprived of her rights and her freedom. Tawakkol's assertion that human civilization is the fruit of the effort of both women and men is irrefutable. And it is hard not to conclude that the lack of harmony in human civilization is largely because women – who have rarely held weapons in battle – are deprived of their rights and freedoms. Tawakkol's approach, therefore, in promoting women's rights and welfare in the course of campaigning for freedom, is at once revolutionary and inspired.

Tawakkol is truly an emancipated soul who perceives the fundamental oneness in humanity as she yearns for an inclusive freedom. She is emphatic that the whole world is one large family, despite differences in nationality, race, culture and language. In her Nobel Lecture, she articulated the spectrum of her grand vision of humanity, which is redolent of the sentiments of Mahatma Gandhi and Martin Luther King:

> Mankind's feeling of responsibility to create decent life and make it worth living with dignity, has always been stronger than the will to kill life . . . this tendency is strengthened day after day with all available means of communication, thanks to the rapid and astonishing development of information technology and the communications revolution. Walls between human societies have fallen down and the lives and destinies of societies have converged, marking the emergence of a new phase, a phase where peoples and nations of the world are not only residents of a small village, as they say, but members of one family, despite differences in nationality and race or in culture and language.

Her optimism is unbending that one day our world will be a planet of peace. She says that she certainly sees the beginning of a humane, prosperous and generous history filled with love and fraternity. She is quite unabashed in expressing her idealism when she says that 'peace will remain the hope of mankind forever and that the best hope for a better future for mankind will always drive us to speak noble words and do noble deeds. Together, we will push the horizons, one after another, towards a world of true human perfection'.

A visionary leader, Tawakkol is clear that the future belongs to the youth and that they should come together to shape the future for the next generation. They should endeavour to curb corruption in their societies, and they should do their utmost to form good governments.

These are not just empty sentiments. While she has adopted an unyielding posture in her quest for freedom and women's empowerment, Tawakkol's humanity and sensitivity are manifest. No one who has had the pleasure of her company could fail to be impressed by her genuine concern for people. As she gifts me two boxes of sweets for my younger siblings, it is hard not to feel that I have joined an enormous extended family; and that this mother of three – the Mother of the Revolution – is taking care.

WANGARI MAATHAI

SAVIOUR OF KENYA'S GREEN BELT

'We can work together for a better world with men and
women of goodwill, those who radiate the intrinsic
goodness of humankind.'

Wangari Maathai was born on 1 April 1940 in the village of Ihithe in Nyeri district in Kenya's Central Highlands in then British Kenya. She was born into a family of peasant farmers of the Kikuyu community, the most dominant ethnic group in the country. The Kikuyu are a people deeply attached to their soil. For them, all boons and banes of life flow from nature, 'their primordial parent'. They call Mount Kenya a 'Place of Brightness' and consider it a sacred place. Many of their celebratory rituals – for instance, childbirth – are connected to the natural world and the seasons.

Wangari's Kikuyu ancestors had been living in Nyeri for several generations. In 1943, however, her family shifted to a white-owned farm near Nakuru town, where her father had found work. Wangari's father had four wives, one of whom he married after her birth. All her siblings and half siblings lived peacefully. They called their own mother '*maitu*', an older stepmother '*maitumukuru*' and a younger stepmother '*maitumunyinyi*'. About her upbringing, she wrote, 'What I know now is that my parents raised me in an environment that did not give reasons for fear or uncertainty. Instead, there were many reasons to dream, to be creative and to use my imagination.'

Late in 1947, they went back to Nyeri because her two older brothers had been studying in primary school there. While in Nyeri, her brother Nderitu one day asked their mother why Wangari was not going to school. It was not a shocking question; educating daughters was a tradition in their family, although it was not a common practice in other Kenyan communities. Irrespective of her mother's response that day, the question changed the course of her life, and she often wondered what would have happened if her brother Nderitu had not asked that question. Wangari's mother was not in a position to pay her school fees, but her daughter's welfare reigned supreme in her mind and she decided to cultivate the village fields for sixty cents a day.

So at the age of eight, Wangari was admitted to Ihithe Primary School. Her first day at school remains etched deeply in her soul. Her cousin Jonothan, nicknamed 'Jono', accompanied her to school. He was older than her and had already learnt to read and write. While walking with Wangari to school, Jono sat down by the side of the road and asked Wangari to sit by his side. He asked her if she knew how to read and write, to which she replied in the negative. He took out a book and wrote a few lines with a pencil and showed it to her. She was amazed. 'Wow, so you can write!' Her cousin then took out an eraser from his bag and rubbed it over what he had written, making the writing vanish. Wangari thought her cousin had performed a miracle, for she had never seen an eraser before. She was delighted to learn from Jono that she too would be able to perform the same miracle at school.

As a child, Wangari was trustworthy and responsible. When her mother had to undergo an operation for the removal of her appendix, Wangari stayed back home. When her mother returned, she was amazed at how much work Wangari had done. Wangari was also kind and brave. Once, she was walking home with her donkey, carrying a load of red kidney beans on her back. While coming down a hill, the donkey slipped and rolled down a slope. Wangari sure-footedly hurried down the slope, with the bag of beans still safely secure on her back, and helped the donkey rise up. She recalls in her memoir that this incident has remained with her throughout her life, saying it reminds her that if one is determined, one can achieve anything.

In her childhood, she spent a lot of time with her aunt, Nyakweya, whom she describes in her memoir as her 'childhood storyteller'. She remembers that Nyakweya would enact the characters while telling her stories and that her tales revolved mainly around good and evil, with good triumphing in the end. Her time growing up with her aunt was an education in itself, as her aunt bequeathed her with a wide knowledge of many oral histories and traditions of the Kikuyu in Kenya. When Wangari was eleven years old, she attended St Cecilia's Intermediate School, a boarding school run by the Mathari Catholic Mission in Nyeri. After her aunt, the nuns at St Cecilia had the greatest influence on Wangari. There she acquired fluency in English, converted to Catholicism and joined the Legion of Mary. Her aunt Nyakweya had always made it her business to tell her that a woman should marry young, saying 'her biological clock kept ticking'. But in the Legion of Mary, Wangari was fascinated to see nuns who were young and pretty and yet had chosen to give up marriage and personal comforts to serve strangers. However, in time, the young Wangari took to the Legion's way of life, and the nuns there became virtually her surrogate mothers. In the Legion of Mary, she adopted the motto 'Service to mankind is service to God' and took a new Christian name, Mary Josephine. Her friends called her Mary Jo. She worked in the school garden, washed and ironed church linen, visited the sick and prayed rigorously. She also excelled in her studies and was later admitted, in 1956, to the only Catholic high school for girls in Kenya – Loreto Girls' High School in Limuru.

In 1952, the Mau Mau rebellion rocked the Kenyan political establishment. The uprising had its origins in the long-festering political and economic conflict between the Kikuyu and the colonial government. The British government in its efforts to urbanize Kenya had seized large swathes of land from local settler communities, especially the Kikuyu, who were heavily dependent on their lands for their livelihoods. The result was resentment and anger against the foreign usurpers, which finally burst forth in the shape of an armed struggle. The Mau Mau rebellion was a pivotal moment in her country's history, and Wangari, in St Cecilia at the time and witness to the fighting, accounts in her memoir, poignantly, the harsh injustices perpetrated by the colonial administration. She remembers how she could not go to school during the time, and had to leave her home along with her family to an emergency shelter.

Wangari recounts that the rebellion was also a fight for Kenyan self-respect. Years of subjugation had eroded Kenyan traditions and replaced them with colonial ones. In the process the Kikuyu's beliefs had become 'primitive', while the British ones 'progressive'. She laments that many Kenyans had been unwitting participants in this psychological warfare and that she herself prayed for the arrest of Mau Mau rebels. The British quelled the rebellion wholly by 1960, but a wound still rankles in the hearts of many Kenyans. In recent times, in 2011, it came to haunt Britain's conscience when survivors of the rebellion petitioned a British court demanding reparations for the abuses that had taken place.

As the Mau Mau rebellion came to a close, winds of change were sweeping across Africa; the colonial era was coming to an end. With freedom around the corner, Kenyan politicians like Tom Mboya thought of providing higher education to Kenyan men and women, to fill administrative posts in the government. They sought help from top politicians in the US, in particular with Senator John F. Kennedy. In September 1960, the Joseph P. Kennedy Foundation agreed not only to fund higher studies of Kenyans in America but also to sponsor their flights to the US. This programme came to be known as the 'Kennedy Airlift' or 'Airlift Africa'.

Wangari was immensely elated at being selected for studying in the United States. She received a scholarship to study at Mount St Scholastica College in Atchison, where she opted for biology as her major and chemistry and German as her minors. She received her bachelor's degree in science in 1964. Thereafter, she pursued her postgraduate degree in biology from the University of Pittsburgh. When Wangari returned to Kenya, she had a new identity: She had added her original name, Wangari Muta, to her Christian name, so she would thenceforth be known as Mary Josephine Wangari Muta, or Miss Muta. It seems Kenya's independence coincided with her own from colonial roots.

After her return to Kenya in January 1966, she was offered the position of research assistant to a professor of zoology at the University College of Nairobi. But when she reached the university, she was told that the job had been given to someone else. Wangari was distressed by this humiliation and realized that she had been discriminated against because of her gender and tribal identity. After a job search spanning two months, Professor Reinhold Hofmann appointed her as research assistant in the microanatomy section of the newly established Department of Veterinary Anatomy at the University College of Nairobi. This was her first job, and she worked diligently on the project assigned to her, which was about the control of desert locusts.

In 1967, she travelled to Germany, to the University of Giessen and the University of Munich, in pursuit of her doctorate. In 1969, she returned to Nairobi where she joined as assistant registrar and continued her research and writing her dissertation. In 1971, she received her doctorate from the University College of Nairobi, and thus became the first East African woman to receive a doctorate. The ceremony was presided over by President Kenyatta, who by virtue of being the head of the state was also the chancellor of the university. However, Wangari was dismayed to note that her achievement had gone largely unnoticed. She felt that the reason for the indifference was her not belonging to a famous family.

At the University College of Nairobi, Wangari became a senior lecturer in veterinary anatomy in 1975 and later an associate professor in 1977, becoming the first Kenyan woman to occupy such high positions. At the university, she vociferously championed the cause of equal benefits for women employees at the university. There were several benefits – housing, free tuition for children and paid holidays – that were being denied to women employees. The university authorities claimed that these benefits were being availed of by the women's husbands and that there was no reason for such benefits to be paid doubly; women employees were advised to take home a basic salary alone. Wangari observed that this amounted to denying a woman her rights as a worker. 'My husband does not help me teach,' Wangari countered the authorities. She formed a union to pressure the university authorities into acceding to the just demands of the women employees. Wangari and Vertistine Mbaya, another professor at the university, were the moving figures of this union. The union also moved court in this regard but did not succeed, as the president of Kenya was the chancellor of the university and could not be impleaded in a court of law. Nonetheless the authorities finally conceded many of the women's demands for equal benefits, and Wangari was satisfied that she had succeeded in winning parity for women employees at the university.

In April 1966, Wangari met Mwangi Mathai, a Kenyan who had studied in the US. Wangari describes him in her memoir as very handsome and a religious man. After completing his education in America, Mwangi served in various companies in Kenya and later entered politics. In May 1969, they married. In the same year, she conceived her first child and son, Waweru. Later in December 1971, their first daughter, Wanjira, was born, and their second daughter, Muta, in 1974. Wangari was a very affectionate mother and enjoyed raising her three children.

Back in Kenya, as one of the few fortunate Kenyan women to have received a formal education, Wangari pioneered a series of civic programmes and initiatives to tackle the many developmental issues of post-independence Kenya. Wangari joined the National Council of Women of Kenya (NCWK), which was founded in 1964 as an umbrella organization of various women's groups, both in urban and rural Kenya. This organization was led by women who had excelled in their professions, businesses or social lives and had carved a niche for themselves in the hearts of Kenyans due to their selfless service to society. She joined the Nairobi branch of the Kenya Red Cross Society and was appointed its director in 1973. When the Environment Liaison Centre, a parallel organization to the United Nations Environment Programme (UNEP), was formed in 1974, Wangari first became a member and later the chairperson of its board. The Environment Liaison Centre's objective was to promote the participation of non-governmental organizations in the work of the UNEP, which was founded in Nairobi in 1972.

As her work progressed in these organizations, news came in that the first UN Conference on Women was going to be held in Mexico City in June 1975. The members of NCWK started deliberating on the issues to be raised at the conference. Wangari noted that almost all discussions were centred on issues of inadequate wood for fencing and fuel, insufficient grazing pastures for cattle and non-availability of sufficient food and potable water. Around this time, at the University College of Nairobi, she was researching the reasons behind the East Coast Fever, which was proving fatal for the imported hybrid cattle. This infection spread through brown ear ticks. As she collected the ear ticks from rural areas and studied them, she also came to observe that the rivers in the locales she visited were muddied with silt, after heavy rains down nearby hillsides had swept away many paths and roads. She had not seen such an extent of soil erosion before. The cows had also become skinny as there wasn't much grass left around for them to forage. She noticed that the lands that had earlier been covered by trees, shrubs, bushes and grass were being ploughed for tea and coffee cultivation. She was dismayed to find that a fig tree that was very dear to her had been cut down for growing tea. She bowed before the wisdom of her ancestors for having planted fig trees, generation after generation, which serve as good soil conservers.

Her many years abroad had not weakened her bond with her native roots, and the Kikuyu's deep connection to the natural world was still very much alive in her. As far as the problems raised by the NCWK women were concerned, it was a no-brainer. She knew that the way to reverse these trends was to attack the root cause of it all – environmental degradation. Independent Kenya's incipient years was marked by its rapid economic growth and population boom, and it was only inevitable that this growth would bring a drastic decrease in forest cover. However, at the same time, it was an urgent need to protect the country's flora and fauna. Wangari's concerns for the environment would thus lead her to found the famous Green Belt Movement.

In 1977, the NCWK accepted her suggestion to plant trees. On 5 June 1977, on World Environment Day, the activists of NCWK marched in a procession from Kenyatta International Conference Centre in Nairobi to Kamukunji Park in the outskirts of the city. There they planted seven trees in honour of historic community leaders. This was the first Green Belt, known as 'Save the Land Harambee' – meaning, 'Let us pull together' – which then became the 'Green Belt Movement'.

As part of the movement, Wangari organized Kenyan women to start tree nurseries throughout the country. The women searched for and planted seeds of trees that are native to their area. She also paid the women a small stipend for each seedling planted. Her efforts at mobilizing women to start nurseries notwithstanding, her movement got a real impetus from the Decade for Women (1975–85) declared by the UN in Mexico City. Her movement, after all, comprised mainly women.

During this time, unfortunately, Wangari's relationship with her husband got strained, and they separated in 1977. Wangari was honest and sincere whereas her husband did not hesitate to beguile. When Mwangi contested the parliamentary elections the second time from Lang'ata constituency, he promised many jobs. Unemployment had become the major issue among voters at the time, and his promise of well-paying jobs no doubt wooed the masses. She was sceptical about Mwangi's promise, but worked hard for his victory, and he emerged victorious. She was elated at his victory as she watched him take his oath of office in the parliament. Later, when she raised the issue of jobs, as was promised during the election campaign, Mwangi told her, 'That was the campaign, now we are in the parliament.'

'But they might not vote for us next time,' Wangari retorted.

'Don't worry. They won't remember.'

Wangari could not believe what she had heard. It was deceit, and clearly the two were not meant for each other. In 1979, after a long separation, Mwangi applied for divorce. He claimed that Wangari was a stony-hearted woman beyond his control. He also accused her of adultery with another member of parliament and claimed that it had adversely affected his health. Maybe quite unsurprisingly, the court favoured her husband. Wangari was outraged by the verdict and, in an interview with *Viva* magazine, referred to the judge who adjudicated the case as 'either incompetent or corrupt'. The interview later led the judge to charge Wangari with contempt of court and sentence her to six months' imprisonment. However, after three days

in Lang'ata Women's Prison in Nairobi, her lawyer compelled
Wangari to issue an apology, and the court found it sufficient
for her release.

After the divorce, Mwangi sent Wangari a notice through his
lawyer, asking her to remove his surname 'Mathai' from her name.
Wangari changed her name, which amounted to adding one more
a to his surname and making it 'Maathai'. By this time, Wangari had
become miserable. She had lost her husband's income and, finding
it difficult to run her household with her university wages, was
forced to send her children to their father's side. Fortunately, she
received an opportunity to work for the Economic Commission
for Africa through the United Nations Development Programme.
Her new assignment was based primarily in Lusaka, Zambia, and
involved extensive travelling in Africa.

In 1979, shortly after divorcing Mwangi, Wangari contested in
the election for the position of chairwoman of the National Council
of Women of Kenya (NCWK). The newly elected president of
Kenya then, Daniel arap Moi, had been trying to undermine the
influence of the Kikuyu, including their voice in voluntary civic
organizations such as the NCWK, at the time. Thus, Wangari was
defeated – by three votes – but was chosen overwhelmingly to be
the vice chairwoman of the organization. In the following year,
she contested the election again for chairwoman of the NCWK,
and was again opposed by the government. But when it became
apparent that Wangari was going to win the election, Maendeleo
Ya Wanawake Organization (MYWO), a member organization
of NCWK that represented the majority of Kenya's rural women
and the main opposition to Wangari's contention – and whose
leader was close to Daniel arap Moi – withdrew from the NCWK.
Wangari was then elected chairwoman of the NCWK unopposed.
After her victory Wangari never looked back. She was re-elected
each time until she resigned from the position in 1987.

In 1982, she decided to contest the parliamentary elections from her home district of Nyeri. As required by law, she resigned from her position at the University College of Nairobi to campaign for office. However, the courts disqualified her from contesting the election because she had not registered to vote in the last presidential elections, in 1979. She contested her disqualification in court, but the judge reconfirmed the disqualification on technical grounds. She, then, applied for the restoration of her university job, which too was denied to her; and she was soon evicted from the university campus and rolls.

Wangari moved into a small home she had purchased earlier, and decided to focus on her work in the NCWK. She poured her heart and soul into the Green Belt Movement. But the NCWK was a volunteer organization and Wangari still was unemployed. A providential escape from penury came when Wilhelm Elsrud, executive director of the Norwegian Forestry Society, walked into the NCWK office one day and said, 'I am looking for Wangari Maathai ... We have heard about the Green Belt Movement, and we want to find out more about what you are doing.' Wangari and Wilhelm discussed the Green Belt Movement and he joined the movement. A few months later, he returned to Wangari offering her the position of coordinator in the Norwegian Forestry Society, and Wangari was employed again. Besides the partnership with the Norwegian Forestry Society, the movement also received seed money from the United Nations Voluntary Fund for Women. The funds helped in hiring more employees to oversee the operations of the movement, and also pay a small stipend to the women who planted seedlings and to their husbands and sons who kept accurate records of the seedlings that had been planted.

Around this time, Wangari received an opportunity to speak about her work in the Green Belt Movement to the activists who had come to Nairobi to participate in the UN's third Global

Women's Conference in Nairobi. She took the delegates around to see the nurseries and to plant trees. She met Peggy Snyder, head of the United Nations Development Fund for Women (UNIFEM), and Helvi Sipila, the first woman assistant Secretary General of the UN. The conference helped expand the Green Belt Movement to outside Kenya. Eventually, with funding from the United Nations Environment Programme (UNEP), the movement acquired a pan-African status, and representatives from several African countries came to Kenya to learn how to set up similar programmes in their own countries to combat desertification, deforestation, water crises and rural hunger.

The movement received widespread acclaim from around the world and earned Wangari several awards. The government of Kenya, however, tried to separate the Green Belt Movement from the NCWK, asserting that the latter should focus solely on women's issues, and not environmental ones. The Kenyan government felt threatened by Wangari's growing popularity among Kenyans and feared that Wangari would use it for political gain. Thus, the demand for the separation of the NCWK from the Green Belt Movement was aimed at her alienation. Consequently, in 1987, she put down her papers as chairwoman of the NCWK and decided to focus her attention on the Green Belt Movement.

In 1988, the Kenyan government upped the ante against Wangari and the Green Belt Movement. It invoked a colonial-era law that prohibited groups of more than nine people from meeting without first obtaining the government's permission. The Green Belt Movement, however, held meetings without the government's permission and even started pro-democracy awareness campaigns, such as registering voters and pressing for constitutional reforms.

In October 1989, Wangari came to know about a plan to construct the sixty-storey Kenya Times Media Trust Complex in

Uhuru Park, which was to house the headquarters of the ruling
Kenya African National Union (KANU) party and the *Kenya
Times* newspaper. The complex was to have an auditorium,
galleries, trading centres and shopping malls, as well as parking
space for 2,000 cars. There were also plans to raise a large statue of
President Daniel arap Moi. She vigorously opposed the project and
wrote many letters in protest to the *Kenya Times*, to the office of
the president and to several others. She wrote to Sir John Johnson,
the British high commissioner in Nairobi, urging him to intercede
with Robert Maxwell, a major shareholder in the project.

The government refused to respond to her inquiries and
protests, and instead branded her, through the media 'a crazy
woman' and claimed that the project was, a magnificent work of
architecture and was being opposed by only an 'ignorant few'.
Her protests, however, caught the attention of the world media
and generated worldwide criticism of the Kenyan government's
policies and aims. Jolted by the resulting tide of international
opprobrium, the government slammed Wangari's writing letters
to foreign organizations and called the Green Belt Movement 'a
fake organization' and its members 'a bunch of divorcees'. It was
suggested that if Wangari preferred writing to Europeans, she
should live in Europe. President Daniel arap Moi said that those
who opposed the project had 'insects in their heads', and urged
Wangari to be a proper woman as per African tradition. The
government, then, forced her to move the office of the Green Belt
Movement into her home and propped up several frivolous cases
of financial mismanagement against the Green Belt Movement.
Despite this torment, her protests achieved the desired impact
when foreign investors chose to cancel the project in January
1990.

Later she learnt that the government could engineer a coup,
as it had – she suspected – in 1982, when 300 Kenyan Air Force

personnel threatened to bomb the State House and take control of the civilian government. To prevent such a move, a pro-democracy group known as the Forum for the Restoration of Democracy (FORD) called for general elections. That very evening, she learnt that one of the group's members had been arrested. She knew that she was next in line and confined herself to her home. But her house was surrounded and, after three days, the police arrested her after breaking into her house. She was charged with sedition, treason and spreading malicious rumours. However, the government later bowed to the pressure from several international organizations and eight American senators, including Al Gore and Edward M. Kennedy, who threatened severe diplomatic repercussions, and she was released on bail after a day and a half in jail. In November 1992, the Government of Kenya withdrew all charges against her.

Upon being released on bail, in February 1992, Wangari and others took part in a hunger strike in a corner of Uhuru Park called the Freedom Corner. Their aim was to force the government into releasing all political prisoners. On 3 March 1992, the fourth day of the strike, the police forcibly removed the protestors, as President Daniel arap Moi labelled Wangari 'a mad woman' who was 'a threat to the order and security of the country'. The attack drew international criticism. In June 1992, during the ongoing lengthy protest in Uhuru Park, both Wangari and President Daniel arap Moi met in Rio de Janeiro while attending the UN Conference on Environment and Development (Earth Summit). There, the Government of Kenya accused her of inciting women against the government – even to strip – at Freedom Corner. The government demanded that she not be permitted to speak at the summit, but the Kenyan government's objections were overruled, and she was chosen to be the chief speaker at the summit. This was no mean achievement, and it incensed the Kenyan government no end.

In the December 1992 multiparty elections, the first of its kind in Kenya's history, she performed a key role in uniting opposition members against the ruling KANU, under the alliance Movement for Free and Fair Elections. She was chosen to head the alliance. However, despite stiff resistance, the KANU intimidated and manipulated the people to win the elections and retain control over the parliament. The government reportedly even engineered ethnic clashes in many places. Even though the government had severely restricted her movements, Wangari travelled to many of these places marred by the clashes to stop the disturbances and help restore peace. Once, former Soviet leader Mikhail Gorbachev invited her to a meeting of the Green Cross International – an environmental organization that he founded – in Tokyo. After Wangari conveyed to him that she would not be allowed to leave the country and was in hiding, Gorbachev pressured the Kenyan government to allow her to travel freely.

In the 1997 elections too Wangari made concerted attempts to unite the opposition. This time, however, popular opinion was in favour of her joining the political fray. She was at first reluctant to contest the elections, but with the encouragement of her supporters decided to contest. They had advised her to implement what she had been preaching through the Green Belt Movement by entering politics. She was urged to think of how much she could have achieved if she had been a parliamentarian. Besides, she had already been tempted before by the prospect of entering politics for public service. She wanted to prove that politics had opportunities for good souls too. Thus, less than two months before the elections, she decided to contest for the parliamentary seat from Tetu, which included her native village,

Ihithe, and also run for president as a candidate of the Liberal Party.

Her intentions were widely questioned in the press, which was favourably disposed towards the ruling KANU. And, further, it played down her candidature and projected her as a spoiler to another woman candidate, Charity Ngilu. A day before the elections, a rumour was widely circulated by the media that she had withdrawn from the election and had urged her supporters to vote for other candidates in both elections. The news made headlines on polling day and resulted in Wangari's garnering only a few votes. And while she lost the elections, the KANU registered an impressive victory. This chicanery, however, did not shake her. She remarked, 'A woman politician needs the skin of an elephant.' She took consolation in the fact that she would not have been able to do much as a member of the opposition if she had been elected to the parliament, and went back to the Green Belt Movement with even greater resolve to accomplish her goals.

In 1998, a blatant case of massive land grabbing came to her notice. The arap Moi administration and its cohorts were casting lots among themselves to apportion prime forest land – in Mau Forest, Karura Forest, Mt Kenya National Park, Kabiruini Park – for their private constructions. The most important and serious case of such land grabbing was to happen in Karura Forest, where the government planned the biggest sale. The threat to the huge forest was grave, and Wangari was furious. She knew the importance of Karura Forest to the locals. Karura Forest was a tract of 2,500 acres of natural forest that acted as a catchment area for local rivers and housed rich species of flora and fauna. Wangari announced a mass agitation against the government's policies.

By this time she had already become the government's arch-enemy, and now with her launching a campaign against land grabbing she had drawn the government into a mortal combat.

She sought permission to enter the forest to plant trees and protest against the construction there, but the government refused, citing security reasons. But she did not relent, and eventually succeeded in planting two trees at the gate of the forest. On the following day, she found that the two trees she had planted the previous day had been uprooted. She and other members of the Green Belt Movement had earlier entered the forest and planted a few seedlings. These seedlings had to be tended to, and so Wangari and other members of the Green Belt Movement entered the forest through the marshlands to water the seedlings. They were caught by the police, who nonetheless allowed Wangari to take water from a nearby stream and water the young seedlings. Thereafter she was escorted out. The Karura Forest episode hit the newspapers the next day and soon catapulted her to worldwide fame.

In another such episode, during a scuffle with encroachers, she tried to assert her right to plant seedlings on public land. She was clubbed on the head and was critically injured. She was rushed to Nairobi Hospital where a doctor informed her later that she was lucky to have escaped death despite the fatal blow. She learnt that the thugs who had attacked her were goons hired by the politicians who wanted to usurp forest land. The attack brought international condemnation on the Kenyan government, as well as swelled sympathy and support for Wangari's cause. Many students from the University College of Nairobi pledged their solidarity with the Green Belt Movement. Finally on 16 August 1999, unable to withstand the mounting pressure on him due to Wangari's relentless struggle, President Daniel arap Moi – to her great surprise – declared that he would ban all allocation of public land forthwith.

Nonethelss, Wangari continued mobilizing members of the Green Belt Movement and raising awareness on land grabbing. In

March 2001, in a village called Wanguru, she erected a billboard warning that a particular plot of village land was likely to be grabbed. Suddenly the police arrived on the scene, carjacked her and took her to the Wanguru Police Station, where she was pushed into a crowded, dirty cell. The situation was very dismal. Just a couple of days prior to this incident, President Moi, while inaugurating a women's seminar in Nairobi, had shamelessly told the women present, 'Because of your little minds, you cannot get what you are expected to get.' His remark followed a string of human rights violations and abuses of power and caused a lot of anger among Kenyan women. After her arrest, her supporters faxed and emailed the news of her arrest to friends and supporters around the globe. Again, international pressure was brought to bear on the Kenyan authorities and it was ferociously attacked in the world media. The authorities did not have a choice; they had to charge her in a court or release her; and since the authorities could not establish any charge in court, she had to be released eventually.

Around this time, Wangari had another tryst with jail. She was with two of her friends inside the compound of the Department of Forests when suddenly the police appeared and placed them under arrest. When she demanded to know on what grounds they had arrested them she was told that she was holding an illegal meeting. Unmindful of her friends' protests, she was taken to a nearby police station and locked up. But upon the intervention of some members of the opposition, she was, again, released. Wangari said that the intention of the police was to humiliate and intimidate her, and that, while they might humiliate her, they would never succeed in intimidating her.

Wangari campaigned for the parliament again in the 2002 elections. This time, the entire opposition united under the National Rainbow Coalition and adopted her as their candidate. On 27 December 2002, the Rainbow Coalition defeated the ruling KANU, with Wangari recording a thumping victory in Tetu garnering an overwhelming 98 per cent of the votes. In January 2003, she became assistant minister in the Ministry of Environment and Natural Resources and served in that capacity till November 2005.

In enjoying the friendship and partnership of many international groups, Wangari may have been extremely fortunate to escape the wrath of state repression. That, however, does not take away from Wangari's own political astuteness. She cleverly employed international journalists and activists to instil a sense of accountability in an otherwise irresponsible administration, who had largely remained unchallenged for forty years since Kenya's independence. It is also important to keep in mind, while judging Wangari's work, that her political machinations were intended not just to further immediate political goals but also to make way for larger, more extensive social changes, especially regarding climate change, sustainable development and a cultural renewal of the Kenyan people who had long reeled under the colonial yoke.

On 8 October 2004, Ole Danbolt Mjos, chairman of the Norwegian Nobel Committee, announced that she had been chosen for the Nobel Peace Prize for 2004. It was for her 'contribution to sustainable development, democracy and peace'. The Norwegian Nobel Committee paid her a glowing tribute in a statement it released: 'Wangari stood up courageously against the former oppressive regime in Kenya. Her unique forms of action have contributed to drawing attention to political oppression, nationally and internationally. She has served as an inspiration for many in the fight for democratic rights and has especially encouraged women to better their situation.'

Wangari was the first African woman and environmentalist to win the prize. About the conferment of the Nobel Peace Prize, she wrote, 'I was not prepared to learn that I had been awarded the Nobel Peace Prize; I wonder whether anybody ever is. The news hit me like a thunderbolt. How was I supposed to handle it? How did this happen? How did they find such a person as me? I could hardly believe it.'

During the course of her valiant fight against the government, Wangari was recognized worldwide, with several international awards being conferred on her. In 1991, she received the Goldman Environment Prize in San Francisco and The Hunger Project's African Prize for Leadership in London. She was conferred the Edinburgh Medal in April 1993. In May 1993, she was conferred the Jane Addams International Women's Leadership Award, and in June 1993, she was invited to attend the UN's World Conference on Human Rights in Vienna.

In December 2009, in recognition of her deep commitment to the environment, the United Nations Secretary General Ban Ki-moon named Professor Wangari a 'UN Messenger of Peace'. In 2010, she was appointed to the Millennium Development Goals Advocacy Group to galvanize worldwide support for the group's undertakings. In the same year, she founded the Wangari Maathai Institute for Peace and Environment Studies in collaboration with the University College of Nairobi, to bring together academic research in land use, forestry, agriculture, conflict resolution and peace studies.

Besides being a leading environmentalist, she was second to none in her love for freedom. Reminiscing about her days of agitation at Uhuru Park, she wrote, 'When I see Uhuru Park and contemplate its meaning, I feel compelled to fight for it, so that my grandchildren may share that dream and that joy of freedom as they one day walk there.' Despite being a university professor, she was deeply attached to her roots and soil. She loved criss-crossing the fields, the rivers, and did not mind working in the fields with her knees deep in the mud. She wrote:

> Although I was a highly educated woman, it did not seem odd to me to work with my hands, alongside rural women. Some politicians and others in the 1980s and 1990s ridiculed me for being so. But I had no problem with it, and the rural women both accepted and appreciated that I was working with them to improve their lives and the environment. After all, I was a child of the same soil. Education, if it means anything, should not take people away from land but instil in them even more respect for it because educated people are in a position to understand what is being lost. The future of the planet concerns all of us and we should do what we can to protect it. As I told the foresters and the women – you don't need a diploma to plant a tree.

Wangari was also a person with global concerns, as are many Nobel peace women. At the start of the twenty-first century, she joined the Jubilee Coalition, a worldwide campaign to write off debts owed to rich countries by poor countries. In April 2000, in Nairobi, several hundred activists of the Green Belt Movement marched towards the office of the World Bank with a petition to write off Kenya's debt.

On 25 September 2011, after a prolonged battle with ovarian cancer, Professor Wangari took leave of this planet at the age of seventy-one. The world remembers her fondly. This simple yet emphatic woman remained inexorably wedded to the dreams of the common rural woman. She walked a sublime path with absolute humility, a path for each one of us to tread – to secure abiding world peace with justice and compassion.

Huruka Maitu Wangari – Rest in Peace, Mama Wangari.

SHIRIN EBADI

Harbinger of an Islamic Renaissance

'I want you to imagine for a moment that I have suffered a
heart attack and have been rushed to the hospital.
Wouldn't that be terrible? It would be much worse than
my arrest. So please keep all this in perspective.'

When a woman whose life has been blessed by good fortune and remarkable talent encounters adversity, it may just be that Providence is giving her an opportunity. For only in confronting adversity may her heroic potential, an innate human gift, come to the fore. And only through her heroic potential may her greatness expand, rising beyond limitations in ways she could scarce envision. Such is the case with Shirin Ebadi, a person uniquely enabled by talent and circumstance to confront injustice and tyranny in her country.

Shirin Ebadi's warmth and humility are quite a contrast to her reputation as a formidable legal mind and dogged campaigner for human rights. It is difficult for me to imagine I am with a woman whose life's work has entailed confronting one of the most feared regimes of the Middle East. I am taken aback by her unassuming manner and utter absence of affectation. She is simply authentic and present to her company, which is as overawing as it is refreshing. As we chat and sip coffee in one of Shirin's favourite haunts in London, I even forget for some time that the lady sitting before me is a Nobel Prize winner. Indeed, no one there seems aware of her achievements. When I quietly inform one of the waitresses that Shirin is a Nobel Peace laureate, she is surprised and thrilled, proud that such a great lady is her regular customer.

Shirin Ebadi – Iranian lawyer, human rights activist, former judge and founding member of Defenders of Human Rights Center in Iran – was the recipient of the Nobel Peace Prize for 2003. She is the only Iranian and the first Muslim woman to receive the award. Shirin was born in Hamadan, a city some 360 kilometres south-west of Tehran, on 21 June 1947. Her father, Mohammad Ali Ebadi, was head of the registry office of Hamadan, the city's chief notary, and a law professor with several commercial law books to his credit. Her family moved to Tehran in 1948, and there Shirin received her early education in Firuzkuhi primary school. She later attended Anoshirvan Dadgar and Reza Shah Kabir secondary schools.

Shirin fondly recalls the loving family life of her childhood. She says that her parents filled their household with affection and kindness, which helped cultivate her gentle demeanour and fostered love between her and her siblings – two sisters and a brother. It also imbued Shirin with empathy for her fellow human beings, which is essential for a rewarding public life. In her memoir, she pays tribute to her father's devotion to her mother: 'To this day, I have yet to see a man adore a woman more devotedly than he did my mother.' Certainly, her formative years equipped her well to face the challenges she would later contend with, and gave her a sound moral foundation upon which her activism and legal advocacy would be based.

Raised in a patriarchal society where sons are groomed to expect primacy over the family's women, Shirin was fortunate to have experienced none of the strictures suffered by many of her sisters in Iran. Rather, she enjoyed privileges at par with her brother. Her father, upon hearing of Shirin's childhood spats with her brother, would simply smile and say, 'They are children. They will make up themselves.' Her father's reluctance to favour his only son not only spared Shirin the low self-esteem that dogged many other Iranian women in the prevailing patriarchy but also instilled within her an essential confidence. Shirin considers her enlightened upbringing her most valuable inheritance.

Uncanny events, or situations engendering revelations and spiritual awakenings, often happen to those whom Providence calls to greatness. It so happened with Shirin. Her mother had fallen seriously ill and Shirin was deeply worried. She recalls that she climbed the stairs to the attic to pray to God to heal her mother, so that she could go to school. There, deep in communion with the Divine, an eerie sensation passed through her body.

She immediately knew that God had heard her prayers, and her mother began to recover. Shirin's faith in God grew enormously, and she declares that it has never been shaken since.

After completing secondary school, Shirin studied law at the University of Tehran. Her choice of law as a profession was influenced in no small measure by her father. It would lead her to become a judge – one of the first female judges in Iran – while only in her early twenties, in 1969. Whether by divine design or sheer coincidence, her position brought her to confront the regime of Shah Mohammad Reza Pahlavi, an absolute monarch, when she signed a protest letter objecting to the constitution of a mediating council by the Shah. This governmental body was to adjudicate cases outside the regular judicial system. Although Shirin and other judges did not face any imminent threat after writing the letter, it became clear to them all that by signing the protest letter they had leapt into the tumult of Iran's degenerating political scene. Disaffection against the Shah's regime was rising, and Ayatollah Ruhollah Khomeini, who hurled his choicest invective at the Shah from exile in Iraq and France, would be quick to capitalize on his opponent's unpopularity.

Public opinion irrevocably turned against the Shah's regime after the arson attack on the crowded Cinema Rex in the city of Abadan on 19 August 1978. This horrific terrorist act claimed the lives of somewhere in the order of four hundred people. Though the true identity of the perpetrators still remains shrouded by allegations and counter-allegations, the Iranian public at the time suspected the hand of the Shah's secret police. The episode served to convince Iranians that the Shah would cling to power even at the cost of people's lives, and moves to depose him gained momentum. The Ayatollah then called upon Iranians to expel the ministers of the Shah's government from office. A few days after Ayatollah's announcement, Shirin, along with other judges and officials, barged into the minister of justice's office. He was absent. A senior judge sitting there was astonished to find Shirin in the ranks of the rebels. He asked her whether she knew that the very people she was inciting to rebellious activities would eventually take her job away if they came to power. Shirin promptly retorted that she would rather be a free Iranian than an enslaved attorney.

The words of the senior judge would prove prophetic, however, and Shirin would taste the bitter fruit of the revolution. In the meantime, a few days after the massive uprising against the Shah, the entire country was paralysed, and the former monarch had to flee for exile on 16 January 1979. Then, on 1 February, Ayatollah Ruhollah Khomeini returned to Tehran to a tumultuous reception. By December, a new, theocratic constitution had been adopted and Ayatollah Khomeini was firmly entrenched as the Supreme Leader of Iran. The constitution was based on the concept of *velayat-e faqih* (rule of the jurist), which held that Muslims require guardianship by the leading Islamic jurist, the Supreme Leader (Ayatollah). Ayatollah Khomeini accordingly became the Supreme Leader and remained in that unchallengeable position until his death some ten years later.

After the Islamist victory, Shirin went with a group to confer with Fathollah Bani-Sadr, the newly appointed provisional overseer of the Ministry of Justice, at his office. Upon finding that Shirin was not wearing a headscarf, Bani-Sadr asked her whether out of regard for Khomeini, who had graced their country by his return from exile, she should not cover her hair. Shirin was taken by surprise. She rejected his counsel and left, wondering and worrying as to what was to be in store for women under the new Islamist dispensation.

She never imagined the indignities and atrocities that were in store for her and her Iranian sisters. And she could scarce have believed that these would be perpetrated by the revolutionaries themselves, whose victory she and her husband Javad, had celebrated by bellowing 'Allahu Akbar' from their house's rooftop. The first such indignity came after she returned from a short vacation in New York, when the Purging Committee asked her to report to the legal office. There, she was informed that she was to be summarily removed from office as a judge and assigned the post of a clerk typist. Shirin could now see that whereas the Shah's ouster was sought for the cause of the dispossessed, the Ayatollah Khomeini's dispensation itself had become the dispossessor. One member of the Purging Committee had been her junior until the previous year.

Shirin was gutted. The very people she had supported had now shown themselves to be inimical to basic women's rights which she had enjoyed since childhood. After reaching her home she fell on the shoulders of her sister and sobbed inconsolably; but she did not give in. Perseverance, the intrinsic attribute of her character, soon surfaced and she decided to report at the legal office. She declared that in protest, however, she would do no work, because she had been demoted against her will. She continued this protest for a few weeks. Until this time, little did Shirin suspect that the revolution would affect her well beyond her losing her station; it would intrude menacingly into every aspect of her life, divesting her of rights and even threatening the basis of her relationship with her husband. She would soon understand, to her horror, that under the new regime Javad – her equal life partner and the love of her life – could very easily become her oppressor by law.

The new Islamic dispensation under Ayatollah Khomeini was buttressed by an Islamic Penal Code, which was foisted upon the people of Iran overnight, in 1979. It drastically altered the very nature of male–female relationships; and the value of a woman's life was effectively reduced to half that of a man's life. A woman's testimony in a court of law was now afforded only half the weight of that of a man's testimony. If a woman was injured or killed in a road accident, her family would receive only half the compensation to which a man's family was entitled under similar circumstances. And no woman could seek divorce without the permission of her husband.

Provisions of the Islamic Penal Code that Shirin found particularly galling permitted her husband Javad to arbitrarily divorce her, to keep three more wives in their marital home along with her and to take away their future children at his whim. It was abundantly clear that the Islamic Penal Code would persist despite widespread misgivings too. In one television appearance, Ayatollah Khomeini sought to suppress all resistance against the new Islamic Penal Code by declaring that anyone opposing it would be termed 'anti-Islamic' and would be punished accordingly.

Shirin had set her own terms for marriage, and she now saw the legal sanctioning of women's subjugation – and potentially, her own. Before agreeing to marry Javad, she had assessed his integrity and matrimonial compatibility for six months. She had then asked that they test the strength of their bond of love by remaining apart for a month. Only after assuring herself that she and Javad were truly made for each other had she married him. Upon the imposition of the new penal code, however, Shirin felt that she had been reduced to little more than a vassal, and she became thoroughly perturbed by her disempowerment.

She could do nothing at this time for other women – Ayatollah Khomeini's televised pronouncement hinted at dire consequences for those opposing the new laws – but she could assert her freedom in her own household. Indignant at the nullification of her legal rights in her relationship with her husband, she decided to take action to personally reinstate them. She asked Javad to make a deposition before a notary, testifying that he would grant her the right of divorce and also custody of their future children if they ever chose to separate.

Shirin's decisive action in response to the change in personal laws under the Islamic Penal Code is understandable to anyone who has known freedom. For his part, Javad refused to take advantage of the superior status that the new Islamic Penal Code had instantly bestowed upon him. As incensed as his wife at the tyranny of the new government – and determined that his marriage would not suffer – he happily complied with Shirin's request. The notary advised him against the contract, but this enlightened man retorted, 'My decision is irrevocable. I want to save my life.'

The new dictates of the Islamic Penal Code, which pervaded virtually every aspect of life in Iran, continued to disturb Shirin. She was driven to distraction by a lack of meaningful work – she was, after all, a lawyer and former judge, now relegated to some of the more menial office duties. She became increasingly disenchanted and even depressed. Thus, just one day after she completed fifteen years of service, which entitled her to a pension, she submitted a request for voluntary retirement. The request was promptly accepted; for her bosses, it was as a case of good riddance of an undesirable female employee.

As if the Islamic Penal Code was a lesser onslaught on the liberties of Iranians, a greater calamity awaited them. Ayatollah Khomeini was determined to spread his revolution in the entire region, proclaiming that Islam knows no boundaries and that nationalism was only a worldly emotion. His tacit support for sectarian divisions in Iraq unsettled Saddam Hussein, the country's infamous president, who saw an opportunity for at once quashing Shia aspirations within his country and expanding his borders.

Under the mistaken belief that Iran had been sufficiently enervated by the revolution and that Iraq's forces would prevail,

President Hussein ordered an attack on Iran in September 1980. Hussein could not have been more mistaken. Hostilities finally ceased in stalemate on 20 August 1988 with Resolution 598, a UN-brokered ceasefire, after seven years, ten months, four weeks and one day of war. The Iran–Iraq War (also called the Gulf War) was the longest conventional war of the twentieth century; and it had all but obliterated a generation of Iranian and Iraqi men.

The conflict began with Iraq's MiG 23 Floggers bombing Mehrabad Airport, as well as other strategic locations in Tehran on 22 September 1980. Soon the Iraqi campaign battered eight more Iranian cities. The main thrust of Iraq's offensive was in southern Iran, where its oilfields were located. The Ayatollah declared the war a *Jang-e tahmili* (imposed war); Shia's 'innocent' defence against a despot. In doing so, Khomeini portrayed Hussein as a modern-day Yazid, the seventh-century Umayyad caliph who had Prophet Muhammad's grandson, Shia saint Imam Husayn ibn Ali, and his entire family slaughtered in the ancient Battle of Karbala.

War is often most calamitous for women and the young. Hussein was well equipped with Western weapons and chemical agents, which Iran, being the most populous country in the region, countered with its own more limited armaments and its greatest asset: the living flesh of its youth. At the same time that Khomeini was invoking the symbolism of Jang-e tahmili to impassion the youth of Iran, the newly formed people's militia or *basij* was being readied to face the enemy. While officially this comprised volunteers over the age of eighteen, in the desperate days of the war, hordes of old unemployed men, some approaching eighty years of age, and boys as young as twelve were sent to the front, often armed with little more than their faith. They were equipped with miniature copies of the Quran, portraits of Ayatollah Khomeini and the first Shia Imam, Imam Ali; and their belief that heaven awaited them were they blessed to be martyred. The more prescient carried their funeral shrouds.

Thus, in many thousand-legged straight-line formations, devout and patriotic Iranian boys would advance on Iraqi positions – without air or artillery support and sometimes with only their fists for weapons – crying 'Allahu Akbar'. The cream of the next generation's men became flesh-and-blood minesweepers, martyrdom achieved with each bursting explosion. On occasions, the tide of these children carried a wave of surging, bloodied flesh over Iraqi lines, engulfing the enemy with fervour and squandered humanity. Then, the terrain was fit for the advance of regular Iranian soldiers.

The exigencies of war left the nation grieving and battered, and there was no space for dissent. Shirin feels that moderate Iranians were caught in an emotional tangle. On one hand, they felt cheated by the Islamic revolution which had deprived them of even their fundamental personal freedoms. On the other hand, they felt compelled by their patriotism to join the war where, perforce, they had to side with the agents of the revolution. Adding to Shirin's despair, her close friends deserted Iran, one by one, despite her pleading and disavowal. Almost daily she blackened her address book with crosses eclipsing the names and addresses of her close friends. Crossing out an address meant that this friend had died to her, each new desertion battering Shirin's heart more heavily than the one before. Shirin's spirits plunged to perhaps the lowest depths of despair when one of her dear cousins and a very close friend departed, just after she was removed from the bench.

Iranian women were caught between the war with a belligerent neighbouring state and a civil dispensation which was routinely hostile. Shirin, along with her female compatriots, had to come to terms with living under the tyranny of the Komiteh, the morality police. Officers of the Komiteh, who often wielded more power than the civil police, patrolled Iran's cities to enforce an inflexible code of conduct on citizens; and women, especially those who took liberties with the Islamic dress code, bore the brunt of their harshness. Women were regularly harassed by the Komiteh for the most minor of sartorial infractions and awarded summary, draconian punishments.

Shirin personally experienced the Komiteh's bizarre regime of terror and its thuggery towards normal and even pious Iranian women. In the spring of 1989, she had travelled to Ramsar, a small town near the Caspian Sea, to celebrate Persian New Year. While walking near the town square, a Komiteh officer spotted her and beckoned her to board a minibus parked there. Shirin's protests notwithstanding, the police officer pulled her by her arm and roughly pushed her into the minibus. There, she found three women huddled inside, all arrested for innocently violating the Islamic dress code. Shirin's fault was that she was found wearing a long coat, baggy pants and a headscarf which, as per the whims of the morality police, somehow breached the code. One of the women already arrested and put in the minibus was a retired schoolteacher who had reportedly sinned for having worn slippers, due to her swollen feet. She only hardened the stern attitude of the Komiteh officer when she protested that nowhere in the Quran is it stated that wearing slippers is a crime for women.

There were innumerable instances of the morality police harassing women – their special focus – as well as all other Iranians – whether Muslims, Christians or Jews. Things had come to such a sorry state of affairs that if ever a dating couple wanted to go for an outing, they would take with them a small cousin or some other young relative. Thus disguised, they might pass for a family and be ignored by the morality force for defying the ban on a girl's moving with an unrelated man.

One of Shirin's closest friends, Soraya, suffered the Komiteh's injustice in an event fairly typical of those times. For what most would consider harmless and innocent behaviour, Soraya was detained and endured an ordeal for which she had no means of redress. She, her fiancé and his two friends ran afoul of the Komiteh after they went together to her home to visit her mother. The morality police arrested them all, took Soraya away and interrogated her male companions separately. They were suspected of being members of the Mojahedin-e Khalq Organization (MKO), an opponent of Ayatollah Khomeini's Islamic revolution. Theirs was a grave predicament: Shirin's own brother-in-law, Fuad, endured seven years' imprisonment and was executed in 1988 for little more than his membership of the MKO.

Once the arresting officer learnt that Soraya, her fiancé, and other male companions were not a threat to the government, they were not released, however. They were charged for travelling together while being unrelated and unmarried. The officer tried to persuade Soraya to confess that she had been engaged in sexual relations with all the men. The judge even offered to take Soraya as his 'temporary wife' if she confessed her guilt. Soraya shouted at the officer, saying that she had not had physical contact with any of her male companions, including her fiancé.

Notwithstanding the triviality of the purported offence, the judge pronounced his judgment against Soraya, finding her guilty of violation of Islamic law (for moving together in public in the company of unmarried and unrelated males), and ordered that she be summarily given forty lashes. Before any officer could raise his hand to carry out the punishment, she admonished the judge for not knowing shariat fully, according to which a woman can be given corporal punishment only by another woman. The judge, humiliated because he could not counter Soraya's argument and piqued by her highlighting his mistake, pronounced instead a sentence of eighty lashes on her fiancé. Her fiancé was promptly forced to lie on the floor and the eighty lashes were delivered – without the flagellator keeping the Holy Quran under his arm so that the blows would be softened, as the Quran prescribes. Soraya's fiancé's wounds from the flogging were so severe that blood began oozing from them, provoking Soraya's hysterical condemnation of the judge.

Soraya's case is illustrative of the grotesque and arbitrary cruelty that the Komiteh regularly inflicted upon innocent people, especially women, for any liberty they took with regard to their personal conduct. Young women routinely drew the Komiteh's ire and summary retribution for such venial 'offences' as wearing lipstick. The Iranian people commonly believed that the morality police officers harassed people simply because they did not have anything else to do. And their harassment was especially brutish and gratuitous. A renowned poet, Ahmad Shamlou, wrote the poem, 'Strange Times, My Darling', exposing the antics of the morality police in targeting the innocent in the name of Islamic law.

The fallout from the introduction of the Islamic Penal Code and a host of other oppressive measures, particularly against women, created negative effects on Iranian society. The age at which a girl could marry was reduced to a farcical nine years, and the government offered inducements for couples to marry, such as grants of free furniture. The country was at war, and the Ayatollah and his inner circle perceived a larger population to be an advantage for Iran. Family planning clinics that had been established during the Shah's regime were shut down and the price for birth control pills was artificially inflated tenfold.

The result, despite the horrendous casualties of the Iran–Iraq War, was the highest rate of population growth – in excess of 3 per cent per annum – in the world. Already burdened with a costly, protracted war, the economy eventually stagnated with the expense of the increased population. Even the most ardent supporters of the Islamic revolution could not ignore the effect of the government's policies. But it was only in the late 1980s, at the end of the war, that Ayatollah Khomeini issued fatwas making contraception widely available and respectable for Iran's conservative citizens.

The government also made some moves towards liberalism that saw Shirin being granted a licence to practise law in 1992. The disorder of the justice system, though – as with other spheres of governance in those years – was so pervasive that it was not the brilliance of a lawyer's arguments that decided a case. It was the quantum of his bribe.

Assaults on women's liberties seemed interminable too. All were traceable to the Islamic Penal Code, which had in some respects reduced the worth of Iran's women to half that of its men, and in others seemed to result in its complete nullification. The judiciary's egregious handling of an aggravated rape and murder of a child in 1996 was a clear demonstration of the Islamic Penal Code's injustice, and it brought Shirin to centre stage of the inevitable struggle against unjust and outlandish laws. An eleven-year-old girl named Leila Fathi was collecting wild flowers in the hills near her home in a small town in north-western Iran, when she was brutalized and her young life extinguished by sexual predators. She was raped and then killed by a heavy blow to her head, and her body was tossed down a hill. Three men were arrested for the crime. The prime suspect confessed and hanged himself in jail. The other two accused were convicted of rape and were awarded death sentences, though they had pleaded not guilty and claimed to have only helped in disposing of the young girl's body.

The Islamic Penal Code came in the way of executing the death sentence in a perverse manner. According to the code, a woman's worth is equal to half that of a man's. Islamic law also grants the right to a homicide victim's family to either seek legal punishment for the guilty or to receive financial compensation (*diyah*, or blood money), which is the traditional compensation due for the shedding of blood. Article 209 of Iran's Islamic Penal Code, however, provided that 'If a Muslim man commits first-degree murder against a Muslim woman, the penalty of retribution shall apply. The victim's next of kin, however, shall pay to the culprit half of his blood money before the act of retribution is carried out.' Thus, the Islamic Penal Code that stipulates that a woman's worth is just half that of a man's intruded in the dispensation of justice in this case, leading to a bitter paradox: The victim's family was asked to pay approximately US $18,000 blood money to their young daughter's killers, and hence were penalized instead of the murderers.

Leila's family would not submit easily to this travesty of justice. Her father sold whatever little material possessions he had, including a mud hut, to gather the blood money. The court, however, found whatever money the family could fetch for their meagre belongings to be insufficient. In the vain hope of reclaiming their lost honour, the family instead lost everything. With a view to raising more money, Leila's father offered to sell his kidney at a clinic, which the doctor declined. Then her handicapped brother offered his kidney, which was also declined.

The doctor whom Leila's father and brother had approached for kidney donation was appalled by the injustice at this turn of events: Here were two poor men, attempting to sell their kidneys simply because their murdered daughter and sister could receive justice. He approached the judiciary and threatened to publicize the case worldwide through Médecins Sans Frontières (Doctors Without Borders) if action was not taken to rectify the situation. Galvanized by his threat, the judiciary agreed to facilitate the execution by making good the deficit of the diyah from the state treasury. With legal wrangling and manoeuvring, though, the case had dragged on for well in excess of a decade, and Leila's family were ultimately denied justice.

Shirin represented Leila's family and decided to showcase the events to illustrate the injustice of various provisions of the Islamic Penal Code for the nation's women. She wrote an article, in language easily understandable for common people, which was published in the magazine *Iran-e Farada*. Shunning all sophistication, she wrote that if a highly educated woman, a holder of a PhD degree, were killed in an accident and an illiterate gangster were hurt and suffered an injury to his testicle, the worth of his injured testicle would be considered equal to the life of even such a highly educated woman. Her words laid bare the Islamic Penal Code's deep prejudice against women. The article mortified the educated classes of Tehran. Shirin was stunned to discover that her audience had been shaken from their torpor; the prejudice against women embedded in the Islamic Penal Code had become a hotly discussed topic among Tehran's citizenry.

For her efforts, Shirin began receiving threats from radical elements led by a notorious parliamentarian. Nevertheless, the brewing rancour against the discriminatory laws convinced the regime to soften its stance somewhat. Any direct challenge to government authority, though, was still met with an iron-fisted response. Shirin was verily throwing a challenge to the powers that be, and it is little wonder that a judge, during a hearing, warned her to refrain from castigating the sacred laws of Islam.

The Islamic Penal Code was not only discriminatory and harrowing for women; children suffered also. In accordance with the Islamic Penal Code, a father was awarded custody of children in the event of divorce as a matter of right, whether he be a drug addict, a criminal, a perpetrator of physical abuse or a person with insufficient means of livelihood. Shirin read in a newspaper a horrifying tale about a little girl named Arian Golshani, whose custody had been granted to her father by the court after her parents' divorce. The girl's mother had petitioned the court for her child's custody on the grounds that her drug-addicted ex-husband was violently abusive towards Arian. The court had, however, thrown out the petition for being antagonistic to the fundamentals of Islamic law.

Arian subsequently died a miserable death at the hands of her father, stepmother and stepbrother. An autopsy revealed that she had haemorrhaged and died after being kicked by her stepbrother after prolonged, depraved abuse. A photograph of her starved, emaciated body, burnt by cigarette butts and disfigured by bruising, shocked Iranians when it was published. It was a horrific picture, and an indictment of Iran's senseless family laws. Many in Tehran were moved to tears by her tragedy, and some 10,000 people attended her memorial service in September 1997. Shirin later recounted: 'The women left the funeral chanting, "This law should be changed."' At the memorial service, Shirin implored the congregation: 'Anyone who is against the law of Iran take all the white flowers and throw their petals on the street.' She recalled, 'After a few minutes, we saw the street all white'.

The government could not afford to ignore the public's reaction to Arian's horrific and needless death. Within months new laws were ratified to allow judges to award custody to another relative or the state where a child's parents were unfit for proper parenting. Shirin had successfully mobilized support to change blatantly unjust laws which favoured men's primacy over common sense and children's welfare. She was not satisfied, however, because the law still held to a patriarchal right to custody and left much to the discretion of judges.

Shirin took up the case of Arian's murder in court and received worldwide attention. Newspaper reporters, broadcast journalists and many well-meaning people thronged at the courtroom.

Although Arian's father and stepbrother were on trial for brutally murdering Arian, the focus of the case was on two issues: First, the unjust law that granted custody of Arian to her murderous father; and second, the fairness of the law in making it mandatory for the girl's mother to pay for the execution of justice. Shirin asked the court how it could be fair that taxes paid by the people should go to murderers. Because the photo of the murdered girl in the newspaper had jolted the conscience of many people and the case had received attention from every quarter, the court did not rule that Arian's mother bear the outrage of diyah. The judge sentenced Arian's stepbrother to death, and her father and stepmother to imprisonment for one year. Arian's mother asked for the suspension of Arian's stepbrother's execution because he, living with his father rather than his mother, had himself been a victim of the same law.

Although it is true that a kite flies not with but against the winds, rising against the winds of the Islamic revolution and weathering their ferocity required nerves of steel. Amidst the frantic scurrying of the educated classes to leave Iran, Shirin was the very epitome of steadfastness. Many of her colleagues had good reason to leave. In the Shah's regime, the much-feared SAVAK (Sazeman-e Ettela'at va Amniyat-e Keshvar, Organization of National Security and Information) had engaged in all manner of torture, intimidation and liquidation of dissidents – including supporters of Ayatollah Khomeini. Its successor in revolutionary Iran, SAVAMA, was essentially a reconstituted SAVAK. Their methods, along with their structure and personnel, remained largely unchanged. And their targets – intellectuals and activists whose political leanings were not to their liking – were much the same as those before the revolution.

SAVAMA, later renamed VEVAK (*Vezarat-e Ettela'at va Amniyat-e Keshvar*), then VAJA, or alternatively Ministry of Intelligence or MOIS, unleashed waves of terror to firm the revolutionary government's grasp on power in its early years.

In the late 1980s, it began a campaign of targeted assassinations against the government's opponents, which were later dubbed the 'chain murders'. MOIS's victims were, for the most part, those of secular dispensation: intellectuals, writers, poets, lawyers and journalists. Perhaps in excess of 100 prominent Iranians and their family members were assassinated, some in a brutal manner and others in ways which left some doubt as to the cause of death. Even Ahmad Khomeini, Ayatollah Khomeini's son – who died of heart failure in March 1995 – may have been murdered, years after his ouster by Iran's hardliners. His son Hassan later alleged that his father had been poisoned by Iranian agents.

Their means of killing were variously stabbings, car crashes, shootings in staged robberies and poisoning, with the intention of obscuring any link between the deaths. One of the favoured methods of assassination was to inject potassium or alcohol into the body of the victim to induce a heart attack. 'Cardiac arrest' thus claimed numerous victims with no history of heart ailments.

A case in point is the mysterious death of Ahmad Mir Alaei (1942–1995). Mir Alaei was a prominent writer, translator and signatory of an open letter from the Writers' Association of Iran to the government, which was highly critical of its repressive policies. He left home early on 24 October 1995 to meet someone at a bookstore; but he never kept his appointment. He was scheduled to deliver a lecture later that day at the medical school in Isfahan. Strangely, the students were informed that his 2 p.m. lecture had been cancelled. His body was discovered at 8 p.m. that night. The official cause of death: cardiac arrest.

Other, more audacious plans to rid the nation of dissidents were put in play. In the summer of 1996, an attempt to kill twenty-one writers and poets shook the literary world. A group undertaking a tour to Armenia to attend a literary conference narrowly escaped a crude but ingenious plot to assassinate them under the guise of a vehicle accident. On 8 August, the driver of their bus tried to steer it over a precipice in the Hayrun Pass in north-western Iran, leaping out before its passengers would plunge to almost certain death in the ravine below. It was the sheer presence of mind and split-second action of one of the writers that saved him and his fellow passengers.

These incidents, and a plethora of other suspicious deaths of moderates of Iran's learned elite, deeply troubled Shirin and her colleagues. The whole intellectual class, especially the members of the Writers' Association of Iran – novelists, writers and poets – was under siege. Shirin was a prominent member of the association, which had written several letters to the government. These letters clarified that their objective was non-political and they wanted only the right of freedom of expression. Some of those who had signed such letters, including Ahmad Mir Alaei, were killed or disappeared under highly suspicious circumstances. Other members, such as Shirin, felt as if death lurked all around her. Whenever she had to attend a meeting, Shirin adopted a circuitous path and changed her modes of conveyance to evade the shadow of intelligence men and thwart the intention of assassins. Perhaps it was only her vigilance that kept her alive through these years.

The judicial system had become a farce. The insidious power of the Ministry of Intelligence meant the roles of investigator, prosecutor and judge had, in effect, merged. Though all writers, intellectuals and journalists were kept under constant fear of liquidation, those who were perceived as particularly threatening to the regime were specially targeted. In this climate of oppression, it was unthinkable that anyone could stand against the might of the state. Shirin, however, continued fighting for justice for those killed for espousing freedom of expression. She also represented those whose lives had been destroyed by malicious prosecutions; the dissidents facing questionable prosecutions, which if successful, would usually entail a death sentence. This work required extraordinary valour. It is a rare human being who forsakes her own welfare for that of others.

The stories of Shirin Ebadi's courage in taking up the cause of political dissidents whom the state seemed hell-bent on eliminating are legion. There was a litany of cases of state persecution that no one but Shirin came forward to defend, often pro bono. One such case was that of a mild-mannered journalist, Faraj Sarkuhi. Sarkuhi was targeted partly because his family was in Germany and a German court had issued arrest warrants for Ali Fallahian, the Iranian minister of intelligence, for his role in the murder of dissidents at a Berlin restaurant in 1992.

In 1996, Faraj was on his way to Tehran's Mehrabad Airport to board a flight for Germany when he was kidnapped and imprisoned by MOIS. With tears flowing and fear writ large on his face, his mother approached Shirin for help. Shirin defended Faraj, and with a broad campaign involving public and international pressure, she secured his release in 1998. She successfully argued that his case could only be heard in an open court; that the secret 'trial' his captors had conducted was legally invalid. Her audacity seemed to know no bounds. She even accompanied Faraj to the passport office in Tehran in order that he secure a passport. With his passport in hand, Faraj left Iran for Germany, where he was granted asylum.

The brutality of MOIS's campaign of systematic liquidations exceeded itself in 1998, and the 'chain murders' could no longer be kept from the public's attention. In the late summer and autumn, a brazen and particularly ferocious series of murders rocked Iran. First, the mutilated corpses of seventy-year-old Dariush Forouhar (Secretary General of the opposition party, the Nation of Iran Party) and his wife Parvaneh Eskandari were discovered at their home in Tehran on 22 November. Both had died in a bloody, vicious attack: Dariush had been tied to a chair and multiple stab wounds inflicted on his aged body. His wife, who was upstairs, had been stabbed to death in a similarly shocking manner. They had anticipated their murders. Before her death, Parvaneh Eskandari had told Human Rights Watch in New York, 'We are living with the fear of being killed. Every night when we go to bed we thank God the Almighty for His blessing of living another day.'

On 10 December, Mohammad Mokhtari's mysterious disappearance in Tehran a week earlier was solved when his body was identified at the coroner's office. Mokhtari was a mythologist, journalist and a member of the Writers' Association of Iran. Mohammad Ja'far Pouyandeh, a notable writer and prolific translator, was found dead just days later. He had been working on a book titled *Questions and Answers about Human Rights* at the time of his death. Both men had been strangled and their bodies dumped. The manner and timing of these crimes inevitably raised suspicions and an outcry from the braver activists of Tehran's intellectual community. This focused attention on the questionable manner of Majid Sharif's disappearance and death of a 'heart attack' just weeks earlier.

Sharif, a translator, had evidently been poisoned and his body placed on the side of a road in Tehran that it would appear his death had been of natural causes. He had written articles for a subsequently banned monthly magazine which criticized government policies. His would be tallied as another death in the 'chain' – as would scores of others, with time. The chain murders would later be traced as far back as November 1988, when Dr Kazem Sami Kermani, Iran's former minister of health, was stabbed to death by an unknown assailant in his clinic.

Shirin was instrumental in exposing the Ministry of Intelligence's involvement in the killings.

Dariush Forouhar's and his wife Parvaneh's killings would finally bring the chain murders to light, with their daughter approaching Shirin to represent her family. Shirin readily agreed and worked assiduously to collect evidence for an exposé that would shake the very foundations of the state. The evidence revealed that the couple had been assassinated, along with numerous other members of Iran's intelligentsia, by a division within the Iranian secret service. Even Shirin, a seasoned lawyer and inveterate campaigner throughout some of the bloodiest years of her country, found the voluminous files for the case chilling, its pages 'dark with descriptions'. She was horrified to discover a document recording an assassin's declaration, 'Shirin Ebadi is next'. It seems she had only been spared by the coming of Ramadan; the killer was instructed by his superiors to wait until the end of Islam's holy month before dispatching her.

The subsequent public furore led to President Khatami hastily convening a committee to investigate the murders. The committee found that a gang of 'rogue' intelligence agents led by Saeed Emami (Eslami), a former deputy intelligence minister, had carried out the killings. On 6 January 1999, the Ministry of Intelligence issued a brief, shocking statement conceding that 'a small number of irresponsible, misguided, headstrong and obstinate staff within the Ministry' had carried out the assassinations. Emami subsequently died in custody, purportedly by his own hand, by ingesting hair-removing cream.

Shirin fought for the couple valiantly and ultimately Dariush Forouhar's and Parvaneh Eskandari's surviving assassins were convicted and sentenced – though the sentence awarded was not commensurate with their heinous crimes. After the court's verdict, the family members of other murder victims began approaching

Shirin as their last hope in the face of a system hopelessly riven with extremist ideology and injustice. As her popularity and renown for her activism grew, the government's menacing attentions increased correspondingly. Shirin felt that like an inescapable shadow, death was chasing her everywhere. Realizing that her arrest was imminent, she wrote to her family on 21 June:

> My dear ones,
>   By the time you read this, I will already be in prison. I want to assure you that I will be fine. I will be released and unharmed because I have done nothing wrong. Can you please do something for me? I want you to imagine for a moment that I have suffered a heart attack and have been rushed to the hospital. Wouldn't that be terrible? It would be much worse than my arrest. So please keep all this in perspective.
>
> *Ghorban-e hamegi*, with love to all.
> Shirin

Shirin was imprisoned late in 2000, albeit for only twenty-five days. Her 'crime': allegedly recording an extremist's confession detailing the support prominent conservative figures lent to vigilante violence and forwarding the tape to President Khatami and the head of the Islamic judiciary. She was exonerated at appeal.

In any event, the intelligence community was hardly chastened by the scandal of the chain murders, and it continued to commit atrocities against dissidents with abandon. Of the several other cases of state-sponsored killing that Shirin pursued was that of a lady named Zahra 'Ziba' Kazemi-Ahmadabadi, a friend of a mutual friend. Ziba was a photojournalist who held both Iranian and Canadian citizenship. She had been arrested on 23 June 2003 on suspicion of espionage while taking photographs of a demonstration at Evin Prison in north-western Tehran. Ziba was interrogated, raped, tortured and battered by prison security and intelligence agents while in custody. She died from blunt force trauma to her head, nineteen days after she was arrested.

The Iranian government alternately stated the cause of Ziba's death as a stroke or head injuries after she had sustained a fall. The Canadian government requested that her body be returned to Canada and, unconvinced by their implausible explanations for her death, demanded that her murderers be punished. Tehran refused to hand over Ziba's body. Iranian authorities were well aware that their preposterous attempts to conceal the crime would be undone should the extensive injuries she had suffered – all unmistakable signs of torture – be documented by an autopsy. These included broken fingers, missing fingernails, crushed toes, extensive bruising, lacerations, a broken nose and a fractured skull. The Iranian authorities' obfuscation and lack of lawful handling of the case angered the Canadian government, which went as far as to recall its ambassador in protest. Indeed, Ziba's murder foreshadowed a prolonged period of icy diplomatic relations between the two countries.

In the face of mounting international pressure, on 30 July, the Iranian vice president Mohammad Ali Abtahi all but conceded that Ziba had died of maltreatment at the hands of government agents. This was cold comfort for her family. Ziba's mother, Ezzat Kazemi, had seen the evidence of torture on her daughter's brutalized remains, and the Iranian government persisted in denying her justice. She came to Shirin in the face of a peculiar development: the authorities had procured her signatures on a power of attorney, ostensibly so that Ziba's killers could be hunted and brought to justice. The signatures, however, were used as Ezzat's consent to not litigate the death. This compounded her misery beyond the limits of tolerance, and she approached Shirin that she and her murdered daughter receive justice.

Ziba's case received unprecedented international attention. Shirin had fought a number of similar cases earlier, but this case provided her a timely opportunity. Now, with world media attention assured – Ziba's case had, by now, become an international cause célèbre – she could showcase the Iranian government's conduct towards those citizens it considered subversive. She could finally impress upon the world how her nation's security apparatus hounded, incarcerated, tortured and even murdered innocent people; and how it did so with impunity. She did so not to damage her country's reputation, but in the desperate hope that condemnation of Iran's government might help end, or at least curb, its excesses.

While Iran's human rights abuses were aired before the world by the subsequent trial, there would be scant change in the nation's hard-line approach to dissent. The government seemed indignant at the worldwide opprobrium Ziba's death generated, even going so far as to describe the Canadian government's stance on the issue as 'biased and unjust'. Moreover, the trial was conducted with little regard for due process. And the judge failed to convict either of the intelligence officers charged with the crime, because the court could not determine who had delivered the fatal blow. The acquittals were just as Shirin had anticipated. She had insisted during the trial of one of the accused, Aghdam-Ahmadi, that he was not Ziba's murderer and requested that relevant witnesses be examined in court to determine the true murderer's identity. Predictably, her request was denied.

After winning the Nobel Peace Prize in 2003, Shirin continued to represent victims of state oppression. Her eminence made it more difficult for the Iranian authorities to muzzle her dissent, and her championing the cause of dissidents in Iran antagonized the authorities to their wit's end. Although she was inwardly fearful, she betrayed no signs of weakness. Rather, she was steadfast in confronting the repressive and deadly factions within her government that had subverted the rule of law and were purging the country of those refusing to conform to their ideology.

While Shirin's bravery was met with almost universal acclaim, the threats against her continued. In 2008, shadowy forces in the government redoubled their efforts to silence her with a slew of threats. These included a threatening message pinned to her Tehran office door and an ominous handwritten note that said: 'Shirin Ebadi, your death is near.' The threats demanded that she desist from making speeches abroad, from seeking the West's support, from appearing abroad without the Islamic headscarf, from questioning the Islamic Republic's punishments and from defending Iran's minority Baha'i community.

Shirin initially braved the threats, as she was accustomed to. But when the official Iranian news service IRNA broadcast a spurious claim in August 2008 that her daughter Narges Tavakkolian had converted to the Baha'i faith – a capital offence in Iran – Shirin knew her days in Iran were numbered. The government was targeting her daughters in an effort to quiet her voice of protest. She attributed the veiled threat to her having agreed to defend the families of seven Baha'is who had been arrested in May 2008 and publicizing her cases internationally. She agonized with fears that her daughters could even be hauled up and brutalized for having polished nails or some other flaw in their dress.

The government was not content to let its campaign against Shirin rest on threats alone. In December 2008 her office and the premises of her Defenders of Human Rights Center were raided and the centre closed, and her home and office were attacked by pro-government 'demonstrators' on 1 January 2009. At this time, she decided she had no alternative but to leave her motherland. After enduring demotion, war, threats and all manner of government harassment over three decades following the revolution, she resolved for her family's welfare to seek asylum in the West. Since June 2009, Shirin has lived in exile in the UK.

The Iranian government has appeared not the least mollified by her exile. In November 2009, Iran's Revolutionary Court allegedly took Shirin's Nobel Peace Prize medal and some other mementoes from a bank box, although the Iranian government has denied these allegations. The government seems to have done a volte-face here, with a view to saving itself from universal derision for this petulant act. It was not above other fairly unconscionable behaviour, though. Realizing that Shirin was not yielding to its coercion and would continue to lecture overseas about the serious shortcomings in Iran's human rights, the authorities turned their sights on Shirin's sister. Iran's Ministry of Intelligence briefly detained Shirin's sister Noushin, in December 2009. Noushin, who was never politically motivated, was detained for no other reason than to pressure Shirin to cease her human rights activities.

Since her exile, Shirin has redoubled her efforts for improving human rights and the rule of law in Iran. She has cautioned European Union nations against restoring ties with Tehran's government without asking it to first improve its human rights record. On human rights, Shirin has posed a volley of pertinent questions to European Union nations: 'Are you willing to shake hands with a government that stones women? Are you going to trust a government that executes its political opposition? Are you willing to compromise standards of human rights that you believe in for your own security?'

Countering Shirin, a spokesman for Iran's UN Mission, Alireza Miryousefi, said that Iran's recent presidential election was free and fair and that the Islamic Republic of Iran has embarked upon the path of democracy and respects the rule of law. Shirin, however, is wary of these statements. She says that even though Iran's president, Hassan Rouhani, claims that his quest is to change the condition of human rights in Iran and was elected on the strength of this promise, there has been no perceptible change in the state of affairs there. Rather, the number of executions in Iran since Rouhani's election doubled from a year earlier, when Mahmoud Ahmadinejad was still in power. In support of her claim, Shirin quotes from the International Federation for Human Rights (FIDH) report, which claims that more than 200 people – some of whom were minors – were executed between 14 June and 1 October 2013: near double the executions that took place in the same period in 2012. She said that opposition activists are still languishing in jails and that persecution of religious and ethnic minorities has not abated.

This brave Nobel laureate does not resile from discussing about the more sensitive topics with me. More than three decades after the Iranian revolution, Shirin remains critical of Ayatollah Khomeini's declaration that Islam knows no boundaries, that nationalism is only a worldly emotion and therefore, Muslims of the world should unite. She told me that she does not believe in freedom of religion as much as 'freedom is religion'.

Unsurprisingly, Shirin has often faced accusations from conservatives that she is working to undermine Islamic law. Shirin is at pains to stress that she is not against Islamic law. She tells me the problem is that the Iranian government interprets Islam incorrectly; it wants the people to blindly believe in the government's incorrect interpretation and does not accept any other interpretation of Islam. She assures me that a correct interpretation of Islam is more liberal, and states that religion and government must be kept separate.

Shirin says that though she is Shia, she has equal respect for the Sunni creed, and for other religions. She also believes that with a correct and liberal interpretation of Islam, Muslims can have respect for all religions. Upon my asking her, she lists non-democratic countries, prejudice towards minorities, and racial forces as being inimical to world peace. She conveys to me her happiness regarding the Arab Spring, whose rapid spread in the Muslim world demands that dictators, absolute monarchies and corrupt local governments institute human and democratic rights.

She also makes clear her views on the proliferation of weapons of mass destruction. A nuclear bomb, she says, can never bring security to any country. She feels that people do not need strategic weapons. They need food. They need jobs. She states that all countries, including India and Pakistan, should destroy nuclear weapons. She regrets that the world focuses more on nuclear energy than human rights and that no attention is being paid to the violations of human rights in Iran. As a result, she says that human rights conditions are worsening there. Moreover, Shirin is staunchly critical of America and European countries for having imposed sanctions against Iran which, she asserts, only cripple the lives of ordinary Iranians. She stresses that sanctions should be intended to weaken the government – but not the people.

Shirin has personally suffered the effects of these sanctions. US law places publishing restrictions on foreign writers from countries the United States has embargoed. Shirin, whose memoir was subject to these laws, was convinced that they were unjust and discriminatory. True to her principles, she successfully challenged the law in a US court in 2004, and her book was published in America.

She suggests that if Iran is barred from using US and European satellites, it would impact the Iranian government more effectively than sanctions, because it would result in the closing down of its propaganda microphones. She also advocates confiscating the assets of senior Iranian officials and ministers who have siphoned off the country's funds. She said that senior government officials and ministers should face travel bans and that their assets should be confiscated. She wants world powers to be firm in applying pressure on the Iranian government to improve its human rights record.

I wonder if other women can summon the courage to stand up and say 'I dare' as Shirin has in her decades of confronting her government's tyranny. My endeavour is to ask the youth of the world to dare to emulate Shirin and fight oppression wherever it occurs, however mighty be the perpetrators. It may be in your neighbourhood, in your community, in your state or in your country. The challenges are many, and opportunities are manifold; but men and women with Shirin's spirit are in short supply. We need to emerge as ones who may dare in the same spirit as Shirin – or, indeed, Malala, Suu Kyi, Mairead, Betty, Karman, Jody or Rigoberta – so that lasting peace in the world becomes an imminently achievable goal.

Shirin's journey – from the day of her removal from the bench to the day she was awarded the Nobel Peace Prize – has been extraordinary. Her constant endeavour has been to impress upon the authorities the need to harmonize the interpretation of Islamic law to further the cause of democracy, equality and human rights. She desires that such a change come to Iran from within and peacefully, and it is for this she has maintained widespread appreciation and support in her country.

Her concerns are not limited to Iran, though. Shirin knows that non-violence is a more effective weapon to wield than violence, throughout the world. She holds Mahatma Gandhi in the highest esteem, and declares him worthy of the world's eternal veneration. While giving a speech to schoolchildren in Mumbai after a meeting of the World Social Forum, Shirin became the first international figure to propose an International Non-Violence

Day. She suggested 30 January, this being the date that Gandhi fell to an extremist ideologue's bullet. Her suggestion was supported by Sonia Gandhi, president of the Indian National Congress, and by Desmond Tutu. Eventually, 2 October was adopted as a day of observance on 15 June 2007, with the UN General Assembly passing a resolution making this a worldwide day for remembering Mahatma Gandhi as an apostle of non-violence.

Shirin reveals herself as a woman of global concern in our meeting. I am somewhat taken aback when she inquires about Sharmila. For a moment, I am left wondering which Sharmila Shirin is referring to, before it dawns on me that she is inquiring about Irom Chanu Sharmila, the Iron Lady of Manipur. Sharmila had been on a hunger strike since November 2000, demanding abrogation of the Armed Forces (Special Powers) Act, 1958, (AFSPA) which was enacted by the Indian government to counter insurgency in Manipur and some other states. This act vests in the armed forces the right to arrest any person without warrant and also search houses and other places without warrant. Irom Chanu Sharmila has spearheaded a campaign for the abrogation of this law, citing endless instances of its misuse by the armed forces. In August 2016, she ended her sixteen-year fast to bring change through electoral politics. However, she lost the elections thereafter, garnering a meagre total of ninety votes from the people she had fought for.

Shirin expresses her surprise to me at how a human being could remain on hunger strike for so long. She appears to have deep respect for Irom Chanu Sharmila for her dedication and unrelenting struggle against state repression. Shirin's regard for Sharmila leads me to conclude that genuine activists transcend all boundaries; they are one on the issues of universal importance, like human freedom.

JODY WILLIAMS

FREETHINKER WHO BANISHED LANDMINES

'… The landmine is eternally prepared to take victims. … it is the perfect soldier, the "eternal sentry".'

Jody Williams, a teacher, feminist and dogged activist for peace, came to prominence for her innovative campaign to ban landmines. Jody's efforts culminated in an international treaty banning anti-personnel mines, which was approved by the vast majority of countries' representatives during a diplomatic conference held in Oslo in September 1997. Just weeks later, Jody was awarded the Nobel Peace Prize, along with International Campaign to Ban Landmines (ICBL) 'for their work for the banning and clearing of anti-personnel mines'.

A decade earlier, Jody had honed her skills and acumen doing humanitarian work during the bitter, grinding Salvadoran civil war. There, she had witnessed the Salvadoran army's repression and gross violations of its citizen's human rights, and had made efforts to educate her compatriots about the state of affairs in Central America. Her work also involved overseeing an endeavour to heal the broken bodies of children caught in the vicious guerrilla fighting between the government and rebel forces.

Significantly, although she would later garner a reputation as a confrontational proponent of the cause of peace – she once threatened to 'publicly fry' the Canadian foreign minister if he backed away from his commitment to the ban on landmines – she demonstrated her ability in El Salvador to make diplomatic efforts towards her goal, even where it appeared almost a lost cause.

Little in Jody's early life gave indication of her later commitment to the cause of victims of war. She was, it seemed, a quiet, ordinary Catholic girl from an ordinary middle-class American family. Jody was born to Ruth Williams, formerly Colvin, and John Clarence Williams, on 9 October 1950. As for most in the New World, hers is a mixed heritage: her maternal grandmother Marianna Bertolino was an Italian immigrant who arrived in infancy during the early twentieth century with her parents, and her paternal grandmother was Scottish. Her mother's Italian family, with its closeness and

strict adherence to Catholicism was a powerful early influence –
John was prevailed upon to embrace the church, as was customary
in the family – and the strong family ties have remained.

Jody is the second of five children in her family. John and Ruth
Williams initially raised their children in Poultney, Vermont,
a picturesque town amidst a wooded, undulating countryside.
Summers are warm, and autumns or falls in the rural north-
east of the United States are a kaleidoscope of russet, orange-
red and magenta tingeing the landscape, giving way to chilled,
snowy winters. When Jody was in grade two, the family moved
to Brattleboro, a larger town some 70 miles (110 kilometres)
from Poultney. While she has travelled extensively throughout
her career and lived at times in Central America, Jody's heart
has remained in Vermont throughout. In many ways, this was an
idyllic setting for a childhood.

The cohesiveness of Ruth's family seems to have given Jody
a strong grounding, but she attributes much of her character
to her father John and her maternal grandfather Ralph Colvin.
She remembers her grandfather as confident and strong; one
who 'did not suffer fools gladly' – a description that may be just
as apt for Jody herself. Her father John Williams was a child of
the depression. Enduring a bleak young life marked by poverty
and harsh living conditions, he was forced to leave school by
his mother in his early teens to work to help support his seven
younger siblings. John grew with a stark hatred of inequality, and
a corresponding dislike for the Republican Party. The latter was
on account of his thankless duty of collecting Depression-era
relief cheques from the local grocery store, whose owners were
Republicans.

Not content with dispensing the welfare in a demeaning
manner, the store owners took an illegal 'cut' from each cheque.
And they would brook no criticism: if anyone complained at their

theft, they would simply take more or withhold the next month's cheque. This injustice left a deep impression on John, and in later life he always showed concern for the common person – the 'little guy', as he put it. And he became a staunch Democrat. In later years, when he owned a grocery store, he hung posters for the party in the store window, despite his father's remonstrations that he would lose his Republican customers. John was adamant in his political beliefs, and it seems that he lost neither business nor respect for this in Poultney.

Ironically, war and military service brought its own salvation to John, as it did for many American children of the Great Depression. John joined the navy at the age of seventeen, and he enjoyed there far better living conditions than he had known: indoor plumbing, flush toilets and running water. Upon returning from duty in World War II, he met Ruth Colvin. Ruth would always tell Jody of how her heart had skipped in exhilaration at seeing John in his white navy uniform. She would often recount their meeting with dramatic flourishes that made it new in the telling, and declare that whenever she unexpectedly saw John in the intervening years, she would experience that same feeling.

John soon approached Ralph Colvin to ask for permission to give Ruth an engagement ring on her sixteenth birthday. Ralph was not opposed to the match, but Ruth was still at high school. And besides, there was time for marriage later – she had to go to college. The smitten couple was in no mind to wait, though, and John sensed that if Ruth went to college unattached, she would be lost to him. Not long after Ruth's sixteenth birthday, the pair took a clandestine day trip to New York and after lying about Ruth's age, they married before a Justice of the Peace. John dropped Ruth back to her home the same evening, and her family were none the wiser; that is, until some months later.

The charade inevitably fell apart when Ruth became pregnant. Ruth's family absorbed the shock of the imposture – the Colvin family was notable for standing by its members – and they happily embraced John as their own. John shifted into the Colvin family home, carrying with him his meagre belongings in a brown paper bag. Months later, Steven, Jody's elder brother was born. Jody arrived just short of three years after Steve, and by the age of twenty-three, Ruth had given birth to two more children: Mary Beth and Mark. Nearly nine years after Jody, Janet was born.

Despite a loving marriage and supportive extended family, home life for Ruth and John Williams was not without its challenges. Steve was born profoundly deaf due to a bout of German measles Ruth had suffered during her pregnancy. This, and his resulting learning difficulties and descent into mental illness in adolescence strained the family, and profoundly affected Jody and her other siblings. Aside from special schools and the practical interventions that were available for the deaf in the 1950s, Ruth resorted to prayer in the hope that her son's condition would improve.

Prayer and strict adherence to the Catholic faith pervaded the Williams family; and its rigour and belief in a greater purpose seem to have imbued Jody's later work, if not her lifestyle. Her campaigning against landmines can be viewed as something of a spiritual quest, and she conducted it with religious fervour.

Jody's church education began early. She attended classes for catechism, and received her first communion when she was seven years old. The Catholic religious instruction in the 1950s America was, not to put too fine a point on it, focused as much on punishment as salvation. Jody was taught less of Jesus' love and forgiveness than the Ten Commandments and the kinds of sins and their consequences. The church maintained in those times that at the age of seven a child became able to exercise her free will to make moral choices, and was therefore capable of avoiding sin. It taught with the intent of inculcating good behaviour and godliness in children; and surely, the church gave support and succour to its people. But a rigid emphasis on sin left generations of people wracked with torment over even quite trivial matters.

Jody's early religious education left her with lingering guilt about all manner of ordinary childhood behaviour. She began to believe that she could not escape the inferno, for whatever she did seemed to be sinful. She would conjure images of hell whenever she committed such mundane wrongs as hitting her younger siblings. Jody recalled in later years: 'Sometimes the simple act of living felt like running temptation's gauntlet, as if hydra-headed demons of evil were waiting at every turn, trying to lead me sinfully astray.'

As part of the 'baby boomer' generation in the United States, Jody was among the first to openly question her religious beliefs, to intellectually challenge church teachings in a manner that would have been unthinkable just a generation earlier. First, she questioned why her dream of becoming the first woman pope was impossible. In her young, fanciful imaginings, she carried herself to the Vatican, where she stood, resplendent in ecclesiastical robes, bowing to receive the papal crown. Why could only boys become pope? Was a girl's faith in God any less than a boy's? Young Jody wondered.

As she grew, Jody became disenchanted with the Catholic Church on account of its demanding blind faith in church dogma. At the age of seventeen, she fell out with a parish priest who taught catechism. Besides several other issues, Jody raised her doubts as to the pope's infallibility, to which the priest had hardly any answer. He grew so impatient with Jody that he served her the ultimatum that if she did not accept the infallibility of the pope, she could be excommunicated from the Catholic Church.

Jody felt herself duly excommunicated, and hence was freed from attending catechism – and from the rigmarole of contemplating lists of sins and attending confession.

By that time, Jody's hallmark directness had begun to show itself, and just as it was evidently too much for an ordinary parish priest to bear, her approach would later test the mettle of senior international diplomats. But Jody had been a quiet, sensitive child. She feels that two pivotal events in her early years evoked her assertiveness. They concerned injustice, and conjured in her a latent, righteous indignation that would later be brought to bear on those who would thwart a long-overdue ban on anti-personnel mines.

Jody's brother Steve suffered on account of his disability, and she was acutely aware of his pain and tribulations. Moreover, Steve suffered for his disability at the hands of bullies, most notably the neighbours in Poultney, Billy and Bobby, who seemed to take sadistic pleasure in harassing him. Jody felt they were evil souls, richly deserving of 'a special place in hell'.

One day she and Steve were bicycling around their neighbourhood when the two boys emerged from behind thick bushes to hurl stones and empty tin cans at them. A can hit Steve on the head, and blood began pouring down his face from its wound. Steve pedalled quickly away towards home, screaming in pain, assuming that Jody was following. But Jody, who was in her early years of primary school at the time, had stopped to confront his tormentors. Her usual quietness evaporating, she dumped her bicycle on the road and charged towards them, screaming. Little did it matter that they were bigger and stronger than her and would likely give her a beating. She was determined to make them pay for hurting her brother, and the bullies fled.

Another incident later in her primary school years evinced her natural inclination for taking the part of the 'little guy'. The

Williams family moved from Poultney to Brattleboro when Jody was in grade two so that Steve could attend a school for the deaf, and Jody attended Green Street School in the town. There, she had a face-off with a common school bully. David was the quintessential popular kid; the leader in every sport and primary school hero. Almost every girl had a crush on this young Adonis, and he controlled the recess and lunchtime games. Michael, in contrast, was one of the more pathetically gawky students: His ears protruded from his head like those of an elephant, and he was invariably the last to be picked for any team. In one recess game, all the children were standing in a circle to play kick ball, when David gave the skinny Michael a hard chest bump, sending him careering out of the circle.

Jody seethed as David enjoyed a hearty laugh, watching the hapless Michael struggling for balance. She was outraged as much at David's cruelty as she was at Michael's inability to defend himself; the smaller boy just withdrew from the scene without uttering a word in protest. While Michael was not Jody's friend, she could not stay quiet for the brazen humiliation he had suffered. She stepped forward to confront David, and with her voice quivering in as much fear as anger, she asked David why he bullied those who could not stand up for themselves. To Jody's surprise, David backed down and beckoned Michael to come back and rejoin the game. He never bullied Michael again, either. Jody began to ponder how people could be helped if others could overcome their fears and take action in the face of injustice. She noticed too that each time she plucked up the courage to speak against a wrong she witnessed her courage grow.

By the time Jody was only twelve, she was seized by the prevailing mood of fear with the cold war, as the superpowers lurched towards open confrontation. Jody and her siblings were part of the 'duck and cover' generation. The children of the 1950s and early 1960s were taught in regular drills to dive under their school desks at the sound of an air-raid siren in the hope that this would save them in a nuclear attack. One can surmise the emotional toll on the children, who may only have dwelt on an ever-present threat of nuclear holocaust. Jody recalled that 'Fear seeped deep into the marrow of my bones.' It seemed her fear was grounded when the Cuban Missile Crisis brought the world perilously close to a nuclear conflagration in October 1962, when America detected the USSR's deployment of missiles in Cuba.

Jody was angry with Nikita Khrushchev and the USSR for precipitating the crisis. She transported herself in her adolescent daydreams to the General Assembly of the United Nations, where she could force Nikita Khrushchev to publicly acknowledge that he was indeed a communist. Then, through the sheer power of her eloquence, she would convince him of the merits of democracy so that he would return to the Soviet Union to free its citizens from communism's grip. Although Jody reminisces on her pre-adolescent flight of fancy with no small mirth, it demonstrates her nascent idealism that would come to the fore in later decades.

Around the time of the Cuban Missile Crisis, the Williams family was beset with its own dramas, which were no less harrowing for Jody and her younger siblings. Steve, Jody's elder brother, began to show marked signs of mental illness, and his sporadic, sudden fits of violence terrorized the family. The particular object of his violence was his mother, whom he would beat and even at times attempt to strangle. Jody too would feel the heat of his rage, particularly when she intervened to defend her mother. Steve's bouts of fury would end just as suddenly as they had begun, and he would apologize profusely for his behaviour. A period of institutionalization had some effect, but it was not until years later that Steve was diagnosed with schizophrenia.

Perhaps the continuing dramas with Steve drove Jody to absorb herself in study, to succeed. She acquired a bachelor's degree in humanities from the University of Vermont in 1972 and then received a master's degree in teaching Spanish and English as second Languages from the School for International Training (SIT), Brattleboro, Vermont, in 1976. She began teaching remedial English in the Paralegal Training Program in Washington in 1980, which provided free courses to children of farm workers, preparing them for careers in paralegal services. In 1984, Jody finished her second master's degree in international relations from Johns Hopkins School of Advanced International Studies in Washington DC. Her natural concern for the 'underdog' and the dispossessed, which was given ample expression in her perseverance and love for Steve over his trying adolescence and beyond, seems to have destined her for a humanitarian career.

Jody's romantic life followed a more tortuous path. During her final year of high school, Jody fell in love with Claude, a high-school classmate. Their relationship was intense, as teenage romances tend to be, and they quickly became inseparable. By all accounts Claude was a genial, decent young man, and he soon became a member of the extended Williams family. Claude would take Jody and her siblings to school and return them in a somewhat dilapidated Ford Thunderbird, with its finned bodywork and stuffing protruding from torn upholstery. He even began to work for John, who had by this time bought a vending machine business. Jody's relationship with Claude, though, would wax and wane over the following years as Jody studied away from Brattleboro. The couple would break up at Jody's instigation, then reconcile – only to break up again. It seems Claude was her link to a stable, loving family life that was familiar and reassuring, yet the yearning for a more adventurous existence, a 'hippy' lifestyle and travel, beckoned strongly.

As an undergraduate in the late 1960s and early 1970s, Jody was transformed from a serious, somewhat uptight girl to a questioning, independent-minded feminist. Upheaval was the order of the times, and activism on campuses against America's involvement in the Vietnam War and in military incursions in Cambodia led to violent clashes between National Guard troops and student demonstrators. Four young students' lives were extinguished by rifle fire from overzealous guardsmen at Kent State University in Ohio on 4 May 1970. Two of the students killed were simply walking to class, and nine others were wounded in this tragic and unwarranted fusillade.

Jody participated in a more peaceful protest in the Vermont legislature building. It was to be the first of her many campaigns. She felt empowered by being part of a widespread protest movement, involving some four million students, that brought campus life to a halt in May 1970. Universities throughout the country closed in spring to forestall further violence. The country, along with the youth of the era, was shaking loose of the last vestiges of innocence that remained from the 1950s. Even Jody's nationalistic, pro-war father changed his stance as the casualties in Vietnam mounted, and he worried that Claude and his son Mark would be drafted for military service.

Despite undergoing quite a radical transformation during her undergraduate days, Jody became determined to marry Claude – against her better judgement and much to the chagrin of her friends. She was married at the age of twenty-one, immediately after her final exams. But it soon became clear that while there was some bond between the pair, they had altogether different ways of thinking and preferences. Claude seems to have been indulgent, absorbing her partying and rejection of his surname, the latter still a rare choice in those years, with some aplomb. It seemed, though, that they were more like congenial roommates than husband and wife, and at the instigation of Jody's sister Marty Beth, Claude decided to file for divorce. Jody's first quest to maintain her independence and feminist beliefs within the confines of marriage was over, and it would be near two decades before she would enter matrimony again. The marriage had lasted all of three years and four months.

After her divorce, Jody left for Mexico for teaching practice which was required to complete her degree from SIT. There, she became involved with Carlos, a younger man from a wealthy local family whom she had met while he was teaching intensive English courses. Carlos had been raised on a luxury ranch in Veracruz, where his family kept their prized Swiss cows and Arabian horses. Though Jody lived with Carlos for some time, and much as he was a kind and generous man, she felt marrying him would be another mistake. Aside from her misgivings about living as an outsider, an expatriate, she felt alienated by Carlos's elitist, racist attitudes towards the region's impoverished native workers. She felt shocked by his saying, 'they are poor because they want to be', 'they are lazy; they don't like to work'. After spending two years in Mexico, she left Mexico and came back to the United States, filled with sadness at having left Carlos behind, weeping on the front step of their apartment.

Back in the United States, she chose to live in Washington DC, in part motivated by a vague notion that she should be doing 'international work'; and Washington DC is certainly an international city. It was here, on a chilly, damp day in February 1981, that she would be drawn towards the humanitarian work in which she would excel. As Jody was descending the escalator of a Metro station in Washington DC on the way home from teaching remedial English, someone thrust a cheaply printed pamphlet in her hand. She was transfixed by its title: 'El Salvador: Another Vietnam.'

Jody was perplexed at this comparison – enough to attend a meeting of CISPES, the Committee in Solidarity with the People of El Salvador, that the pamphlet had advertised. The meeting was a life-changing event. There, she was apprised of the bitter conflict between the military-led government of El Salvador and the Farabundo Martí National Liberation Front (FMLN), a coalition of five left-wing guerrilla organizations. She quickly learnt of how in December 1980, the previous year, four American churchwomen, Catholic nuns and lay missionaries, had been raped, beaten and shot dead by El Salvadoran National Guardsmen, their bodies then buried in shallow roadside graves. The brutality of this atrocity was matched by its brazenness; two of the women had dined with the US ambassador, Robert E. White, on the evening prior to their deaths.

At the meeting, Jody heard of the bravery of the martyred Óscar Romero, the Archbishop of San Salvador and champion of El Salvador's poor. Incensed by the atrocities of the government forces as the nation's civil war raged, the archbishop had written an open letter to President Carter on 17 February 1980. He urged the president 'to forbid that military aid be given to the Salvadoran government' and asked for his assurance that America not 'intervene directly or indirectly ... in determining the destiny of the Salvadoran people'. In his sermon on 23 March 1980, Romero called upon Salvadoran soldiers, as Christians, to obey the commandment, 'Thou shall never kill.' The following day, the Archbishop was assassinated – shot in the heart by a 'death squad' member as he celebrated Mass. In one account of his killing, he was slain as he raised the chalice at the altar; a diabolical sacrifice of a true man of God.

Jody also became apprised of the 1979 Sandinista revolution in neighbouring Nicaragua which had toppled the dictator General Anastasio Somoza. She was shocked to discover that the United

States had occupied Nicaragua in the 1930s and had supported dictators from the Somoza family until the revolution. It became clear to Jody that the pain and suffering in El Salvador and Nicaragua was due in no small part to America's interventionist foreign policy, which was becoming more aggressive with Ronald Reagan's victory over Jimmy Carter in the 1980 presidential elections. Jody was indignant at the US espousing democracy while supporting dictators and militaries in neighbouring countries that suppressed the democratic aspirations of their peoples.

The pamphlet could not have come to her hand at a more opportune time. Jody was galvanized into action. She joined hands with two CISPES activists, Robert and Stewart, and helped to organize a protest outside the infamous Watergate Hotel where General Jose Guillermo Garcia, the Salvadoran minister of defence, was staying. They also held a demonstration near the Inter-American Defense Board on Sixteenth Street to oppose the US training of Salvadoran troops. Jody soon began writing the organization's newsletters. One of the main activities Jody undertook at CISPES was helping to arrange a march on Washington. On the appointed date in March, tens of thousands of people assembled to oppose the intervention of the United States in El Salvador. The protest was a triumph, and Jody, though utterly terrified of public speaking, gave a stirring speech that earned her praise.

There was a disturbing development at the event, however. Jody discovered to her dismay that one the several volunteers at the CISPES office was an FBI spy, when she saw him on duty at the protest. She wondered what the government could possibly gain by spying on CISPES, which was, after all, merely holding an open protest. It seemed that paranoia reigned in the US government with regard to its Central American policy. The White House would whip up its fanciful rhetoric during the Reagan years in portraying the Sandinistas as a 'cancer' in Central America; one that if left unchallenged, could overtake Texas and from there, spread throughout the United States.

Driven to pursuing a broader agenda than just El Salvador, Jody left CISPES. Without any clear plan for her career, she undertook a master's degree in international relations at the prestigious Johns Hopkins School of Advanced International Studies (SAIS). Despite her challenges – Jody had to work part-time jobs and struggled to finish the course – she graduated late in 1984, and her proud parents came to Washington DC to celebrate her achievement.

Jody did not want to follow the graduates' well-worn paths from Johns Hopkins to investment banks, think tanks or tenured government positions. She was still gripped with a desire to work for alleviating the needless suffering in conflict-ravaged Central America, and she leapt at an opportunity to work in the Nicaragua–Honduras Education Project (NHEP). The NHEP was conceived by Cora Weiss, an eminent philanthropist from New York who would in later years be nominated for the Nobel Peace Prize five times.

The purpose of the NHEP was to enlighten US journalists, philanthropists, elected officials and other notable people about life in the troubled Central American countries through guided study trips. On these trips, the delegations would not merely imbibe the culture and be given a guided tour. They would interact with people of the various classes and backgrounds in both the countryside and the cities of Nicaragua, thus garnering an understanding of the region beyond the narrow, often contentious perspectives of the American media. They too would gain at least some first-hand knowledge of the impact of the US interventions and of the counter-revolutionaries on the lives and livelihoods of the people. Trips also visited Honduras, where the

CIA-sponsored Nicaraguan counter-revolutionaries, the Contras, were based.

On the first trip to El Salvador, Jody and the tour group witnessed signs of the kind of human rights violations that pervaded the country at the time. As they drove in a convoy of minibuses, Jody saw a military jeep speed past them, carrying a bound and blindfolded youth. The captive was on his knees, with two soldiers training their automatic weapons at his head. The violence implicit in this scene haunted Jody, and she wished only that she had had a camera on hand. While in Nicaragua, the groups met government as well as opposition representatives, businessmen, priests and human rights organizations along with farmers, and in Honduras they even met Contra representatives. America had learnt its lessons in Vietnam and it did not send its men to El Salvador or Nicaragua. Instead, it sent millions of dollars in military aid and extended other logistic support, to the military-dominated government in the former and to the rebel Contras in the latter.

The NHEP's trips afforded numerous elite Americans a greater understanding of the region, and doubtless caused many to question the merits of their country's gung-ho foreign policy. After witnessing the shambolic state of the infrastructure in Managua, Nicaragua's capital – not to mention the nation's administration, which was pitiable – few of those undertaking the tours could have perceived the Sandinistas as capable of threatening the North American continent. The NHEP, however, suffered from funding shortages almost from its inception, and it closed in mid-1986.

Jody was philosophical at the demise of the NHEP, and quite undeterred from her quest to improve the situation for the people in the war-stricken Central American countries. She had worked for the organization Medical Aid for El Salvador, a Los Angeles–based charity fostered by a number of A-list celebrities, for nearly two years on a contract basis. First, Jody had overseen the sending of medical supplies to El Salvador in November 1984, following an earthquake that had devastated the country on 10 October. As many as 1,500 people had died and ten thousand were wounded in this catastrophe, which only served to compound the miseries of conflict. After NHEP's closure, Jody accepted a full-time position at Medical Aid for El Salvador.

Her primary duty in the organization was to administer the charity's Children's Project. In this project, children wounded in the war would be brought to the United States and provided free medical care facilitated by donations. In El Salvador, Jody worked with the Archdiocese of San Salvador to coordinate the children in need of treatment. In the US, Jody sought doctors and hospitals which were willing to offer medical care for the children. Numerous doctors and twenty-one hospitals pledged their support. Jody further undertook to enlist the many households needed to host the children and their parents while they were in the United States for treatment.

Besides the obvious humanitarian aspect of its work, Medical Aid was intent on raising public awareness in the United States of the war's impact on civilians, particularly on the rural poor. In this sense, at least, it was a continuation of Jody's work in NHES. Jody was honing her natural skill for publicity, diplomacy and persuasion in these years, and it would certainly stand her in good stead for her later campaign to end the affliction of anti-personnel mines. She even secured free flights on the now-defunct Pan American Airlines and United Airlines for the children and their families visiting the United States for treatment.

Despite the fairly innocuous nature of Medical Aid's activities in El Salvador, Jody faced danger in the country. El Salvador's notorious 'death squads' under Major Roberto D'Aubuisson waged a campaign of terror: death, torture and disappearance against anyone unsympathetic to their cause – even foreign aid workers engaged in helping the poor. Indeed, as Cynthia Arnson, a writer on Latin American affairs for Human Rights Watch would later observe, 'The objective of death-squad terror seemed not only to eliminate opponents, but also, through torture and the gruesome disfigurement of bodies, to terrorize the population.'

D'Aubuisson had risen from the military to political power, presiding over some of the nation's most heinous human rights violations, including the mass murder of 600 civilians, the killing of Archbishop Romero and the egregious rape and murder of the four American missionary women in 1980. At one time, death squads even went so far as to surround US ambassador Robert E. White's residence in an attempt to intimidate him; and this, in a country purportedly allied to the United States.

Jody later recalled that the menace in San Salvador of those years was palpable. Ironically, Nicaragua, the bastion of the communist 'cancer' the Sandinistas, felt far safer. San Salvador was a place where 'you learnt to sit with your back against the wall', and Jody had assumed all manner of other habits and routines to assure her safety. She would walk facing oncoming traffic so that she would be alert to abduction attempts, which were routinely conducted from death squads' vehicles. Along with the rest of the Medical Aid staff, she was ensconced in a 'safe' hotel for her stays in San Salvador, and she felt relatively secure in its sanctuary. She had hurriedly retreated behind its high, locked gates one night after being followed in her jeep and menaced by a group of men who appeared to have been death squad members.

Though Jody made every effort to keep safe from the death squads, even she could not escape their violence. In San Salvador, the nation's capital, Jody suffered one of the most horrific events of her life. Her trauma was such that it would take years for her to heal: to confront the incident, to talk openly of it.

On one sweltering Sunday afternoon in 1988, Jody was relaxing, reading a book by her hotel pool. Shaded by palms, the pool was secluded in the hotel's walled compound, and with most locals at home with their families, she had the pool and quietude for her sole enjoyment. Jody was somewhat taken aback when three men in their late twenties or early thirties broke the tranquillity, diving boisterously into the pool and indulging in banter designed to get her attention. Jody simply continued reading, but predictably, the men eventually approached her and engaged her in conversation. Jody was guarded with them, unsettled by their overconfidence, and gave non-committal responses to their asking about her work in El Salvador.

One of the men invited her to dinner in a restaurant that evening. Against her better judgement, she consented. At the restaurant, they indulged in meaningless chatter, but when Jody asked her dinner partner his profession, he revealed that he was a member of the most notorious of El Salvador's death squads. The man, it transpired, was one of Major Roberto D'Aubuisson's minions.

Horrified by the death squad member's subsequent manic rantings about the communist threat of the FMLN, Jody beat a hasty retreat to her hotel. Just as she cursed herself in the hotel room at her folly for accepting the dinner invitation, there came a knock at her door. As she opened it, the death squad member she had left a short time earlier was before her, and he roughly pushed her inside the room, locking the door behind him. While he shoved her, his words virtually spitting from his mouth with hatred, Jody was defenceless against him, and had only her inner strength to sustain her. She recalls that there was not a modicum of passion in the man as he raped her. Jody endured his brief assault as if a minute had turned to hours. He departed a short time later with a warning: 'Watch out. I know who you are.' As if to prove the point, he drove up to her the following day as she walked in another part of town and called out to her, his face contorted with a sadistic grin, 'Want a ride?'

Jody would later learn that her rapist was the nephew of the hotel owner. The whole event was an act of vicious, cold-blooded violence; a disgusting attempt to break Jody's will to make her contribution to El Salvador's people. It is tribute to Jody's resilience that she did not let the rape destroy her or her resolve. It was years, though, before she could bring herself to discuss the attack with anyone; and that person would be her future husband, Goose.

Afterwards, she saw that sharing her experience could benefit other women, a vast majority of whom had suffered sexual violence. She courageously read a monologue dealing with her rape before an audience of 2,000 women at a 'V–day' event in New York City on 19 June 2006. Jody urged the women not to let horrible experiences ruin their lives, stressing that she had not let the rape ruin hers. In a later interview with Eve Ensler, the American feminist best known for her play *The Vagina Monologues,* Jody imparted wisdom for self-empowerment when she asserted, 'I don't feel rage ... I feel righteous indignation. But I am not angry.'

Jody Williams's stoic realism sustained her as conditions in El Salvador deteriorated towards the end of the decade. In 1989, the civil war intensified, and some of the nation's expatriate humanitarian workers fled lest they become casualties themselves. As the government forces came under military pressure, death squads became increasingly ferocious. Jody was not among those departing the country. Her dedication is redolent of Henri Frederic Amiel's profound observation, 'Self-interest is but the survival of animal in us, humanity begins in a man only with self-surrender.'

Unsurprisingly though, Jody's worried parents pleaded with her to return to the US. But Jody was determined to stay and continue her work. Her thoughts and her motivations for staying, which were elucidated in a letter to her parents in June that year, evince the kind of tenacity and unbending commitment to a cause that is innate in Nobel Peace laureate women:

12-6-89 Continental flight to L.A. 3:40 PST

Dear Mom & Dad,

I write to apologize for being sharp last night. I appreciate your concern for me, but I would ask you to please direct it towards the people I care deeply about in El Salvador, who are suffering and who do not have the luxury to leave as I do.

My work is not 'work'. It is born of a commitment to stand with the poor. I know that sounds strange coming from an 'elitist' ex-Catholic like myself. But I guess I have to blame you two for your beautiful faith that is not oppressive but is an example of how it should be. And Stephen John. And Michael in 4th grade.

I know what I do and why I do it and am happy with the choices I have made in my life. I do not take irresponsible actions – I'm no John Wayne.

But I ask you to trust me and support me. It is hard when I have to reassure you and explain myself. I need your support so I can give mine to those who really need it in El Salvador.

Yesterday I was getting aggravated with a woman that I have been working with in Iowa. Perhaps I was being a bit overzealous – hard to imagine, I know – when she said, 'Jody, I understand what you are talking about. My brother is in Zacamil. I have asked him to come home. I worry about him.

He told me he would stand with the people as witness until he was deported. He asked me to pray for those who cannot leave.

Gwen is a nun. Her brother is a priest. Needless to say, it brought me back down to earth very quickly. (By the way, Zacamil is one of the hardest hit areas of the capital – aerial bombardments, army raids, etc.)

All of this to say, I love you, I understand your concern. But I am no fool. Trust me. Pray for others who have no hope. No escape.

On that cheery note, I end. See you at Christmas.

P.S.: It is a beautiful sunset on the plane. The world is so beautiful. Why do we humans make it so ugly?

The fighting only worsened in the following months, with the rebels launching a major offensive against the government on 11 November 1989. With the element of surprise in their favour, the FMLN seized much territory in the countryside, entered San Salvador and took control of some poorer areas there. Running street battles raged as government troops tried desperately to drive the rebel forces out of the nation's capital. They even resorted to shelling residential neighbourhoods that were believed to be supporting the FMLN. The grim situation in San Salvador was perhaps no better illustrated than by the desperate floor-by-floor gunfight between government and FMLN forces in the Sheraton Hotel on 21 November 1989; that, and the wanton murder of six Jesuit priests and their housekeepers at the University of Central America several days earlier by a death squad.

Despite the heavy fighting, Jody arrived in San Salvador with two planeloads of medical supplies for her charity. Shortly afterwards, Jody learnt that uniformed police officers had broken into her office in her absence. They had left the office intact, but

Jody and her assistant knew they must quickly take precautions. They desperately burned and dumped pamphlets that advocated peace through national dialogue, before the 6 p.m. curfew that evening. In those desperate times, even these might give the police or army cause for retribution. Salvadoran police and army units were raiding and looting churches throughout the country with abandon, and dozens of foreign aid workers accused of assisting the FMLN were being rounded up and deported.

On 25 November 1989, the day that police had broken into the Medical Aid office, President Cristiani issued an order that non-governmental organizations were not to be raided by police without authorization from the high command. On the very same day, police raided the house of Jennifer Casolo, a US church worker living in El Salvador, and weapons were allegedly uncovered. Casolo was arrested and paraded before the press, accused of running an FMLN safe house. She was detained, and threatened with being charged as a terrorist. It appears that the evidence against her was planted: an unnamed US administration official would later describe the case against Casolo as a 'frame-up', and charges against her were dropped in December. For a few weeks, though, Casolo's plight seemed grim indeed. The government appeared to be using the case to threaten and intimidate all foreign aid workers in the country.

A week after Jennifer Casolo's arrest, and despite President Cristiani's order, the Medical Aid office in San Salvador was ransacked and vandalized. Virtually everything in the office was taken. Jody arrived at the scene to find the lining of the walls torn away, the ceiling smashed and concrete paving in the yard behind the office broken. It appeared that those raiding the office had been searching for weapons, and after coming up empty-handed, had resorted to looting the charity. Even soda pop bottles, the kind that could be returned for a refund, had been taken.

In this atmosphere of state-sponsored terror, and with the very real prospect of her suffering the fate of Jennifer Casolo, it seems quite remarkable that Jody did not retreat from El Salvador for her own safety. Indeed, as was her way, she confronted the situation in a constructive and ultimately rewarding manner. When the FMLN's offensive was blunted and some normality returned to San Salvador, Jody's indignation at the raid on the Medical Aid office demanded satisfaction. On 5 April 1990, Jody telephoned the office of Colonel Inocente Orlando Montano, El Salvador's vice president of public security, to schedule a meeting.

That she chose to call to schedule a meeting with Montano that morning says much for her courage, not to mention her sense of outrage at the looting of Medical Aid's office. Colonel Montano was one of the most feared men in El Salvador at the time. The head of the dreaded Belloso Battalion, Montano was implicated in countless gross human rights violations throughout El Salvador's civil war, including the killing of the six Jesuit priests and their housekeepers in November the previous year. In a sense, Jody was walking into a lion's den.

To Jody's surprise, Montano called her to a meeting that very day. And to her greater surprise, she and her assistant met not only Montano: they sat opposite the heads of the national guard, the treasury, the fire brigade and the police – all donned in camouflaged uniforms. Jody gave a short presentation to Montano and the other department heads on Medical Aid's activities, and raised the looting of Medical Aid's office. Montano claimed not to know who was responsible, describing the raid as a 'mistake'. He nevertheless accepted a list of the items taken in the raid and gave a commitment to 'investigate' the matter. Jody thanked them all, and she and her assistant left.

Perhaps Montano and his colleagues could not help but admire Jody's direct approach – her courage, her assertiveness – and had thus decided to cooperate with her and Medical Aid. She was, they would well have known, one of the more hardy foreign non-governmental organization personnel who had not fled during the darkest hours of the November 1989 offensive. There was a changed mood in El Salvador too at the time of Jody's meeting with Montano. The government had now reconciled itself to the reality that its military force could not subdue the FMLN. And with glasnost and perestroika reigning abroad – the Berlin Wall had fallen on 9 November 1989, days before their offensive, and the cold war was over – the rebels' hopes for international support for their armed revolution were dashed.

In any event, the meeting would yield dividends quite beyond Jody's expectations. A couple of months after Jody's meeting with Montano, Medical Aid in Los Angeles received what the organization would later call their 'golden letter': an official communication from the Salvadoran minister of defence acknowledging the charity's work and stating that the charity had the full support of El Salvador's military. The letter was an unqualified coup: it allowed the charity to conduct its work virtually free of government interference.

Despite her triumphs at Medical Aid – or indeed, on account of them – Jody began to feel drained. While she continued to travel to Central America, she sought alternative employment. The military campaigns, the death squads; the ineffable human rights violations of a desperate, repressive government; the traumatized population – all had taken their toll on Jody. Her time in Central America seems to have convinced her, nevertheless, of the need for vigorous, targeted advocacy for peace: campaigns which at once cajoled and coerced governments to effect change, the likes of which she would later employ in worldwide initiatives.

In November 1991, Jody received a telephone call from Thomas Gebauer, the head of Medico International, a German humanitarian relief organization that had collaborated with Medical Aid on some projects in El Salvador. He asked Jody to host him for a brief stay in Washington, which Jody felt was strange, but she anyway agreed, and collected him from the airport. The next day, he asked her to drive him to a short meeting with Bobby Muller, the executive director of the Vietnam Veterans of America Foundation (VVAF). Jody had met Muller before when she had given a talk about the El Salvador war at the VVAF. Muller was a charismatic, wheelchair-bound dynamo, whose debilitating injuries sustained during the Vietnam War had inspired him to become a leading peace activist.

Little did Jody suspect that she would be involved in the meeting, and that it would profoundly change her life's direction. Indeed, she had brought a book with her so that she could sit outside and keep herself entertained while the two men met. She was quite taken by surprise when they asked her to join them. Gebauer and Muller were passionate about their shared project: an endeavour to train landmine survivors in Cambodia to make prosthetic limbs for others in the country maimed by the weapons. They drew Jody into their discussion, the thrust of which was that although their cause for ameliorating suffering of landmine victims was worthy, it was like 'trying to stop a haemorrhage without even a Band Aid on hand'. Landmines contaminated much of Cambodia, and were a blight on a poor country trying to return to a peaceful existence after years of bloodshed.

It did not take long for Muller to reach the crux of his presentation. Animatedly, he declared that the only real solution to landmines' needless destruction was a worldwide ban. And they considered Jody just the right person to lead a campaign for a ban. Jody was quite bemused at the suggestion. She had no real background with landmines, and found guns and nuclear weapons at least as abhorrent. Why would landmines merit a campaign any more than the other weapons that killed and maimed just as landmines did?

Muller's reasoning was compelling on this point; he had evidently given the matter much consideration. He remembered the terror landmines had inspired in the soldiers when he served in Vietnam. But landmines not only caused horrific injuries in battle and left broken soldiers who had to be evacuated with great difficulty from the site of their injuries. Like silent, tiny sentinels, they remained poised for decades to maim whomever trod their ground, regardless of whether their victim was a soldier or a child; and indeed, mindless of whether the conflict for which they had been deployed remained. The inherent indiscrimination of the landmine was its greatest terror. And it too often wreaked destruction on civilians going about their ordinary business, long after peace had returned. Farmers in paddy fields, children playing or collecting firewood or mothers foraging for their children's meals were their regular victims.

Jody seems to have been caught with Bobby Muller's infectious enthusiasm, and intrigued by the potential of advocacy on an international scale, she had agreed within the hour to initiate a campaign to ban anti-personnel mines. She later mused that Thomas and Bobby had evidently discussed her suitability at length with others, and they would well have known that for her '"No" is not the end of possibilities; it's an obstacle to be overcome.' She was thus suited to leading any seemingly impossible quest.

Jody initially surmised that the campaign would take somewhere in the order of a decade, but she plunged headlong into the project nevertheless, starting with a three-month contract as a consultant for the VVAF. Her duty during this time would be to become conversant with all aspects of the landmine issue. She also began by contacting all the numerous non-governmental organizations and international bodies whose support would be crucial for the campaign, and elicited their support. She met several prominent dignitaries belonging to New York–based Human Rights Watch (HRW), Physicians for Human Rights (PHR) in Boston and Asia Watch.

Just months before Jody's meeting with Thomas and Bobby, Asia Watch and PHR had published *The Coward's War – Landmines in Cambodia,* an in-depth study of the impact of landmines. This report was written by Eric Stover and Rae McGrath. McGrath, a former soldier and anti-personnel mine expert, would work with Jody extensively in the coming years. Jody also contacted a prominent politician from her home state Vermont, Senator Patrick Leahy, whom she felt would be sympathetic to a landmine ban.

Particularly intriguing for Jody was that international law already existed to purportedly curtail the use of landmines. The Convention on Certain Conventional Weapons (CCW) is a UN-sponsored treaty that had been prompted by war. It contained provisions in its Protocol II that should have all but nullified anti-personnel mines' threat, at least to civilian populations. The CCW was signed by fifty member states, and entered into force on 2 December 1983. This was a salutary lesson for Jody, for despite all the good sense and sentiment of the protocol, it was woefully ineffective in reducing the abomination of landmines. Of the countries which had signed the CCW, a few had ratified it; and others ignored it anyway. The CCW's failure underpinned Bobby Muller's conviction that the only way to stop landmines killing and maiming civilians was a blanket international ban.

Indeed, anti-personnel mines contaminated more than eighty countries, and they were endemic in Cambodia, Afghanistan, Angola, Mozambique, Iraq, Somalia and the vast region known as Kurdistan covering parts of Iraq, Iran, Turkey, Syria, Armenia and Azerbaijan. Moreover, at least fifty-four countries were producing and selling landmines. Jody quickly concluded that she would have to target the many landmine manufacturers, who sold these ghastly weapons for as little as fifty cents apiece, and even gave them away, at times, as a 'sweetener' along with purchases of more expensive weapons.

Despite the enormity of the task set for her, Jody was captivated, and after three months, she decided to launch an international campaign against landmines. Though at this time she had only the support of VVAF and Medico International, she began to talk of the 'international campaign to ban landmines', which quickly became ICBL. She constituted a campaign advisory committee and enlisted the support of prominent people known for their concern about landmines to serve as members. Though the committee itself did little, the eminence of its members lent considerable credibility to the campaign in its first year. But though the name ICBL implied an international effort, it was, in its earliest stages, only an international collaboration insofar as the American VVAF and the German Medico International had joined in founding it. And the ICBL had, Jody later quipped, an 'international staff of one. Me.'

The ICBL was granted an early fillip by Senator Leahy and Congressman Evans, who managed a shrewd and carefully orchestrated campaign of their own. They whisked a bill through both houses of the American legislature that became law in October 1992, which mandated a one-year moratorium on the export of landmines. The world's great superpower making a distinction between landmines and other weapons underscored the gravity of the ICBL's quest internationally, and it helped people believe that a blanket ban on landmines could be successful.

This was crucial in the early days of the ICBL campaign, because Jody found those she approached in the diplomatic field quite incredulous at her overtures. She would be routinely palmed off to junior staff members when she approached various countries' missions at the UN, and if it were not for her tenacity, she would certainly have been quickly discouraged. At any rate, on 6 October 1992, a meeting in New York with representatives of four of six organizations that would become the backbone of the ICBL charted the way forward for the new coalition. From this meeting, the ICBL formally began, and Human Rights Watch (HRW), Medico International, Handicap International, Physicians for Human Rights (PHR), Vietnam Veterans of America Foundation (VVAF) and the Mines Advisory Group would pool their resources for the common goal of ridding the world of the dreaded landmine.

The diverse range of skills and expertise in the ICBL was to be decisive in its success; the credentials of key players in the movement were impeccable. The Mines Advisory Group was already engaged in demining, and the imperative duty of coordinating efforts of decontaminating areas of mines would naturally fall on them. Handicap International provided prostheses to landmine victims throughout the world. PHR and HRW collaborated in releasing a second report – *Landmines: A Deadly Legacy.* The ICBL relied heavily on publicity for the cause, and it helped enormously to have international celebrities on board. The first of many eminent people to lend their voices to the ICBL was former US president Jimmy Carter. As the campaign gained currency and momentum, numerous non-governmental organizations called for a ban on landmines in their own countries.

Beyond the Americas, the first major tactical victory was the European Parliament passing a resolution in December 1992, calling upon all its member states to declare a five-year moratorium on the export of landmines and also on training in their use. France followed the US in declaring its own three-year moratorium in February 1993. The French Landmine Campaign gave further impetus to the cause when it convinced the nation's foreign minister to make an official request to the Secretary General of the UN to pass a resolution calling upon all countries to implement similar moratoriums.

Jody understood that support for the ICBL was needed from all quarters, and especially the august humanitarian organizations of the world. She had sought the backing of the International Committee of the Red Cross (ICRC) at the ICBL meeting in October 1992, but though there was sympathy within the ICRC, its overt support was not immediately forthcoming. More than a year later, however, on 24 February 1994, Cornelio Sommaruga, president of the ICRC, declared: 'From a humanitarian point of view, we believe that a worldwide ban on anti-personnel mines is the only effective solution.' Jody also met with the executive director of UNICEF in Geneva in April 1993. UNICEF's work with disadvantaged children in war-ravaged countries gave the executive director a profound appreciation of the misery these weapons wreaked on families, and he was particularly keen on assisting the ICBL. UNICEF would co-sponsor the ICBL's second conference in Geneva in 1994; its endorsement would be critical in the success of the campaign.

Although the campaign almost immediately showed promise in the United States and Europe, it was imperative that it reach beyond the West to countries contaminated by landmines. Jody knew well that non-governmental organizations in such countries would be essential for the ultimate success of the ICBL, and that without them, a ban would be meaningless. Keeping in touch with all the disparate non-governmental organizations throughout the world and coordinating their activities could only be described as a Herculean task, but it was one for which Jody was well suited. She made ample use of the fax in the days before the Internet, then took to email to communicate efficiently across time zones.

Jody alternately employed her considerable charm, moral peer pressure and persistence in keeping the non-governmental organization partners in the ICBL to their commitments to the cause. In this, she had to rely on just the right blend of geniality and forcefulness to achieve her goals, because she had no direct control over the ICBL affiliates. Only a common, righteous cause bound them. She wrote later of it being like a 'global chess match'; and evidently, she was a master.

Coordinating global partners' actions and keeping everyone in the campaign abreast of developments is one aspect of the success of the ICBL. Harnessing moral indignation and utilizing sheer force of personality to effect change is another. Jody could be confrontational when she felt it was necessary, which was most often when she was dealing with uncooperative or evasive diplomats, some of whom she regarded with barely concealed contempt. Jody was a peace campaigner with first-hand experience of war's misery, and she knew well of the human suffering that landmines wrought. She was exasperated with the carefully intoned speeches in Geneva that skirted around the issue of the weapon's disproportionate and arbitrary violence. Jody was a straight talker to a fault, and neither dressed up nor softened her words to impress. This was her strength, but it could be a liability when a more considered approach was warranted.

She was indeed fortunate, then, to find a partner in the ICBL whose beliefs almost invariably coincided with hers, yet who was her polar opposite in approach. This partner was Steven Goose. Jody at first called him Mr Goose, because he seemed particularly respectable and formal. Later, she just called him Goose, because Steve was her brother, and she couldn't equate him to Steve. Goose started working with Human Rights Watch in February 1993 and very quickly became immersed in the ICBL. In so many senses, Goose was Jody's foil: She was confrontational, just as he was considerate and conciliatory in his approach. He wore a suit and tie to every event, while she dressed for comfort. She would want to storm out of meetings in protest, but he taught her it was often the last person at the negotiating table who was heard. And despite their differences, they agreed on virtually everything. As time progressed, Jody's relationship with Goose only deepened.

Goose and Jody were the classic 'good cop, bad cop' team, and according to the situation, one or the other or both would attend meetings. Goose's persistence helped Jody from being driven to distraction by posturing at the conferences. She would scoff in her frustration that the 'high point of a day's work was to change a comma to a semicolon' in a document. He would seem less forceful than Jody, but he would always be there, and he would never falter.

The ICBL team, spearheaded by Jody and Goose, would need to work around the diplomatic doublespeak that pervaded international conferences. A major stumbling block for the ICBL was the United States' advocacy of 'smart mines', which the US delegates maintained would not remain deployable for a significant period and would therefore not pose a threat to civilians. Pro-ban countries were not the least impressed with the US stance, and Jody was vexed by her own government's chicanery,

At a reception in a restaurant near the UN headquarters in 1995, a US colonel began discussing the issue with Jody and Goose. He talked of how they were all on the same team – they were all Americans, after all – and they ultimately wanted the same thing, which was to protect the victims. As the colonel continued with his smooth talk, Jody became increasingly angry. She told him in no uncertain terms, punctuated with expletives, that they were not 'on the same page': she and Goose wanted to ban landmines, and he wanted to protect his landmines. Goose intervened to conciliate, but to no avail. Jody had, by this time, long endured the blatant double dealing of government delegates, and she would not tolerate the colonel's unctuous attempt to sway them.

In any event, President Bill Clinton had already called for the eventual elimination of landmines in his address before the UN General Assembly in September 1994. It seemed that the emphasis was actually on the word 'eventual', and the US military were intent on clinging to their 'smart mines', which no one in the pro-ban countries believed would reduce landmines' misery. Jody and the ICBL team called upon Clinton to eliminate landmines immediately. Indeed, Senator Patrick Leahy had already proposed a 'comprehensive ban'; the US administration was clearly divided on the issue.

In Europe, nevertheless, the ICBL was steadily moving towards its goal, and countries were venturing beyond moratoriums to outright bans. The Netherlands agreed to destroy its stockpile of landmines in November 1994. In March 1995, Belgium became the first country to pass a national law proscribing anti-personnel mines, and it was followed by Norway and Austria in the ensuing months. Perhaps the most memorable event of the ICBL campaign for Jody was the march at Brescia in Italy in September 1994. She was at first reluctant to attend the march, because it seemed few would turn out, and she didn't relish the plan to march to Castenedolo, the town where Valsella's landmine production facility was located. At first, it seemed that the march would be a small group, and it would be a perfunctory event. But Jody discovered, to her astonishment, that the march route would take them all of 17 kilometres. She was even more astonished at their numbers swelling exponentially along the way. Jody looked back at the marchers to discover that she could no longer see the stragglers at the end of their ranks, such was their number.

When they arrived at Castenedolo's town square, music and several thousand people welcomed them. But more moving was the protest of four Italian women, workers in Valsella's landmine factory, who silently held aloft a banner with the words, 'We will not feed our children by making landmines that kill other people's children.' Sadly, not a single man from Valsella's landmine factory accompanied these heroic women. This surely evinces the need for women to take a far more assertive role in the peace movement; and it shows that women's protests can be powerful in their own right, without men's participation.

The campaign to ban landmines in Cambodia, which was launched in August 1994, was perhaps even more poignant. The campaign's manifesto was a letter from four landmine survivors working at the Centre of the Dove, a Jesuit vocational training centre for the disabled, which was a chilling plea for a landmine ban:

> We are amputees.
> Before, we were soldiers,
> Members of four different armies
> That laid landmines that blew the legs
> Arms and eyes off one another.
> Now we teach and learn together at the Centre of the Dove
> We beg the world to stop making mines.
> We beg the world to stop laying mines.
> We beg the world for funds for clearing mines
> so that we can rebuild our families, our villages and our country again,
> Hem Phang, Klieng Vann, Tun Channareth, Suon Creuk.

Though the number of pro-ban countries was increasing, the United States stuck to the defence of its landmines, and some other countries did not want to depart from the existing, and ineffectual, CCW landmine regulations. The Cambodia conference in June 1995 saw a surprising development, however. China, which was not the least inclined to a ban on landmines, made a quiet announcement via its delegates that it would cease the export of landmines. It appears that the ICBL was making progress even where it was least expected.

Nonetheless, the negotiations at the Vienna conference in September 1995 ended without any tangible result, besides a broad agreement for further talks. The ICBL had managed to secure the cooperation of pro-ban countries there, though, that would later pay dividends. In 1995 Jody somehow found time to co-author a book, *After the Guns Fall Silent: The Enduring Legacy of Landmines*, with Shawn Roberts, which examined the impact of landmine contamination on the social and economic lives of people of four countries. The book added to the veritable mountain of empirical evidence against anti-personnel mines. There was no doubt too of the common idea of the ICBL. But the activists would need to break the impasse that had developed, or the campaign risked losing momentum.

A change in tactics would shake the diplomats from their torpor and denial in the proceeding review conference in Geneva in April and May 1996. The conference was attended by about 150 campaigners from twenty countries, and landmine survivors were given ample opportunity to relate their experiences. Some enterprising campaigners had arranged loudspeakers near the review conference to issue the sound of a landmine explosion every twenty minutes, highlighting to the delegates that every twenty minutes a landmine was killing or maiming somewhere in the world. There was a greater emphasis on publicity, and the diplomats could hardly fail to be impressed by the message. 'Ban Mines' stickers were pasted liberally throughout the city, and posters adorned buses throughout Geneva. In solidarity, and to sustain pressure on the respective governments, Austrian campaigners brought six tonnes of shoes to the Austrian parliament, symbolizing the countless shoes landmine survivors could no longer wear. In Paris, Handicap International raised a 'shoe pyramid' in front of the Eiffel Tower.

The ICBL stepped up its pressure with an orchestrated publicity campaign in the international media. In its newsletter, the ICBL also exposed the duplicity of some governments which were posing as pro-ban in public but were covertly anti-ban. The column was titled, 'The Good, the Bad and the Ugly'. The ICBL became more openly confrontational towards intransigent delegates, warning that their governments would face a backlash in their countries for failing the movement. Strangely, the US, still batting for its smart landmines, had invited Goose and Jody to be part of the US delegation in the Geneva deliberations. Both demurred. Perhaps the most significant development in Geneva was that Canada officially broke its customary solidarity with the US on landmines. The Canadian government's volte-face in support of the ban rekindled the ICBL team's hopes of an imminent ban treaty.

Canada began to take a proactive role in banning landmines, sponsoring a conference in Ottawa in October 1996. Canadian minister of foreign affairs Lloyd Axworthy made a startling announcement at the conclusion of this conference. He stated that Canada was committed to a landmine ban, and asked the other countries at the conference to return there the following year to sign a treaty which, he said, Canada would sign if only one other country signed. Axworthy's pronouncement was a bold public challenge, and quite a diplomatic risk. But it gave a sense of urgency to the cause, and strove to cut through the seemingly interminable diplomatic to-and-fro of the preceding years, when there was clearly a broad consensus for a treaty.

While the ICBL was thrilled at Lloyd Axworthy's courageous announcement, the weight of expectation fell squarely on the organization. Jody and her team were acutely aware they would have to capitalize on the lead given by the Canadian government and build the impetus for a treaty. The result would be what Jody and her team called the '1997 Landmine Ban World Tour' – a frenetic series of events and conferences across the globe to build support and international pressure for a landmine ban treaty. A significant part of the effort of that year was to build support in Africa, the most mine-infested continent, for a comprehensive landmine ban. May 1997 saw a conference on landmines in Kempton Park in South Africa, attended by forty-one nations of the continent. Thanks largely to the lobbying and seeking of grass-roots support by the ICBL, the conference ended with some level of support from all nations but Egypt, which nonetheless expressed its desire for an 'eventual elimination' of anti-personnel mines.

It appeared that the Egyptian government was echoing the sentiments of its ally America, motivated in part by a desire to appease the US, and doubtless also in cognizance of the country's losses against Israel in the Six Day War of 1967 and the Yom Kippur War of 1973. Egypt's fears of giving away any advantage to a belligerent neighbouring country were echoed with the Finnish anti-ban sentiment, which was predicated by a desire to retain landmines as a defence against any future Russian attack. The Finnish position was also influenced strongly by history: the Finns had suffered greatly in the series of Russo-Finnish wars in the early and mid-twentieth century. Finland had ceded territory and paid punitive reparations to the erstwhile Soviet Union in 1944 to secure an end to the last debilitating conflict.

Jody could see that these countries' positions on landmines were not based so much on future concerns as preoccupations with their last wars. The US, however, seemed intent simply on retaining its armoury. The military, which was not always in agreement with the nation's elected officials, seemed to fear that if landmines were taken from their arsenal, other weapons may also face sanction. For the US government, the ICBL campaign seemed to be far more than a ban on landmines. It was a potential threat to the nation's vaunted military supremacy.

The Oslo conference began on 31 August 1997, with a US delegation intent on derailing the ICBL. Coincidentally, it was the day of Princess Diana's death in Paris. This was to have some bearing on the conference, as Princess Diana had lent her support to the ICBL months earlier. Her iconic pictures with landmine survivors in Angola and Bosnia had helped the cause immeasurably, though some later suggestions that her championing the landmine ban was crucial to the treaty seem more based on sentiment than evidence. Princess Diana's passing away appeared to cast a pall over the British delegation, though, which had by now broken ranks with its American allies on the issue.

The pressure of the US to bend negotiations to its will was met with a determined ICBL, which was learning ever more ingenious ways of conveying the evils of anti-personnel mines. At the Brussels conference three months earlier, some clever and enterprising activists rigged up a simulated minefield outside the conference centre, and delegates had to run the gauntlet of sensors tripping the sounds of mines exploding as they entered. It was surely comical; but it served its purpose. Once inside the building, the delegates had to confront the landmine survivors, whose presence could barely fail to press the point of the weapons' senseless violence.

At the Oslo conference, the US was apparently resorting to clever manoeuvring to negate the effect of the treaty. Just as it seemed the negotiations appeared to be drawing to a successful conclusion, the US managed to secure a delay in proceedings. Worse, their pressure appeared to be softening Canadian resolve for a treaty; Canada supported the US delay. A Canadian reversal appeared a very real prospect, and Jody was outraged. In a conversation with the head of the Canadian delegation, Jody swore and threatened to 'publicly fry [the Canadian] foreign minister' if his government reneged on its commitment to a landmine ban treaty.

This, along with the firm resolve of other nations, finally overcame active US opposition at Oslo. The US withdrew, and the conference considered the final wording of the Convention on the Prohibition of the Use, Stockpiling, Production and Transfer of Anti-Personnel Mines and on Their Destruction, or the Mine Ban Treaty that would be signed in Ottawa just months hence. After a few tense moments when Japanese delegates took the floor to discuss fresh proposals, the chairman twice asked, 'Does this conference approve this text?' And when no one raised an objection, he brought his gavel down to approve the treaty. Jody and the ICBL had prevailed. It was a little after noon on Wednesday, 17 September 1997.

Much has been spoken about Jody's contribution to the landmine ban treaty. Indubitably, her passion and commitment drove her work, and inspired a concerted international effort that would perhaps have not been successful without such a charismatic leader. Her approach, which could be variously blunt and confrontational, and engaging, firm and supportive according to the situation, was instrumental in achieving a treaty that many just a few years earlier had considered a quixotic fancy. Jody's speeches rallied people to action, and her forcefulness headed off attempts to mire the treaty in endless palaver. Indeed, a member of the Finnish delegation approached her once to confess that on occasions when he attended meetings with her, she would appear in his nightmares. While some would find her manner of dealing with the ICBL campaign off-putting, none would question her commitment, and she earned the respect of many of her opponents.

Jody's commitment to the ICBL stemmed from a rare devotion to humanity that found expression throughout her career. Only such devotion can turn the seemingly impossible into the possible, as was acknowledged by Francis Sejersted, chairman of the Norwegian Nobel Committee, who paid the tribute to Jody thus:

> There are those among us who are unswerving in their faith that things can be done to make our world a better, safer, and more humane place, and who also, even when the tasks appear overwhelming, have the courage to tackle them. Such people deserve our admiration, and our gratitude. We are delighted and honoured to welcome some of them to the Oslo City Hall today. Our warm welcome to you, the representatives of the ICBL, the International Campaign to Ban Landmines, and to you, Jody Williams, the campaign's strongest single driving force. You have not only dared to tackle your task, but also proved that, the impossible is possible. You have helped to rouse public opinion all over the world against the use of an arms technology that strikes quite randomly at the most innocent and most defenceless. And you have opened up the possibility that this wave of opinion can be channelled into political action.

On 10 October 1997, less than a month after the approval of the treaty text in Oslo in September, the Norwegian Nobel Committee announced that it would award the Nobel Peace Prize in two equal parts to Jody and the ICBL. The Mine Ban Treaty was opened for signing on 3 December 1997 in Ottawa. Tun Channareth received the shared Nobel Peace Prize on behalf of the ICBL and Rae McGrath delivered the ICBL's Nobel Lecture. Jody became the tenth woman and third American woman recipient of the Nobel Peace Prize at the award ceremony in Oslo on 10 December 1997. In addition to the Nobel Peace Prize, another prize Jody received from her time leading the ICBL was Steven Goose. She married Goose in Geneva, that city where they had spent so much time together, on 13 May 2001.

Jody served as a founding coordinator of the ICBL from 1992 until February 1998. She acted as a chief strategist and spokesperson for the ICBL, which she developed from two non-governmental organizations. From functioning as the only staff member, she created an international powerhouse involving some 1,300 non-governmental organizations in more than ninety countries that supported the campaign. The ICBL's success will perhaps serve to guide future generations in how a movement can achieve its aims in a relatively short period of time. Jody has shared her experiences of the ICBL in her autobiography, *My Name is Jody Williams – A Vermont Girl's Winding Path to the Nobel Peace Prize*.

Jody has lost none of her characteristic directness in the intervening years. Nearly two decades after her Nobel Peace Prize, she remains passionate about human rights and government policy. She tells me with some satisfaction that the signatory governments are obeying the Mine Ban Treaty. This, she explains, is because the campaign is still active today; as the non-governmental organizations are active, the governments abide by the Mine Ban Treaty. Indeed, she says, it is one of the most properly observed international treaties. The reason is that the non-governmental organizations did not declare victory and melt away when the Mine Ban Treaty was successfully negotiated in 1997. They have been telling the governments that they are going to continue to make sure that they abide by the law they created.

In February 1998, Jody handed the role of campaign coordinator to Liz Bernstein, who kept the ICBL vibrant until December 2004, when Sylvie Brigot was appointed to the position. Jody meanwhile assumed the role of campaign ambassador, and it is in this role that she continues to speak and promote the cause of the Mine Ban Treaty around the world. As a result, as many as 160 countries signed the treaty by 2012, and some 44 million stockpiled landmines have been destroyed. Despite these laudable achievements, Jody regrets that America has preferred to remain in its pseudo-majestic isolation in refusing to sign the treaty. But she notes with some satisfaction that America has not used anti-personnel mines since the Gulf War in 1991. It hasn't exported mines since 1992, it stopped producing mines in the mid-1990s and has destroyed millions of mines it had stockpiled. Nevertheless, Jody regrets that successive US governments have yielded to military pressure to retain landmines in its arsenal.

Jody continues to be with the ICBL in spirit, but is presently the chairperson of the Nobel Women's Initiative, launched in 2006 by six women recipients: Betty Williams, Mairead Maguire, Rigoberta Menchú Tum, Dr Shirin Ebadi, Professor Wangari Maathai (now deceased) and Jody herself. Liz Bernstein, whom Jody has long admired and worked with since the early ICBL days, has been the executive director of the Initiative since its inception. The primary object of the Initiative, besides helping each other's projects in their respective spheres of activity, is to help women and amplify their voices of protest wherever they feel persecuted. Jody informs me during my interview with her that only grass-roots activists are members of the Initiative as per the laws of the Initiative, explaining the exclusion of Aung San Suu Kyi of Myanmar and President Ellen Johnson Sirleaf of Liberia from the

Initiative. Jody regrets that there is no such thing as a Nobel Men's Initiative. She said men never think about coming together. It is the women who have formed the Initiative for the empowerment of women and espousing women's causes.

When I ask Jody why the focus of the Nobel Women's Initiative is not on seeking a ban on nuclear weapons, she says that though she has spoken personally for a ban on nuclear arsenals at many international forums, her focus – and also the focus of the Nobel Women's Initiative – is on the empowerment of women. She holds that women's voices must be heard, be included and be part of all discussions in order to change our world and save our future. She has an enlightened concept of security. She regards human security as far more important than national security. She says that for ensuring human security, there is an urgent need for making food, medicines, good jobs, education and safe drinking water available to every human being. If we can shift thinking from national security towards human security, someday there could be sustainable peace with equality and justice.

War, Jody declares, is not inevitable. War is a choice. For men, it is a business. Men make a good deal of money from war. Jody also expresses her grave concern over the growing use of rape as a weapon of war. Five years ago, the Nobel Women's Initiative began a campaign to stop rape and gender violence in conflict and is bringing together non-government organizations to work together to pressure governments, armies and the UN to stop rape in war. She is happy that the British government has taken a significant lead in this respect.

When asked to spell out her advice to the world's youth, Jody informs me that the world talks about science and advancement but does not talk about morality and ethics. We need to start discussion on morality and ethics, and not just science, technology and advancement. She says that she cannot tell anybody what to do and how to do it. All that she suggests is to find a group of people, a non-governmental organization, and volunteer a few hours a month to see how you feel and how you can bring about change. She says there is no point in thinking about changing the world or worrying about the problems in the world. It is about doing something. We need to do something in order to make a difference to the world. Every single thing we do does actually matter.

Jody expresses her grave concern about the plenty in the hands of a few and almost nothing in others' hands. She says poverty, which is the direct outcome of an unequal economic system, has to be addressed as a priority. She says that the world is beset with myriad problems, and the Nobel Women's Initiative cannot work on all of them. The Initiative has chosen to work with women around the world and to work for sustainable peace. Jody tells me that there are organizations working for children, some are working on nuclear issues and some others are working towards climate change. It is not possible to do everything, and if one tries, one will probably not do well. She says that the other concern of the Nobel Women's Initiative is disarmament, in the same way as the campaign against landmines was created.

Jody considers herself fortunate, she tells me, for stumbling into a way of life that allowed her to work on what she cared for. She says that she enjoys many ordinary things in life, and cooks dinner with her husband. She is governed by the same human emotions as others, and at times, cannot withstand others' anger.

Jody has been teaching since 2003 at the Graduate College of Social Work at the University of Houston, Texas. Since 2007, she has been the Sam and Cele Keeper Endowed Professor in Peace and Social Justice there. It seems she takes to teaching as she takes to activism. Jody is highly unassuming, easily accessible; and she remains a down-to-earth activist for each cause she holds dear. She declares that every human being is capable of bringing change in the world. She has aptly said, 'I think there is a myth that if you want to change the world, you need to be sainted like Mother Teresa or Nelson Mandela or Archbishop Desmond Tutu. Ordinary people with lives that go up and down and in round circles can still contribute to change.'

With the efforts of other grass-roots activists in Jody's mould, the day will not be far when sustainable peace with equality and justice becomes a reality. In the New Testament, in the Gospel of Matthew, there is a thought-provoking verse (5:13): 'Ye are the salt of the earth; but if the salt have lost his savour, wherewith shall it be salted?' Likewise, if woman as a creator becomes oblivious of her obligation to protect her creation, who can beckon her to do her duty?

Renewing her call for action, Jody told *Real Leaders* in June 2015:

> The image of peace with a dove flying over a rainbow and people holding hands singing kumbaya ends infantilizing people who believe that sustainable peace is possible. If you think that singing and looking at a rainbow will suddenly make peace appear then you are not capable of meaningful thought or understanding the difficulties of the world.

Jody's life story holds a message for the youth of the world. The message is clear and eloquent. It is that you do not have to be devoutly religious. You do not have to possess a saintly demeanour, you do not have to belong to an aristocratic class and you do not need to possess riches. All that you need is to create a desire to work and work for others instinctively. Jody's example is a call to action. In the words of Swami Vivekananda, we have to 'Awake, arise and rest not till the goal of abiding peace with equality and justice is achieved'.

RIGOBERTA MENCHÚ TUM

CRUSADER FOR INDIGENOUS RIGHTS

'What I treasure most in life is being able to dream. Even
during my most difficult moments, I have been able to dream
of a more beautiful future.'

Each woman Nobel Peace laureate is unique in her own way, but all of them have a story of valour and perseverance to tell. Yet, Rigoberta is an enigma of an altogether different hue. She shot to worldwide fame when, at twenty-three, in 1981, she published her first book, *Mellamo Rigoberta Menchú y así me nació la conciencia* (My Name Is Rigoberta Menchú, and This Is How My Conscience Was Born). The book earned her several international awards, and has been translated into more than twelve languages, including English and French. In 1998, she penned another volume, *Rigoberta: La Nieta de los Mayas* (*Crossing Borders* in English).

Rigoberta's book narrated the harrowing tale of the suffering of Guatemala's indigenous peoples during the Guatemalan civil war. She said that she wrote the book to bring international condemnation upon the Guatemalan army. She soon caught the world's attention and, in 1983, two American film-makers, Pamela Yates and Newton Thomas Sigel, came to Guatemala to film *When the Mountains Tremble*, a documentary film about the civil war between the Indian guerrillas and the Guatemalan army under dictator Jose Efraín Ríos Montt. They met Rigoberta Menchú, a young Quiché peasant and asked her to relate the stories of atrocities committed by the Guatemalan army towards its people. In the film, Rigoberta narrates the large-scale suffering and misery the poor Mayans had to face, first under Spanish rule and thereafter under succeeding dictatorships. The Guatemalan civil war had resulted in the deaths of 14,000 Guatemalans, majority of whom were Mayan peasants.

It may seem counter-intuitive, but this author of many books and the central focus of a film by some of the most renowned film-makers, and a Nobel Peace laureate, has never been to school. There are twenty-three indigenous ethnic groups in Guatemala, and she was born in the Quiché ethnic group. She was born in a village called Chimel. The nearest town, Uspantan, was

24 kilometres away, and, as there were no roads suitable for vehicles, everyone travelled mostly on foot. The village was situated in a mountain, and everything they carried was either on horseback or on their own backs. Earlier, her parents had lived in a town, but they had to leave because their house had been forcibly occupied by a Ladino (people of mixed – Spanish and American Indian – descent) family.

Her father, Vicente Menchú Perez, was born in the Santa Rosa Chucuyub village in El Quiché. He had a troubled childhood, as his father had died when he was still a child. Vicente's mother took him along with his two brothers to Uspantan and, there, started working as a servant for the wealthiest family in town. As the boys grew, the rich man refused to offer them food, saying that Vicente's mother did not work enough for him to feed her sons. Eventually, Vicente's mother gave Vicente, her eldest son, away to another rich man.

Vicente would toil a lot in that rich man's fields, but in return he would receive merely food for his sustenance. Always dirty and in tatters, Vicente was kept away from the rich man's family. He could not bear the humiliation and left the rich man's house to find work in the nearby coastal estates. There, he started earning enough money, and even sent some of his earnings to his mother. Under grievous circumstances, his mother had been forced to serve as her employer's mistress, but when Vicente started earning enough, his mother left her employer and joined Vicente in the coastal estates, along with Vicente 's brothers.

Around the time, the military started conscripting young boys to fight the growing movement of guerrilla insurgents called the Guatemalan National Revolutionary Unity. Vicente was taken away by soldiers, leaving his mother and two brothers to fend for themselves. When he returned after a year in the army, he found his mother seriously ill, and could not arrange for her medicines.

His mother soon died, and his brothers went their different ways in search of work.

It was at this time that Vicente met Rigoberta's mother, Juana Tum Kotoja, and they married. Juana also belonged to a poor family. But Vicente was hard-working, as was Juana, and together, they founded a village up in the mountains. Since the land belonged to the government, they had to seek permission before settling there; Vicente had to pay for clearing the land and building a house. It was here that Rigoberta was born, as the sixth child to her parents, on 9 January 1959. Rigoberta's parents were already in financial straits by then – their crops were only just enough for their family to sustain themselves – and with the inclusion of a sixth child, it became harder to run the household. However, hard work, as Rigoberta says, ran in the family bloodline and they would successfully weather the many storms of life.

In Rigoberta's community, a child begins its life on the very first day of its mother's pregnancy. As per the custom, the day a woman learns about her pregnancy, she has to approach the village leaders with her husband to tell them that she is going to be blessed with a child. She offers her child to the leaders to act as the child's second parents. The leaders then pledge to take care of the child as its second parents, should the need arise. The leaders are referred to as 'abuelos' or 'godparents'. The child's parents and grandparents put in concerted efforts to find suitable abuelos; so that in the event of the child 's becoming an orphan the godparents will nurture the child. Custom also requires a neighbour of a pregnant woman to visit her every day and take care of her. When the pregnancy advances to the seventh month, the mother goes out into the fields or the hills to introduce her child to the natural world. At the same time, she has to carry on with her domestic chores, so that her child is aware of the hardships of life. When the baby is born, her husband, the village leaders and the couple's parents should be around her. The birth of a new child is considered significant, and at least three couples from the parents' families should be present during childbirth. The child is received in person by a midwife or a grandmother. During the first eight days, the community meets all the household expenses.

The Quiché customs are based on a feeling of fraternity. If empathy ran that deep, there would hardly be any need for national boundaries and weapons of mass destruction. But regrettably, Rigoberta's own country was engulfed by a civil war that lasted thirty-six years, from 1960 to 1996. The war was fought fiercely between the descendants of European immigrants and the American Indian population.

When Rigoberta was a little girl, her mother used to take her to the plantations – on her back, wrapped in a shawl, like most women plantation workers. Rigoberta was only eight years old when she started working in coffee plantations. She picked 35 pounds of coffee a day and earned twenty centavos. At the tender age of eight, she began earning as much as an adult. When she was ten, she started working in cotton plantations. If she was ever short of money and any of her siblings offered to help, she would refuse, saying she wanted to manage her life on her own; and as a result, she learnt to live independently from a very early age. However, no one could see then that her early development in the plantations would be the beginning of her future greatness.

Their living conditions in the plantation were so filthy – and their skin so sunburnt – that no driver would drive them to the plantations. The lorries belonged to the plantation owners, but the drivers, or *caporales*, oversaw the farm workers. The caporales would stand by the workers to see how hard they worked, chastising them if they were slow or were resting. Workers were asked to bring their own plates, cups and water bottles, and food was provided only to those who worked to the satisfaction of the caporales, and if someone could not, whatever the reason, no food was provided. The workers' children were also not given food, and the children's mothers had to share their rations with their children.

Every plantation had watering holes called cantinas where workers could buy liquor. Many workers spent most of their earnings in these cantinas, and many would even lapse to debt. As debts piled up, most workers ended up owing all their wages to cantinas. Rigoberta's father too owed all his wages to a cantina. In addition to debts the workers owed, the corrupt overseers also charged workers for things they had never bought or for losses they had never caused. Rigoberta would ask her mother why they suffered so much at the hands of the caporales, and her mother would say that she would understand when she grew up.

Poverty spins hundreds of tales, and Rigoberta's family's story was one of them. Back in the village from the plantations, her family suffered the curse of poverty. Often Rigoberta and her siblings fell sick, and Vicente could not take them to the plantation. The only way of making a consistent income was by collecting *mimbre* (wood) from the nearby mountains. So even though they all were sick, all of them went to cut wood.

After they had collected 50 quintals of wood, having spent seven days in the mountains, they would dry the wood. Their dog acted as their guide, and in its absence they would often lose their way. After collecting the wood, the walk back home lasted three days, often without any food to eat; while they could, they had to feed on *bojones* (shoots of palm trees). In fact, sometimes they even had to leave some of the wood behind, as they could not carry all the wood when it rained. Being back home, however, was no respite either, as they now had to take the wood from their village to the town, and from the town to the capital, and still bear the cost of transporting the wood the family had collected in seven days.

Rigoberta recounts that among all her siblings, she was her father's favourite, and her father would choose her to accompany him on his journey to the capital. Once, when they reached the man to whom her father sold the wood, the man refused to buy it. Her father then went looking for another buyer, but, on finding no one, was forced to sell the wood to the first man at half the price he had earlier quoted. Fifty quintals of wood fetched Vicente a mere twenty-five quetzals. Her mother nearly fainted on hearing the money the wood had fetched for the family. Hunger was soon staring the family in the face, and so they had to return to the plantation they had left.

The working conditions at the plantation were poor. There were about 400 workers at the plantation, and there was only one toilet. Everyone made a beeline in the morning to use the toilet. Flies hovered around because filth was scattered everywhere. There was additionally the danger of chemical poisoning, as many of these cotton and coffee plantations used chemical fertilizers and pesticides indiscriminately. Rigoberta would lose her eldest brother, Felipe, to pesticide poisoning at the plantation.

Her younger brother Nicolas, whom her mother used to carry wrapped up in a shawl on her back, died of malnutrition when he was only two years old. Her mother wanted to bury her brother at the plantation, but the caporales would only let her if she paid them money. Her mother had no money. As the body started rotting, and on seeing that no help was forthcoming, her mother decided to pay the overseers and bury her son at the plantation. As recompense, she agreed to work without pay for over a month. But before her mother could approach the overseers, a man brought a suitcase-like box, put her son's body inside it and buried him.

It enraged the overseers no end, and they ordered her mother to leave the plantation. Rigoberta's mother did not even know the name of the town where they had been living, and suddenly found herself deserted. Somehow they managed to reach their home in the Altiplanos – a mountainous region in Guatemala.

Tragedy befell Rigoberta around this time when her dear friend Maria died from pesticide poisoning at a plantation, and she lost all her zest for life. She told her mother that she wanted to die. Her mother but reprimanded her for being so cynical. However, the desire to end life was strong in her. She had many questions to which she could not find satisfactory answers. She thought of seeking the help of a few priests she knew, but she did not know Spanish and hence could not converse with them. She told her father that she wanted to learn to read, but her father could not help, as there had not been the money or the availability of a school nearby. She then asked her father to send her to the priests, but he did not agree, saying that Rigoberta would then have to move away from her community.

Rigoberta, however, was determined to learn to read. Around this time, a plantation owner asked her father to send Rigoberta to him to work as his maid. The plantation owner offered Rigoberta twenty quetzals a month to be his maid. However, her father refused. He knew that the rich treated their maids badly and felt that his family should live together even if it meant that they had to suffer together. Her elder sister had once worked for the same plantation owner, and when Vicente had gone to see his daughter, after a month, he had found that she had been ill-treated. Nevertheless, this was the opportunity Rigoberta had been waiting for. She knew she was made of a much tougher mettle and that she would survive what her sister could not. Thus, she persuaded her father to let her replace her sister and work as a maid in the capital, so that she could learn Spanish.

At the plantation owner's house, Rigoberta was humiliated and insulted. Her clothes were shabby, her skirt was dirty and her blouse was literally a rag. She did not have shoes. In fact, she had never worn shoes in her life. While Rigoberta was fed only beans and a hard maize cake, the owner's dog was fed lavishly with meat and rice. But the worst embarrassment of all was when the mistress of the house would throw her out of the house every Saturday and ask her to come back on Sunday evening. Rigoberta was caught in a dilemma. On one hand, she found her subhuman living conditions intolerable, and on the other hand she had to learn Spanish. She resolved not to accept defeat.

Her ordeal at the plantation owner's house ended unexpectedly one day when her brother came to take her back home. Her father had been imprisoned. After two decades Vicente had made his family's land worthy of cultivation, and the land had started yielding good produce. But one day a few landlords descended upon their land, along with a few inspectors and engineers. They claimed that they had come on government orders to 'repossess' the land. Vicente had been jailed because he had been waging a relentless battle against the landlords who in fact wanted to deprive him and his community of their lands.

It was obvious that the military government and the landlords had made a deal to divest the American Indian villagers of their lands. Not one to roll over and accept defeat, Vicente and other villagers at his settlement approached the Institute for Agrarian Transformation (INTA) for help. The authorities at the INTA, however, made Vicente sign a piece of paper, of which Vicente knew nothing of what was going to be written thereon. To their utter dismay, the INTA had committed treachery. The INTA claimed that

Vicente, on behalf of all the villagers, had conceded that the villagers had no objection to the takeover of their lands by the landlords. Vicente and the villagers approached lawyers, but the lawyers were interested only in extracting a heavy fee. The ensuing struggle saw engineers and inspectors visiting their lands more than twenty times, and each time they had to be fed with expensive delicacies even Rigoberta's family and neighbours had not tasted before.

The villagers' extending them lavish hospitality notwithstanding, they were ousted from their homes and had to leave the village in 1967. As the villagers lost their livelihoods, their animals starved to death; and the famished and destitute villagers were forced to feed on plants to satiate their hunger. However, Vicente was a spirited man and did not relent at any stage. He took the matter to a judge. But the landlords bribed the judge; and Vicente was arrested. He was accused of having compromised state sovereignty. Whatever little remained with his family was soon spent on arranging for lawyers and an interpreter. Unfortunately, the interpreter had also been bribed by the landlords, and he manipulated the statements given by the villagers. The interpreter wrote on behalf of Vicente and other villagers that their land belonged to the landlords, and that the landlords had paid Vicente and other villagers for the cultivation of their land. The worst, however, was yet to come: Vicente was sent to the state prison in El Quiché.

When Rigoberta visited her father in Santa Cruz prison, she was horrified to see the condition of the inmates. She realized that if her father served the full eighteen years of his sentence he would go mad. Vicente, however, had begun working inside the jail and saving some money, which he could send to his family, so that they could get him released. Rigoberta's family and the entire village worked hard for Vicente's release. Rigoberta's family's earnings were already depleted, but what was left of it was immediately spent on lawyers and other legalities. Rigoberta herself worked for a whole year, without going home even once. The landlords, however, were not to give in so easily, as they identified Vicente as the mainstay of the Quiché. Vicente was taken to court every five days and pressured to plead guilty to the charges against him. The landlords never failed to grease the judge's palm whenever Vicente appeared in court, and the judge obligingly ordered her father's retention each time. Nonetheless, the concerted efforts of Vicente's family and the villagers ultimately succeeded, and Vicente was released.

Their troubles were far from over, though. The landlords' henchmen kidnapped Vicente. Rigoberta's brother, who witnessed the kidnapping, was able to mobilize the villagers quickly. The villagers followed the kidnappers, who, seeing that they were outnumbered, abandoned him and fled. Before abandoning him, however, the kidnappers had severely beaten him up, breaking several of his bones. Vicente was left unable even to walk. He was taken to hospital, and the doctors advised hospitalization for at least nine months. But the villagers decided to bring Vicente back to the village, so that they could guard him against any future kidnapping attempts.

Vicente was kept hidden in a secret place. After about eleven months, he was brought home. Though battered physically, his determination to overcome his enemies grew stronger. His hate for Ladinos – to which ethnicity the landlords belonged – also grew feverishly. Vicente sought help from the labour unions this time, but the Ladino landlords were becoming more and more hostile towards him, and he was arrested again in 1977. This time, the case against him was worse: he was accused of being a communist and a subversive, for which he could be sentenced to life imprisonment. He had now become a political prisoner.

However, over the period, the community had grown wiser, and the whole community – priests, nuns, villagers and unions – stood behind Vicente. Protests were organized against Vicente's arrest, and soon the community's pressure secured Vicente's early release. Vicent's faith in his community had paid off. He always knew that his community was his strongest pillar of support, and often urged his family and friends to stick together in one strong bind. He had told Rigoberta, 'I'm your father now, but later the community will be your father.'

Vicente's latest time in jail was a defining turning point in his life. In jail he met other political prisoners who had been imprisoned because they had defended peasants' rights. One of them had advised Vicente, 'We must fight the rich, because they have become rich with our land, our crops.' Vicente realized that he had to fight the battle not only of his community but also of the entire peasant underclass. Rigoberta witnessed her father's metamorphosis from a plantation worker to a mass leader, and this would impact her in a big way.

Though sympathetic towards the Catholic priests and nuns who had helped her and her community, Rigoberta regretted the church's fatalism and teachings, especially regarding acceptance. According to her, the church establishment, who had never toiled in the fields or experienced gnawing hunger, would not be able to empathize with the struggles of Indian peasants. The poor, therefore, were not to be content with the promise of a kingdom of God in their afterlives, and had to strive for a better life here on earth. To this end, she resolved to found a church that taught its faithful to fight injustice rather than accept it. She envisioned

God as the emancipator of the poor and exploited. The Bible, Rigoberta argued, calls upon men and women to fight hunger and poverty and improve the human condition.

Thus, in accordance with her new faith, Rigoberta decided to organize her villagers to thwart the soldiers who, at the behest of the landlords, had regularly invaded and looted their villages. She along with others villagers set up traps for them. In one instance, the villagers trained a pretty girl from the village to flirt with soldiers. Later, during a raid, the girl approached the last soldier to enter the village and engaged him in conversation. Just then Rigoberta and another villager pounced on the soldier, 'Drop your weapons!' The terrified soldier was easily overpowered, and was later blindfolded and taken to the village.

Having prepared her village against similar attacks, she shifted to other villages to teach the people there how their villages could also be defended against invaders. Her father was very proud of her, but advised her to be vigilant. She recounts how in some villages hundreds of women were raped and impregnated by soldiers. Once, she travelled to a village where many of her friends resided. She was deeply distressed to learn that her friends had been raped and impregnated by soldiers, and felt miserable for being unable to relieve their plight. One of them would have an abortion despite Rigoberta's numerous pleas to mother the child, because the child had not been to blame. But the girl could not fathom feeding the child when she hated the soldier whose child she had been bearing.

Rigoberta organized the people in her friends' village and taught them methods of self-defence she had honed in her own village. She made the villagers shift to a camp up in the mountains. When the army raided the village at night, they could not loot anything, as the villagers had taken all their belongings with them. The villagers had also left traps at the doors of their houses. Each trap consisted of a pole, and a big pit more than ten feet deep. A pole was laid across the pit, and then a board on the pole, so that when anyone stood on the board, he would fall in. In the morning, the villagers found that a soldier had fallen to Rigoberta's traps.

The villagers threw him a rope and pulled him out of the pit. The captured soldier disclosed that he had been recruited to fight communists. The soldier, however, had no idea why he had to fight the communists. Rigoberta told the soldier that he was, in fact, fighting his own people for the sake of the rich. The soldier expressed his heartfelt regret and promised the villagers that he would leave the army.

In 1978, she formed the Peasant Unity Committee (CUC). In the same year, she visited her home in the Altiplanos. Vicente had also returned home clandestinely, as the army, under the influence of the landlords, had launched a massive manhunt for him. If he had been caught, he would have been killed instantly. The evening after Vicente returned home, a grand fiesta was organized in Rigoberta's village. Her father announced that he would be leaving the community, because his children could now fend for themselves. He was needed in other places and must, therefore, leave his village. He told the villagers that he might not return.

Her mother also bid adieu to the villagers, as she too felt she was needed elsewhere. The villagers were pained, but at the same time were heartened that Vicente and Juana were leaving for a noble cause. Vicente often said that the traditional hat the Quiché wore was not just to cover the head but also to think about the community and bring about the changes desired by the community. Rigoberta also resolved to leave the village. Thus, by the close of the evening's fiesta, the three of them had bidden farewell to their beloved village.

The following day, Vicente left for El Quiché, and Rigoberta left to work in the CUC, where her principal task was bringing together peasants and other marginalized peoples of Guatemala. She travelled extensively, during which she stayed with nuns, who taught her Spanish, and interacted with workers from plantations – sugar, coffee and cotton – on the southern coast. Many of the workers she met promised to carry on her work in the CUC in their villages and also to get more people to join the CUC. During her travels, she rushed from one place to another, overcoming linguistic barriers and developing relations with many women – relationships sometimes as close and intimate as with her own mother. Her travels, thus, suffused her with an understanding of the country's diverse facets, through her increasingly widening acquaintance.

In one of her travels, Rigoberta visited her *compañero*'s (co-worker) at her house. She had only a a thin blanket with her and had not realized that it would be a terribly cold night. She hoped that her compañero would lend her a shawl or something to keep herself warm, but she was surprised to find that the family had nothing to protect themselves from the biting cold. By midnight the chill froze them all. Her jaw became stiff from cold. She had never suffered such a biting chill before. Seeing her predicament, her friend offered her a mat. She, however, refused because she did not want any special treatment. She kept thinking about the miserable plight in which the family lived, one which she had never experienced before. That night Rigoberta realized that human beings have greater resilience than they believe they have. She realized that not only the American Indians but also Ladinos suffered the same plight.

Initially she had been full of hatred for Ladinos, for she had considered them cruel and exploitative. Later she realized that not all Ladinos were alike. It was not a struggle between Ladinos and American Indians; in fact, it was the perennial struggle between the rich and poor. The same was confirmed to her by the participation of Guatemalans in the CUC, the majority of whom were Ladinos.

Many Ladinos had joined the CUC and had actively participated in the organization's efforts to unite the country's underclass. She realized that the Ladinos needed the CUC as much as did the American Indians.

Gradually the organization Rigoberta had helped build acquired greater dimension, and a fierce battle was soon in the offing, because the poor were now determined to protect their interests and the landlords and rich were determined to deprive them of their rights.

In 1974, General Kjell Eugenio came to power by promising the people many things – hospitals, schools, roads and many more. However, once he came to power, he gave free rein to the landlords and turned a blind eye to their reign of terror. Plantation owners imposed unbearable restrictions on workers. Organizing the peasants in such a dismal situation was indeed challenging for Rigoberta and others in the CUC. Moreover, the government refused to recognize the CUC as a representative body of the plantation workers. The CUC, however, refused to be bogged down and carried on with their work clandestinely. In response, the government unleashed a witch-hunt for CUC leaders, especially in El Quiché.

Of the myriad gory incidents during Kjell's tenure, the massacre of 106 peasants in Panzos town, on 29 May 1978, was the worst. The government had discovered oil in Panzos town and had started excavation in peasants' lands after having usurped them. The peasants marched in protest along with the CUC leaders against the government's move. The government killed men, women and children indiscriminately, and Panzos wore a deserted and ghastly look, with blood splattered on its main squares. Rigoberta felt as if she also had been killed in the massacre because the brutality had numbed her consciousness. Although the massacre had been reported in the newspapers, it did not receive its deserved attention.

In 1978, Fernando Romeo Lucas Garcia came to power replacing Kjell. Lucas Garcia proved to be worse than Kjell. He ordered mass killings, so much so that each day clandestine cemeteries were raised for the disposal of the dead. The terror was so frightening that only few would even come forward to claim the bodies. Pushed to the brink, the peasants and workers joined hands and organized a grand rally under CUC leadership, and over 70,000 workers attended.

As Rigoberta witnessed massacres, her own family would fall victim to the tyranny of the military government. Her sixteen-year-old brother was kidnapped on 9 September 1979. When Rigoberta and her parents had left their village, her brother had stayed back. The army had found him organizing villagers. It was said that he had been with a girl when the army had caught him. Rigoberta's mother would later learn that her son had been betrayed by someone from their own community, that the boy was taken some 2 kilometres away, and was beaten up severely on the way. He could not walk; he could hardly stand. He was bleeding so profusely from his face that he could hardly see.

The real torture, however, began when he was taken to the army camp. He was subjected to brutal torture to get information about his family and other guerrilla fighters. There, stones were pushed into his eyes. His fingers and the cheeks on his face were chopped off; his skin was burnt. The soldiers not only tortured him but also ensured that he wallowed in seething pain. For this, they would force-feed him a few loaves of bread, so that he would not die.

At the camp, there were twenty other men and a woman who were similarly tortured. The woman was raped too. On hearing about Rigoberta's brother's kidnapping, Rigoberta's parents and brothers arrived home. The military announced that the guerrillas they captured would be punished publicly. The place chosen for administering the punishment was Chajul village, which was a long way off. There, the army made sure that all villagers were present to witness the punishing. The army officers told the attendant crowd that the guerrillas were being punished for being subversives, and that if anyone indulged in their ways they too would be dealt with in the same way. When the lorry carrying the guerrillas arrived, the prisoners were taken out one by one. Their faces were badly scarred, bloody; and none of them could walk – the soles of their feet had been hacked off. One army officer thundered about communists leading people astray. He claimed that communists from the Soviet Union, Cuba and Nicaragua had entered Guatemala, and that the communists would face death. It was a dreadful scene to witness, and everyone around was in tears.

Rigoberta's mother recognized her son, whereas no one else from the family could recognize him. He had multiple cuts on various parts of his body. His scalp had been peeled off. But it was the woman who had received the worst torture. Her genitals were mutilated. One of the nipples of her breast had been chopped off. The other breast had been entirely cut off. Her ears had also been cut off. The gruesome scene sent shivers down the spines of everyone present. Children clung to their mothers and cried in horror.

Rigoberta's mother, putting her life in great peril, surged ahead to embrace her son, but was stopped by her father and brothers. Her father, though, betrayed no sign of his inner turmoil. The soldiers made the prisoners stand in a line, poured petrol on them and set them ablaze. They screamed and begged for mercy, but the soldiers were deaf to their pleas. After setting them on fire, the soldiers shouted, 'Long live the fatherland! Long live Guatemala!

Long live our president! Long live the army! Long live Lucas!' It was horrifying.

People ran in all directions to fetch water to douse the burning bodies, but it was too late. The bodies twitched, and eventually even the last shred of life left their tortured bodies. The scene was beyond tolerance, and many wanted to strike back, risking their own lives. Some had raised their weapons but realized that there could be a holocaust, as the army was well armed, and even had airplanes flying overhead. Rigoberta was shattered, not only for her brother but also for all the other tortured American Indians. After the bodies had been burnt, the villagers collected blankets to cover the corpses. Her mother hugged and kissed her son's body. A Christian burial was arranged for all the dead. Back home, Vicente infused new blood into the family. He declared, 'I may be old, but I am joining the guerrillas. I will avenge my son.' Her mother was devastated and sometimes showed signs of madness, but she too recovered like her brave husband. She said, 'If I start crying in front of the neighbours, what sort of example will that be?' The family went again in different directions to continue the great work each of them had undertaken. Rigoberta went back to organizing the peasants and workers for the CUC. She felt that it was the only way of mitigating the people's suffering and preventing such crimes.

Around this time, a demonstration was being planned by students, workers, unions, peasants and Christians, which was to take place in January 1980, protesting the military's repression in El Quiché, where news of daily kidnappings of boys was being reported. Rigoberta's father met her in November 1979 and asked her to attend the demonstration. In the meantime, Rigoberta got busy with her compañeros in mobilizing people. The marchers in El Quiché demanded that the military government be dismantled. To show the world the terror the army had let loose on the

Guatemalan people, the organizers brought several orphaned children to the demonstration. Peasants came from far and wide, most of them from El Quiché.

On 31 January 1980, the peasants occupied the Spanish embassy, but they could not have foreseen the horrors that awaited them there. The peasants were burnt alive. Rigoberta would lose her beloved father to this ghastly massacre. However, she always knew what fate had in store for her father. What she dreaded the most was that he should be caught alive and subjected to the cruelties her brother had been subjected to. Nevertheless, seething at the injustice, Rigoberta steeled her resolve to fight the government harder.

Rigoberta's mother, Juana, was kidnapped on 9 April 1980. She had come back to her village because eight compañeros in the village, who were active in the CUC, had been burnt alive at the Spanish embassy. She was the leader of the village and had thought that her village needed her at that critical moment. Her mother was raped repeatedly by army officers, and when she fainted from the brutality, she was injected with a serum to revive her consciousness and again raped and disfigured, repeatedly. The officers left her totally deformed, with several cuts on her body. Her body was then infested with worms; she succumbed to the torture shortly thereafter. After she died, soldiers urinated into her mouth, and her body was abandoned to be eaten by wild animals and dogs. It was a matter of great solace to Rigoberta that her mother had finally died and would not be tortured any further.

I find it difficult to compose myself whenever my thoughts drift to Rigoberta. I constantly wonder how she could reconcile herself to her fate – how she could witness so stoically the lynching and burning of her brother, and the burning of her father at the Spanish embassy, how she could stomach her mother 's suffering at the hands of the army, and, after everything, how she could so bravely say: 'With the help of our ancestors, we must prevail over the times we are living in.' Such ghastly tragedies in one's life should have driven one to insanity, but here was a tigress who braved such personal calamities in magnificent fashion.

Undoubtedly, her saintly mother was a crucial influence on Rigoberta. Her mother was kind and friendly, and a nature lover who treated even maize cuttings reverentially. She would tell Rigoberta that maize cuttings fed and nourished humans and therefore deserved respect. Rigoberta's mother was also a hospitable and generous host; whenever someone visited her, she would offer them something – be it a home-made drink or tortilla with salt. Her mother would tell Rigoberta, 'You must always know how to give, because a person who gives will also receive when the time comes. When you are in a difficult situation, you won't have to face your troubles alone. You will always receive help, even if it is not from the same person you helped. There will always be people who will hold you in high esteem.'

Although illiterate, her father had the sagacity of a statesman. Her mother too was not far behind. Her mother, Rigoberta says, believed that no evolution, no change can be achieved through a movement in which women did not participate. The people respected Rigoberta's mother. When she went to meet her son, captured by the army, all women of the village accompanied her, braving their own torture and death.

Rigoberta's mother possessed many other virtues of head and heart. She was hard-working and a perfectionist. Rigoberta recalls that her mother would always be found making mats, weaving clothes, plaiting straw, making earthen pots or tending to animals. She knew many herbal medicines and served in the village as a nurse. Rigoberta, however, was more attached to her father than her mother while she was growing up.

After the Spanish embassy burning, the need to bring the struggle to a decisive and profitable end became more urgent. In February 1980, 80,000 peasants, including workers from sugar and cotton plantations, participated in a peasants' strike. Initially the strike was started by about 8,000 peasants, but soon the numbers swelled and grew tenfold. The workers struck work for fifteen days. The strike was meticulously planned. The peasants marched under the banner 'the thirty-first of January popular front', so named in honour of those who died in the Spanish embassy burning on 31 January 1980, and was ready to die together.

The CUC, the Revolutionary Workers' Group and a host of other fronts by students and revolutionary Christians formed the Vicente Menchú Revolutionary Christians, after Rigoberta's father, whom they perceived as their national hero. In El Quiché, many priests joined the front. They had lost faith in the Catholic Church's call to forgive, as the government did not seek forgiveness when it killed.

Rigoberta went into hiding in 1981, for she would have been killed if she was found. Her compañeros flew her to Mexico. In Mexico, she built popular support for the resistance in Guatemala. She received immense support from a few Europeans too. Later, when the military government in Guatemala eased their witch-hunt against subversives, Rigoberta returned to Guatemala. Back home, she was eager to join the CUC, but the CUC had many able leaders, and so she opted to work for the Vicente Menchú Revolutionary Christians.

After the Guatemalan civil war, Rigoberta started a campaign to have members of the Guatemalan political and military establishment tried in Spanish courts. She filed a criminal complaint in 1999 in a court in Spain. Earlier the courts in Spain had refused to admit cases from Guatemala, as legal routes had first to be exhausted through the judiciary in Guatemala. Rigoberta's massive efforts to bring the perpetrators of the genocide in Guatemala to justice bore fruit on 23 December 2006 when Spain called for the extradition of seven former members of Guatemala's government on charges of genocide and torture. They included former military rulers Jose Efraín Ríos Montt and Oscar Mejia. Spain's highest court had ruled that cases of genocide committed abroad could be tried in Spain, even if no Spanish citizen had been involved.

Having won the battle against the military establishment in Guatemala, Rigoberta expanded her activities across the globe. She is a member of PeaceJam, an organization devoted to producing young leaders for the cause of mutual human concern and community building. She is a member of the Foundation Chirac's Honour Committee, founded by former French president Jacques Chirac to promote world peace. She is also an active member of the Nobel Women Initiative with fellow women Nobel recipients. Rigoberta also ran for the presidency of Guatemala in 2007 and 2011, but lost both the elections. Over the years, she has emerged as the chief leader and advocate of American Indian rights and ethno-cultural reconciliation, both in Guatemala and in the Western hemisphere. Rigoberta also heads Salud Para Todos (Health for All), a company that provides affordable generic medicines to the people of Guatemala. After receiving the Nobel Peace Prize, she established the Rigoberta Menchú Tum Foundation, which aims to promote the rights of indigenous people across the world. She has also served as the official spokesperson of the United Nations International Decade of Indigenous Peoples. Since 2004, she has held the position of goodwill ambassador for the peace accords in Guatemala.

Rigoberta was awarded the Nobel Peace Prize in 1992, in recognition of 'her work for social justice and ethno-cultural reconciliation based on respect for the rights of indigenous peoples'. She spiritedly espoused the cause of American Indian peasants in Guatemala, even in the face of mounting threats to her life. Her personal sufferings notwithstanding, she did not harbour any ill will or prejudice against her oppressors. In her Nobel Prize acceptance speech, she famously spoke of bringing out 'all shades and nuances' of the Guatemalan mosaic – Ladinos, Garifunas (ethnic group of African Carib descent on the Atlantic Coast) and American Indians.

AUNG SAN SUU KYI

THE GREAT GENERAL'S DAUGHTER

'It is not power that corrupts but fear. Fear of losing power
corrupts those who wield it and fear of the scourge of power
corrupts those who are subject to it.'

On 13 November 2010, at 5.30 p.m. Myanmar Standard Time, an upright, delicate-looking woman wearing a lilac-coloured Burmese dress emerged from her home; her prison for one-and-a-half decades of the preceding two. At the gates of her compound, an ecstatic crowd of thousands of well-wishers waited, many wearing T-shirts sporting the slogan 'We stand with Aung San Suu Kyi'. Aung San Suu Kyi, the world's most famous woman prisoner of conscience, was now a free woman.

Hundreds surged forward to greet her as she stood on a platform behind the steel gates of her former prison. Someone from the crowd handed her a flower, and she placed it in her hair – she was rarely seen in public without flowers adorning her tresses.

Aung San Suu Kyi tried to speak, but was drowned out by the din of the crowd chanting her name and singing Myanmar's national anthem. When the assembly finally calmed, she spoke without triumph or bitterness, but with humour and intimacy to those who regard her as Daw Suu (Daw meaning 'Aunt', being an honorific) or Amay Suu (Mother Suu):

'I have to give you the first political lesson since my release. We haven't seen each other for so long, so we have many things to talk about. If you have any words for me, please come to the [National League for Democracy] headquarters tomorrow and we can talk then and I'll use a loudspeaker.'

She was not under any illusions as to the challenges ahead. Indeed, she was painfully aware of the ethnic and political divides that had dogged Myanmar for generations: 'People must work in unison. Only then can we achieve our goal.'

Five years later to the day, on Friday, 13 November 2015, Daw Aung San Suu Kyi made her first significant step in achieving her aims when her party, the National League for Democracy (NLD), won 348 seats across Myanmar's two Houses of parliament, 19 more than the 329 needed for an absolute majority. While it was anticipated, the NLD's was a thumping victory. Aung San Suu Kyi was free to form a government, handpick a president and pass legislation. The half-century of military dominance of Myanmar's affairs was now at an end. And though the challenges of this complicated, verdant land remain, Myanmar's aspirations, and the hopes of her citizens, are once again vested in a leader of the people.

Seldom have a country's aspirations been more endowed upon one person than Aung San Suu Kyi in Myanmar. It is rare too that the mantle of a national hero father has fallen to his daughter rather than son, as it has with her. Doubtless, to understand Aung San Suu Kyi, one must understand her father, Aung San, father of the nation of modern-day Myanmar. Despite barely remembering Aung San – Suu Kyi was little more than two years old when he was assassinated – Aung San's place in her life and family lore has remained as powerful as it has in the nation's. She is, in a very real sense, fulfilling the destiny promised by her father.

Certainly, Suu has accepted her lot as her father's child with characteristic equanimity, and the same forbearance that has seen her prevail through decades of hardship. She has embraced it, rather than denied it or laid claim to her own, disparate identity. In an interview with Steven Erlanger of the *New York Times* published just as her political star first ascended, in January 1989, she stated, 'I don't pretend that I don't owe my position in Burmese politics to my father ... I'm quite happy that they see me as my father's daughter. My old concern is that I prove worthy of him.'

Doubtless, Suu Kyi's leadership qualities and determination are reminiscent of her father, not to mention her obvious physical resemblance. Her non-violent, conciliatory style, however, contrasts with Aung San's pragmatism as he steered his country toward independence during World War II. And her careful inflexions, her tutored English with its international accent borrows little from Aung San's forthright, even blunt, style.

Much of Suu Kyi's polish may be ascribed to her education and unofficial exile in the years after her father's death; Aung San's youthful lack of sophistication and poor English were challenges he worked hard to overcome. Her stout adherence to Gandhian non-violence, at any rate, owes much to a broad understanding of her country's history; an understanding garnered from decades of living abroad and observing her nation as an outsider, as it were.

Gandhian non-violence, though, is perhaps appropriate for Suu Kyi on more than just moral and practical grounds. Aung San died at a youthful thirty-five. It seems that in non-violence, the means by which she has overcome tyranny, Suu Kyi has faithfully continued her father's political evolution, cut cruelly short by the assassin's bullets. Aung San's last, successful efforts for Burmese independence after the carnage of World War II, involved campaigns of peaceful civil disobedience against the British.

By then, the mercurial leader had progressed from student revolutionary to anti-imperialist communist, head of Burma's army, then social democratic politician – a remarkable development, even in the crucible of war.

Underpinning Aung San's political activity throughout was unflinching patriotism, which was perhaps inevitable, given his heritage. His grandfather, Bo Min Yaung was a patriot who fought against the British annexation of the country with the Third Anglo-Burma War of 1885. Aung San's mother's uncle had been executed by the British for rebellion. And education was as much a family trait as nationalism; Aung San's ancestors were mostly scholars.

Aung San was born to U Phar, a lawyer, and his wife, Daw Suu, in Natmauk, Magway district, in central Burma, on 13 February 1915. After attending a Buddhist monastic school in his home town and Yenangyaung High School, on the western side of

Magway district, Aung San began his study in Rangoon University in 1933, where his eldest brother Ba Win had prepared his path.

In university, Aung San quickly showed his determination, mastering English as he cut his teeth with student politics. Aung soon became editor of the students union magazine, then president of both the Rangoon University Students Union and the All Burma Students Union, and later a leader of a group of revolutionary nationalist students.

When unrest on the nation's oilfields in 1938 resulted in a nationwide general strike, Aung was involved in an ill-fated student march in the capital, which ended when one of his colleagues was killed in a police baton charge. Aung himself was seriously injured. The civil unrest of this period was later to be glorified as 'Revolution 1300', 1300 being the year 1938 in the Burmese calendar – though ugly sectarian strife reared its head with clashes between Buddhists and Muslims.

Aung left Rangoon University in October 1938, and became general secretary of the Dohbama Asi-ayone (We Burmese) or Thakin Party. Aung, along with other nationalist compatriots, assumed the title of Thakin (lord and master), to signify self-determination for the Burmese people. This was an ironic act, because Englishmen insisted on being addressed as Thakin by the Burmese. The young nationalists intended to highlight that the title had been wrongfully appropriated by the British.

The Thakins would not be satisfied with mere symbolic gestures, however. Neither would they confine themselves to peaceful agitation, such as that championed by Gandhi in India. In August 1939, Aung San co-founded the Communist Party of Burma (CPB) with other Thakins. World politics was by then hurtling towards disaster. While war erupted in Europe on 1 September 1939, it had already raged in Asia for more than two years with the Second Sino-Japanese War. With Great Britain under siege as the German Luftwaffe pounded southern England, the Thakins resolved to seize this opportunity to wrest their homeland from the British Empire.

Aung and another Thakin, Hla Myine, secretly flew to Amoy, now Xiamen in Fujian province, China, in August 1940. There, they intended to elicit support for a Burmese uprising against the British from either the communists under Mao Zedong or the nationalist Kuomintang led by Chiang Kai-shek.

Fate was to lead them further east, to a more dangerous patron. Fujian had by that time fallen into Japanese hands, and a Japanese military spy by the name of Suzuki Keiji got wind of their mission. Aung and his companion were soon intercepted in Amoy and persuaded to fly, under the cover of arrest, to Tokyo in November 1940. There, they were offered the resources of the Japanese Imperial Army to 'liberate' their country from the British Empire.

That the two young Burmese nationalists – professed communists, no less – were quickly swayed to accept the fascist Japanese overtures, says as much of their commitment to ridding Burma of the British as it does of their naivety. Despite his misgivings about the Japanese's intentions, Aung San returned to Burma disguised as a Chinese sailor, and began recruiting for the new Burma Independence Army (BIA). What came to be known as the 'Thirty Comrades' of Thakins, spent much of the following year in rigorous training on the island of Hainan. Among them was Ne Win, the future military dictator of Burma.

The new army was soon to show its force. Aung Sun and his comrades joined the Japanese campaign to oust the British, leading a 50,000-strong force of recruits and irregulars, victorious into Rangoon in March 1942. The BIA was reorganized as the Burma Defence Army (BDA) under the Japanese and later renamed the Burma National Army (BNA), but was still headed by Aung San.

Aung San and the other Thakins, in any event, became swiftly disillusioned with the Japanese. Indeed, later accounts suggest they secretly resolved to evict them as early as 1942.

The source of their discontent was, as is common, broken promises. As a condition of their support of the Japanese invasion, the Thakins extracted an assurance from the Japanese high command that Burma be declared an independent state. A provisional government was to be formed when their combined forces took Moulmein (now Mawlamyine), the main trading centre and seaport in south-eastern Burma. The alliance was irreparably damaged, when after taking control of Moulmein on 31 January 1942, the Japanese refused to abide by their agreement. And despite a Japanese declaration of an independent Burma in August 1943, it was patently obvious that Japan intended that the country become independent in name only; that it remain a vassal state to the Empire of Japan.

Worse still was the treatment meted out to ordinary Burmese citizens by the Japanese forces. As an ardent follower of Aung San later explained to Field Marshal Sir William Slim, the British commander in the Burma theatre, 'If the British sucked our blood, the Japanese ground our bones!' By the time the war had ended, some 250,000 civilians had been killed. Some were killed in fighting, while others died from ill-treatment while they were in pressed service to the Japanese, building roads and railways. Many died from malnourishment and disease.

In the intervening years, Aung San played his hand adroitly, continuing to pay obeisance to the emperor of Japan while he bided his time. Ba Maw was declared head of state, and his cabinet included both Aung San as war minister and the communist leader Thakin Than Tun as minister of land and agriculture, as well as the socialist leaders Thakin Nu and Thakin Mya. Aung San went so far as to attend a ceremony in Tokyo in March 1944, where he was decorated by the emperor and promoted to the rank of major general. This, when in early 1943 he had secretly let his intentions of ousting his Japanese masters be known to Major Hugh Seagrim, a legendary British agent in hiding in rebel Karen territory in Burma.

The Japanese could only have suspected that moves were afoot against them. Aung San was bold enough on 1 August 1944 to speak publicly of his contempt for the Japanese brand of independence in Burma, and in the same month the Anti-Fascist Peoples Freedom League (AFPFL) was formed. Throughout, the Japanese forces were deployed to corral the major portion of the BDA forces around Rangoon and Mingaladon.

It was all to culminate in one of the most masterful political and military volte-faces of the century. Aung San asked the permission of the Japanese commander-in-chief to allow the Burmese forces to engage the allied paratroopers in the delta, which the commander granted with deep appreciation. On 17 March 1945, Aung San took a pledge with senior Japanese officers at Rangoon City Hall to fight the allies with the beleaguered Japanese forces. To the tune of a Japanese military band, Aung San's army marched out of the capital towards the front. Once in the countryside, however, the forces scattered and headed in the opposite direction, regrouping at prearranged locations in lower and central Burma. Ten days later, they launched a series of determined attacks on their former allies.

By this time, Aung San was married and had two sons. In the months after he had led his forces into Rangoon with the Japanese in March 1942, he had suffered from malaria, and was admitted for treatment and bed rest at Rangoon General Hospital. There, he met Ma Khin Kyi, a senior staff nurse. He was immediately taken by her firmness, her beauty and dignity – and she with his charisma. They were married on 6 September 1942. Around the same time, Khin Kyi's sister married the communist leader Thakin Than Tun. Aung San and Khin Kyi were soon blessed with a son, Aung San Oo ('Oo' meaning 'first') and then a year later, their second son, Aung San Lin.

Shortly after Aung San's forces' stunning defection from the Japanese cause, Khin Kyi, now heavily pregnant, made her way from Rangoon with her two young sons to Hmway Saung village on the Irrawaddy delta. She was disguised so as to avoid capture; the reprisals from the Japanese for Aung San's betrayal would perhaps have been horrific had she been apprehended. Surrounded by five of Aung San's most loyal troops, she took refuge in the village. Allied forces, with Burmese support, took Rangoon on 3 May, just hours before the onset of the monsoon, and an allied victory was a fait accompli.

On 19 June 1945, four days after Lord Louis Mountbatten staged an elaborate victory parade in Rangoon, Aung San and Khin Kyi's first daughter, Suu Kyi, was born in Hmway Saung village. Her name appropriately means, 'strange collection of bright victories'. Another daughter, Chit, was subsequently born, but died within a few days of her birth. Soon after Suu's arrival, Aung San sent Khin Kyi a note to tell her the capital was liberated, and she could return.

One of the more remarkable personal encounters of wartime leaders was that of Aung San and the British commander, Field Marshal Slim. Nearly two months after he had dramatically switched sides against the Japanese, on 16 May 1945, Bogyoke (Major General) Aung San paid a visit to Field Marshal Slim in Rangoon, dressed in his near-Japanese uniform, complete with sword. In a bold move, he announced to the startled British commander and his staff that he was, as leader of the AFPFL, entitled to status of an allied commander, and not that of a subordinate.

Slim could only have been astounded at Aung San's audacity. Only three years earlier, Aung San's forces had helped inflict a humiliating defeat on Slim's, hounding them all the way past the country's northern border. But there he was, demanding equality as an allied leader. Slim took a firm approach, telling Aung San that he was wanted for murder – he had personally executed a village headman for betrayal – and asked him if he thought he was taking a risk in visiting him and demanding equal treatment. Aung San replied, 'No. ... Because you are a *British* officer.' Slim could not help but laugh.

Impressed with his chutzpah, Slim was soon taken by Aung San's disarming candour. Slim then suggested that the only reason that Aung San's forces were now siding with the British was that they were winning, to which Aung San replied, 'It wouldn't be much good coming to you if you weren't, would it?'

It was this combination of directness, honesty and competence that made Aung San the Burmese people's natural choice as leader. In Suu Kyi's infancy, their post-war family home at 25, Tower Lane in Rangoon became the focus of all manner of political parleying and discussion. Bogyoke, as he was popularly known, was the heir apparent to lead the country's first independent government, and he was honest – brutally so – to the last. In February 1946, he told the British governor, Sir Reginald Dorman-Smith, 'How long does a national hero last? Not long in this country; they have too many enemies.' He went on to say that he only had eighteen months of life left, at best.

Aung San was remarkably prescient, but not the least fearful as he set about rebuilding his war-ravaged nation. He organized an All Burma Conference in January 1946, with participants from fifteen political parties and representatives from Burma's different ethnic groups in attendance. The Women's League was one of the participants. The conference passed eight resolutions, of which the fourth was that all men and women of eighteen years or above would have the right to vote. This allowed Burmese women to participate in politics equally with men for the first time.

Aung San's party won an overwhelming majority of 248 of 255 seats when it contested the elections for the Constituent Assembly on 9 April 1947. Little more than three months later, Aung San met his end. He was chairing a meeting in the Secretariat Building in Rangoon on 19 July 1947, when five men in fatigues, armed with automatic weapons, burst into the room. Aung Sun stood as the assassins opened fire, bullets ripping open his chest. Seven members of the governing council and one bodyguard were killed along with him, including his eldest brother, Ba Win, who was the interim minister of trade. The event would be commemorated in Burma as Martyr's Day, a national holiday on 19 July every year.

Less than a year before independence was granted, Burma had lost its founding father, and greatest hope for stability. U Saw, a bitter political rival and former prime minister, was later convicted and hanged for the murder. While there seems little doubt that U Saw ordered the assassination, rumours of British complicity persist, decades later: A certain Captain David Vivian was sentenced to five years' imprisonment for supplying guns and ammunition to U Saw, but later escaped.

Aung San's death was as devastating for his young family as for the fragile democracy he had fostered. Aung San had refused an army pension, which would have amply provided for his family. The outpouring of sympathy for her loss could do little to help her make ends meet, so Khin Kyi was forced to resume work, albeit in an administrative role. Suu Kyi and her brothers were cared for in her absence by servants in the Tower Lane family home.

While Khin Kyi was doubtless grief-stricken by the loss of her husband, she was not the type to allow herself to wallow in mourning. Suu Kyi later described her as a 'highly disciplined' perfectionist, who maintained her household with strictness as much as love. Suu Kyi's famous, upright posture was developed at home in her childhood. Her mother taught her children to not simply sit up straight at the dinner table: their backs must not even touch the chair. She would give her children deportment lessons, making them walk in the grounds of their home with their backs erect.

There was at least some consolation for the three children's loss of their father. Khin Kyi's father, a Christian convert, stayed with the family for the rest of his life, and he was a loving, indulgent grandfather – the perfect foil to a disciplinarian mother. Suu Kyi bonded strongly with him, and thus says she never felt the absence of a male figure in her childhood. And though Ma Khin Kyi was somewhat severe with her children, Suu recalls that she was always available for them while she was home. She made every effort to connect with them, to answer their questions, impart her knowledge of Buddhist practice and educate them.

Suu also shared a strong relationship with her brother Lin. Lin was only a year-older, and the two shared a room. He was adventurous and fun-loving, while their elder brother Oo was inclined to be remote. Lin showed her how to scale the building to the glass-walled pavilion atop the house, and the pair would whisper in their room at night before they slept.

Suu thus has mostly fond memories of her early years, aside from the tragedy which struck her family when she was nearly eight years old. On 16 January 1953, Lin drowned in a pond at their Tower Lane home, apparently while trying to retrieve his sandal from the mud.

Personal tragedy was to be a persistent theme in Suu Kyi's life, and the effect of this loss would be hard to quantify. Later in life, when she was faced with hardship or trouble, she would confide in her friend and assistant Ma Thanegi, 'Oh, how I wish Ko Ko Lin were here! He was so brave and clever, he would have made a great leader.' Lin's death left Suu feeling alone and isolated; feelings that surely characterized her later years of house arrest.

Her distant relationship with her eldest brother Oo, which has remained cool throughout their lives, was little consolation for her too. It was surely not helped by Suu's suspicion that Ma Khin Kyi favoured her son over Suu; a suspicion confirmed when Khin Kyi gave Oo a ruby ring Suu had long admired. Suu had to reconcile herself, just as so many women must, to the reality that she was second in her mother's affections to her brother.

After Lin's death, the family moved to a home donated by the government. U Nu, independent Burma's first prime minister, had already taken steps to ensure a suitable role was given to Khin Kyi – she was appointed director of the Women and Children Welfare Board and later chairperson of the Social Planning Commission and the Council of Social Services. He now saw to it that Bogyoke's family was suitably housed. A former merchant's villa, the home at 54, University Avenue, was decent by perhaps any standards, and it boasted a frontage to Inya Lake, the largest lake in Rangoon.

It is a sad irony that the property given to Suu Kyi's family in recognition of her father's contribution to the nation, that his surviving children would be well accommodated, would later serve as his daughter's prison.

For the time being, the University Avenue home would be where the young Suu would grow and learn. She attended first a private Catholic girls' school for her primary education, then the English Methodist High School, which was the institution of choice for the children of Rangoon's elite. Suu recalls being more inclined to 'running away and hiding instead of doing [her] lessons'.

She was a keen Girl Guide – Khin Kyi was the national founder of the movement, and Suu is remembered by her school friends, quite incongruously with the graceful woman the world now knows, as something of a tomboy. Early in her life, she felt the urge to follow her father's ways. Everyone referred to Aung San as Bogyoke, which means general, and she aspired to become a general herself. It was quite some disappointment to the young Suu to discover that the Burmese army had no place for women soldiers.

There was, of course, much learning for her otherwise. Her school was staunchly English, despite being enrolled with many former revolutionaries' children, and the students were forbidden to speak their mother tongue in all but the Burmese class. Children were also required to attend church, even though there was no pressure to convert to Christianity. For the young Suu, this exposure to Western culture and the rigours of the English language was ample preparation for the next phase of her life, and indeed her later political career.

As Suu Kyi grew into adolescence, the country her father had died for had descended into anarchy. During the war, the country suffered perhaps as much grievous loss as any in the Asia theatre, with horrific civilian casualties and its infrastructure laid waste by the Japanese and Allies' campaigns. In its wake, internal divisions were rife, and the one man who was dynamic and practical enough to lead this land of competing tribal, ethnic and religious groups had been killed.

Aung San's successor, the charismatic and charming U Nu, was hardly cut out for the role. Immediately following the war, he had eschewed politics for writing. As one of the few AFPFL leading lights to escape the assassination plot of 19 July 1947, he was thrust into the nation's leadership. The challenges in keeping peace alone were too much for him.

In 1948, an insurgency of the Karen, a people mostly from the hills bordering the eastern mountainous region and Irrawaddy delta of Burma, threatened to overthrow the government. Rebellions simmered not just with the Karen, but other ethnic groups, communist factions and some regiments in the army. Thakin Than Tun, Suu Kyi's aunt's husband and head of the Communist Party of Burma, took up arms and seized a large area in the Pegu Mountains north-east of Rangoon, with the support of Chinese communists.

Opposing forces from the exiled Kuomintang (nationalist) Chinese government were also a bane for the fledgling democracy in Burma. Driven from China by the victorious People's Liberation Army, Kuomintang forces had taken refuge in eastern Burma and established bases there. It was not until 1961, with Chinese government support, that the Kuomintang was finally evicted; driven back into neighbouring Laos and Thailand.

Throughout the post-war years, U Nu's government dithered and bickered. The AFPFL, which was at best a loose coalition of competing political and personal interests, splintered until, in 1956, it was returned to power with a humiliatingly diminished majority. U Nu resigned as prime minister, and left former prime minister, Ba Swe, to fill his shoes for some nine months while he set about rebuilding the AFPFL. When he resumed office, U Nu and Ba Swe fell out, and the AFPFL split into two factions: the Clean AFPFL under U Nu and the Stable AFPFL headed by Ba Swe.

U Nu barely survived a no-confidence motion of his own party on 8 June 1958. Beset by political intriguing, insurgency and with the nation's economy in tatters, U Nu asked the army chief of staff General Ne Win on 26 September 1958 to take office in a 'caretaker government'. Ne Win was sworn in as prime minister on 27 October 1958. In the subsequent February 1960 general election, U Nu's Clean AFPFL won a landslide victory over the Stable AFPFL. U Nu was returned to power, and renamed his party the Union Party.

The factional infighting, however, had done its damage. Written by the journalist Sein Win in the months after Ne Win had assumed power, the book *The Split Story – A Recent Account of Burma's Political History,* was scathing in its judgement of Burma's dominant political party:

> Division of the 'loot' had always been the cause of dissensions among the political parties and [the] AFPFL succumbed to this disease as early as in 1946. ... The main cause of the rift that rent asunder the AFPFL was personal feuds as a result of rivalry, jealousies, and distrust among the colleagues who, after long years of power, became intoxicated and succumbed to blind conceit and power corruption.

It seems General Ne Win was himself intoxicated by the power he held when he was prime minister. Elections were conducted in February 1960, and General Ne Win stood aside for the victorious U Nu on 4 April 1960. He plotted his return, though, and on 2 March 1962, seized control of the government in a coup d'état. U Nu was detained in an army camp outside Rangoon, which the new regime euphemistically described as 'protective custody'. The former prime minister, Ba Maw, President Mahn Win Maung and Justice U Myint Thein were likewise incarcerated.

Although the coup was described in the Western media as 'bloodless', there were at least two eminent casualties, and both were of royal extraction. Independent Burma's first president's seventeen-year-old son, Sao Mye Thaik, was shot dead, and Thibaw Sawbwa Sao Kya Seng, a highly regarded aristocrat and politician, disappeared mysteriously after being stopped at a checkpoint near Taunggyi. It was later reported Thibaw Sawbwa Sao Kya Seng had been killed.

While these murders were repugnant, it must be said that two killings in the commission of a coup d'état is fairly unremarkable, or even moderate, in a historical context. Burma has an unenviable history of political repression, spanning centuries before the upheaval of the post-war years. Indeed, an orgy of political killing indulged by the country's last monarch, Thibaw Min, provided the British some moral pretext for their conquest of Burma in the 1880s.

Ne Win seems to have wished to portray himself as a benevolent dictator when he took power, and at first largely confined himself to imprisoning and exiling his opponents. But with the onset of student protests in Rangoon University in July 1962, his approach changed dramatically. When police arrived in army jeeps and arrested peaceful student protesters on 7 July 1962, other students rushed to the scene, and skirmishes broke out between the police and the students. Tear gas failed to quell the unrest. Then, in a ghastly escalation of the violence, hundreds of troops from the No. 4 Burmese Rifles Battalion surrounded the campus, and opened fire on the unarmed students.

As many as one hundred students perished in just minutes, though the official figures count only fifteen fatalities. Somewhere in the order of 3,000 students was arrested. But Ne Win did not let it rest there. At dawn on 8 July 1962, the army dynamited the historic Rangoon University Students Union building, a symbol of Burmese nationalism ever since the anti-colonial struggle, and closely associated with the nation's father Aung San. Students, some of them wounded from the previous day's shootings, perished in the building.

Shortly afterwards, Ne Win delivered a five-minute speech on Burma's radio, in which he presented the incident as the work of a traitorous group of communist students. He concluded his speech with an ominous statement that would echo his later threats: 'If these disturbances were made to challenge us, I have to declare that we will fight sword with sword and spear with spear.' Never mind that the army fired thousands of rounds from automatic rifles, at students throwing stones and a few Molotov cocktails.

If there was any doubt as to the nature of the military regime before the brutal Rangoon University crackdown of 7 July, there would be none now. Ne Win demonstrated that he was prepared to risk public opprobrium in order to exert control over the populace and quell dissent. But while he was willing to clamp down on anyone who might cause unrest or annoyance to his dictatorship, Ne Win knew Khin Kyi posed a particular challenge to him.

Khin Kyi's assassinated husband was the most venerated man in Burma: virtually every town, at least with a sizeable ethnic Burman population, boasted its own 'Bogyoke Aung San' road or square. Portraits of the nation's dead hero abounded; he symbolized hope for the people, and his widow, an intelligent, forthright and articulate woman in her own right, could well do likewise in his stead. She had already proved her political mettle, briefly representing Aung San's erstwhile constituency, Lanmadaw in Rangoon in 1947–48, and in later campaigning for U Nu's Clean AFPFL.

Naturally, Ne Win could not afford to risk public outrage by taking action against Aung San's family overtly. Instead, well in advance of his coup, he had hatched a shrewd plan to neutralize Khin Kyi as a political force, while giving every appearance of honouring her. He engineered her appointment as Burma's first woman ambassador to India – indeed, the first Burmese woman in modern times in any ambassadorial post – in 1960. It may only be said that this was an appropriate position for her, given her talents and background, but her new role kept her well away from Burma's political scene. Thus began Aung San Suu Kyi's long, unofficial exile from her motherland.

Suu Kyi was fifteen-and-a-half when she and her mother left for India. In a sense, the timing of Khin Kyi's appointment was fortuitous: the young Suu had a good basic education, and was ready to expand her view of the world. In Delhi too she was in friendly surrounds: Prime Minister Jawaharlal Nehru had met Aung San in London, and the two great nationalist leaders shared a warm rapport. When Khin Kyi and Suu Kyi arrived in 1960, Nehru generously prepared one of his family bungalows for them: In Lutyens's erstwhile Delhi Imperial Zone, the bungalow at 24 Akhbar Road would temporarily be named 'Burma House'. Later, it would serve as the Congress party headquarters.

Ironically, while Ne Win was busy stripping Indian merchants of their wealth and expelling them from Burma, Khin Kyi and Suu Kyi were extended every courtesy by Nehru and the Indian government. Naturally, Nehru would have known of Khin Kyi's private opposition to Ne Win. Suu met Indira Gandhi, who would become prime minister later that decade, and struck up a lasting friendship with her son Rajiv, Indira's successor when she was assassinated in 1984.

Suu spent the final two of her high school years in a rather stern convent school run by Irish Catholic nuns of the Convent of Jesus and Mary. As with her earlier schooling, it was a strictly English-medium education, laced with Christian religious teachings and practice. Suu's school friend, Malavika Karlekar – Malavika and three others, Anjali, Kamala and Ambika, were Suu's constant companions – remembers her as being correct, obedient and strictly supervised by her mother. While it seems her trademark erect posture was well established by then, her friend rather surprisingly recalls the teenage Suu Kyi as somewhat plain in her school uniform and plaits. And at least for now, she was more inclined to a career in literature than politics.

After graduating from high school, Aung San Suu Kyi attended Lady Shri Ram College, which then was a fairly new college for humanities, exclusively for young women. There, despite her literary bent, she studied political science. However limiting this may have been, political science was perceived as the most suitable subject for women in the decade before feminism's rise in the West. Doubtless, it would stand Suu in good stead for her final career. In any event, the young Suu did not abandon her literary ambitions. Her creativity blossomed at Lady Shri Ram; she wrote plays and acted as she studied.

Given that Suu Kyi's education had been almost entirely in English, and her literary tastes were decidedly British – she read Jane Austen, George Eliot and Rudyard Kipling voraciously in her schooldays – it is perhaps unsurprising that she felt a strong urge to study in England. Delhi of the 1960s still nurtured some nostalgia for the British Raj too, and perhaps this was another factor in the lure of an English university education.

Suu thus only spent one year at Lady Shri Ram, and much of that year was spent applying for courses in England and preparing to move there. The British high commissioner Sir Paul Gore-Booth and his wife Lady Pat Gore-Booth happily agreed to act as her guardians in England. Suu would in time become like a daughter to the Gore-Booths, and it was through them she would meet her future husband.

Suu Kyi was accepted at St Hugh's College, Oxford, to study politics, philosophy and economics. Her first taste of Oxford was a shock for her, just as her arrival made quite a splash at St Hugh's.

It was 1964: miniskirts for women and long hair for men were de rigueur in fashionable circles, and The Beatles were topping the charts. The sexual revolution was just getting under way, and moral standards carelessly cast aside. Yet Aung San Suu Kyi seemed quite unaffected by the licentiousness of it all, and still dressed traditionally, in a *longyi* and *aingyi* (a wrap-around skirt and blouse). In the staunchly Anglo-Saxon world of Britain in the swinging sixties, Suu was exotic, beautiful – and unequivocally conservative.

Suu's college friends remember her as unshakeable in her moral convictions, just as they acknowledge her humour. When one asked her, 'Don't you want to sleep with anyone?' Suu replied, 'No! I'll never go to bed with anyone except my husband. Now, I just go to bed hugging my pillow.' Needless to say, her reply evoked a chorus of laughter from her more adventurous friends. Her almost puritanical streak was not simply of sexual mores, though. She exhibited already a strong sense of right and wrong in all areas of her life, and was forthright with her views, especially about her country.

She retained a powerful foundation of Buddhist philosophy too that could perplex her lecturers at times. When the distinguished philosopher Mary Warnock discussed John Locke's proposition that one is only the same person as that person whose past acts one can remember, Suu's rejoinder was enigmatic, but definite. She said, 'But I am my grandmother,' then smiled and refused to be drawn further on the issue. Of course, she was named for her paternal grandmother as well as her mother, but there was more to Suu's declaration than this.

Notwithstanding Suu's steadfast adherence to her beliefs, she was greatly changed in her first year at Oxford. Her friend Malavika had followed her from Lady Shri Ram in Delhi, and was amazed at Suu's transformation into a sophisticated woman at St Hugh's College. The plain ponytail was dispensed with, and in its place Suu wore her hair in a fringe, though still with her trademark jasmine pinned to her tresses. She sometimes wore skin-tight white trousers, and rode a chic Mouton bicycle with small wheels from the girls-only college to town and the main Oxford campus.

Not to be left out, Suu also partook of some rites of passage, but only in the most decorous manner. She indulged in the college tradition of going absent without leave at night at least once. While many of her more intrepid friends were attending risqué parties, Suu's outing was a respectable dinner date, after which her gentlemanly companion chivalrously helped her back into the college over the garden wall. There was never a more demure flouting of college regulations.

Suu once tried alcohol too, which was likely the most daring act of her time at St Hugh's. With some of her more worldly friends, she retired to the bathroom with a bottle of wine, and within moments had forsworn alcohol forever. It was, it seems, just a matter of curiosity for her.

While at St Hugh's, she took pains to learn to punt, which was an essential skill for an Oxford summer. But of all her experiences of those years, the most formative was not at Oxford. It was in a trip to see her family friend Dora Than E, who had been one of Burma's early singing stars. Ms Than E was working for the United Nations in Algeria, and Suu flew there to stay with her in the summer of 1965, shortly after Houari Boumédiène's deposing of the nation's president, Ahmed Ben Bella, in a cleverly orchestrated and bloodless military coup. Suu witnessed the suffering of the Algerian people, and spent some weeks labouring in a large relief camp. The experience was tangible, rather than the mere political theory she was studying at the time, and so much more compelling.

Back at Oxford, her study of politics, philosophy and economics, which was not her choice but her mother's to begin with, had lost its interest for Suu. She tried to transfer to forestry, which was her first choice, but this was rejected by the Oxford authorities, as was a later request to study English. Suu eventually graduated with a less-than-stellar third-class degree in 1967, which was more an indication of her lack of interest in her subjects than her intelligence.

Just as she was completing her degree, in the spring of 1967, Suu had the first of many unfriendly dealings with Ne Win and his regime. The dictator invited, or rather, summoned Suu and her brother Oo to his Wimbledon home for an audience; while his people languished in poverty, Ne Win enjoyed his overseas homes and a lavish lifestyle. Suu snubbed Ne Win, with the excuse that she had study for exams to attend to. Aung San Suu Kyi was already showing her independence and courage, even in her early twenties.

In the same year, Daw Khin Kyi retired from her ambassadorial post and returned to Burma. She had become increasingly estranged from the regime, and her wayward brother-in-law Than Tun's insurrection could only have complicated matters. However principled, her daughter's failure to accept Ne Win's invitation could not have helped her cause either. But Khin Kyi was fundamentally opposed to the hardship Ne Win was inflicting on their people anyway.

The government under Ne Win was imposing a bleak vision of socialism and autarky on Burma's people, and they were suffering. Industries and businesses, large and small, were nationalized, and the country lurched towards economic disaster. Ne Win's junta found myriad ways, direct and indirect, to suppress any kind of dissent. For Khin Kyi, this came in the form of a large tax bill on her ambassadorial salary when she returned to Burma, despite her meagre earnings being exempt from taxes.

After Suu left Oxford, she returned to the Chelsea home of the Gore-Booths, and found part-time work as a tutor and as an assistant to Hugh Tinker, a Burma scholar. Her time at the Gore-Booths was uneventful in terms of her career, but it was at their home that Suu met the love of her life.

Paul and Pat Gore-Booth had twins, David and Christopher. Christopher had a friend who was one of another pair of twins, Michael Aris, and on one of Michael's visits to Christopher's home, he met Suu.

Michael was a tall, genial academic; a student of Tibetan culture. In disposition, at least, perhaps the easy-going, kindly Englishman reminded Suu of her grandfather. For his part, Michael was immediately smitten with the beautiful, graceful young woman, and he and Suu began a delightful, old-fashioned courtship. While it seems Suu's feelings took a little longer to develop, they were no less intense than his. Indeed, decades later, Suu Kyi and Michael Aris's romance and marriage remain a testament of true love and lasting affection. Their relationship began with geographic separation – endured and grew stronger nonetheless – and finally, ended only with Michael's death, after years of enforced separation.

The couple's first time apart was on account of work. Michael, an expert on Tibet, was recruited to tutor the royal children in Bhutan. He was to remain in Bhutan for six years. Suu went to New York to stay with her surrogate aunt, Ma Than E, where she would turn down a university place in favour of a job at the United Nations. At the UN, Suu was to work in a junior capacity for her compatriot U Thant, the Secretary General of the United Nations. Michael and Suu kept their love alive with a continual flow of airmail letters; international telephone calls in those days were prohibitively expensive, and unreliable, anyway.

In the summer of 1970, Michael visited Suu in New York, and they were formally engaged. The following year, Suu visited Michael briefly in Thimpu, Bhutan, and in the ensuing eight months, she wrote no less than 187 letters to him. In one, she made one condition for their marriage, to which Michael readily acceded: 'I only ask one thing, that should my people need me, you would help me to do my duty by them. Would you mind very much should such a situation ever arise? How probable it is I do not know, but the possibility is there.' It was a request of which neither could have understood the import; Suu Kyi herself could not have comprehended the huge cost of her heritage to her marriage and children.

On New Year's Day 1972, the couple married in a Buddhist ceremony at the Gore-Booth's Chelsea home. Michael and Suu sat crossed-legged on a mat, and a Tibetan lama blew on a conch shell while guests wrapped sacred thread around the couple, solemnizing their marriage. Neither Khin Kyi nor Suu's brother Oo attended: they disapproved of Suu marrying an Englishman. All the same, nothing could stand in the way of the couple's happiness, and the Gore-Booths were only too pleased to act as a surrogate family for the bride.

The newly married couple flew out to Bhutan, where Michael continued his tutoring the royal children. Suu and Michael's sojourn there was perhaps more idyllic than any honeymoon: they lived for the rest of the year in Bhutan, enjoying regular treks through some of the world's most scenic mountain terrain. The king's chief minister gifted Michael and Suu a Himalayan terrier pup, which was appropriately named 'Puppy'. Puppy would remain a family fixture until late in the following decade. In August 1973, Suu discovered she was pregnant, and they decided to return to England. On 12 April 1973, their first son, Alexander was born; they gave Alexander a Burmese name alongside his English: Aris Myint San Aung, to honour his famous grandfather.

Soon after Alexander was born, Michael was asked to lead an academic expedition to northern Nepal, and the young family was away from England for a year. During this time, Suu and Michael took a trip to Burma to introduce their infant son to his grandmother. It was also Michael's first meeting with his mother-in-law.

Daw Khin Kyi was delighted to meet the infant Alexander, and equally pleased with her daughter's affable, learned husband; also impressed with his old-school English manners. On one occasion, she upbraided Suu for wanting to eat in Michael's absence. She reminded Suu that Michael always waited for her to return home before he ate, and prevailed upon Suu to do likewise.

Daw Khin Kyi was by now living a secluded life at the family's University Avenue home – not unlike that Suu would lead there in following decades, under house arrest. While Khin Kyi was not actively persecuted by Ne Win's regime, she surely felt exiled from public life, and rarely ventured beyond the home's gates. She was, nevertheless, a focal point for the politically disaffected who had managed to remain out of jail, and entertained a constant flow of visitors, bringing gossip of the latest intrigues.

Some, it seems, wished the redoubtable widow of Aung San to take a stand in national politics, but Khin Kyi was reluctant. Perhaps she was only too aware of the true character of the tyrant; the lengths to which he would go to maintain power. She must surely have known the truth of the rumour that Aung San had loathed his comrade-in-arms, enough to want him dead. Aung San had reportedly been disgusted at Ne Win's womanizing and excesses, such that during the war, he ordered one of his troops to kill him. It is said that decades later, the hapless soldier still bore the scars of his beating from Aung San, when he failed to carry out his mission.

Khin Kyi's trepidation was well founded. Burma was soon to discover that Ne Win's vindictiveness could not be assuaged, even by death – and the greatest of Burmese heroes would be given no quarter. Suu and Michael witnessed the denouement of one of Ne Win's vendettas while they were on a trip to stay with Khin Kyi in December 1974. It involved the corpse of Suu's former boss, and it sparked a national crisis – a period of bloodletting.

U Thant had retired as Secretary General of the United Nations in 1971, not long before Suu had left the organization to marry Michael. The first non-European to hold the highest office in the UN, U Thant was one of the most skilled diplomats of the twentieth century, and the most admired man in Burma. He came to prominence as Prime Minister U Nu's secretary and adviser, and was then appointed Burma's permanent representative to the United Nations in 1957. He was elevated to the organization's leadership after United Nations Secretary General Dag Hammarskjöld was killed in a plane crash in September 1961.

U Thant spent the following decade at the forefront of world affairs, and curiously, was admired at once by Soviet and US officials. By the time he died of lung cancer in New York on 25 November 1974, he had been conferred no less than two dozen honorary degrees, the Jawaharlal Nehru Award for International Understanding in 1965 and the Gandhi Peace Award in 1972. He would have received the Nobel Peace Prize too had its conferral on him not been vetoed by the chairman of the Norwegian Nobel Committee, Gunnar Jahn. That this most illustrious international diplomat, this man of peace's funeral was to become a flashpoint for violence, was truly, and bitterly, ironic.

Ne Win resented U Thant's success and prestige with the Burmese people. He had never forgiven U Thant too for U Nu's call for the overthrow of Ne Win's government in a press conference outside the UN in 1969, notwithstanding that U Thant had nothing to do with U Nu's address and was in Africa at the time.

Ne Win subsequently insisted that U Thant be considered an 'enemy of the state'.

In any event, when U Thant's coffin arrived on 1 December 1974 on a chartered flight to Mingaladon Airport, there were no government officials waiting, leave alone arrangements for a state funeral that would be usual for such an eminent citizen. Not even a hearse had been arranged for the coffin's transport. Only the deputy education secretary, U Aung Tin was present, but this was on account of his being a former pupil of U Thant.

The situation was to descend into a dangerous farce. An old Red Cross ambulance eventually took the coffin to the Kyaikkasan Grounds, a disused sports field, where it lay on uncut grass for thousands of ordinary people to pay their respects. On the following day, the state media announced U Thant's family had broken the law in their bringing the body to Burma, and made noises about legal action. After some toing and froing, permission was granted for a funeral on 5 December.

Many in the capital were outraged by the regime's disgraceful treatment of Burma's most eminent citizen, and the funeral became a flashpoint for more widespread anger. Disastrous mismanagement of the economy had already sparked social unrest, and August of that year had seen mass demonstrations. These were, naturally, savagely suppressed by the army. The regime's shameful behaviour towards its national hero again galvanized students and disaffected citizens into action.

On the day of the funeral, a crowd of students gathered. After the Buddhist rites were completed, a group of them commandeered the coffin, taking it on a truck to Rangoon University, with thousands marching behind. They kept the coffin in the dilapidated convention hall until the government offered a compromise: There would be a public, but not state funeral, and the coffin would be interred at the foot of Shwedagon Pagoda.

But just as the coffin was to be transported, students hijacked it again, and took it to the site of the former students union building, where they buried it.

After a stand-off, Ne Win responded with force. Troops surrounded the university and lobbed tear gas grenades, then fired live rounds at the students – just as they had done twelve years earlier, in the first months of his regime. After hundreds of students had been killed and the rest rounded up and detained, the military exhumed the coffin, which was reburied at the foot of Shwedagon Pagoda, one of Buddhism's most sacred sites. Martial law was quickly declared in Rangoon and Mandalay. Bizarrely, Ne Win then saw fit to embark on a purge of Western culture, with a slew of bans targeting Western fashions, especially jeans, and long hair for men.

At the time Suu, Michael and Alexander were in Rangoon, on one of their regular visits to see Ma Khin Kyi. In the midst of the unrest, Suu was summoned for an audience with officials of Ne Win's Burma Socialist Programme Party (BSPP), who asked her if she planned to get involved in 'anti-government activities'. With trademark prudence and calm, Suu replied that as long as she was living outside the country, she would never become involved in Burmese affairs. The officials seemed satisfied by her assurance; at least for now.

Back in the UK, Suu devoted herself to her young family, at first in a cottage in Sunninghall, just outside Oxford, and then, in 1977, a cottage near Suu's old college in Oxford. Michael worked on a small stipend from Oxford University, studying his PhD on the historical foundations of Bhutan. In 1977, Suu and Michael's second son was born. They named him Kim, for the adventurous character of Rudyard Kipling's novel that Suu had loved as a teenager.

In these years, Suu adopted a more-or-less traditional role at home, which seems somehow at odds with the resolute, independent character the world would later come to admire. She ran the home with a discipline reminiscent of her mother's when Suu was a child, and seemed proud of her role as a mother and homemaker, despite her feminist friends' misgivings.

She was not the least oppressed, though. Suu's competence in running the household was deeply appreciated by Michael, who seemed quite content for her to have her will. A big-hearted gentleman, Michael knew that he relied heavily on his wife, and never seemed to contradict her.

Michael had every reason to appreciate Suu. She cooked nutritious meals on a budget, and ironed all Michael's clothes – even his socks. She found every means to economize, as Michael's fellowship was barely adequate to support the family. Suu bought fabric at sales, carefully tailoring dresses for herself, and instead of buying drapes, stitched her own. Friends in Oxford recall her in those years, riding her bicycle home, loaded with vegetables and groceries in plastic bags; she and Michael could not afford to run a car.

In a sense, these straightened circumstances prepared Suu Kyi well for the privations she would suffer later under the military regime in Burma. She resolutely maintained her family's dignity in Oxford, and gave every appearance of style, while she and Michael were often down to their last few pounds.

After Michael obtained his doctorate in 1978 and subsequently received a full fellowship at Oxford's Wolfson College, the family's financial challenges eased, and the family moved into their home in Park Town, in central North Oxford. The boys were growing up, and Suu began to ponder her future beyond that of a homemaker. She evidently enjoyed her time as a stay-at-home mother, but there came a time when this hardly seemed sufficient for her. She confided her frustration to a friend, Ann Pasternak Slater: 'Is this my destiny, to be a housewife, the partner of an Oxford don?'

Far be this a confession of resentment toward Michael's career achievements. Indeed, Suu happily took it upon herself to help Michael with his work, and co-edited one of his books. It was simply that her creative energy needed an outlet, beyond that of her family duties. Her feelings are familiar to many intelligent, competent women, whose children have grown beyond needing their undivided attention.

Suu's first career moves after marriage were to fulfil her old ambition to write. She penned three children's books, about Burma, Bhutan and Nepal, then dedicated herself to writing a short biography of her father, which was published by the University of Queensland Press in 1984. She took a part-time job in Oxford's Bodleian Library, then decided to engage in study again, enrolling in a one-year course to prepare for an MPhil degree in Burmese literature at SOAS, the School of Oriental and African Studies, University of London. While at SOAS, she obtained a research fellowship offered by the Centre for South-east Asian Studies, at Kyoto University in Japan. There, in the 1985–86 academic year, she would study Burma's independence movement.

The fellowship was to be a watershed experience for Aung San Suu Kyi, for through academic study, she would come to terms with her relationship with her father as much as her country. In an interview years later, Suu made mention of the intrinsic nature of her relationships with her father and the Burmese nation: 'When I was young, I could never separate my country from my father, because I was very small when he died ... So even now it is difficult to separate the idea of my father from the concept of my country.' And like Aung San more than four decades earlier, her sojourn in Japan would propel her inexorably towards her destiny in Burma.

Curiously, Suu described herself in her Japanese visa application not as a scholar or a writer, but a housewife. Decades later, it seems almost incomprehensible that one of the world's most famous leaders, an icon to millions across the globe and a paragon of women's empowerment, would ever have described herself a housewife.

Anyhow, with an eight-year-old Kim in tow, Suu Kyi travelled to Kyoto, while Michael and Alexander also flew east, to Shimla in Himachal Pradesh, where Michael was to undertake a two-year fellowship at the Indian Institute of Advanced Studies. The family would unite in the holidays.

Suu and Kim stayed in International House, Kyoto University, where Suu came in contact with Burmese students. Her encounter with them was perhaps as powerful an experience for Suu as her study of Burmese nationalism. The students' reverence for her and their expectation that she could contribute to their nation inspired her, and bolstered her determination to return to Burma.

Another incident at this time fired her moral indignation, and that too would drive her back to her homeland. Ne Win's regime was watching Suu from afar: it appears that Ne Win perceived Aung San Suu Kyi a potential threat, well before she entered Burma's political arena. When one of the students Suu had befriended, Koe-chan returned to Rangoon, he was surrounded by soldiers at the airport and arrested. They purportedly discovered a pistol in his luggage – a mildly ridiculous imposture to incriminate him, it seems, on account of his association with Suu Kyi. Koe-chan, a promising young PhD student, was sentenced to seven years' imprisonment in Insein Prison.

The knowledge that Koe-chan had suffered on her account gnawed at Suu, even after she left Japan and was reunited with Michael and Alexander in Shimla. While she had left Japan to freedom and academic accomplishment – she and Michael were fellows of the Indian Institute of Advanced Studies in Shimla – Koe-chan had returned to Burma to languish in jail. The episode played on her mind after their return to England in September

1987, and hardened Suu's resolve against Ne Win's military junta. She had already been encouraged by many, such as the librarian Ko Myint Swe, to help her country. It was only circumstances now that stood in Suu's way of fulfilling her destiny as her father's child.

Other circumstances would soon present themselves; a coincidence of unfortunate situations, that would draw Suu Kyi back from exile and on to the centre stage of Burma's affairs.

It began with a telephone call in late March 1988. Suu, Michael and the boys were about to retire for the night in their North Oxford home – the boys were to go school the following morning – when they received a call from an Anglo-Burmese family friend they called Uncle Leo. Uncle Leo bore terrible news: Daw Khin Kyi had suffered a severe stroke, and was in a critical condition in Rangoon General Hospital. Suu must come at once.

Michael wrote later of that night, 'I had a premonition that our lives would change forever.'

Suu Kyi returned to a family crisis, and a nation in turmoil. General Ne Win and his junta's incompetent and sometimes outright bizarre management of Burma's economy had beggared the nation and impoverished its people. Particularly outlandish was Ne Win's demonetization of currency, and subsequent cancelling, on 5 September 1987, of all 100, 75, 35 and 25 kyat notes, leaving only 45 and 90 kyat notes. Ne Win's diktat was at least partly due to the latter's divisibility by nine, the dictator's favoured number. It was, in any event, unsuccessful in curbing black market activity, the official rationale for the currency cancellation. Burmese citizens reeled under this folly, as much of their savings were immediately wiped out.

The government also issued a decree in December of that year requiring farmers to sell their produce below market rates, so as to increase government revenue. Violent protests in rural areas ensued in the following months. Decades of economic mismanagement had reduced Burma to the status of least developed country, and unchecked corruption at all levels of government rankled with even the most tolerant of Burma's citizens. The absence of any means of redressing people's grievances also fanned discontent; judicial posts were monopolized by Ne Win's cronies, BSPP loyalists.

By the time Suu Kyi arrived to tend her ailing mother, widespread unrest had gripped the nation. After student-led protests in Rangoon in March 1988 were suppressed brutally – as many as two hundred and eighty-two students were killed – the government announced the closure of universities for several months.

At first, the students led the protests – as they almost invariably did in Burma – but the protests were quickly joined by ordinary Burmese people, across ethnic divides. The ranks of students and activists were swelled by lawyers, government workers, Buddhist monks, navy and air force personnel and hospital workers, and the protests fanned out from the capital to regional centres. Demonstrators demanded the abolition of the one-party BSPP monopoly, and multiparty free elections. The regime of the BSPP was under siege, shocked at the scale of the protests. Ne Win was also undermined for the first time, by a highly critical open letter from his former number two, Brigadier General Aung Gyi.

Throughout these months of unrest, Suu Kyi stayed by her mother's side, even sleeping next to her in the hospital. She needed to be with Daw Khin Kyi. The hospital system was in a parlous state, and though treatment was in theory free, the patient's families were forced to provide their own dressings, medicines and the like. Suu Kyi wasn't, however, insulated from the upheaval in Rangoon. While tending to her mother, Suu was deeply moved at the sight of injured protestors in the hospital.

Daw Khin Kyi, at any rate, was partially paralysed by her stroke, and when in July, doctors concluded there was nothing they could do for her, she was discharged to Suu's care at 54, University Avenue. She was to spend her final days bedridden, downstairs in the study, now converted to a sick room. The only lightness to this dark time, as Suu awaited the inevitable, was the arrival of Michael and the boys on 22 July.

The day after this happy reunion saw a peculiar performance by the military strongman Ne Win, who was now in his late seventies. On 23 July 1988, the general convened an extraordinary congress of the BSPP. Before the 1,000 delegates, the aging tyrant gave a rambling televised address, in which he proposed a referendum for the introduction of multiparty democracy, and committed to relinquish power, along with five of his most senior office-bearers. It seemed that twenty-six years of totalitarian government in Burma would soon end. Ne Win's speech concluded with menace, however. He warned that 'if in future there are mob disturbances, if the army shoots, it hits – there is no firing in the air to scare'.

Suu Kyi watched General Ne Win's address on the television at 54, University Avenue, and she was thrilled. For the first time in more than a generation, there was hope for the Burmese people's self-determination. But if she and the protestors were elated at the prospect of the military handing over the reins of power to a democratically elected government, and 'old man' Ne Win and his henchmen retiring quietly, they were soon to be disappointed. Just as quickly as he had made his shock announcement, Ne Win installed his key loyalist Sein Lwin, known widely as 'the butcher', as party head and president.

Sein Lwin had long been unpopular with the Burmese people, and beyond being fiercely loyal to Ne Win, was a strange choice for president. He was implicated in the July 1962 student massacre at Rangoon University, and as commander of the security force riot police (Lon Htein) was ultimately responsible for the killing of students just months before Ne Win's address. Indeed, a group of students was shot, beaten and drowned by riot police in Inya Lake, on the shore adjacent to Daw Khin Kyi's home on 16 March, and forty-one more died in custody after riot police stormed Rangoon University and arrested scores of students the following day.

Ne Win's ploy to exert his influence from behind the scenes through Sein Lwin was transparent, and provoked a new wave of protests. The dictator had misjudged the people's mood: buoyed at the prospect of free elections, the Burmese public was enraged at the mere prospect of being governed by 'the butcher'.

Massive street demonstrations ensued, first in Rangoon, then in other regional cities, culminating in a general strike on 8 August 1988. The date was significant, because in Burmese tradition, the number eight is propitious, and the protests of 1988 would later be referred to as the 8888 Uprising. It was also the fiftieth anniversary of a general strike led by militant students, among whom was none other than Aung San.

Despite hundreds already dying in volleys of fire from security forces in the preceding weeks, the protest and strike received widespread support. It began at precisely eight minutes past 8 a.m. on 8 August 1988, when dock workers at Rangoon port marched off the job. Hundreds of thousands of people from all walks of life then marched on Rangoon City Hall, flouting the regime's declaration of martial law.

Despite a large police and army presence and continued warnings over loudspeakers, the demonstrators descended on Shwedagon Pagoda. A 2,500-year-old holy Buddhist monument in Rangoon, the gilded pagoda has remained a focal point in the capital throughout the ages, and contains enshrined relics, including strands of hair of the Buddha himself. Around the pagoda, and in the streets of the city, the demonstrators remained, in an almost festive mood, for the duration of the day and into the evening.

The joy of the event was to be short-lived, and 8 August 1988 was to become one of the darkest days of post-independence Burmese history. At 11.30 p.m., tanks, armed personnel carriers and two dozen army trucks moved out into the streets, firing live rounds at anyone with callous, murderous intent. By the time the city was quiet at 3 a.m., somewhere between 1,000 and 3,000 Burmese lives had been extinguished.

Predictably, international opprobrium followed, with the US Senate passing a unanimous motion condemning the regime's actions. Under pressure from his compatriots as much from abroad, Sein Lwin resigned on 12 August, and was succeeded briefly by Dr Maung Maung.

Until this time, the uprising seemed uncoordinated; a spontaneous, grass-roots movement. Soon, however, student activists looked for leadership from senior figures in Burmese society, not tainted by association with the government. It was only natural that they would approach Aung San Suu Kyi.

For her part, Suu Kyi had not joined the demonstrations, although she was most sympathetic to the cause of Burmese democracy; 'It's not my sort of thing,' she would later say. She was also occupied in nursing her dying mother, and looking after her sons, who would only leave Burma to return to school the following month. Within days of the 8 August bloodbath in Rangoon, though, she was approached by student representatives, who asked her to lead the protest movement.

Suu Kyi was at first reluctant, but then agreed to open a small office in the dining room of her house, where a group of students and activists would meet to discuss strategy. Meanwhile, in a move which perhaps speaks more of her commitment to non-violence than it does of political naivety, she privately held out an olive branch to the council of state, a coterie of Ne Win's generals. She wrote a letter to the council, asking that a 'people's consultative committee' be formed 'to present the aspirations of the people in a peaceful manner, within the framework of the law.' The proposal was endorsed by U Nu, the last democratically elected leader of Burma.

Needless to say, the letter did not receive even a cursory acknowledgement from the council, and Aung San Suu Kyi was drawn inexorably into the intrigues, factionalism, treachery and outright danger of Burmese politics.

Her entry to Burmese political life was a brief, humble beginning – a speech at Rangoon General Hospital, which she delivered from atop a steel petrol drum. She looked confident and stunning in a white blouse, and promised to speak at Shwedagon Pagoda two days later.

The daughter of the father of the nation had made her opening gambit, and the regime acted quickly and disgracefully. Propaganda leaflets were immediately printed and distributed, some depicting Suu and Michael pornographically. The leaflets referred to her as a 'genocidal prostitute', and told her to leave the country with her 'bastard foreigner' husband.

If regime figures meant to dissuade her, they were to be sorely disappointed. The leaflets served only to publicize her opposition to the government, and may even have hardened people's disgust for it.

On 26 August 1988 at 8.30 a.m., Suu and her entourage of eleven vehicles set out for her debut proper in Burmese public life. The scale of public expectation was evident from the moment they left. Shwedagon Pagoda was little more than 4 kilometres from Suu Kyi's University Avenue family home, but through packed crowds that had gathered in anticipation of her arrival, it took no less than forty-five minutes to reach there.

A crowd of monks flanked the stage, giving their moral imprimatur to the event. The expectation was palpable. The audience was captivated, as curious about the daughter of Aung San as they were passionate for political change. Many were unsure how she would speak – after all, she had spent all but a few months here in the preceding thirty years, and she had never before spoken to a public gathering, leave alone one numbering perhaps a million.

The people were not to be disappointed. Aung San Suu Kyi spoke clearly, calmly and in perfect vernacular Burmese, declaring the people's 'unshakeable desire to strive for and win a multiparty democratic system'. She held aloft a file, and from her father's text, read, 'We must make democracy the popular creed,' that is, she affirmed, ' ... the only ideology which is consistent with freedom.' The crowd erupted with applause, and by the end of her speech, was chanting her name. If there were any doubts as to her nerve, oratory or charisma, these were now swept away with the people's adulation.

Curiously though, Suu Kyi did not attempt to capitalize on her success at Shwedagon Pagoda in the days that followed, and still expressed her reluctance to enter politics. She did, however, make appeals to the army to return to barracks, and made efforts wherever she could to avert mob violence.

Indeed, while there was some danger of Burma slipping into anarchy, with sporadic mob lynchings of government agents and BSPP stooges, people began to self-govern. Monks were seen in central Mandalay directing traffic, and in other parts organizing rubbish collection. Martin Moreland, the British ambassador who befriended Michael and Suu during the 1988 Uprising, later recalled, 'The city of Rangoon, and indeed the whole country, ran disturbingly smoothly without "Big Brother".'

Still, there was no cogent voice of the people: more than a generation of exiling, jailing and harassing dissidents and outlawing any political party other than the ruling BSPP had left the country without any organized opposition. The former prime minister, U Nu, invited derision by claiming that he was the legitimate, elected leader of the country, despite having been out of power for some twenty-six years. And although other prominent dissidents threw their support behind the pro-democracy cause, there was no pre-eminent figure to lead the people's movement.

The regime was eerily quiet too with the government machinery all but still in the days following Aung San Suu Kyi's speech. There were disturbing signs, however, that the army was preparing for a counteroffensive. On the day of her speech, truckloads of soldiers arrived at the Myanmar Foreign Trade Bank and commandeered a hoard of 600 million kyats – enough to pay the army for several months.

At any rate, the putative leader of Burma, President Maung Maung, was himself ready to fall on his sword. He conceded publicly on 13 September that the BSPP 'lacked the experience of making sacrifices, taking risks and working hard to overcome difficulties'. It seemed the junta's fall was inevitable, and Michael exulted to his family that 'the final cracks in the edifice of this monstrous regime are appearing'. He hoped, he informed family members in a faxed message, to be able to bring the boys back to Burma for Christmas.

Read all these decades later, it is hard not to be touched by Michael's optimism, made all the more poignant by the sadness that was in store for him, Suu and their boys.

In hindsight, it is clear that matters could never be so simple. The military, still headed by Ne Win in all but title and name, had much to lose under a civil dispensation. Power, position and corrupt fortunes had been amassed under the BSPP. Rather than the ostensible leadership of Burma, it was the armed forces (Tatmadaw) – or more, the leadership of the armed forces – that was the obstacle to political reform.

There is a curious obverse to Aung San Su Kyi's story, and it is one rarely emphasized. While Aung San Suu Kyi was contemplating her future involvement in Burmese politics, another daughter of a former leader had already been deeply involved with politics for nearly a decade, and was plotting her next move. Sandar Win, Ne Win's favourite daughter, was deeply involved in affairs of state and political manoeuvring throughout the 1980s.

As Ne Win aged, he began to rely heavily on Sandar, who became increasingly powerful by controlling access to her father. She was instrumental in the appointment of Colonel Khin Nyunt, who would later serve as prime minister, as chief of intelligence in the early 1980s. She could thus exert considerable indirect influence in subduing political rivals and tyrannizing dissidents.

Sandar Win would become Aung San Suu Kyi's foil in the drama that would unfold in the later months of 1988. And just as Ne Win, with his womanizing and corruption, contrasted with the monogamous and principled Aung San, the two prominent daughters could barely have differed more. Sandar Win wielded considerable power in the regime, yet had little or no appreciable public backing, whereas Aung San Suu Kyi commanded massive grass-roots support, but had no influence in the regime beyond respect for her father. And while Aung San Suu Kyi was educated in English and had an innate ability to communicate with the masses and international figures alike, Sandar Win's poor English had hampered her study abroad, and was more inclined to rely on her power as the daughter of the nation's most powerful man.

A popular joke of those years had Sandar Win challenging Aung San Suu Kyi to a duel on the street. The pacifist Suu Kyi declined, saying, 'Instead, let us both walk down the street together unarmed, and see which one of us gets to the other end alive.'

Curiously enough, both daughters of Burma's leaders would suffer the state's wrath, though to vastly differing degrees.

In any event, Sandar Win, Colonel Khin Nyunt and other proxies for Ne Win in the regime plotted in the days following Aung San Suu Kyi's watershed speech. On 18 September, in the face of a likely mutiny in the armed services – a number of soldiers had openly marched with protestors, and some 150 airmen gone on strike – what became known as the State Law and Order Restoration Council (SLORC) was formed.

The acronym of this military council was almost laughably redolent of a thriller's evil secret service, perhaps like SMERSH of the James Bond series, but it was no joking matter. Under the head of the armed forces, General Saw Maung, SLORC took power, and it would unleash a wave on terror on the Burmese people, perhaps to surpass even the earlier excesses of Ne Win under the BSPP.

SLORC immediately imposed martial law, and abolished all judicial institutions in the country. Meetings of more than four people were outlawed and arrangements for arrest, sentencing and incarceration of citizens without trial affirmed. Bizarrely, SLORC allowed political parties to form – provided, of course, that they did not hold meetings!

Late on Sunday, 18 September, SLORC quelled demonstrations in Rangoon with shocking military force. Hundreds of armoured personnel carriers with Bren guns and army trucks made their way through Rangoon's streets, troops engaging some protestors in largely one-sided street battles, and casually mowing down others simply for daring to be on the streets. Somewhere in the order of one thousand pro-democracy protestors perished in the following day.

Aung San Suu Kyi was menaced that day too with dozens of soldiers taking up positions outside her University Avenue home, along with a .275 calibre machine gun, and the telephone lines of the home were cut. With characteristic composure, Suu Kyi did not flinch at the loud gunfire in the background, and enjoined her student retinue not to fight, but let her be arrested if forces came to detain her. As the army tightened its grip on the capital and in the regional cities, some 10,000 pro-democracy activists, fearing reprisals, fled to areas held by the Karen rebels near the Thai border. Some later even joined the Karen insurgency.

Suu Kyi would not be moved, nor would she veer from her path of non-violence. On 24 September, with a select group of former army officers and eminent dissidents, she formed the National United front for Democracy, which was soon renamed the National League for Democracy (NLD). Suu Kyi became the general secretary, with former generals Aung Gyi and U Tin Oo assuming the roles of chairman and vice chairman respectively. The central executive committee of the party included veteran journalist U Win Tin, Kyi Maung, a former army officer and Daw Myint Myint Khin, a woman barrister and the head of the Rangoon Bar Association. The party's red flag was emblazoned with a golden 'fighting peacock', which Suu Kyi preferred to be known as the 'dancing peacock'.

Almost immediately, Aung San Suu Kyi's international education, her polished communication and experience in the United Nations came to the fore. She contacted foreign ambassadors, asking that their governments condemn the military's violence against unarmed civilians, including students, children and Buddhist monks. She also made a plea to Amnesty

International to raise the matter at the United Nations General Assembly debate on 27 September.

Next, Suu ran the gauntlet, embarking with her entourage on 30 October, on the first opposition political party campaign in more than a quarter-century. In the following months, she made several tours of the country, speaking at meetings in contravention of SLORC's law against public assembly. Often, huge crowds, thousands of people, turned out to see the daughter of Bogyoke speak. They were not disappointed. Suu Kyi spoke simply and directly, appealing to the people in an often light-hearted manner: ' ... you haven't got a head to nod with – you've been nodding for twenty-six years. The head is there for you to think!'

The admiration Aung San Suu Kyi attracted throughout her tours bordered on hero worship, and was perhaps akin to that experienced by pop stars and cinema actors. Sometimes, it seemed she might be harmed by overenthusiastic supporters, who thrust flowers at her and sprayed her with perfume – often directly into her face. But while she travelled with a group of loyal students she referred to as her 'boys' to protect her, she underwent the rigours and discomforts of the road with them, refusing out-of-turn luxury when it was offered.

At first, the SLORC military junta, which was controlled from behind the scenes by Ne Win and his family, seems to have hoped that the pro-democracy movement would simply peter out. Accustomed to meeting dissent with force, it was nonplussed by Suu Kyi's steadfast adherence to peaceful protest – and her obvious appeal to Western diplomats and media. For the most part, it confined itself in the early days of the NLD, to surveillance; Suu Kyi's speeches and public events were attended religiously by police in plain clothes and government agents.

It seems that the regime also made efforts to sabotage the NLD from within. The former general Aung Gyi, whose initial support for the NLD was crucial, began to undermine the party, by downplaying Aung San Suu Kyi's importance and claiming that it had become infiltrated by communists. Aung Gyi was ousted from the leadership by a committee vote on 3 December, and left the party with a number of former military supporters. Several commentators have suggested that Aung Gyi may have been a regime stooge. But despite causing some disturbance by offering party positions for generous donors and slandering the leadership, he could not derail the NLD's popular campaign.

There were some wild accusations from the regime too, some of which discredited those who levelled them more than their targets. Ludicrously, Khin Nyunt claimed that the communists had intended Daw Khin Kyi to lead the 1988 protest movement – this, while the poor lady had lain stricken in bed since March! In any event, on 27 December, Daw Khin Kyi died at the age of seventy-six, after months at death's door.

Against the backdrop of army atrocities, Khin Kyi's funeral was a powder keg. Violence could very well have eventuated, just as it had at U Thant's funeral more than fifteen years earlier, but for Suu's calls for calm. With her leadership, the 100,000-strong assembly of mourners gave Khin Kyi a dignified farewell. The regime too conducted a ceremony worthy of Bogyoke's widow; General Saw Maung and the intelligence chief Khin Nyunt even visited Suu Kyi at University Avenue to offer their condolences on the evening before the funeral. The strained civility between Aung San Suu Kyi and Burma's military junta, however, could not last.

Aung San Suu Kyi's mother's passing away was a defining time for her politically as much as personally. For the Burmese people, she was now the senior-most member of Aung San's family: her older brother Oo had emigrated to the US in 1973 and showed little interest in Burmese affairs; her commitment to her nation demonstrated she was Bogyoke's worthy heir. And for the regime,

Daw Khin Kyi's death left no illusions as to Suu Kyi's commitment to her country: The lady was here to stay.

In the months that followed, Suu Kyi continued her campaign, touring the countryside. The NLD's reception by the local authorities varied greatly in these months, depending on the inclination and whims of the officer in charge of the district. In places, the army seemed least concerned by the public gathering – one officer even left a message that he had gone fishing, and left Suu Kyi and her NLD cadre completely untroubled by any army presence. At other times, it seemed that the army were preparing to engage a hostile military force rather than an academic, middle-aged woman with a student retinue, who had arrived simply to speak.

In one instance in Bassein, a port town, the NLD group found the streets blocked with sandbags and barbed wire, and the harbour blocked. The townspeople had been menaced, instructed at gunpoint to remain indoors. The Irrawaddy division commander, Brigadier Myint Aung, was particularly affronted by the NLD's presence in the town, and even ordered the group's vehicles impounded. Suu Kyi was unfazed, and even walked calmly into the street from the house where she stayed for the night, and chatted with the soldiers. Her personal charm seemed to break the deadlock.

Charm and good grace were very much a part of Suu Kyi's appeal to the masses. She was at pains to wear ethnic dress to events, which delighted the ethnic minorities, who were often bitterly opposed to the government to begin with.

Her unmistakeable resemblance to her father also had its effect. The people of Burma were thrilled to discover in those months that Aung San Suu Kyi not only looked like her father, she even sounded like Bogyoke Aung San. At their first meeting, U Tin Oo, the former commander-in-chief of the armed forces of Burma whose support in the executive was crucial in the NLD, saw her as a 'female replica' of the great man he had served under as a youth. The people were soon to discover too that along with physical traits, Aung San Suu Kyi had inherited her father's courage.

In the village of Danubyu, on 5 April 1989, the bloodshed that had overtaken the country in the name of 'law and order', very nearly claimed its most famous victim. The village was under the jurisdiction of the infamous Brigadier Myint Aung, and the officers in charge met Suu Kyi and the NLD group with rifles at the ready in front of the NLD office. A certain Captain Myint U forbade the planned meeting in the village, and as their group of perhaps eighty people left, soldiers were ordered to load their weapons and aim at the group. The NLD were not only forbidden from public assembly: they were, it seems, not even allowed to walk away in a group. Aung San Suu Kyi was untroubled by the threat, saying to one of the troops, 'Hey, they are telling you to load, aren't you going to do it, soldier?'

The situation was quickly defused when the group boarded boats on the river to go to outlying villages. But when they returned, a soldier tried to stop them disembarking, and after they landed on the jetty anyway, a military policeman ordered them not to walk on the road. Suu ignored the order, and proceeded with her group along the road. To her, as to any reasonable observer, this was senseless bullying – plain and simple. She continued at the front of the procession, with a young activist carrying the NLD red flag, emblazoned with its fighting peacock.

In seconds, the situation escalated. An army jeep stopped ahead of the group. Several soldiers alighted and levelled their guns directly at Aung San Suu Kyi and her supporters. Captain Myint U walked towards the group, gesticulating and shouting at them to get off the road. Suu Kyi responded by asking her people to walk along the sides of the road, which they did. The captain was not the least mollified by this partial backdown. He threatened to open fire on them, even as they walked on the sides of the road. It seemed that at any moment, there would be a bloodbath.

In a few, definitive seconds, Aung San Suu Kyi exhibited a rare, implacable courage. With utter fearlessness, she strode back to the centre of the road, and straight towards the muzzles that were levelled at her head and midsection. Her 'boys' followed; in seconds she was in front of the soldiers with their weapons, who seemed more frightened that she was, and coolly brushed past them. A major had arrived on the scene, and had ordered, or more accurately, begged Captain Myint U not to fire, calling to his subordinate, 'Don't do it, Myint U, don't do it, Myint U!'

Senior regime figures would have quickly come to know of this event, and it must have given them cause for consternation. If Aung San Suu Kyi was not to be deterred by the threat of rifle fire, of death, what could intimidate her? The lady herself later explained, with trademark equanimity, 'It seemed so much simpler to provide them with a single target than bring everyone else in'.

News of the incident spread, and cemented Aung San Suu Kyi's reputation as a heroine. The Burmese people too began to perceive Suu Kyi in almost mystical terms; she came to be viewed as a bodhisattva, a saint dedicated to alleviating others' suffering.

In any event, it would not be the last time that her life was threatened. And rather than an encounter which nearly turned deadly on account of a junior officer's misjudgement, the next would be a calculated assassination attempt.

There was also the continual harassment Suu Kyi and her entourage were forced to endure. This included soldiers distributing pornographic leaflets, with cartoons depicting the lady in disgusting acts, and making scurrilous, false accusations. Doubtless, though, Aung San Suu Kyi was saved from more egregious treatment, or even death, by her relationship to the father of the nation of Burma. Others in the pro-democracy movement were not so fortunate, and she was quick to champion their cause.

In October 1988, Suu Kyi brought to Amnesty International's attention the despicable practices of forced conscription, where young men particularly were seized, bound and transported to areas under insurgency. There, they were forced to work as porters. Some died from illness and maltreatment, while others were killed in a ghastly manner, after being forced to cross minefields to detonate mines, ahead of the government troops' advance.

In the broader community in the following months, the military junta stepped up its reign of terror, arresting pro-democracy activists and NLD functionaries, and, at times, torturing and killing them. Even so, protests were sustained, sometimes in the most creative manner.

The 1989 one-kyat note is a case in point. Until 1989, virtually every currency note in independent Burma bore the image of the nation's founding father, Aung San. In the new one-kyat note, the designer incorporated some clever subversion that remained undetected until the note was in circulation. The lines of Bogyoke's jaw and cheekbones were softened to morph into a likeness of his daughter, and the concentric petals of the watermark unmistakeably contained the digits 8888. It was a brilliant, creative protest, but one can only imagine the reprisals the bold designer faced from the military for his trouble.

Throughout, Suu Kyi was careful to make a distinction between the corrupt army officers and SLORC, and the better elements within the forces. When, on 2 June 1989, a military spokesman announced that martial law would remain in force beyond the elections scheduled for May 1990, she stated that the

NLD could not participate in elections until the issue of power transfer was resolved. She also stressed that the 'NLD has always said and accepted ... there are officers with the defence forces who are good, who prefer freedom of movement for democracy ... and who wish the defence forces would remain neutral ... [The NLD has] no desire to confront the defence forces.'

The war of words between Aung San Suu Kyi and the Burmese military junta intensified that month, with the junta publishing an eight-page document, accusing Suu Kyi of running a party at the behest of communists, and accusing her, inter alia, of trying to split the army. Four days later, on 26 June, Aung San Suu Kyi threw down the gauntlet when she bluntly accused General Ne Win of alienating the military from the people and making it a body answerable only to him. She set aside her usual circumspection in saying 'the opinion of all our people [is] that U Ne Win is still creating all the problems in this country', and resolved to continue printing and disseminating NLD political pamphlets, in spite of the government's ban.

Until this time, Aung San Suu Kyi had avoided directly confronting the 'old man' or 'number one', as Ne Win was variously known. But as the situation in the nation worsened and attacks on her character intensified, Suu Kyi gave vent to her disgust for the dictator; at least, in her usual measured, calm manner.

It was a bold step. Ne Win was a fearsome character – even in his late seventies. A moody, erratic man, he was prone to fits of blind temper, and trivial issues would often trigger wildly disproportionate responses. He once viciously beat an aide whom he suspected of flirting with his wife. His murderous rages terrified his subordinates, and he thought nothing of killing.

Ne Win had no qualms, either, about inflicting his violence on women. One of his five wives left him after he hurled a heavy glass ashtray at her throat, seriously injuring her. Public opprobrium would not moderate his behaviour in the least too. On Christmas Eve 1975, he went on the rampage when his peace at his Inya Lake mansion was disturbed by a party in a nearby hotel. With a platoon of his soldiers, he burst into the party, beating guests and band members and smashing their instruments. When a European woman stood and remonstrated with him, he took hold of her party dress and tore it down the front, then threw her back into her chair.

Ne Win's predilection for gambling and the occult only served to make him more fearsome and unpredictable. He was widely reported to engage in bizarre practices of *yadaya*, Burmese magical rituals. Terrified of assassination, Ne Win carried a revolver during the day and kept a sub-machine gun by his side at night. He would periodically shoot his reflection in the mirror with his revolver in a bid to avert assassination attempts, or view his reflection as he trampled a dog's entrails when his soothsayer warned him of an impending bloodbath. Stories of his grotesque behaviour are legion. He routinely ordered all dogs slaughtered at a location before he travelled there, simply because his soothsayer had warned him to avoid dogs, particularly those with crooked tails.

A number of whimsical, but ultimately damaging, policies were implemented for yadaya. Besides the demonetizing of currency notes not divisible by nine, one of Ne Win's more outlandish official decisions was changing the nation's roads to right-hand traffic, on 6 December 1970. The dictator decreed this, despite nearly all cars in Burma being right-hand drive. The resulting bedlam on Burma's roads was purportedly due to Ne Win's soothsayer warning that the country had turned to the left.

Of course, yadaya's appeal was not limited to Ne Win: the prime minister he ousted in 1962, U Nu, keenly practised it, as did later leaders. Even in the current decade, Burmese junta members' resort to yadaya at Aung San Suu Kyi's rise would make an absurd spectacle, but more on that later.

Suffice it to say, at any rate, that a rather unstable, paranoid character was still behind the Burmese government's machinations during SLORC's reign, and Aung San Suu Kyi's public censure of Ne Win is testament to her bravery and commitment to the pro-democracy cause. It also upped the ante, with the government making ever more risible claims, such as that the aim of the NLD was to overthrow the government by force. This, despite the overwhelming firepower of the military, and Aung San Suu Kyi's steadfast adherence to non-violence. She abjured violence, and repeatedly appealed for calm and peaceful protests.

Peaceful protest was becoming a deadly undertaking in these months. SLORC had made some fairly unorthodox attempts to bring the country back under the regime's control, including the peremptory renaming of the nation Myanmar and the capital Yangon, along with renaming other cities, on 18 June 1989. It now adopted more extreme, direct measures to quell democratic aspirations.

In July 1989, martial law order 1/89 was passed, giving military commanders in Yangon and the central and north-western military commands the power to conduct summary trials. Fifteen military tribunals were quickly convened. And on 18 July 1989, one day before Martyrs' Day, martial law decree 2/89 was passed. Under this ordinance, even junior officers of the military could arrest political prisoners and administer summary punishment: hard labour, life imprisonment, or execution. The passing of the decree was timed to thwart a Martyrs' Day march that Aung San Suu Kyi and the NLD had scheduled.

SLORC sent army trucks with loudspeakers into Yangon on 18 July, announcing that people may only commemorate Martyrs' Day in ones and twos: any groups larger than five would be subject to order 2/89. With this sobering development, and after a 6 a.m. to 6 p.m. curfew was imposed, Suu Kyi called off the Martyr's Day march with a hastily written circular, which was printed and posted throughout the city, early on 19 July. And when Suu Kyi attempted to leave her home for a private visit to the Martyr's Mausoleum, to pay her respects to her father and uncle and others, she was prevented from leaving the grounds.

The following morning, eleven truckloads of soldiers surrounded 54, University Avenue. Aung San Suu Kyi was comfortable with her fate, and just as her idol Mahatma Gandhi had been before his periods of incarceration, quite at peace that she would be arrested. Alexander and Kim were with her. The three of them looked on with amusement as soldiers with a large pair of scissors cut the telephone line.

Perhaps it was the only amusement of these days, although she and the boys were, despite the regime's crackdown, perfectly relaxed. Suu Kyi's closest aides and supporters, including her personal assistant Ma Thanegi, were arrested and jailed in the infamous Insein Prison. Only she and U Tin Oo were spared from jail, but on 21 July, a SLORC spokesman announced that the pair were to serve at least a one-year sentence of house arrest for ' ... committing acts designed to put the country in a perilous state'.

Suu Kyi immediately demanded that the government imprison her with her supporters. That way, she reasoned, she might be able to afford them some protection from maltreatment. Needless to say, the regime flatly denied her request, and Aung San Suu Kyi embarked on a hunger strike.

She had been on the strike, drinking only water and juice, for three days when Michael flew to Yangon. As soon as his plane landed, it was surrounded by troops, and he was escorted from the tarmac by an army officer. Michael was allowed to go to the

University Avenue home to be with Suu and the boys, only on the proviso that he abided by the same terms of home detention as Suu.

When Michael saw his wife, he was deeply concerned. Suu possessed a waif-like figure naturally, and months of touring and stress had whittled away what little flesh she had. Now, she was emaciated, and fast fading. After some days, Michael managed to broker a compromise, where the military gave a solemn promise not to mistreat the NLD prisoners. He only managed to convince Suu to accept this and break her fast by telling her she would be of no use to the movement dead; the regime had no intention of giving in to her demand. Suu had not eaten for twelve days, and it took many weeks for her to recover her strength.

Michael and the boys stayed with Suu for the following month, all under house arrest. Strangely, the family enjoyed themselves under detention. They could not know that this was to be the last time they would all be together. On 2 September, the boys returned to England to attend school, and it would be more than two years before they would see their mother again. SLORC arbitrarily cancelled their Myanmarese passports, and would not grant any visa on their British passports.

The regime cunningly granted Michael a visa for his next visit, however. Allowing Suu Kyi's husband to see her was a calculated attempt to pull at her heartstrings: the regime hoped Michael might persuade his wife to abandon the NLD and her pro-democracy campaign and return with him to Oxford. Of course, nothing was further from his mind. Michael stayed true to his commitment to Suu before their marriage, that he would support her when her country needed her. When Michael visited Suu that December, the couple enjoyed one of their last times together.

In the months of her isolation that followed, Suu Kyi adopted a strict regimen, which included waking at 4.30 a.m. for an hour of vipassana meditation. She read and wrote, developing herself from within – the regime had taken everything else away from her.

Outside, save for the ongoing armed insurrections, the regime had all but stamped out resistance, and with the military tribunals vested with the power of life and death, any Myanmarese citizen who had as much as held an NLD placard lived in fear. And while SLORC had promised polls in May 1990, with the entire leadership of the NLD imprisoned, there was little that Suu and the party could do but wait.

One of the curiosities of this period is that SLORC allowed an election to take place. In similar situations in other parts of the world, most dictators avoided elections, unless they rigged the result. But SLORC made no concerted effort to tamper with the polls themselves. It may very well be that SLORC considered the NLD a spent force. Or perhaps SLORC was so far out of touch with the people of Myanmar that it felt that its proxy party, the National Unity Party (NUP), stood a chance of winning.

It did, though, go to great lengths to hobble the opposition. Hundreds of thousands of people from city neighbourhoods with a high proportion of NLD supporters were forcibly relocated to hastily constructed, distant townships, which were little more than malarial shanty towns. And aside from incarcerating the entire executive of the opposition – U Tin Oo was sentenced to three years' hard labour – and barring Aung San Suu Kyi from candidature, the junta made it virtually impossible for any opposition to campaign. The NLD's party machinery was crippled, and with contradictory rules and ordinances, NLD activists were reduced to canvassing like black marketeers peddling contraband.

What the NLD activists did have was a manifesto written by Suu Kyi before she was arrested. 'The people of Myanmar,' she maintained, 'view democracy not merely as a form of government but as an integrated social and ideological system based on respect for the individual.' The manifesto set out some broad principles on how the NLD would govern – for what use it would be.

The polls were scheduled for 27 May 1990 – a date divisible by nine, according with the regime's numerological preferences. Select foreign media representatives were even allowed to cover the elections. On the election day, turnout was heavy, with some 72 per cent of the electorate casting its vote. The first results announced that evening, of a landslide victory for the NLD candidate in Seikan Township in Yangondaw, were a clear sign of the voters' intentions. To SLORC's horror, the NLD trounced the NUP, winning 392 of 492 seats, and nearly 60 per cent of the popular vote. What's more, with its allies in the ethnic states, the NLD coalition won a landslide 94 per cent of seats. With all SLORC's patronage, the NUP could only manage to secure a mere ten seats.

Just as it was a stunning victory for Aung San Suu Kyi and the pro-democracy forces, the election was a shocking, unequivocal rejection of Myanmar's military junta. More disquieting still for the military was that in several electorates where soldiers comprised the majority of voters, such as Dagon constituency in Yangon, NLD candidates won.

With its leadership locked up, the NLD could not mobilize grass-roots support, which may well have topped the Burmese military regime. SLORC spent weeks buying time, before claiming that the election had been not been for a government, but for a constitutional convention. The flimsy pretext for this was that the elections were held in a constitutional vacuum: the 1974 constitution had been abolished by SLORC in 1988. SLORC remained in power; it had obviously never contemplated handing over power to an elected government – unless that were a government of its own preference.

All the while, Aung San Suu Kyi remained isolated at University Avenue, except for her following events on television and radio, and receiving letters from Michael and her boys, which were relayed through the British embassy and brought to her by SLORC. But even these meagre contacts with the outside world were to be removed.

Khin Nyunt, the intelligence chief, declared in a news conference on 13 July that SLORC had been 'very lenient' to Suu Kyi by allowing her to receive letters and parcels from her family. Suu Kyi responded to this decisively. She considered it, quite correctly, her right to communicate with her family, and resolved, as a matter of principle, 'not [to] accept any "favours" from [SLORC]'. This became her silent protest against the injustices of the regime; although incarcerated in her home, she was in spirit suffering along with her NLD colleagues in jail. She was now all but cut off from the outside world.

One can scarce imagine the suffering Aung San Suu Kyi would have to endure in the decades that followed. Unlike other prisoners of conscience in the twentieth century such as Nelson Mandela and Anatoly Tikhonovich Marchenko, however, she voluntarily accepted her fate. At any time in her incarceration, she could have thrown in the towel and submitted herself to the comfortable ignominy of exile back to the UK and her family. That she did not and willingly accepted her imprisonment, forced estrangement from her family and other privations demonstrates her commitment to her people as much as it does her courage.

In the wake of the NLD's election victory, SLORC began rounding up and imprisoning its victorious candidates so they would have no chance of forming a government. Some, including

Suu's cousin Dr Sein Win, fled to the protection of the Democratic Alliance of Burma (DAB), a coalition of insurgent forces which was based in Manerplaw, in mountains near the Thai border. There, they declared the National Coalition Government of the Union of Burma.

It was left only to the clergy now to censure the government. On 8 August 1990, the anniversary of the 8888 Uprising, thousands of monks in Mandalay left their monasteries with their begging bowls as often they did, but instead of accepting alms, they held their bowls upside down, symbolizing their spiritual embargo on SLORC. Already deployed in anticipation of unrest in the city, soldiers opened fire, killing four people, two of whom were monks. The monks' sangha or association announced, in response, that the boycott of the regime would continue indefinitely.

SLORC had brutalized each sector of Myanmarese society that had dared to defy it, and it crushed the monks' dissent by raiding monasteries and dissolving a number of them. In a deeply religious country, this could not be without consequence. The crackdown on the monks seems to have precipitated General Saw Maung's subsequent emotional breakdown, which occurred within months of suppressing the monks' rebellion. He was replaced in April 1992 by Than Shwe, who was to rule Myanmar for eighteen years.

Meanwhile, Aung San Suu Kyi was suffering with her home detention. Years later, in November 2010, she told a reporter, 'the first years were the worst ... they threw me in at the deep end'. She has been circumspect, over the years, in talking of the personal cost of her struggle, especially in expressing her feelings about her separation from Alexander and Kim: the regime would likely make use of anything she said; it was, after all, waging psychological warfare against her.

Be that as it may, Suu Kyi fared better than most of her colleagues, and she repeatedly acknowledged this. Her close adviser and fellow NLD executive committee member Maung Thaw Ka died after he was tortured and denied medical care in jail. U Win Tin was jailed and tortured, and eventually served nineteen years of a twenty-year sentence, and an astounding twenty-five year sentence was imposed on Daw Myint Myint Khin.

Still, without the parcels from family and well-wishers, Suu barely had enough food to survive, and from her normal weight of 48 kg, she lost 7 kg, and was a gaunt 41. She developed spondylosis, a degenerative condition of the spinal column, and her eyesight deteriorated. But the regime, despite its best efforts, never broke her mind or her will. She said that she felt her father's presence at times, and was comforted by this. Undoubtedly, her strict regimen, which always included early morning meditation, exercise, reading, writing, playing the piano and sewing – she made curtains, just as she had done years before in Oxford – helped her to cope with her isolation too.

Just as Aung Suu Kyi was coming to terms with her bleak existence at 54, University Avenue, she was to be honoured with the world's most prestigious award for those devoted to humanitarian causes. On 14 October 1991, the Norwegian Nobel Committee announced that she would be conferred that year's Nobel Peace Prize, 'for her non-violent struggle for democracy and human rights'.

Of course, the lady herself could not be at the award ceremony in Oslo on 10 December 1991 to accept the prize, so Alexander and Kim accepted it on her behalf. Alexander delivered a heartfelt speech for her, which was wise beyond his years. The chairman of the committee, Professor Francis Sejersted, said 'She is still fighting the good fight. ... Her absence fills us with fear and anxiety.'

In terms of international diplomacy, the prize exerted much pressure on the Myanmarese government, and SLORC responded by calling Michael in March 1991 into the Myanmarese embassy in London, asking him to persuade Suu Kyi to return to England. When Michael bluntly rebuffed this approach, the junta seconded a prominent monk who had known Suu's family for years, U Rewata Dhamma, to ask Suu directly to leave.

The reply Aung San Suu Kyi gave was befitting of Bogyoke himself. She would do as he proposed and leave Myanmar willingly, she said, on four conditions: the government would hand over power to civilians; all political prisoners would be released; she would be given fifty minutes of broadcast time on government television and radio, and be allowed to walk to the airport.

Needless to say, the government abandoned any further efforts in this vein. But with international diplomatic pressure, particularly from the US and Japan, and with coaxing from the monk, regime figures and Aung San Suu Kyi met in September and October 1994. And on 10 July 1995, she was freed. She had been under house arrest for 2,180 days.

On that day and on the days that followed, Suu and her colleagues would greet crowds at the gates of 54, University Avenue, where she would speak over a public address system. These became weekend appearances, and within months were Yangon's biggest attraction. But despite Aung San Suu Kyi's popularity and her freedom, it was quickly apparent there would be no real progress towards political reform. Suu and her executive pulled out of a fruitless effort to draft a new constitution in November 1995, and it seemed she and U Tin Oo would presently be back in detention.

Aung San Suu Kyi and U Tin Oo retained their freedom, tenuous though it was. The regime seethed at Suu Kyi's weekend speeches, going so far as to threaten those attending the speeches with twenty years' jail. When this failed to dampen the people's enthusiasm for Suu Kyi's appearances, the government placed barricades across the road in an effort to stop them. When Suu and her colleagues simply changed the venue to nearby street corners, the regime turned to its organization of state-sponsored thugs, the Union Solidarity and Defence Association (USDA). On 9 November 1996, a 200-strong mob of USDA goons attacked Aung San Suu Kyi's cavalcade as it left her home, and one car's windows were broken by steel bars. Two years later, in August 1998, her car was forced off the road by USDA hoodlums. The worst, though, was yet to come.

Incidents such as these belied, at any rate, the junta's mere lip service to international opinion in setting the world's most famous prisoner of conscience free, and demonstrated it had no intention of sincerely reforming Myanmar's political system. Suu Kyi showed no fear, however. In an interview with the *Times,* she evinced the same courage that she had when her life was threatened years earlier, saying, 'If the army wants to kill me, they can do it without any problems at all, so there is no point in making elaborate security arrangements.'

A year after the first USDA attack, on 15 November 1997, SLORC transformed into the rather hopefully named State Peace and Development Council (SPDC) – the new name suggested by an American public relations consultancy. Some of the old guard were sidelined and power was more centralized with the top four SLORC generals. By and large, however, the government's approach remained unchanged by this reshuffle.

The day before SPDC rose instantly from the ashes of SLORC, Suu Kyi was held in a car at her gate for eleven hours: the government would not allow her to travel. Stand-offs like this were to become quite common; a focus of significant international media attention. And in the preceding month, a UN special rapporteur's paper on human rights noted 'the absence of any improvement in the overall situation of human rights' in the regime. The paper made mention of 'the continuing violations of basic human rights, including extrajudicial, summary or arbitrary executions, death in custody, torture, arbitrary and politically motivated arrests and detention, absence of due process of law', and the gamut of human rights violations.

It was by now patently clear that Aung San Suu Kyi had only been freed as a concession to regional and international powers. With the lady free, Burma could join ASEAN, lobby for the easing of sanctions that had been imposed in the wake of the 1988 massacres and attract foreign aid, particularly from Japan, and investment. On the matter of foreign investment, Aung San Suu Kyi and the NLD took a firm dissenting stance. They did so in the knowledge that as in Marcos's Philippines, Mobuto's Zaire and numerous other dictatorships, it would be the junta's corrupt leaders who would benefit from foreign investment, rather than the public at large. The NLD also lobbied hard against the regime's promotion of tourism in Myanmar, again on the basis that tourism would not appreciably benefit the average Myanmarese citizen.

In spite of Suu's release, she was still far from free to resume her personal life, and the regime continued its psychological warfare by barring her family from the country for all but a few months in the latter half of the 1990s. At first, when Suu was released in 1995, Michael and Kim were given visas, and they stayed with her at 54, University Avenue. Suu was astonished to see that Kim had now become a young man. He had changed so much since their last meeting that she admitted she could easily have walked past him in the street.

Michael's time with Suu for Christmas 1995 was to be his last visit to Burma, and Suu would never see her husband again.

Michael had spent much time over the preceding years lobbying for Suu and working tirelessly for her – mostly in the background, of course. He kept himself and the boys out of the limelight, as much to protect them and Suu as anything else. The regime had made continual attacks on virtually every aspect of

Aung San Suu Kyi's life, and among the most unconscionable were on her marriage. One of the regime mouthpieces, for instance, the *New Light of Myanmar*, bellowed that 'The *bogadaw* [a pejorative term for the wife of a European] has lost her right to inherit her father's name', because she had 'failed to safeguard her own race'. Michael knew that he would serve Suu far better with quiet diplomacy than by seeking publicity. Still, while lecturing and writing, Michael managed to devote more than half his time to his wife's cause.

Much of Michael's time was consumed in trying to obtain a visa to see his wife. His attempts became more impassioned when, in 1998, he was diagnosed with prostate cancer. To the last, Michael never gave up trying to see his beloved Suu, but he implored her not to come to his side. As his medical state worsened, numerous international appeals were made to the Myanmarese junta, some by luminaries such as UN Secretary General Kofi Annan and Pope John Paul II, that Michael be granted a visa. Unsurprisingly, given the Myanmarese regime's callousness to its citizens and especially Suu Kyi, the appeals went unheeded. The junta disingenuously claimed that it had denied his request, because Myanmar didn't have the medical facilities to take care of him

It is a mercy that Suu and Michael had enjoyed a full and happy married life in their early years together. As Michael's condition deteriorated, he tried desperately to telephone her. Just as the erratic line would finally connect, he would hear her answer, 'Hello,' and the line would be cut. He last spoke with Suu in early 1998. To the end, Michael's support for democracy in Myanmar was unflinching, and his devotion to Suu never wavered. The walls of his home were proudly adorned with Suu's awards and certificates, and above his bed hung a large poster of his wife.

Michael Vaillancourt Aris died in Churchill Hospital at Oxford on 27 March 1999, his fifty-third birthday. Knowing that to depart from the country for any reason, even to attend Michael's funeral, would be to allow herself to be exiled from Myanmar, Suu held a Buddhist ceremony for Michael at her home. Some 1,000 mourners attended. She wore white, and her hair was for once without her trademark flowers. Suu paid heartfelt tribute to Michael: 'I have been fortunate to have such a wonderful husband, who has always given me the understanding I needed'.

Michael had written in *Freedom from Fear*, released in the wake of Suu's Nobel Peace Prize conferral: 'Fate and history never seem to work in orderly ways. Timings are unpredictable and do not wait upon convenience.' His words could not have been wiser, or more accurately described Aung San Suu Kyi's incarceration and belated rise in Myanmarese politics.

Far from blunting Suu's determination, Michael's death seemed to spur Suu Kyi on in her seemingly interminable quest for democracy in Myanmar. Little in the regime had changed, though, only it was now even more abundantly clear to the generals that nothing was going to make the daughter of Bogyoke go away. She continued to embarrass the government too. In September 2000, she tried to travel to Mandalay and was stopped by the army in Dala, Yangon's southern suburb. Suu Kyi responded by refusing to leave her car or turn back, and on 21 September, tried to take a train. Only a 200-strong contingent of riot police could force her back to 54, University Avenue, and to a new sentence of home detention. Such incidents were keenly watched by the international media, and prompted condemnation from numerous governments.

The two top generals in the regime had differing views on how to manage the challenge they must face in Aung San Suu Kyi. Khin Nyunt, the military intelligence chief who made some efforts towards modernizing the nation, favoured engagement and began secret dialogue with the lady. His colleague, the head of the armed forces Than Swe, a dour, unimaginative man, was of the old school, and it was he who would eventually prevail.

Aung San Suu Kyi was released from her latest stint of house arrest on 6 May 2002, and immediately set about continuing her cruelly interrupted plans to travel through the country. Just months earlier had seen a changing of the guard, with an alleged plot to overthrow the junta by Ne Win's son-in-law Aye Zaw Win, the husband of his daughter Sandar Win. The plot was thwarted, exposed on 4 March 2002. Sandar's husband and children were imprisoned, along with the family soothsayer. Just as Suu Kyi was to be released, Sandar Win and Ne Win were sentenced to house arrest – ironically, in their villa on Inya Lake, facing Aung San Suu Kyi's home – with the former 'number one' dying all but unmourned just months later, on 5 December 2002.

Khin Nyunt, for one, would have mourned his former mentor Ne Win's demise. The new political landscape in Ne Win's absence was, paradoxically, more dangerous for Suu Kyi, with the hardliner Than Shwe in the ascendency. Than Shwe had a chillingly direct, and more final means of dealing with the lady.

The previous years had seen the emergence of the USDA, which on account of its lawless, thuggish suppression of pro-democracy activism, has been likened to Hitler's Brownshirts. A large contingent of USDA goons, numbering perhaps as many as 5,000, was involved in a despicable, stage-managed attack on an NLD convoy. The event would come to be known as the Depayin Massacre.

At 7.30 p.m. on 30 May 2003, at Kyi village near Depayin, Suu Kyi's cavalcade was stopped by two old monks at the side of a narrow, potholed tarmac road. The pair asked NLD security if Aung San Suu Kyi would address them, as they and their fellow monks had waited to meet her. She acceded to their request – after all, it would hardly have been fitting to rebuff the holy men. The men, though, were not monks at all, but USDA stooges – Aung San Suu Kyi and her NLD comrades had driven into an elaborate trap.

As the convoy was waiting, two trucks and cars pulled to a halt behind, and USDA thugs alighted from the vehicles, chanting slogans against the NLD. When a group of villagers challenged them, the thugs, along with the bogus monks, attacked the villagers with iron bars, bamboo rods and bats.

At first, it seemed that this might simply be another roughing up to be endured, but it quickly became clear the men in the mob were drunk or drugged, and they attacked with murderous intent. The armed goons turned on the cavalcade, which included NLD personnel on motorcycles and several cars, shattering the cars' windows and brutally bashing the NLD members.

Youth members rushed to the front of the cavalcade and surrounded Suu Kyi's dark-green Toyota Landcruiser to protect the lady, and they too were set upon. Aung San Suu Kyi's driver, Kyaw Soe Lin, pleaded with the assailants, and told them that Suu Kyi was in the car, but they only became more ferocious in their attack. Behind and around the vehicle, women and men alike were bludgeoned until they lay motionless, bloodied on the ground.

Kyaw Soe Lin looked desperately for an escape from the carnage. He reversed and drove forward, as the attackers damaged the vehicle's steering and smashed its headlights and the window next to Suu Kyi. He accelerated the Toyota Landcruiser hard and dodged three trucks which were placed to block the road. Left behind were the bloodied corpses of some seventy NLD supporters and youth security members. U Tin Oo had been dragged from his car, beaten and taken away.

Further ahead, Kyaw Soe Lin encountered a larger armed mob, numbering in the hundreds. He accelerated as he approached, knowing that to hesitate would be fatal. The thugs scattered, but flung stones at the vehicle, smashing its remaining windows. Beyond was a line of policemen with guns at the ready, but he drove through their midst as well, threading the car deftly between trucks which had been parked to obstruct the road.

Amazingly, Suu Kyi asked Kyaw Soe Lin if he was okay. He told her he was fine, and drove through a number of other roadblocks before they reached Depayin. Aung San Suu Kyi had been saved by her driver's skill, her NLD youth security personnel using themselves as human shields – and the miscalculation of her attackers, who had concentrated their attacks on the cars in the middle of the convoy, thinking the lady was in one of them.

Bizarrely, Aung San Suu Kyi was arrested and sent to Insein Jail after this event, and the perpetrators were never brought to justice. Even more outlandish was the bald-faced admission of General Than Shwe. The head of the armed forces, who had at first hidden behind his deputy foreign minister's claim that the massacre was a minor incident caused by Suu's cavalcade, eventually declared that he had ordered the massacre at Depayin with the intention of 'eradicating' Aung San Suu Kyi.

More remarkable still was the lady's reaction to the event. In the months that followed, she indicated that she was willing, despite this assassination attempt, to 'turn the page', and even engaged in behind-the-scenes talks with regime representatives.

Sadly, while the talks showed promise, they came to nothing. Khin Nyunt, who apparently had nothing to do with the attempt on Suu Kyi's life, was ousted on 18 October 2004 in a power struggle with Than Shwe, and detained. The hardliner Than Shwe saw compromise with the NLD as a threat to the status quo, and Suu Kyi remained under house arrest until 13 November 2010.

The lady's release had been due more than a year earlier, but her house arrest had been extended on account of a trivial incident, one that reeks of conspiracy.

In November 2008, a troubled American Vietnam veteran, John Yettaw, swam across Inya Lake and attempted to meet Suu Kyi, but was stopped and turned back at the shore outside her home by her security. Undeterred, and determined to warn Aung San Suu Kyi of an imagined attempt on her life, Yettaw made another bid to meet her at her University Avenue home, on 2 May 2009. This time, he was successful, but Suu pleaded with him to leave. He told her that he could not, as he had stomach cramps. He eventually left on 5 May, and was arrested and detained.

It is very likely that Yettaw, described variously as 'eccentric' and 'a crank', was manipulated by government agents. The regime charged Suu Kyi and Yettaw, and she was sent for trial along with him and her two female companions: she had, the regime alleged, violated the terms of her home detention. Yettaw later testified that he had a dream of Suu Kyi's assassination, and stated that he had gone to see her simply to warn her. For his trouble, he was sentenced to seven years' jail in August 2009, but was freed and deported after three months. The government used the incident as a pretext to prolong Aung San Suu Kyi's detention, along with her companions, for 'only' eighteen months.

The incident and its timing were a fillip for the government. It intended to hold elections the following year; it was convenient to have Suu Kyi incarcerated, and unable to participate in any form. In the elections held on 7 November 2010, the Union Solidarity and Development Party, the successor to the thuggish USDA, won 259 of 440 seats in the Pyithu Hluttaw (House of Representatives); a convincing win, on the face of it, in elections dismissed internationally as fraudulent. The NLD had, in any event, boycotted the elections.

In the campaign period, in which NLD was conspicuously absent, it seems that the junta still perceived Suu Kyi as a threat – at least, enough of a threat to warrant a bizarre public display of a yadaya ritual. In October 2010, Thai prime minister Abhisit Vejjajiva made a state visit to Myanmar. The visiting dignitary could only have been bewildered at his greeting by State Peace and Development Council officials wearing longyis with decorative prints, traditionally worn by women. It seemed the officials were attempting, via this aberrant act, to appropriate the lady's power.

At the time of Aung San Suu Kyi's final release from house arrest, on 13 November 2011, however, the regime appears to have perceived the lady a spent force. The regime had, out of the barrel of a gun, managed to manufacture a semblance of democracy, and it was still firmly ensconced in power. The years that Suu Kyi had spent incarcerated in her home almost incommunicado, though, had seen the beginning of a series of events that would eventually change the political landscape of the country.

When Suu Kyi emerged from her imprisonment, she was astonished at the change in communications since her last real contact with the outside world. She marvelled at the possibilities Facebook, YouTube and the proliferation of the Internet offered. It was such technologies that were now playing their part to effect change in Myanmar.

Political change for Myanmar in this century started not with protests for democracy, but a small-scale, tentative demonstration in Yangon on 22 February 2007, over the rising cost of food and basic necessities. Prices had soared over the preceding months, with a spike in international commodities rates, which caused significant hardship for the poverty-stricken Myanmarese people. The government quickly suppressed this protest, but discontent over living costs festered in the following months. It came to a head after the government, under pressure from record international oil prices, removed subsidies on fuel, unannounced, on 15 August 2007. The cost for diesel and petrol immediately doubled. Food prices rose proportionally, and the Myanmarese people's anguish would not long be contained.

What was to become known abroad as the Saffron Revolution – a misnomer, because Myanmarese monks traditionally wear maroon robes – began in earnest when three monks were injured by troops forcibly breaking up a peaceful demonstration in Pakokku. After a stand-off in the days that followed, on 22 September, thousands of monks marched through Yangon and Mandalay, chanting the *Myitta Thote* (the Buddha's words on loving kindness). In the capital, they marched through a barricade in front of 54, University Avenue, and blessed Aung San Suu Kyi at her gate. From that day, the monks vowed to withhold services from the army: they imposed what may best be described as a spiritual strike.

For daring to appear at her gate and receive the monks' blessing, Suu Kyi was sent to Insein Jail. But in the following days, the protests intensified, with as many as 100,000 joining a demonstration in Yangon on 24 September. The regime responded in just the same manner as it had to such events since 1962: arbitrary arrests, threats, beatings, then murder – cold, brutal force. What set the Saffron Revolution apart from the 8888 Uprising and earlier student protests, however, was the effective reportage, which leaked damning images and narratives to international media outlets and on to the Internet.

Widespread disgust at the government's treatment of monks in Myanmar would not easily be assuaged. To much of Burma's deeply religious citizenry, the ruination brought by Cyclone Nargis on 2 May 2008 – some 138,000 Burmese citizens perished – was divine reckoning for the regime's sins. Aung San Suu Kyi was lucky to have only lost the roof of her home in the cyclone, which was the worst natural disaster ever to hit Burma, though she spent the following nights in darkness along with her people.

At any rate, the referendum for Burma's constitution, which was delayed in districts by the cyclone, was passed the same month, despite allegations of forcible voting and electoral fraud. The regime could take comfort in the provision which bars anyone who has either married or parented a foreign national from holding political office, which was a transparent attempt to keep Aung San Suu Kyi from power. But despite this and the myriad other efforts of the government to break her will, it was clear in the months after her release that Myanmarese citizens continued to look to Aung San Suu Kyi to lead the nation to democracy.

In August 2011, I travelled to Yangon to meet Aung San Suu Kyi, after making contact with her office through exiles who had fled from the military junta. Needless to say, I had kept the purpose for my travel to Myanmar a closely guarded secret: I flew into Yangon International Airport on a twenty-eight day tourist visa, and responded to the probing questions of immigration officers by saying that I wanted to see Myanmar's sights, such as Shwedagon Pagoda. I had booked a room at the Yuzana Hotel, a large, salubrious establishment in Bahan Township, a north-central area of Yangon adjacent to Shwedagon Pagoda.

The hotel was all but empty; the NLD had only forsaken its opposition to tourism little more than a year earlier, and visitors were still scarce in the nation's capital. My Myanmarese contacts in Delhi had advised me not to take a taxi anywhere near the NLD building. They were adamant too that I should not carry a large, professional camera which, they explained, would quickly betray my mission. So on 6 August 2011, I set out from the hotel on foot, dressed in jeans and carrying a small handycam in my bag, just as any tourist might. The NLD headquarters was just a few minutes' walk away from the hotel, towards Shwedagon Pagoda on Shwedongdian Road.

The level of attention a foreigner received in Burma at that time was disquieting for me, to say the least. I felt that I was being watched by many pairs of eyes, as surely I was, but I could hardly tell whether it was on account of simply my appearance, or the government having some intelligence of the real purpose of my visit. Near the NLD office, I was stopped by a uniformed officer, who asked me in halting English, 'Where are you going?' 'To Shwedagon Pagoda,' I replied, and I tried to keep from showing my fear. I felt that at any moment, I would be arrested. He pointed me in the direction of Shwedagon, and continued on his way. He was, it seems, simply being helpful.

When I reached the NLD headquarters, a small, somewhat dilapidated-looking building, I did not hesitate outside. In the lobby, a large, framed painting of Aung San looked benignly down from the wall on three men drinking soup, and other staff members poring over papers. Upon seeing me, one of them said, 'You've come for an interview,' and led me up to the first floor.

Sitting on a chair outside Suu Kyi's office was the redoubtable U Tin Oo, and I spoke with him for several minutes. As we were speaking, the office door opened, and the lady herself emerged, dressed in a green longyi and pale yellow aingyi, with a matching rose in her hair. 'Supriya, I'm running late. Just give me five minutes. I'm so sorry.' She smiled then walked past the two of us and downstairs, a youthful energy in her gait. For a moment, it seemed not that I was to interview the most prominent woman prisoner of conscience of the last century, but I was here to enjoy a friendly meeting with an acquaintance.

I was as much surprised by Aung San Suu Kyi's office as by her unassuming manner. A large refrigerator sat in one corner, and a couple of functional wooden chairs and a table were its only furniture – it was utilitarian, functional; not the least luxurious or even decorated.

The first moments of our meeting were a warm embrace. Suu Kyi sat beside me on one of the wooden chairs, her hand on mine. She could see I was still shaken by my encounter with the officer on the street. In the forty minutes that followed, we spoke, and I recorded our interview.

Aung San Suu Kyi's posture is graceful, and her back still doesn't seem to touch that of the chair. Her accent is attractive, with more English than Asian inflexions, and her voice carries a gentle assurance. She has an intelligent, direct gaze, and the bearing of someone old and wise, yet it seems youthful for her years. In person, away from the glare of mass media, she is warm and engaging too.

One of her staff members took photographs: I had thought it far too risky to engage a photographer in Yangon. For a moment, I mistakenly spoke in Hindi, rather pointlessly asking her staff member to take photographs from the other side of the room, in my language rather than his. Suu Kyi smiled and translated my Hindi into Myanmarese for him. For a moment, I was dumbfounded. She smiled, and said, 'Mujhe Hindi pata hai, chinta na karen. (Don't worry, I speak Hindi)'. For the following few minutes, we conversed purely in Hindi, Suu Kyi reminiscing about her time in Delhi and inquiring about my family. I was surprised at her proficiency: she spoke Hindi without an accent and with the ease of a native speaker.

Towards the end of my interview, Suu Kyi asked where I was staying and when I would be leaving Myanmar. She seemed genuinely concerned for my welfare. After a farewell at her office door, I again spoke with U Tin Oo outside her office. A slim, astute-looking man in his mid-eighties who looked at least ten years younger, he smiled kindly and shook hands with me as I left.

'You are a very fortunate child,' he said, 'because you are going away alive.' His words unnerved me, but I surmised U Tin Oo was simply emphasizing the danger his compatriots faced in pursuing democracy in Myanmar. I wasn't taking any chances, though. His staff advised me to keep my interview notes safely hidden when passing immigration at Yangon International Airport. When I returned to Delhi, an email from Aung San Suu Kyi's office awaited me, asking if I had arrived safely.

After my interview with Suu Kyi was telecast on the Times Now network by Arnab Goswami, I learned that a senior officer in the military junta had made some fraught telephone calls to Myanmar's embassy in India. The officer, I was told, was apoplectic with rage that a young female reporter had managed to interview Aung San Suu Kyi and leave the country without detection.

My interview with Suu Kyi was well worth the risk, and it gave me an invaluable perspective on the nature of this rare, brave woman. Apart from her warmth, which was as pleasant as it was unexpected, I was impressed most with Aung San Suu Kyi's complete lack of pretension. She is humble and unaffected; she is calm, and seems completely at ease with herself and her place in the world. Perhaps more significantly, the lady has the air of someone who has lived through much pain – without the misery of scars, but with wisdom and strength.

The 2012 Myanmar by-elections were to be the first elections in which the NLD would participate in twenty-two years – indeed, since its 1990 landslide win. The regime's antipathy of proper representative democracy remained, and there was little question that the government was holding the polls with the purpose of getting sanctions lifted. Before the polling day, the NLD complained of the gamut of irregularities, including vote-buying, fraudulent voter lists and bias to the election commission. Voter lists contained the names of deceased people too a fact Aung San Suu Kyi highlighted publicly. Still, the government invited foreign observers for the election, although it cunningly only brought them to Myanmar a couple of days before the actual polling.

By then, there had been much controversy. Two days before the by-election, Suu Kyi stated that the voter irregularities were 'beyond what is acceptable for democratic elections'. She said the vote could not be considered 'a genuinely free and fair election', and underscored that acts of violence had been perpetrated against NLD party members. On the day of polling, 1 April 2012, the NLD complained that ballot papers had been coated with wax, to allow the election commission to rub out and change votes for the NLD.

The by-election campaign was gruelling for Suu Kyi, and she had cut short her canvassing due to exhaustion, which was in no small part due to the heat. She did, however, make an official televised address on 12 March, in which she pledged her commitment to reform the 2008 constitution and ensure more adequate protections of basic democratic rights. Some parts of her speech, in which she criticized the army's repression of Myanmar's people by law, were censored.

Notwithstanding the challenges Aung San Suu Kyi and her party faced, the election result was a resounding victory for the NLD: It secured a spectacular 40 out of 45 parliamentary seats. Aung San Suu Kyi, speaking outside the NLD headquarters to a cheering crowd of supporters bearing red and white roses and banners, described the victory 'a triumph of the people'. She spoke in Burmese and English in holding out an olive branch to the regime and other parties: 'We invite all parties who wish to bring peace and prosperity to our country [to work together].'

The Myanmarese people, after half a century of military rule, were now beginning to find their voice in democracy.

A few months after the electoral victory, the lady was to enjoy a more personal triumph. On 16 June 2012, Aung San Suu Kyi finally delivered her Nobel Lecture at Oslo City Hall, more than two decades after being awarded the Nobel Peace Prize. Thorbjørn Jagland, chairman of the Norwegian Nobel Committee, recalled how, when more than thirty laureates assembled to celebrate the peace prize's hundredth anniversary in 2001, 'we left one chair empty [for her]'.

Suu Kyi delivered a warm, thoughtful speech that was at times self-deprecating, and received a rousing, standing ovation. She made reference to her suffering under house arrest, particularly her separation from her sons and husband: 'to be parted from those one loves' – the fifth of six great aspects of suffering in Buddhism. It was a rare mention from Suu Kyi of the personal cost exacted by her long and lonely campaign for democracy. Her reunion with her sons was, it seems, not easy. Still, Kim accompanied her at the Nobel Lecture. Days later, on 20 June 2012, Suu Kyi returned to Oxford, after an absence of more than twenty-four years.

The campaign of Bogyoke's daughter was not over, however. The following June, Aung San Suu Kyi publicly stated, 'I want to run for president, and I'm quite frank about it.' Her frankness found ears in all international media outlets, prompting speculation about how she might negotiate her way around the clauses of the constitution that were specifically written to deny her power. The answer was to come after her party blitzed its opposition in the 2015 elections.

On 1 April 2016, a bill creating the position for her of State Counsellor of Myanmar, which is akin to the office of prime minister, was passed by Myanmar's Upper House of parliament. It was passed by the Lower House on 5 April, and the following day, became law when it was signed by President Htin Kyaw. It seems fitting that Aung San Suu Kyi's legitimate government could, by due process of law, circumvent an outrageous provision of the constitution that had been contrived simply to deny her rightful office – that too by a government that had not been properly elected.

Just a few years before, when she was released from house arrest in 2010, few observers gave Aung San Suu Kyi any hope of achieving her ends. She was old, or at least past her middle age, and had been away from Myanmar's political scene for too long, they reasoned. For many, including those in the country's military junta, she seemed destined to become a footnote to Myanmar's history – to fade into relative obscurity. But the same consistent, firm and unwavering approach to non-violence and democracy that had sustained the lady through years of hardship and earned the enduring affection of her people, carried her from the oblivion of house arrest, to the heights of her country's government.

In this new period of political freedom, she was courted by international government figures such as Prime Minister David Cameron of the UK and President Barack Obama of the US. Her status as a nation's leader, along with the honours she has received over the years, made her one of the world's most eminent, respected persons. At the time of writing, in addition to the Nobel Peace Prize, she had been awarded the Rafto Prize, Sakharov Prize, Jawaharlal Nehru Award, Order of Australia, US Congressional Gold Medal and Presidential Medal of Freedom. She had also been made an honorary citizen of Canada.

The lady herself, though, is at pains to be truthful about her human limitations. In an address to the Lowy Institute for International Policy in Sydney in November 2013, she said that she saw herself 'as a politician, not as an icon', and that she was 'no saint of any kind'. She stressed that she does believe, however, 'there is such a thing as an honest politician', and that was what she aspired to.

Perhaps she has felt an undue pressure to be more than a politician; to be a saint in a world damned by imperfection. In any event, it appears that sainthood has been the yardstick by which Aung San Suu Kyi has been judged in recent times, especially since she assumed public office in 2016. International press articles such as the *Economist*'s 'Aung San Suu Kyi – the halo slips' of 15 June 2013, made it abundantly clear that nothing less than saintly conduct was expected of the lady – even within the context of governing a fragile, emerging democracy dogged by poverty and generations of ethnic-based conflict.

Aside from criticizing Suu Kyi's approach to economics, the article made mention of her failure to denounce discrimination, and violence by Myanmar's security forces, against the Rohingya Muslim minority in Burma's Rakhine state. Criticism flared into open condemnation against Aung San Suu Kyi in 2016, when the army launched a bloody crackdown on Rohingya militants. Reports filtered out of Myanmar of widespread atrocities by the armed forces as some 50,000 Rohingya refugees fled across the Bangladesh border.

On 29 December 2016, a group of eminent international figures, including no less than thirteen Nobel laureates, wrote an open letter to the United Nations Security Council, requesting action to address the 'ethnic cleansing and crimes against humanity' perpetrated against the Rohingya. The letter amounted to a damning censure of Suu Kyi by her fellow laureates, but the lady remained diplomatically quiet about the issue.

Her first year in power was, unsurprisingly, turbulent. It seems too that forces inimical to democracy were still at work, with NLD lawyer and constitution expert Ko Ni gunned down outside the airport on 29 January. Three former army officers were subsequently implicated in the assassination. Aung San Suu Kyi's speech to commemorate the anniversary of her taking office struck an almost defensive note, acknowledging a lack of progress and offering to step down 'if someone or some organization can do better than us'.

Perhaps observers would best be reminded of Aung San Suu Kyi's rare qualities, as well as take realistic stock of her situation. Suu Kyi has come to power in a nation divided by ethnic unrest, with limited power according to the constitution. The army and police are not under her control as in a normal civilian government – indeed, the army commands 25 per cent of parliamentary seats by reservation – and the nation's economy still languishes from decades of mismanagement and corruption. The venerable Aung San maintained three years of silent diplomacy before he rid his country of invading forces. It may well be that Bogyoke's daughter, who has proved her courage and integrity equal to her father's, is likewise waiting for the opportune time to bring peace, implement democratic reforms and ensure lasting prosperity for her nation.

ALVA MYRDAL

AMBASSADOR OF ETHICS

'If only the authorities could be made to realize that the forces
leading them on in the armament race are just insane.'

Alva Myrdal, Swedish sociologist, diplomat, politician and staunch proponent of disarmament, was born on 31 January 1902, in Uppsala, Sweden. Alva was widely known for her work with her illustrious husband, Gunnar Myrdal, a recipient of the Nobel Memorial Prize in economic sciences along with Friedrich Hayek in 1974. In her middle age, she became renowned as one of the century's most eminent intellectuals and activists.

Alva was the eldest of the five children of Albert and Lowa Reimer, a middle-class couple whose idealism and ambition would ultimately find expression through their daughter. As was her name, a blend of her parents' names, Alva was blend in the crucible of her parents' expectations and dreams. Indeed, her attractive name could not only have carried an actor to stardom; it was like the woman herself – new and inspired, a break from patriarchal norms that no longer served her country or culture. Her husband Gunnar Myrdal's family had changed their patronymic surname 'Pettersson' to the more exotic 'Myrdal' in honour of their family farm, Myr, in Dalarna. And it was with Gunnar Myrdal's active support and collaboration – in a wife–husband partnership that was one of the most prominent in the intellectual sphere in the twentieth century – that she would achieve greatness.

Alva's parents had wished for a boy before Alva's birth. When her brother Folke was born in 1906, the four-year-old Alva saw in his effusive welcome into the family how utterly different life was for a male child. Alva's parents commissioned a clay sculpture of Folke's features, when no such honour was even considered for their two daughters. Attention was lavished on the infant Folke, whom Alva and her younger sister Rut, born in 1904, nicknamed 'the gold dumpling'. Alva and Rut would secretly discuss engineering an 'accident' to break the sculpture. Alva clearly felt her lower social station, as a female, at a young age, as this was for most intelligent, ambitious women of that era, an issue Alva would encounter throughout her life. It would drive her to define the role of women in modern society, to cut a new path for women that would emancipate them as much as it benefitted society at large.

Notwithstanding their preference for male children, Alva's parents were decidedly modern and progressive. Modernity and idealism were hallmarks of Alva's upbringing, as was her home environment that was, for the most part, austere. Her parents changed their family name from 'Jansson' to 'Reimer', breaking from Nordic patronymic tradition. Lowa Reimer followed all the latest child-rearing fads. Alva claimed that she had been one of the first babies to have been subjected to 'controlled crying', and that her health as an infant had suffered as a result. Alva would later distance herself from her family, at a young age, more due to a tenuous emotional relationship with her mother than due to physical hardship.

Alva's thinking was, undoubtedly, influenced by her parents', especially her father's. Both of Alva's parents were politically conscious and active, and Albert, an atheist, was particularly imbued with the emerging socio-democratic ethos at the end of the nineteenth century. Albert was an insurance agent and, later, a building contractor, whose commitment to his principles led him to eschew wealth. He built a number of collective homes, for families to share, and insisted on selling them as cheaply as he could. To him, the making of profit was immoral.

As the family's fortunes waxed and waned, Albert's working without remuneration would bring him into conflict with Lowa, who liked a more salubrious lifestyle. The Reimers moved from house to house in the early years as their family grew – Alva's sister Maj was born in 1909 and brother Stig, the youngest in the family, in 1912 – living in homes that Albert built until the moisture in their walls dried. Alva's childhood was thus quite unsettled, and moving from place to place was run-of-the-mill.

After several such moves, and in the year that his youngest child was born, Albert built a cooperative store in Stockholm's suburbs. The cooperative's board meetings in the Myrdals' well-appointed apartment above the store were rich with political discussions, and the young Alva eagerly sponged up the many insights that emerged during the debates. She later recalled the wonderment she had felt listening to the idealistic exchanges by the dining table or while reading the forbidden books she had smuggled out of her father's locked cabinet. The commitment to proper procedure at these meetings – due debate of issues, taking minutes and moving and passing motions – was a most useful lesson for Alva's later public life.

The Reimers enjoyed a comfortable life in Stockholm; therefore, Alva and her siblings were gutted by their final move: leaving Stockholm in 1914 for Lowa's father's farm in Eskilstuna, a town 110 kilometres away from Stockholm. Despite their father's enthusiasm for the rural idyll, their stylish and increasingly delicate mother was not the least inclined to a farmer's life. The labour-intensive agricultural practices of the early twentieth century were quite a rude shock for the children. Alva would never completely adjust to life in the countryside, though her siblings would enjoy it.

As Alva entered adolescence, the emotional distance between her and her mother, which began in her childhood, widened. Alva's childhood was marred not so much by parental neglect as by fundamental difficulties in her relationship with her mother. She later described her childhood as 'hellish'. Though Lowa was committed to her children's well-being, she was overbearing, tainted by her own hypochondria and failing health. Being the eldest child, Alva suffered the brunt of Lowa's discipline, as she was rarely given the freedom to make her own decisions. Before Alva's birth, Lowa's sister and brother had died of tuberculosis and Lowa had developed a pathological dread of the disease. Such was her fear that her children would be struck with tuberculosis – which was almost invariably fatal in the years before antibiotics – that she never kissed her children. She even forbade 'excessive reading' on grounds that it could harm her children's eyes, an injunction that maddened Alva, who loved to read. Any untidy or messy game was quickly stifled too. Alva and Rut would wish that their mother had gone out for work so they might get some playtime. 'Dear God, please let mother get a job,' both would jokingly pray before going to bed. Lowa intruded into everything they did. Perhaps in this generation, Lowa's behaviour may be described as obsessive–compulsive.

Lowa's health was fragile, and she spent much of her adult life bedridden. Alva and Rut thus bore much of the responsibility of raising their infant brother Stig – a responsibility they nonetheless relished. Likewise, Alva enjoyed her time at school, for the freedom she enjoyed to go outdoors and play games with the boys. But her education was of little interest to Albert and Lowa. While her mother was adamant that Alva not leave home to attend school, her father was indifferent. He would not mind if Alva could manage her studies on her own, and did little to encourage her.

Apart from her parents' lack of interest, a significant obstacle to Alva's intellectual progress was the education system in Sweden. It was not until 1928 that schools in Sweden accepted girls. This was the first of many piercing injustices she would face in her intellectual career, and it seemed only to harden her determination to succeed. She possessed an almost compulsive desire to learn, and it soon became apparent that, in any event, nothing could come in the way of her acquiring knowledge. Alva later described her teenage self as 'the most naive idealist imaginable'. But her idealism, coupled with youthful energy, undoubtedly drove her intellectual development.

Perhaps she was destined to educate herself by unconventional means. She wrote poetry and corresponded with Per Sundberg, her former teacher from Stockholm, who, despite his youth – he was just twenty years old when Alva was fourteen-and-a-half – possessed a mature mind and was quite the philosopher. Their correspondence lasted for three years and diversified Alva's interests, mundane and profound, infusing Alva's mind with an appreciation for subtlety and intellectual rigour. In her early teenage years, Alva became an autodidact, devouring the few books she could afford with her meagre earnings from sewing and embroidery and making clandestine trips to the town library to read. Secrecy was necessary for this quite innocuous act, because her mother did not let Alva take books from the library, fearing Alva might contract tuberculosis from the books' dirty pages.

Alva would bring library books home, hidden under her long skirt. She would take the books to the attic and conceal them under old newspapers or sawdust. When her mother was not around, she would go and read quietly, shunning the daily farm chores for learning. She became so immersed in her personal study that she even pilfered discarded school books from a neighbour's outhouse. The books were destined for use as toilet paper, but to her delight, she discovered that some of the books had translations of Shakespeare's plays.

Alva also studied astronomy by correspondence, and even learnt Esperanto – just the kind of intellectual pursuit that would have made her father proud – but she refused to abandon her dreams of a formal education. At first, she undertook courses at the town's commercial institute, where she studied English and Swedish literature, along with shorthand, bookkeeping and typing. This also helped her find work with Eskilstuna's tax office, where she was engaged in her first formal employment, at the age of fifteen, for the salary of 160 crowns per month.

Academical education is one aspect of a person's development, but moral education is another. As Alva was completing her courses and working on her first job, the impact of World War I bore heavily down on Sweden's people, even though the country was officially neutral in the conflict. In the autumn of 1916, food shortages threatened the country and famine loomed large. Rationing was introduced. Facing starvation, a significant proportion of the urban population abandoned the nation's cities and foraged in the countryside for food. The following year saw hunger riots, and Albert, as a member of the Food Board of Eskilstuna, was charged with overseeing the equitable distribution of wheat and potatoes in the region.

Albert's interests conflicted with his wife's motherly instincts, and the ethical and emotional aspects of the bitter quandary would shape Alva's thinking throughout her life. Lowa's concern for her children got the better of her, and she simply could not bear to see her children starving. Flouting the austerity of the grain rations, she stole some grain from the farm's granary and ground it for her children in a small hand mill. When Albert discovered her secret, a family row erupted. He would not be moved by Lowa's emotional remonstrations that she must feed her hungry children. 'What was more important for the children', Albert thundered, 'the lasting lesson of justice or their temporary hunger?'

Alva inherited her father's unwavering commitment to his ideals. Alva only did what she perceived to be right, regardless of the consequences. In an interview in 1971, she said, 'I think that if I don't do so, I don't increase the proportion of goodness in the world. For me, this supplants religion.' Although she also inherited her mother's passion for fine clothes and surrounds – and would, as she found success, indulge this passion – she remained altruistic throughout, even donating most of her Nobel Peace Prize money for peace research.

Achieving success was never plain sailing for Alva, however. And though she would be lauded as a prototype 'superwoman', a paragon of womanhood who somehow managed to balance career, family and passion, it was not without great personal cost.

With laudable self-determination, the teenage Alva arranged a loan from a family friend and sought admission to a boarding school. She was overjoyed upon receiving an acceptance letter. It was mandatory, however, that she be referred by her parents. When Alva approached her mother for her reference, Lowa became furious and tore up the application. She was sure that Alva would 'go astray' if she went to boarding school; she might, Lowa thought, even get pregnant. Alva was mortified by her mother's response. She felt as if Lowa had destroyed her entire future.

For his part, Albert was not anti-intellectual. He was fond of Rousseau and held Strindberg's revolutionary writings in high regard. But he harboured deep suspicions about formal education, which he felt was laced with middle-class and elitist values. Although he was not the least interested in Alva's further studies, and even less interested in defying his wife, he was moved by his daughter's helplessness. As one who valued liberty almost as an article of faith, he understood that Alva's yearning for education needed his support. He mobilized the parents of other girls and requested the town school board to open a separate school for girls.

The board authorities acceded to the request, but demanded an exorbitant fee for their troubles: 900 crowns per annum for each girl's tuition, as opposed to 80 crowns for boys in the existing school. Moreover, the girls were not permitted to use the same facilities as the boys and had to be accommodated in makeshift classrooms. The course too was no small challenge for Alva, as she had known neither French nor German and had to learn quickly these languages for the syllabus. As if her situation were not difficult enough, her parsimonious father demanded that Alva repay whatever money he had paid to the town school board for her education. For this, she had to continue working at the tax office. However, she could stay home while studying, an arrangement which her mother could not object to. She applied herself to her studies with characteristic determination and received her matriculation with highest honours in June 1922.

During the years of her schooling, in 1919, Alva met Gunnar Myrdal. Their first encounter was the stuff of romantic novels. One morning, Albert called Alva and Rut to prepare coffee for three tramps who had spent the night in the hayloft. The girls rolled over in their beds and went back to sleep. Their grandfather then said the tramps in the hayloft were university students. One can imagine their grandfather and father sharing smiles and chuckling as Alva and Rut awoke with a rush. They hastily got out of bed, tidied their hair, dressed, prepared coffee and rolls and carried the breakfast to the students. One of the students was Gunnar Myrdal.

Alva fell in love with the handsome and charismatic Gunnar at first sight, mesmerized by his magnetic personality and scholarly demeanour. Gunnar was no less attracted to Alva, as much for her personality and cheerful disposition as her beauty. Both had found an equal: an intellectual partner, soulmate and lover. In the following days, they made plans for a life together, and thus began one of the most illustrious intellectual partnerships of the twentieth century.

At that time, Gunnar was pursuing a degree in law from the law school of Stockholm University. He completed the degree in 1923 and, thereafter, began his practice while undertaking further studies, eventually receiving a juris doctor in economics in 1927. Until she met Gunnar, Alva had not considered marrying, and, compelling as their relationship was, marriage was a foregone conclusion for the couple. Inspired by fanciful notions of love she had garnered from novels, Alva would merge with the formidable entity that was Gunnar. It was a familiar pattern for an intelligent woman of that era, and, certainly, the world was better for their union. But subsuming some parts of herself for what she believed to be the greater good would eventually take its toll. In later years, she wrote, 'How have I come to displace my own self in order to fit in with other selves? Where does one self merge with the other?'

In these two questions, Alva sketched perhaps her greatest personal quandary and, indeed, one that most women grapple with in life's drama. It would define her relationship with her husband and her children, and she would often find, as women are apt to, that she would play the peacemaker and make compromises to fulfil the myriad roles she had assumed. She would not be subjugated by her husband, as many women of those times were; hers was to be a creative and enriching partnership. She continued her studies, earning a *filosofie kandidat* in Scandinavian languages, literature and the history of religion, which was equivalent to a bachelor's degree, in 1924, from the Stockholm University. Alva and Gunnar had planned on marrying in 1923, but Albert had prevailed on Alva to finish her degree before their wedding. They were married on 8 October 1924.

Marrying an intellectual of Gunnar Myrdal's stature would ultimately be as rewarding for Alva as it was challenging. Her own intellectual development advanced with his, and there is every indication that Gunnar believed his wife to be his equal. But he thought highly of himself, as many aspiring to greatness are inclined to, and remained engrossed in fulfilling his dreams. Alva – his love, muse, adviser and friend – was left to deal with life's mundanity. Not only did this come in the way of her pursuing her own dreams; it subjected her, at times, to enormous pressure. Alva Myrdal's life exemplifies the struggles women face in fulfilling their life goals.

Alva and Gunnar's son, Jan, was born in 1927. Two daughters would, in time, join the Myrdal family. Neither Alva's nor Gunnar's parents were wealthy, and nor were Alva and Gunnar's earnings sufficient to afford the services of a maid or a cook. Alva was thus heavily burdened with domestic drudgery in the years when she and Gunnar were establishing themselves as academics of note and, later, doyens of public policy. Their earlier years, Gunnar would later recall, comprised 'just the right combination of the hardest of toil and pure creative joy', but he was speaking of his own creative joy, and not Alva's. For her, it was mostly toil: she had to at once rear her little son, undertake her own study in psychology and carry out secretarial and research duties for Gunnar. She had suppressed her own creativity for Gunnar's and in her hopes that he would attain greatness, and that she would, too, with him.

Alva and Gunnar's finances were precarious in their early years together. They subsisted entirely on meagre stipends, and any surplus seemed to dissipate as they helped Gunnar's cash-strapped father. To help their finances during their postgraduate studies, Alva and Gunnar approached the Rockefeller Foundation for study fellowships in the United States. Both were accepted. While Alva was to study the methodology of social psychology, Gunnar was to study the methodologies in economics and the social sciences. The fellowship granted stipends of $750 each for Gunnar and Alva for the 1929–30 academic year, which was almost the average American income. The young couple could enjoy a comfortable living for the first time in their independent lives.

They decided to leave Jan, who was by then a toddler, in the care of their parents on their respective farms. This was a fairly common practice in that era for those with a city job or who had to travel overseas, and Alva was reassured by her paediatrician of their decision. She would, however, later describe this compromise for her husband and her career as a mistake, and it would have grave consequences for their future relationship with their only son. Alva's fretting over her studies at the expense of her little son's welfare was in contrast with Gunnar's indifference. He was thrilled to relive the togetherness of their first years as young students: he would have her all to himself, and he could concentrate his energies on the development of his yet inchoate economic theories that would, in time, make him famous.

Before undertaking their fellowships in the United States, Alva and Gunnar had gone to London. Gunnar there began his classic *The Political Element in the Development of Economic Theory*, which would be published in 1930. Alva, meanwhile, wrote a critique on Freud's theory of dreams, and also a treatise on emotional factors in education. In her critique, she pointed out some inconsistencies in Freud's theory of dreams, but concurred with most of his observations of psychoanalysis.

Alva and Gunnar's time in the US laid the groundwork for their future greatness. Immersing themselves in the dark chapters of American history afforded them invaluable, and sometimes shocking, insights into the workings of class, government and social policy. The stark inequalities they witnessed underpinned Gunnar's theoretical work in economics. But more than that, it gave impetus to their later shared quest for a practical social democratic state in Sweden.

The couple arrived in the US for fellowship studies in mid-October 1929, just days before the most calamitous stock market crash in history. Two of the greatest economic and social thinkers of the century thus had, as it were, a front-row seat to the unfolding of the Great Depression. On Black Tuesday, October 1929, Wall Street's dramatic crash signalled an inexorable slide in the value of stocks and wiped billions of dollars from the market and left millions in penury. Alva and Gunnar were impressed with the American 'frontier spirit' but were shocked at the inability of the government to address the deteriorating economic situation much beyond issuing slogans through loudspeakers and on billboards. Alva and Gunnar were profoundly disturbed by the jarring contrast of dishevelled crowds of hungry poor queuing up at soup kitchens and the conspicuous indulgence of the rich – a state of affairs quite at odds with the shared responsibility for poverty in Sweden.

Alva and Gunnar would later state that they had been 'radicalized' by their experience in the US and, thereafter, became devoted to government initiatives that fostered greater social equality. For his part, Gunnar became hardened against the failings of a free market, writing in *The Political Element in the Development of Economic Theory* that, in the still-unravelling Great Depression, 'laissez-faire had lost because of events, not intellectual criticism'.

In the US, Alva devoted herself to more than a dozen research topics in education, child psychology and child development. But when her sponsoring professor expired and she had to abandon her project on Freud's theory of dreams, it seemed that her career aspirations had been sidelined. Alva was not one for complaining, though, and when Gunnar was offered a position as an assistant professor at the University of Geneva, Gunnar and Alva set off to Switzerland in September 1931 with their son, Jan, and Gunnar's younger sister Mela.

Their sojourn began promisingly enough, with a road trip, in the family's shiny black Oldsmobile from the US, to a scenic villa by Lake Geneva. But the most traumatic months of Alva's life would follow. After a late-term miscarriage, she suffered a serious infection, and for weeks her life hung in the balance. She underwent a bungled operation and was told by her physician that she must have a hysterectomy. Alva rejected the doctor's advice. She would not, she declared, be subjected to any procedure that would render her infertile. In asserting her reproductive rights, she foreshadowed feminist movements for female reproductive rights that emerged in later generations.

Her firm stand surprised Gunnar, and it dismayed the doctors, who would need to take special care in their subsequent remedial operation. But for herself and her unborn children, she would be proved correct, with time. In the short term, she faced months of convalescence, and the disconsolate Gunnar's energy was expended in carrying her from room to room of their new house and caring for her.

It would take two years for Alva's health to recover and her recurring fevers to abate. However, her irrepressible mind could not be subdued by ill health, and after the Myrdals' return to Stockholm, Alva found herself deeply engaged in seeking meaningful solutions to the problems facing her country's women and children. She wrote articles on parenting, children's education and the problem of underpopulation facing Sweden. She and Gunnar also set about formulating policies which would later be adopted by the Swedish Social Democratic Party. The party would, in time, provide a platform for Alva's ideas aimed at establishing a more equitable, just and progressive society. She found an ideological ally in the Social Democratic Party leader Per Albin Hansson, who was elected prime minister in 1932. Like

Alva and Gunnar, Hansson wanted every citizen to be afforded basic rights and necessities as a matter of course.

Alva and Gunnar saw the welfare of Sweden's citizens as inextricable from that of the nation. One of the major issues facing Sweden in those years was a falling birth rate. In 1934, Alva and Gunnar wrote *Crisis in the Population Question* (*Kris i befolkningsfrågan*), in which they advocated extensive social reforms to address the nation's dwindling population. They stated that a larger population was necessary and cautioned that if the trend of Swedes' having fewer children continued '[Sweden] would at the end of the 1970s have almost twice as many elderly people in relation to individuals in the working ages now'. This would inevitably lead to a catastrophic decline in the nation's production. They stated that couples should be persuaded to give birth to at least three children, and proposed that families with three or more children be provided free medical care, free school lunches, more affordable housing and subsidized rent. Other recommendations in Alva and Gunnar's book included easy access to contraceptives, sex education in schools, education loans, maternity leave and government allowances for children.

One of the more radical assertions of the book – and undoubtedly Alva's most controversial contribution to Sweden's public policy – concerned eugenics. Alva suggested that those 'hereditarily defective or in other respects deficient' should be sterilized. Alva's idea was by no means original; it had been the subject of considerable debate and was deliberated on by the Swedish Royal Commission on Population in 1929; it either existed as or became public policy in much of the Western world by the mid-twentieth century. Whether on account of Alva's suggestion or existing public discourse, compulsory sterilization – most of which would be conducted on eugenic grounds –

was implemented in 1934. The practice was only abandoned more than four decades later, in 1975, with the Swedish state subsequently paying damages to its victims.

At any rate, *Crisis in the Population Question* created uproar. It was immediately the subject of intense public discussion, and study groups were formed across the country to consider the book's proposals. Sweden's more conservative elements thought its suggestions scandalous, a threat to morals and culture, and some in the political left rejected the idea that people should be encouraged to have children. Thankfully, the robust self-confidence of the book's assertions was matched by Alva's and Gunnar's conviction in the book's cause, for it would have a profound impact on their lives – personally as well as professionally. Gunnar's mentor Cassel publicly denounced their work, and a fellow academic even urged his wife to shun Alva. Alva and Gunnar came to be known as the notorious 'Myrdal Couple', and all manner of eponyms for the pair gained currency in the wake of the book's publication: To 'myrdal' became an expression for 'having sex'; an apartment building with many children was known as a 'Myrdal building'; children were light-heartedly referred to as 'Myrdal sprouts'. Alva's daughter Sissela recalls that she was dubbed 'Krisan' (little crisis) for the continuing storm of debate the book provoked.

Indeed, Sissela's birth was timely for Alva. After miscarriages and traumatic medical complications in Geneva, Alva could show the nation that she was practising what she preached when Sissela (later Bok) arrived on 2 December 1934, just as the furore over the book raged. Alva and Gunnar would have one more child, Kaj (later Fölster), in August 1936. She had fulfilled her procreational duty towards her country – perhaps, in adhering to her book's suggestion that Swedish families of all classes consist of three children.

Alva's own commitment to her ideals here was mirrored by a powerful consensus in the nation for change. And insofar as Gunnar and Alva's writings became a virtual handbook for the Swedish Social Democratic Party government's foundation of the country's welfare state, known as *Folkhemmet* (the people's home), the book was a roaring success. Alva's and Gunnar's intellectual credentials were firmly established and elevated along with Folkhemmet, and their influence on Swedish society was assured by decades of public policy based on their seminal work.

Alva and Gunnar were equally adamant that their radical proposals in *Crisis in the Population Question* were necessary for the nation to redeem itself. But though Alva had perhaps contributed the greater part of the social aspect of the book – as she travelled the country, giving speeches and writing countless newspaper articles in support of its tenets – Gunnar was ultimately afforded more recognition. He was made chairman of the Housing Commission and a member of the newly formed Population Commission in 1935. He became a member of parliament too, and was asked to serve in other public capacities where perhaps Alva's expertise was superior, as it was in housing.

The injustice and sexism were noted by Alva, as it was by Gunnar. When Gunnar received some offers, he would suggest that their offer was better made for Alva. Gunnar then would be met with replies that evinced the spirit of the times. The embarrassed representative of the authority in the subject would explain that they had surely meant, by their offer to him, that Alva too would be involved in their organization. It would be years before Alva's brilliance would be recognized and sought in its own right.

Alva's energy and intellect would not be contained by others' expectations, however. She was instrumental in founding a training college for preschool teachers – Socialpedagogiska

Seminariet (the Seminary for Social Pedagogy) – in 1936. For her, social change could only be facilitated by an educated population, and for this, she saw instilling community values and fostering the abilities of young children as crucial.

Only two years after the opening of the school, in 1938, Gunnar was invited to the United States to undertake social research. The result of his labours – delayed by the events of World War II – was *An American Dilemma: The Negro Problem and Modern Democracy*, which would be published in 1944. Alva, meanwhile, worked on *Nation and Family*, in which she deliberated on Sweden's social progress. The book also denounced racial discrimination, asserting that it militated against democracy's basic principles and espousing gender equality and equal pay for equal work.

Alva's achievements by this time had been bringing her international attention, and she would eventually be named 'Sweden's most admired woman' several times. But she never assumed any aura of superiority; on the contrary, she exhibited humility and a clear, straightforward commitment to her ideals and proposals. Her courage too was evident, though, unlike other women recipients of the Nobel Peace Prize, her mettle was never tested under the fire or duress of repressive governments.

Gunnar and Alva's decision to return to their country after Germany's invasion of Norway and Denmark on 9 April 1940, however, surely evinces the couple's unwavering commitment to their country and ideals. Their decision bordered on foolhardiness given the state of affairs in Europe at the time. Both were strident in their criticism of National Socialism, and Nazi Germany had almost the entirety of Europe in its grasp. Had Sweden's government not maintained neutrality or collaborated with Hitler in the manner of Norway's traitorous leader Vidkun Quisling, Alva and Gunnar's plight would have been dire indeed.

Adhering to their other ideals was not so straightforward for Alva and Gunnar. While they had been sermonizing in print and during public appearances about child psychology, child education and childcare, their own family was far from a paragon of domestic harmony. A series of compromises, most of which Alva had made for Gunnar, led inevitably to Alva's family's suffering. One such decision was to leave her children behind in Sweden to join Gunnar in New York in 1941, after he returned there to continue work on *An American Dilemma*. By the time Gunnar and Alva were back in Sweden in 1942, fifteen-year-old Jan had been in open rebellion against his parents. Alva's attempts to smooth over the increasingly violent altercations between Jan and his father proved futile. After one such incident, in which Gunnar had chased Jan around a table and Jan had threatened him with a chair, Jan left home. Much to his eminent parents' disappointment, Jan refused to join university and instead sought work as a journalist. Jan eventually became an activist, commentator and writer.

Jan's estrangement from Alva and Gunnar would, in time, become permanent and a source of much pain for his parents later in their lives. In 1966, Jan wrote and directed the controversial film *Myglaren*, whose scheming and manipulative central character's career bears more than a passing resemblance to his father's. And in his parents' final years, in 1982, Jan would publish a book *Barndom* (*Childhood*) that chronicles his tortured relationship with his parents. Needless to say, Alva and Gunnar were distraught at the book and its revelations.

This drama was decades away, though, and Alva's most productive years were ahead of her. During the war, she helped the Swedish diplomat Count Folke Bernadotte plan his White Buses Missions to repatriate Jews and foreigners, whose release from Nazi captivity he had negotiated, and in 1946, she was asked to join the Swedish School Commission. She was, however, still living in Gunnar's slipstream, and in 1947, when Gunnar was appointed the head of the UN Economic Commission for Europe (ECE) in Geneva, it seemed she would be relegated to playing the role of hostess for her powerful husband. All would soon change, and Alva would chart her own course in the coming years. It was in 1949, when she was forty-seven years of age, that she would really come into her own.

This was the year when she left to head the Secretariat's Department of Social Affairs in the United Nations, in New York. For the first time, her skills as a diplomat were put to use. She highlighted to those she encountered the practical importance of their decisions; and her engaging intellect rarely failed to impress. Now, she was no longer the adjunct of the great Gunnar Myrdal. She was a powerful, sought-after voice in international affairs and the senior-most woman in the UN – at an age when most women of her generation were settling into a middle age of unfulfilled dreams and drudgery.

From her new and exciting surrounds of New York, Alva wrote to Gunnar's sister, 'I have never had this chance to do what I can and be what I am; it is an "unfolding" that almost astonishes me.' For all the years until this time, she felt that her career path was like 'a meandering ribbon running alongside' Gunnar's. From this time, Alva's career would, at times, race ahead of her husband's.

As iron sharpens iron, Alva's years working with Gunnar had honed her intellect and tempered her rational perspectives. Their collaborations had been mutually beneficial, and she had become a visionary very much his equal. Now, as ever, Alva would not shy away from unpalatable truths. She approached the challenges she saw in the world with the same gusto she had for those of Sweden, and her assessments were forthright and topical. In 1950, in a lecture at the famous American liberal arts college for women Mount Holyoke College, she lamented: 'It seems incredible that more than half of this world's inhabitants go hungry today ... that about half of them, because of their illiteracy, are unable to participate in the life of our century. It might as well be 1350 as far as they are concerned ...' In the coming years, she would contend with some of the most compelling issues facing humankind with similar clarity and sense of purpose.

In the same year, Alva moved to Paris to head the Division of Social Sciences at UNESCO. In contrast to her championing procreation in Sweden nearly two decades earlier, she saw a need to avert an impending population explosion in the world and made efforts to promote a worldwide initiative for family planning. Her efforts were ultimately thwarted at the World Population Conference in Rome in 1954 by a strange – and perhaps unprecedented – tag team of the Catholic Church and Soviet bloc countries. Their delegates strived to prove that population itself was not an issue and advocated social and economic reform. Alva was bitterly disappointed. An opportunity to alleviate suffering of the world's poor and empower women had been squandered in favour of political manoeuvring.

Alva's UNESCO duties brought her to India in December 1952, where she met India's first prime minister, Jawaharlal Nehru, at a UNESCO conference about Gandhi. Alva and Nehru would become close in the following years. In their first encounter, she managed to startle the notoriously disengaged politician with an otherwise bland speech. She referred to UNESCO's goals as Gandhian goals and made mention of the Gandhian call to conscience. The great Indian leader had apparently dozed off, as he sat listening to the usual procession of pleasant homilies that such events oblige. But when Alva said, with characteristic forthrightness, 'And the truth must be the same, in whatever circumstances one speaks it, whether it concerns Korea or Kashmir,' the great statesman of the subcontinent awoke with a start. Her reference did not offend Nehru in the least, though. He invited Alva to lunch the following day, and they would remain friends until his death on 27 May 1964. Alva later described their friendship as 'an affectionate relationship that never became a relationship'. Speculation as to the exact nature of that relationship aside, Nehru's framed picture accompanied Alva as she lay bedridden and dying more than three decades after they met.

During her years at the UN, Alva finally completed *Women's Two Roles: Home and Work* with her friend and sociologist Viola Klein. The book, which was published in 1956, dealt with the conditions and choices facing women in the US, England, France and Sweden. Alva had shelved the project for years while she grappled with the more immediate issues plaguing women of the world's poorest nations. Perhaps her work at UNESCO afforded her a more rounded and mature perspective on the issues of womanhood.

In any event, the book proposed a timeless approach for women to adopt for balancing the numerous roles they would assume in their lives. Alva knew from her own experiences the opposing forces women often unsuccessfully negotiated as they juggled a career and family duties. Women, Alva and Viola suggested, could happily devote their lives to their families yet enjoy a fruitful and satisfying career if they chose to consider their lives in stages. Simultaneously assuming the roles of mother, wife and career woman could be a debilitating experience. Women may offer their children the nurturing they require in their children's first nine years while preparing themselves for a different role – like a 'new life' – in the workforce. This would not allow the full expression of their talents, but it would ensure that their abilities were not wasted to society and that their families enjoyed the company of a fulfilled mother and partner.

Underpinning the book's assertions was Alva's frank self-evaluation – understanding garnered from her life's tribulations and mistakes. Alva and Viola understood that a combination of factors in more affluent countries – medical advances that led to greater longevity and contraception that allowed women greater management of reproduction – had freed women from the bondage of endless pregnancies and the likelihood of death during childbirth. Women must be as free to express their aspirations as men. In this sense, Alva was a forerunner of many eminent women later in the twentieth century. Partnered with a man whose views were decidedly feminist for the times – he had made abortive efforts to study gender inequality after writing *An American Dilemma* – she was achieving success beyond the imaginings of her sisters of earlier generations. But she was only too aware of the toll exacted on her young children by her absences and remoteness as she held centre stage in Sweden's national discourse. Older and wiser, she concluded that women can satisfy the numerous aspects of their being – but not at the same time.

In 1955, Alva returned from service in the UN to that of her own country, when she travelled to Delhi. She would be Sweden's first woman ambassador to India, Ceylon and Burma for the following five years. In the Indian capital, she quickly became reacquainted with Prime Minister Nehru. Her visits to his residence, Teen Murti Bhavan, where she met his widowed, shy daughter, Indira, were followed by a deeper interaction. Indeed, the widower Nehru – his wife Kamala Kaul Nehru had died of tuberculosis in 1936 – would call upon Alva, at times, to host formal gatherings at his home. Attractive, urbane and an excellent speaker, she was eminently suited to the role. Her nationality too had some bearing on her close relationship with Nehru, the nature of which would have been unthinkable for an emissary of one of the world powers of the time. India had emerged as the leader of the Non-Aligned Movement; it was India's defence minister V.K. Menon who coined the term 'non-aligned' in 1953. Sweden's long-standing policy of neutrality allowed a more cordial relationship with its diplomats than those of Britain, the United States and the Soviet Union.

Perhaps unsurprisingly, given her spirit of humanitarianism, Alva's interest in the social policies and initiatives of India's first government in the early years of Independence far exceeded any regular ambassadorial obligation. She became utterly engrossed in Indian affairs and culture and immersed herself in the study of the country's history and traditions. Alva felt inspired by Nehru's idealism, just as were millions of Indians of the time. She went so far as to accompany the Indian prime minister to a number of village projects or agricultural developments he visited. When she travelled alone, Nehru would later seek her impressions and assessments of her trip. Alva's ambassadorship was thus characterized by 'engaged neutrality', as she described it, and it was a resounding success. On a personal level, it was likewise. She found in the dynamic Indian prime minister the foil for Gunnar's rational and academic genius, later referring to Nehru as 'the light man in my life'.

From 1956, Gunnar joined Alva in India for a series of visits. His observations there would form part of his epic work *Asian Drama: An Inquiry into the Poverty of Nations*, which was published in 1968. He too came to admire Jawaharlal Nehru and enjoy his friendship. While Gunnar seemed happy that they would return to Sweden, 'learning to grow old together' – and Alva had no career plans beyond writing of her experiences on the subcontinent – Alva was sad to leave India in 1961. She could scarce know that she would spend her 'retirement' years engaged in some of humanity's most pressing concerns.

Back in Stockholm in April 1961, Alva was busying herself with writing lectures on shared world responsibility for poverty when she was approached by Minister for Foreign Affairs Östen Undén to prepare a report. The report would contemplate proposals for disarmament that he could present to the UN General Assembly later that year. The world at this stage was faced with a very real threat of nuclear catastrophe. The erection of the Berlin Wall in 1961 was just weeks away, and the cold war would reach its climax with the Cuban Missile Crisis in October 1962, little more than a year later. In the following months, the Soviet Union declared that it would resume nuclear weapons testing, and the United States responded in the same vein. Alva Myrdal's attention towards disarmament was timely indeed; there could have been no worthier cause for her genius in diplomacy and public policy.

At first, Alva was overawed by the enormity of the task before her. Her work in the post-war years had, she later wrote, been predicated on building a better world, which had 'left [her] as rather an idle bystander' in the debate on nuclear weapons proliferation. Still, this was perhaps just the challenge she needed, and her formidable intellect was quickly trained on the issue. The result of her endeavours was the Undén Plan – a proposal for a 'non-atom club', which would consist of nations free of nuclear armaments, setting an example to others.

The report suggested that all non-nuclear nations would be equally devastated in the event of a nuclear catastrophe and should join hands and oppose nuclear proliferation and begin creating nuclear weapons–free zones, such as the one later created by treaty in 1967 in Latin America. In November 1961, Alva was elected to the national parliament, and in 1962 asked to lead the Swedish delegation to the United Nations Disarmament Commission. She would serve on the commission for the following twelve years. Her rational approach, which she shared with Gunnar, left her with no illusions as to the willingness of the major powers to commit to disarmament. But her penchant for compromise, coupled with an indefatigable resolve, gave her strength for persevere in finding ways of reaching towards this almost impossible objective. In contrast, Gunnar's trademark bluntness and inclination for controversy made him quite unsuited for such a role.

Alva established herself as an astute politician and persuasive speaker in these years. Her courtly demeanour, attractive appearance and elegant dresses – coupled with her natural sense of style and drama – helped to create a public persona that furthered her cause. She was keenly aware of the power of image and publicity, and Gunnar would oblige by posing with her for crafted public photographs. He seemed quite content to play a supporting role, as she had often done for him. Driving all her efforts, though, was her commitment. She felt more uplifted by her role in pursuing disarmament than for any of her other numerous endeavours.

It was just as well. Although much publicity and diplomatic efforts were launched for their cause by the eighteen-member Disarmament Commission, neither the United States nor the Soviet Union seemed the least swayed from their course of acquiring weapons of mass destruction. In the decade between 1962 and 1972, the number of intercontinental ballistic missiles (ICBMs) prepared for deployment increased more than fivefold: from 500 to 2,600. In their dogged quest to amass weaponry that could spell doom for humankind, the powers seemed to have entered into some kind of tacit alliance. Alva saw hope in the short term only for test bans, which would serve to at least mitigate the nuclear threat.

The outcome of exhaustive negotiations in Geneva was a treaty banning nuclear weapons testing in the atmosphere, in outer space and underwater, known as the Partial Test Ban Treaty (PTBT). The treaty was ratified by the major nuclear powers in August 1963. Alva was assured by the relevant governments that the ban on atmospheric, underwater and outer-space testing would be followed by a later complete ban on nuclear testing, but she soon saw that the nuclear-weapon nations remained committed to underground testing. Still, her efforts in bringing the opposing sides together to endorse the PTBT saved immeasurable harm to the environment and the world's people – harm that is unavoidable with atmospheric testing.

Alva also succeeded in persuading the Swedish government to constitute the Stockholm International Peace Research Institute (SIPRI) in 1965, which would give sound data about nuclear proliferation. When she was made minister for disarmament in January 1967 – the first such ministership in the world – Gunnar took over as chairperson at SIPRI. Their collaborations never ceased. Both saw development and disarmament as inextricably linked, and Alva would continue with her social activism within Sweden while being part of the government. She was instrumental in Sweden's declaration to renounce nuclear, and later chemical and biological, weapons.

At the end of her tenure as the Swedish representative on the United Nations Disarmament Commission, Alva expressed her frustration, saying, 'May I end this last official statement of mine by asking my colleagues: "When is some action for disarmament to start in earnest?"' As with many great people, her ideas and work outlived her, and proposals she made during her time on the committee would see the light of day decades later.

After her retirement from the commission and government, she again took to the field of education, lecturing in sociology at several schools in the United States, such as the Massachusetts Institute of Technology, Wellesley College and the University of Wisconsin–Madison. She also remained actively engaged in peace activism. She castigated both the United States and the Soviet Union in her book *The Game of Disarmament: How the United States and Russia Run the Arms Race*, which was published in 1976. In this book, Alva laid out a road map for total disarmament. She advocated an end to stockpiling, deployment and use of all weapons. She stressed the importance of ending warfare against civilians and the environment and proposed the demilitarization of oceans and space. Alva also staunchly opposed foreign military bases.

In her book, she stated that she had been constrained from openly articulating as a commission member; and her criticism had been withering. She charged the United States and the Soviet Union with indulging in irresponsible behaviour in pursuing nuclear supremacy and with having conspired to avoid disarmament. She asserted that arms control had been merely a euphemism – one employed to convey the false impression that the superpowers were interested in abandoning or at least moderating their dangerous race for military advantage.

Alva called for a world disarmament conference, which would be preceded, she suggested, by demanding two principal security guarantees from the nuclear powers: first, a promise not to initiate any act of nuclear warfare; and second, a guarantee not to attack with nuclear weapons any country and, especially, those countries that possess a nuclear arsenal. At such a conference, she proposed the powers to agree to begin quantitative disarmament, to end qualitative improvements in nuclear and conventional weapons and to prohibit production, stockpiling, deployment and use of all chemical weapons.

She did not expect the superpowers, however, to move forward on nuclear disarmament of their own volition. She suggested that the unresponsive superpowers be bypassed and other nations come forward for executing arms limitation agreements. She wanted an international verification agency to be put in place to monitor chemical and nuclear tests. Alva believed a freeze on the development of all types of weapon systems to be a prerequisite for any realistic disarmament policy.

The perseverance and urgency with which Alva championed disarmament evinces her deep commitment to humanity's welfare. She passionately warned of the threat of mass destruction if nuclear proliferation was not brought to an end. She had written in the preface to *The Game of Disarmament* the stark words: 'The ruin of the planet is there for all to contemplate'.

For her pivotal role in furthering the cause of nuclear disarmament, Alva was conferred the Nobel Peace Prize in the year 1982, along with Mexican diplomat Alfonso Garcia Robles. Chairman of the Norwegian Nobel Committee, Egil Aarvik, paid rich tribute to Alva Myrdal in his presentation speech in Oslo on 10 December 1982:

> Alva Myrdal's commitment to the service of disarmament has long since established her international reputation. The many awards and other marks of high honour she has received testify to her standing in the international community. Her commitment, moreover, reveals a tremendous span, both in terms of time and spheres of interest. As far back as the 1930s, she played a prominent part in developing the modern Swedish welfare state. She was a staunch champion of women's liberation and equal rights. She has proved a brilliant diplomat, and was the first woman to be appointed head of a department in the United Nations.

By this time, Alva was nearly eighty-one and ailing. Despite being stricken with bouts of aphasia – and needing her daughters to be present to read her lecture should she be unable to speak – Alva declared in her stirring lecture on 11 December 1982:

> I have always looked at the world's development as a battle between the forces of good and evil. Not, therefore, simply expressed as a battle between Jesus and Satan, since I don't see the development as limited to our own cultural sphere. Rather perhaps the metaphor about Ormazd, the good, and Ahriman, the evil. My personal philosophy of life is that of ethics.

She noted in the lecture that 'many countries persecute their own citizens and intern them in prisons or concentration camps. Oppression is becoming more and more a part of the systems'. She also stated that 'the age in which we live can only be characterized as one of barbarism. Our civilization is in the process not only of being militarized but also of being brutalized.' She expressed satisfaction that 'a mighty protest movement, speaking the language of common sense, in more and more countries, has now arisen to confront all these forces engaged in the armament race and the militarization of the world'. She stated her belief too that 'leaders ... will be forced some day, sooner than later, to give way to common sense and the will of the people'.

She condemned the employment of science and knowledge for destructive pursuits, stating, 'It does not just happen. It is disclosed by science that practically one half of trained intellectual resources are being mobilized for murderous purposes'. But despite the misuse of resources for weapons which endanger humankind's survival, Alva did not lose hope for better understanding between nations. She observed in her Nobel acceptance speech, 'We can hope that men will understand that the interests of all are the same, and that hope lies in cooperation. We can then perhaps keep peace.'

Alva tried to spur the good in world leaders and called upon them to come together for nuclear disarmament. She stressed that 'inventions and great discoveries have opened up whole continents to reciprocal communication and interchange, provided we are willing'. She reminded leaders of the impossibility of victory in nuclear war in her Nobel Lecture, and called upon them to appreciate that 'War is murder. And the military preparations now being made for a potential major confrontation are aimed at collective murder. In a nuclear age, the victims would be numbered by the millions. This naked truth must be faced'. Alva's commitment to peace was afforded even greater significance when she dedicated her share of the prize money to two projects – against Gunnar's wishes. One project was a study of nuclear weapons deployed at sea, and the other a study of the ethical aspects of the 'culture of violence', with a focus on what Alva termed 'anti-violence'. She deposited the prize money in a bank account in her own name so that she would be free to use the funds on these cherished projects. They would be her last contribution to the world.

Alva Myrdal has rightly been hailed as the conscience of the disarmament movement. Besides the Nobel Peace Prize, Alva also received, along with Gunnar, the West German Peace Prize (1970), the Albert Einstein Peace Prize (1980) and the Jawaharlal Nehru Award for International Understanding in 1981. Alva breathed her last on 1 February 1986. Her work continued though, and test bans that she had proposed decades earlier were finally agreed to in 1996. At least part of her vision was facilitated by Mikhail Gorbachev, one of the heroes of the last century, whose reorientation of Soviet strategic aims brought the end of the cold war.

The works of a writer of Alva's insight are timeless, and her material is highly thought-provoking. Among her most thought-provoking works is, curiously, a letter to her daughters in April 1983, in which she elucidated questions one should ponder:

> How is one an individual, and how is one's fate shaped in interaction with other people?
> How does one in turn contribute to forming these other people?
> How close can one really be to other people?
> How do I become myself?
> How have I really been with you?
> How have I come to displace my own self in order to fit in other selves?
> Where does one self merge with another?

In this letter, she also gave voice to her regrets. Cautioning her daughters, she wrote:

> This has become a problem now that I have lived so long. I can see, as if in a fifty- or sixty-year rear-view mirror, the completely preposterous displacements that have taken place between what I have become, and done, and what I should have been able to, perhaps ought to have planned. But I did not plan it. To a large extent, life just became.

Furthermore, she made mention of her feelings regarding the changed status of women:

> Of course this is especially clear in a historical-sociological perspective now, when living conditions have become so different. If 'then' had been 'now' I would of course never have taken the name 'Myrdal'. Even now, after the passage of the new laws concerning names, I am tempted to call myself Alva

Reimer Myrdal. Why should the genes from the female side be denied?

The life of Alva Reimer Myrdal carries clear lessons for women of this century: Educate yourself first, no matter what trials and tribulations you may face. Struggles in childhood may ultimately help achieve dizzying success. And middle age can be the most rewarding time to pursue career ambitions – it need not be a time for self-recrimination or inactivity. Women should not be compelled to choose between career ambitions and family. Greater flexibility must be afforded the world's women so that they may fulfil their potential at home and the workplace, for the benefit of themselves, their families and society at large.

A rich tribute to the memory of Alva Myrdal would be in women ensuring greater gender equality. If today's women assert themselves as Alva did, 'giving the genes from the female side their due', the welfare of humanity will be assured. Half of the world's people may find their voice, a voice holding the promise of a new generation. And with the innate understanding of the value of creation that women possess, humankind may only then march towards world peace.

MOTHER TERESA

BORN DARLING OF HUMANITY

'... In our wholehearted, free service to the poorest of the
poor, the starving and destitute – it is Christ we touch.'

Mother Teresa enhanced the prestige of the Nobel Peace Prize. A true saint, she tore apart dualities of all kind: fame and shame, good and bad, life and death, happiness and sorrow. She has rightly been hailed by the world as the 'Saint of the Gutters'.

Mother Teresa was born on 26 August 1910, in Skopje town of Albania, to Nikollë Bojaxhiu and Dranafile Bojaxhiu. She, however, considered 27 August as her birthday because it was on this day that she had been baptized. She received her first Communion when she was five-and-a-half years old. The youngest of three children, she had a sister, Aga, and a brother, Lazar.

Her father passed away when she was only eight years old. He died under dubious circumstances, and it was rumoured that he had been poisoned by Serbian agents. His death brought the family to the brink of penury. Dranafile, Teresa's mother, battling depression at the time, struggled to raise her children. Nonetheless she started a small business selling embroidery, and faced the financial crisis with fortitude.

Dranafile was a devout Christian and never turned away anyone who came to her for help. About her mother, Teresa said, 'She taught us to love God and to love our neighbour.' Teresa and her mother spent most of their time at their parish. Teresa was so deeply imbued with Christian values that she thought of becoming a nun when she was only twelve years old. Teresa was fascinated by stories of the lives of missionaries and their service to the poor in Bengal. However, her mother did not approve of the idea, as she was too young.

Teresa was a good student, and was articulate and had a calm demeanour. She loved to teach and, so, gave religious instruction to children at her parish. However, she loved spending time at church, praying, the most. As time passed, the desire to be a nun acquired more and more urgency in her, and after six years she received her call to be a missionary. Her religious instructor, Father Jambrenkovic, told her that a call of God would be accompanied by a feeling of deep elation and joy. Teresa now had no doubts, and this time, her mother did not object to Teresa's decision to become a nun. She told Teresa, 'Put your hand in His and walk all the way with Him.' So, Teresa applied to the Loreto order in Bengal, an order of nuns that worked for spreading literacy in India.

Teresa left home in September 1928. Bidding a tearful farewell to her friends and relatives at Skopje railway station, she left for Zagreb, where she spent a few days with her mother and sister. Then, she bade farewell to her mother at Zagreb railway station – the last she saw of her mother. However, before leaving for Bengal, Teresa went to the Loreto Abbey in Rathfarnham, Ireland, to learn English, the language the Sisters of Loreto used to instruct schoolchildren in Bengal.

On 6 January1929, she reached Calcutta (now Kolkata). After spending a few days there, she travelled to Darjeeling, about 650 kilometres north of Calcutta, where she learnt Bengali and taught at St Teresa's school close to her convent. On 24 May 1931, she took her religious vows as a nun – vows of poverty, chastity and obedience. After completing her novitiate there, Sister Teresa, as she was then addressed, was asked to teach at St Mary's School, supervised by Loreto Convent in Entally, eastern Calcutta. She spent seventeen years in the school, both as a teacher and as a principal. In the school, Sister Teresa taught geography, history and catechism. Teaching was Teresa's passion, her only love other than her love of Jesus. She was a dedicated teacher who sacrificed all her comforts for the care of her schoolchildren. While teaching, she was humorous and witty and often narrated many anecdotes from her life.

In 1943, the Bengal famine tore apart her heart, as she could not stand to see the death and starvation all around her. She was also deeply disturbed by the communal violence that broke out in 1946, owing to the demands of the Muslim League under the leadership of Muhammad Ali Jinnah. On 16 August 1946, violent riots erupted in Calcutta lasting four days. Food became scarce, and Sister Teresa had around 200 starving children with her.

Sister Teresa was inspired by Father Henry, a Belgian priest who worked for the poor. Father Henry believed that prayer without action is worthless. Sister Teresa was deeply touched by Father Henry's teachings, and developed a similar faith in the importance of action. On 10 September 1946, while she was travelling from Calcutta to Darjeeling, she felt an ecstatic sensation. She felt that Jesus had called on her to nurse the poor and the sick. She felt that God did not want her to remain confined to Loreto and had earmarked her for a higher purpose. Mother Teresa says, 'The message was quite clear. It was an order. I was to leave the convent. I felt God wanted something more from me. He wanted me to be poor and to love Him in the poorest of the poor.'

There were many hurdles in her choice. The first was that it required her to leave Loreto, which was no less painful than her severing relations with her own mother and siblings when she had decided to become a nun. The second hurdle was that she needed the Church's permission to leave Loreto.

She had two options for seeking permission. She could either seek permission from the Vatican directly, which would be final and binding, or she could seek permission from the Archbishop of Calcutta. She opted for the latter, because she thought it would be convenient. But it turned out otherwise. The idea did not go down well with the Archbishop of Calcutta, as he could not permit a lone European woman to move on the streets of Calcutta when political and communal strife was rampant. To err on the side of caution, she was sent to Asansol, a city about 280 kilometres from Calcutta. But here, again, God intervened when Father Henry declared, 'His Grace had confided in him that a mother was coming for the poor. She would work not in a convent, in big schools, in colleges or in hospitals but in the slums and in the streets.'

The issue of permission travelled to the Vatican, and she was granted the Indent of Exclaustration for one year; after a year, it would be decided whether she should be allowed to continue her work or be asked to return to Loreto. The news gladdened Mother Teresa, and soon spread like wildfire in Loreto and among other Christian missionaries in Calcutta. She, then, got her religious habit blessed by Father van Exem. It was a white saree with blue borders which she wore with a rosary. Since Mother Teresa was to work in the slums, Father van Exem advised her to undertake medical training, and Mother Teresa went to the Medical Mission Sisters in Patna, Bihar. She wore the habit while leaving the Loreto convent on 17 August 1948 to love and nurse the poor and the sick. All the Loreto Sisters were proud of Mother Teresa, and Sister Rozario remarked that Mother Teresa had brought glory not only to Loreto but also to God.

Back from Patna, she started a small school in the slums of Motijhil near Dumdum, north Calcutta, in 1948. While she left as a principal from St Mary's School, here, in the new school, she did not even have a roof over her head. There were no tables, chairs, books, pencils or any other amenities necessary for running a school. All she had in the name of a school were twenty-one shabbily dressed children.

The children were first instructed in cleanliness. She also washed some students. Seeing Mother Teresa's commitment to the children, the people of the slum came forward to provide books and slates by collecting money. The attendance grew to fifty-six in just one month, and three teachers volunteered to help. The students were taught Bengali and arithmetic. Girls were taught needlework as well. Mother Teresa christened the school 'Nirmal Hriday' – 'pure Heart'. The children were taught to develop a nirmal hriday, and speak well with their parents and siblings at home. Later she opened another school in the notorious slum of Tiljala, east Calcutta, in December 1948.

Once, while returning home, she stopped at a church on the way in the hope of getting some donation to her work. The priest at the church treated her rudely and told her to start begging. She left, her eyes filled with tears. Nonetheless she was not disheartened. The humiliation of being turned away proved to be a blessing in disguise, as she now realized that there is grace even in begging to help the poor. Mother Teresa would say, 'If the ultimate humiliation is for me to beg, so be it.' All she needed for begging was the ability to sustain humility, of which Mother Teresa possessed an inexhaustible store. In fact, this was the logical outcome of her vow of poverty.

She soon opened a dispensary and started visiting chemists and asking them to donate medicine. She would often face nasty abuse. The two most common diseases she encountered were tuberculosis and leprosy. Once, she met a leper who had been abandoned by her family. She had lost fingers in both hands and could not cook. Mother Teresa nursed her affectionately. She would also visit an education officer for developing her Motijhil school. Awed by her dedication, the education officer would tell her, 'Sister, I admire you and envy you. Your love for these destitute classes is great, and here we, of this country, do nothing for our own. Go to the prime minister and tell him about what you have been doing. He should do this work with his government.' But Mother was not impressed by the empty words. She wished that he had provided her with the assistance she had approached him for.

Mother Teresa thought her faith alone could sustain her in the field of service. However, her working alone in the slums made the local clergy highly uncomfortable. Their rumblings had reached Mother Provincial in Entally. Mother Provincial loved Mother Teresa, and she asked Mother Teresa to come back to Loreto. But Mother Teresa stopped visiting Loreto thereafter, so that she might not succumb to the temptation of an easy life there. Mother Teresa remarked:

> Mother Provincial's desire is for me to go back to Loreto, but I know God wants my work. If the rich can have the full service and devotion of so many nuns and priests, surely the poorest of the poor and the lowest of the low can have the love and devotion of us few. 'The slum sister', they call me, and I am glad to be just that for His love and glory.

Around this time, the Archbishop of Calcutta, Ferdinand Perier, who had been keeping tabs on Mother Teresa's work, decided to support her in her mission. The Archbishop of Calcutta was convinced that Mother Teresa's work was informed by the will of God. The Archbishop asked Father van Exem to prepare a constitution for a new congregation which would be called 'Constitution for the Missionaries of Charity'. On 7 October 1950, the constitution was approved by the Sacred Congregation in Rome. Father van Exem read the constitution during a Mass celebrated by Archbishop Perier himself:

> For more than two years now, a small group of young women, under the guidance of Sister Teresa, a lawfully uncloistered religious of the Institute of the Blessed Virgin Mary, have devoted themselves ... to helping the poor, the aged and the sick, in our metropolitan city, who, crushed by want and

destitution, live in conditions unworthy of human dignity.
Those who join this Institute, therefore, are resolved to spend
themselves unremittingly in seeking out, in towns and villages,
even amidst squalid surroundings, the poor, the abandoned,
the sick, the infirm, the dying ...

In Christianity, the creation of a constitution and a vow, as was
outlined for the Missionaries of Charity, is a rarity. It speaks volumes
of Mother Teresa's resolve to return God's love and compassion by
loving Him in His oft-ignored manifestations. Only a saint can find
Christ in the broken, starving and destitute, and Mother Teresa
identified wholeheartedly with these suffering souls. On one
occasion, Mother Teresa met the Lieutenant governor of Delhi at
this residence, and when the governor offered her a cup of tea, she
adamantly refused. Many years later, when Navin Chawla, Mother
Teresa's biographer, asked her about the refusal, she had a bizarre
explanation. She said that wherever she or her sisters went, people
often thanked them and offered tea or a cold drink or some eatable,
which they, of course, could not afford. She said she could not
refuse the hospitality of the poor and accept the hospitality of the
rich. This way, she explained, nobody would be hurt.

In 1952, with the help of Indian officials, Mother Teresa
opened the first Home for the Dying, converting an abandoned
Hindu temple into Kalighat Home for the Dying (or Mother
Teresa's Home for the Dying Destitute), a free hospital for the
terminally ill. The poor who sought refuge in the home received
medical attention and a dignified death, according to the rituals
of their faith. The Quran was read when a Muslim inmate was
dying; Hindus were given gangajal (water from the Ganga); and
Catholics were administered the last rites. About offering the poor
a good death, Mother Teresa said, 'A beautiful death for people
who lived like animals but died like angels – loved and wanted.'

In 1955, she opened the Nirmala Shishu Bhavan, a home for orphans and homeless youth. Mother Teresa tried to establish a Shishu Bhavan in all the leprosy centres that her mission had opened. She insisted that one of the greatest diseases is loneliness and emphasized the need for opening more and more such Shishu Bhavans for children.

Mother Teresa was always among the first to reach places affected by strife. She reached Beirut in August 1982 when the Lebanon–Israel war had grown fierce. She found that a number of mentally ill children were trapped amidst heavy shelling, thirsty and hungry. Mother Teresa and her sisters, ignoring all warnings, went in a Red Cross van to rescue the children. Seeing them, the fighters ceased fire and allowed them to rescue the children.

Mother Teresa's relationship with Pope John Paul II, then head of the Catholic Church, is well documented. She looked up to him and called him 'Holy Father'. The Pope in turn held Mother Teresa in high esteem and was highly appreciative of her work based on the Church's core values. He allowed Missionaries of Charity to set up soup kitchens for the poor of Rome, a testament to how valued Mother Teresa was in the Catholic world.

Mother Teresa has received widespread acclaim across the globe. Various roads and buildings have been named after her. The most famous of them is Albania's international airport. Her birthday is a public holiday in Albania. In the country of her adoption, India, she was recognized for the first time with a Padma Shri award (the Order of the Lotus), the fourth highest civilian award in India, on India's Republic Day, on 26 January 1962. Mother Teresa was the first person of non-Indian origin to be conferred the Padma Shri. She was not inclined to accept the award, because, humble as she was, she believed that she had done nothing to deserve it. On returning to Calcutta, she adorned the medal around the neck of a small statue of Virgin Mary at Nirmal Hriday in Kalighat, whom she believed deserved the prize. She would later be conferred India's highest civilian award, the Bharat Ratna (the Jewel of India), in 1980. She was also conferred the Ramon Magsaysay Award in 1962 and The Order of Merit, the highest award of the British monarch, in 1983.

The chairman of the Norwegian Nobel Committee, Professor John Sannes, revealed that what had motivated the committee to confer the Nobel Peace Prize on Mother Teresa had been a comment made by the president of the World Bank, Robert S. McNamara: 'Mother Teresa deserves the Nobel Peace Prize because she promotes peace in the most fundamental manner – by her confirmation of the inviolability of human dignity.' She refused to attend the Nobel banquet, but agreed to receive the Nobel Prize 'in the name of the poor', to which the Norwegian Nobel Committee agreed.

She expired on 5 September 1997. After the death, the Holy See soon initiated her beatification, the first step towards canonization. Canonization of a person requires proof of miracles having occurred with the intercession of the person. In 2002, the Holy See recognized a miracle. A tumour in the abdomen of a Bengali woman, Monica Besra, was reportedly healed after her abdomen had been touched by a beam of light emerging from a locket containing Mother Teresa's picture. Monica Besra confirmed that this miracle had indeed taken place before her eyes and cured her. Mother Teresa was beatified on 19 October 2003, bestowing on her the title 'Blessed'.

Some critics accuse Mother Teresa of being a Catholic fundamentalist, whose aim, according to them, was evangelization and who contacted the vulnerable poor to convert them to Christianity. Mother Teresa had also, controversially, opposed abortion, going against the feminist advocacy of female reproductive rights. About abortion, Mother Teresa opined, 'The greatest destroyer of peace is abortion, because if a mother can kill her own child, what is left for me to kill you and you to kill me?' It is pertinent here to note here that Catholicism does not regard perfection as a precondition to sainthood. Vatican journalist John Allen has rightly observed, 'In reality, declaring someone a saint does, indeed, reflect a judgement that he or she lived a holy life, but it is not tantamount to a claim of moral perfection. It does not mean they never made mistakes or were utterly free of blind spots.' Mother Teresa was an unorthodox nun. She did not wear her habit and wore a coarse sari woven by lepers. She wanted to identify herself with the destitute to whose service she had committed herself. In her mission to serve the people, she took after Mahatma Gandhi, who wore only a loincloth and was called a 'half-naked fakir' (half-naked mendicant).

Mother Teresa always used charcoal for cooking food, the fuel the poor used. She never watched television or listened to the radio, as she would say, 'We have the reality.' The reality of life led by the Missionaries of Charity was indeed harsh. Mother Teresa made it binding upon all missionaries to go out into the streets, because the poor could not come to them. She also refused remuneration for her work. She once refused a millionaire when he offered her a large sum of money on the condition that she could use the interest accrued from the principal. That would have given her mission a considerable financial boost, but she asked him, 'What is the use of that money if I can't use it when and where it may be needed? I don't want my work to become a business. It must remain a work of love.'

She firmly believed that God would provide her with all she needed to continue her work. She urged her missionaries to serve people on the strength of their faith rather than on the strength of the funds they would have collected from the rich. It is no wonder, then, that her missions are now running hospitals; homes for persons with AIDS, leprosy, tuberculosis; soup kitchens; dispensaries; mobile clinics; counselling programmes for families and children; orphanages and schools.

She spent thirty years in Calcutta and founded her first mission overseas in Venezuela, in February 1965. Her missions spread to as many as 129 countries during her lifetime. And she never forgot to give each of her visitors her business card, on which the following lines were printed:

The Fruit of Silence is Prayer
The Fruit of Prayer is Faith
The Fruit of Faith is Love
The Fruit of Love is Service
The Fruit of Service is Peace

Mother Teresa

BETTY WILLIAMS

WOMAN WHO ENDED THE TROUBLES

'Every war that was ever fought represents life needlessly
wasted, a mother's labour spurned.'

Betty Williams was born on 22 May 1943 in Belfast, and was baptized as a Catholic. Her mother was a housewife and doting mother; her father earned his livelihood as a butcher. She did her early schooling at St Teresa Primary School and her higher studies at St Dominic's Grammar School. Though Catholicism marked the ambience of her home, tolerance and respect for others were thickly weaved into the family's fabric. When Betty was a child, she once referred to a person as 'a Protestant', and was immediately chastised by her mother, who said, 'I do not ever want to hear "Protestant" or "Catholic" in this house. Christians are what we are.'

When Betty had just entered her teens, her mother suffered a stroke, and the responsibility of taking care of her mother and her eight-year-old sister, Margaret, fell on her. The stroke had not only rendered her mother invalid but also financially ruined the family. Nonetheless, the family put up a brave face. Betty adopted a rigorous schedule for housekeeping besides taking care of her mother and young sister. She would feed and bathe her mother every morning, and escort her sister to her school. She continued with her own schooling too. She even helped her mother walk and coached her to speak, the ability to which her mother had lost as a result of the brain haemorrhage she had suffered. As a result, Betty matured beyond her years. Her early years laid the foundation for her future struggles in life, especially her heavenly ordained struggle for peace after witnessing a gruesome tragedy on Finaghy Road, in which a woman and her three children were killed in a car accident.

Though Catholic, Betty did not conform to Church dogma. She often disregarded the Church hierarchy of Northern Ireland. Defying religious traditions of Ireland, Betty, at the age of eighteen, married Ralph Williams, a Protestant and an Englishman. Ralph was an engineer with the merchant navy.

He had met Betty at a dance and they had fallen in love. Betty's decision to marry Ralph was bold, as such unions had been unheard of in Ireland and sometimes people had even been killed for marrying a person of a different faith. Her first child Paul was born in 1965, and is now a retired footballer. Her daughter Deborah was born in 1972.

After her wedding, she had to stay in Belfast because her husband was in the merchant navy and was often away. Betty cared for her children as Ralph was at sea most of the time. He earned a handsome salary, but Betty continued to earn independently. She held, 'I've always earned my own way ... not so as to be independent but in order to keep my mind active. I don't believe that women should cut themselves off from the world when they become wives and mothers. They should keep their minds open always and learn new things. And that was what I was doing, quietly, off in a corner.'

While working as a waitress, she had many bitter experiences because of her assertive nature. Betty told me that she was fired fourteen times for being discourteous to overbearing customers. She says, 'I was fired practically every Saturday night, after the rush hour.' Besides her work life being in disarray, she also had to suffer discrimination as a Catholic. She remembers the ruthlessness with which the English soldiers treated the Catholic community in Northern Ireland during the Troubles. She recalls, 'If a single Provo [IRA Provisional] did something in our area, the soldiers harassed us for six months. It really was infuriating.'

The Troubles refer to the ethno-nationalist conflict that began in the late 1960s and ended with the Belfast Good Friday Agreement in 1998. The Troubles were triggered in 1968 when young Catholics demanded civil rights, an immediate end to 'colonization' of Northern Ireland (also known as 'Ulster') by England and, particularly, by Protestants of England. The issues which emerged and needed to be resolved were the constitutional status of Northern Ireland; the relationship between Unionists or Protestant Loyalists, who wanted Northern Ireland to remain with the United Kingdom, and the Irish nationalists or Republicans, who were mostly Catholic and wanted to join a 'United Ireland'. The Irish Republican Army (IRA), a militant organization of Irish Republican volunteers, was formed to carry out an armed struggle to achieve the political aims of a United Ireland.

Witness to the many ignominies the Catholic community faced during the Troubles, Betty flirted with the idea of violent struggle for a brief period of time; like for instance, when she found that her sister's house had been destroyed while her sister and her husband had been away. She herself had a harrowing time at the hands of the army when she was arrested as an IRA suspect, during which she witnessed, with her own eyes, how the English soldiers dehumanized their victims. She was taken to a military prison and interrogated by soldiers. Betty describes her plight thus: 'I was sitting in the middle of a room, on a chair and this woman kept walking around me. It was extremely unnerving, and I was very irritated. I was certain I was going to be beaten at any moment.' Though not beaten, she was insulted and abused profusely and accused of many wrongdoings she had not committed.

She understood then why people revolted and joined the IRA. Her sympathies for the IRA had grown and she helped them whenever she could. On one occasion, she helped a few IRA cadres cross the border. She says, 'One night, I had a badly wounded man in the trunk of my car and drove him across the border. It was a risk I took because I regarded the IRA as our salvation, as our only means of surviving.'

However, on seeing the devastation on Bloody Friday, 21 July 1972, when the IRA had set off twenty-two bombs and killed and seriously wounded several people, her honeymoon with violent thinking ended abruptly. She now condemned violence of all nature. She confronted many IRA members she knew and urged them to eschew violence. Once, in a bizarre incident, she was beaten up in her own home by two women IRA activists who could not countenance her advice on peaceful means of protest. Yet another incident that eroded Betty's faith in the IRA took place, one day, in 1973, when she was shopping and she heard a gunfire. Later, a twenty-year-old British soldier would breathe his last at Betty's feet. Betty said, 'For the first time, I realized that the British troops are human beings too.' Betty knelt down beside the dying soldier and prayed for his departing soul. However, her people were not happy. Betty says, 'The women of Falls Road let me know that they were furious with me, because I had tried to open the gates of heaven to that poor boy's soul! That too was a lesson for me. I learnt that people had obviously lost their sense of the value of human life.'

From sympathizing with the IRA she went on to fully denounce violence and become convinced of the virtues of pacifism. Her transformation was not all plain sailing though, as she would suffer several pangs of doubt regarding her choices. She says, 'I've always had to exercise strict control of myself so as not to fight back. In fact, I still have to struggle for self-control.' But the death of three children on Finaghy Road, on 10 August 1976, removed all doubts from her heart. She says, 'The IRA adopted the slogan, "Peace with justice". But I could see no justice in what they had been doing…' Betty had no experience of being a peace activist and had been working as an office receptionist until the tragic accident on Finaghy Road turned over her life.

Although fundamentally same, people are different in the way they respond to happenings around them. On 10 August 1976, Anne Maguire was walking on the pavement with her three children when a speeding car suddenly swerved towards them. The driver, Danny Lennon, a nineteen-year-old IRA fugitive had been trying to escape, after having stolen a blue Ford, and was shot dead by the pursuing British army patrol. His car ploughed into Anne Maguire and her three children. Eight-and-a-half-year-old Joanne and her six-week-old brother Andrew, who was in his pram, were killed instantly; and John, just two-and-a-half years old, was hospitalized and succumbed to his fatal injuries the very next day.

Several people on the road witnessed the incident, but they all went their different ways. But the world witnessed the grace and magnanimity of Betty's soul. Betty Williams, who was driving home after visiting her mother, heard the crash and rushed to the site of the accident to care for the children and their mother. The tragic scene sent shivers down her spine. She tells me that she is still frequented by nightmares of that tragic day. The mother, Anne Maguire, sustained serious injuries. She valiantly endured the pain and recovered from her injuries, but became so psychologically distraught on losing her children that she later committed suicide.

Inevitably, the task of identifying and burying her three dead children fell to Anne's devastated and traumatized sister Mairead Maguire and Anne's husband. On hearing about the empathy Betty Williams had shown towards her family, Mairead invited Betty to the children's funeral. Meanwhile Betty, traumatized by the incident, started mobilizing people to bring an immediate end to the long-standing sectarian hostilities between the IRA and the British army. The conflict between Protestants and Irish Catholics had battered many lives, and Betty's family was no exception.

Betty's grandfather, who worked as a riveter in a shipyard in Belfast, had been thrown overboard by Protestants who had heard that his son was going to marry a Catholic woman. Betty's cousin Danny, an eighteen-year-old medical student, was shot dead by Protestants when he was entering his home after work. The hail of bullets traced a bloody outline of a cross on his chest. Four months later, another of Betty's cousins was blown away while driving past an exploding car. The car had been abandoned by IRA militants on the roadside. Betty rued, 'The Protestants killed one of my cousins, and the Catholics killed the other.'

After living through such horrific incidents, Betty's convictions had been shaken. The persecution of Catholics by Protestant soldiers had hounded Betty's conscience, and her faith in peaceful protest had eventually become tense. About her turbulent mind at the time, she said, 'I didn't think about the question of a United Ireland. I was only concerned about what I saw before my very eyes, about what was happening to Catholics in the ghettos. There was injustice everywhere. The whole system seemed to be rotten, and the only solution seemed to be an armed uprising against the enemy.'

The day of the Finaghy Road accident, 10 August 1976, was like any other day in Ulster. In 1976 alone, 300 killings had been reported. Reporter Richard Deutsch described the day of the Finaghy Road accident thus: 'A couple of dozen automobiles and trucks were stolen to use in building barricades. A few vehicles were burnt. There was a "small" disturbance in front of a police station in West Belfast. A bomb scare in a bus depot. A few cases of arson. All in all, it had been a normal day by Belfast standards.' But no one knew that the incident on Finaghy Road would start the end of the Troubles that took around 1,600 lives. It had changed Betty forever.

She decided to fight the mindless violence that roiled Ireland during the Troubles. She led thousands of citizens in a march, chanting, 'Enough is Enough!' and demanding an immediate end to the killings. When John succumbed to his injuries the next day, fifty women from Andersonstown and Stewartstown marched with prams protesting the IRA's violence. In the evening, Mairead rushed to Ulster Television studio and made an impassioned speech, on air, urging Protestants and Catholics to end violence. The whole of Belfast was electrified. Meanwhile, Betty Williams tore a few empty pages from her son's notebook and rushed out of her home. She started banging on people's doors, yelling at women who opened, 'Sign this!' When asked why she had been demanding signatures, she immediately wrote on the papers in her hands, 'Petition for Peace'. Within two days, she collected 6,000 signatures.

She did not immediately know what she should do with the papers. Then it struck her: She immediately phoned a local Irish newspaper and told them the story. It was the newspaper's front page the next day. She also appeared on BBC television, appealing to the women of both north and south Ireland, of England, Scotland and Wales to join her in a rally at the spot where the children had been killed.

On 13 August 1976, the children were buried at Belfast's Miltown cemetery. The following day, a Saturday, thousands joined a peace rally marching along Finaghy Road. Some members of the Irish Republican Army disrupted the peace march, abusing the marchers verbally and physically. Betty and Mairead were accused of being 'dupes of the British'. On the day of the funeral, the two women met Ciaran McKeown, a committed pacifist and well-known reporter for the *Irish Times,* and elicited his support for their movement for peace. After Ciaran assented, they together formed the Peace People, an organization for promoting non-violence in Northern Ireland and the rest of the world.

The opposition they faced, and the labels they were slapped with, did not deter the two determined women. They led a march the following week in which as many as 35,000 women participated and protested against the disruption to the peace march. The goals of the movement were to bring an immediate end to the mindless sectarian violence in Northern Ireland and the violence of the IRA and all British paramilitary operations.

Ciaran McKeown, who had become the guiding spirit behind the Peace People, penned the 'Declaration of Peace People', a charter outlining the objectives and functions of the Peace People:

- We have a simple message to the world from this movement for peace.
- We want to live and love and build a just and peaceful society.
- We want for our children, as we want for ourselves, lives of joy and peace – our lives at home, at work and at play.
- We recognize that to build such a society demands dedication, hard work and courage.
- We recognize that there are many problems in our society that are a source of conflict and violence.
- We recognize that every bullet fired and every exploding bomb makes that work more difficult.
- We reject the use of the bomb and the bullet and all techniques of violence.
- We dedicate ourselves to working with our neighbours, near and far, day in and day out, to build that peaceful society in which the tragedies we have known are a bad memory and a continuing warning.

Betty Williams converted her own home into an office for the Peace People. On 21 August 1976, over 50,000 people gathered for a rally at Ormeau Park, to sloganeer for peace in Northern Ireland. This was unprecedented both in numbers and in spirit. It was in this rally that the 'Declaration of Peace People' was first read. Thereafter, rallies for peace were held throughout Northern Ireland for the next three months every Saturday. In all those rallies, women were the heroes, leading the marchers from the front. And in choreographing them, Betty and Mairead strained their every nerve. The people had come in their own chartered buses to attend the rallies, and Mairead leapt from one bus top to another giving stirring speeches to the assembled crowd.

The Peace People's rallies garnered immense popular support, drawing in support groups and activists from various parts of the country. Of the many prominent voices that declared solidarity were Women Together, an organization of Catholic and Protestant women, who backed the Peace People's call to end violence. However, they refrained from lending support to a rally on Shankill Road, a region dominated by Protestants, because they feared that the rally would be attacked by Loyalists. The Peace People, however, decided to go ahead with the rally as they considered it important to show that the people on Shankill were peaceable, and against violence, and that they would work together for peace and reconciliation.

Thus, ignoring all warnings, and despite the threat of violence, over 25,000 Catholics and Protestants, mainly women, walked along Shankill Road on Saturday, 28 August 1976. People from all walks of life participated in the rally; and the most rapturous moment was when several nuns wearing their religious habits joined them. The marchers welcomed every nun with an intimate hug. It was a euphoric moment for everyone on Shankill Road, and would be etched deeply in the memory of everyone present.

The peace marches were quickly gathering steam. Every Saturday for the next three months, Betty and Mairead led a peace march. As many as sixty-six peace groups had been formed by September 1976. The number eventually rose to more than a hundred. The movement had caught the imagination of the people so widely and deeply that there was a huge drop in violence during the second half of 1976, whereas the first half of 1976 was the worst period of sectarian violence during the Troubles.

The notable peace marches, for their participation and spirited sloganeering, were the Derry–Londonderry double march, the London march, the Boyne march and the Falls Road March. The Derry–Londonderry march, held on Saturday, 4 September 1976, was characterized by Protestant women's marching on one side of the River Foyle and Catholic women marching on the other. They converged on the Craigavon Bridge, while, simultaneously, around 50,000 protestors marched in solidarity in Dublin. The Falls Road rally was marred by violence, after bottles and stones were thrown at the marchers. The attacks became fiercer and more violent when the march neared Falls Park. But the marchers braved the attacks as they felt that the success of their movement lay in the successful culmination of their march.

The Peace People led their last march of the campaign on 5 December 1976, along River Boyne. The protesters from north and south Ireland met at the Peace Bridge. Rallies were also held throughout Britain, finally ending in London. One was held at Trafalgar Square, where Joan Baez sang 'We shall overcome', the anthem of the African American Civil Rights Movement (1955–1968). The song was first published in September 1988, in People's Song Bulletin, by its guiding spirit and director, Pete Seeger, and its appeal has since remained.

As the Peace People concluded its marches, Mairead, Betty and Ciaran emerged as the holy trinity of the peace movement. Prominence in the movement, however, went to the two women, as they had been the ones who had first picked up the gauntlet. Moreover, Ciaran had a philosophical dispensation, and his articulation of ideas fascinated only the intellectual class, and did not inspire the common people, on whose support lay the success of the movement. Nonetheless, Mairead shared with me her deep regard for Ciaran McKeown and her feeling that the trio should have been nominated for the Nobel Peace Prize. She told me that Ciaran had left the Peace People because of personal reasons.

Betty Williams and Mairead Maguire were awarded the Nobel Peace Prize for the year 1976. But, in 1980, the very trust between activists of various creeds that had been crucial to the success of the Peace People had begun to fray. The main reason for their falling apart was disagreement over the use of the award money, though earlier some strains had developed in the movement because of prison justice. This impacted the mutual relationship between the two women irreconcilably. The movement could not be carried any further. Betty Williams resigned from the Peace People in 1980. The two spiritual sisters were separated. Nonetheless, each one walked her own chosen path towards peace and remained highly active towards securing peace in the world.

Betty possesses both sublime anger and compassion. In January 2002, while delivering a lecture to students at Miami University, Betty said she had been so overpowered by profound anger at the 9/11 attacks that she wanted the terrorists to be instantly nuked. In another speech – this time, in Brisbane – at the Earth Dialogue Forum, on 24 July 2006, she expressed, quite flippantly, her anger at President George Bush and his policies:

> I have a very hard time with this word 'non-violence', because I don't believe that I am non-violent. Right now I would love to kill George Bush. I don't know how I ever got a Nobel Peace

Prize, because when I see children die, the anger in me is just beyond belief. It is our duty as human beings, whatever age we are, to become protectors of human life.

When I asked her how she could espouse non-violence and also, at the same time, think of killing George Bush, she answered:

This is strange – that one line that hit [me]. That is what usually happens with the newspapers. They use one line and they don't use the rest of what you said. I didn't say that I would love to kill George Bush, but I actually meant to say 'I could kill George Bush'. I was so angry, and I followed that up by saying that, as a matter of fact, hundreds of times I felt that I wanted to kill a person who had hurt a child, but that doesn't mean I will do it. That's what actually I said ... He [Bush] is a war criminal, and he should be taken to the courts. Yes, I can feel that kind of anger if someone hurts a child. Yes, I could honestly haul them for doing it, but I don't mean I will ... Hey, if George Bush can slaughter hundreds of thousands of people including children, have I not the right to be angry at that? ... Nobody takes on power. I take it on. ... Robert Kennedy said 'Speak truth to power'. I speak truth to power every day because that allows others to tell their truths.

Betty thus shows us that she is an ordinary human being, all flesh and blood, governed by petty instincts of hatred and vengeance. What set her apart, however, is her willingness to learn and her courage to change.

She was the driving force behind the widespread protests that ended the Troubles in Northern Ireland. In 1978, she left the Peace People, the organization she had been so instrumental in founding and the organization that was the focal point of peace activism in Ireland, and shifted to the United States in 1980. Since then she has been vigorously espousing the cause of helpless children suffering from disease, malnutrition, illiteracy, child prostitution and other forms of exploitation. For this, Betty has formulated her own 'Declaration of Rights for Children', along the lines of the Peace People's charter – the 'Declaration of Peace People' – and intends to start a petition campaign after having secured over a billion signatures. She says she will knock on the door of the UNO for the adoption of a charter on human rights for children. She rues that children do not have a political voice and is presently engaged in creating one for them. Her declaration reads thus:

- We, the Children of the World, assert our inalienable right to be heard and to have a political voice at the United Nations and at the highest levels of governments worldwide.
- We, the Children of the World, must live with justice, peace and freedom, but above all, with the dignity we deserve.
- We, the Children of the World, require a Marshall Plan, a Geneva Convention and a World Children's Court of Human Rights which meets regularly to listen to the testimonies as to what is actually happening to us. We intend to provide our own testimonies.
- We, the Children of the World, demand the right to be taken to safe shelters in situations of war.
- We, the Children of the World, consider hunger, disease, forced labour and all forms of abuse and exploitation perpetrated upon us to be war.
- We, the Children of the World, have had no political voice. We demand such a voice.
- We, the Children of the World, will develop our own leadership, and set an example that will show governments how to live in peace and freedom.
- We, the Children of the World, serve notice on our abusers and exploiters, whoever they may be, that from this day

hence, we will begin the process of holding you responsible for our suffering.

She has been travelling worldwide and has founded the first city for orphaned refugee children, called the 'City of Peace'. Located in Basilicata, Italy, it was built by the World Centre of Compassion for Children International, with Betty as its president. The aim of this organization is to raise awareness for child rights and save children from war, hunger, social and economic exploitation. This city was inaugurated on 25 June 2012 by His Holiness the Dalai Lama, a fellow Nobel Peace laureate. Betty told me that she would shortly establish another City of Peace in Ghana. Each City of Peace will have state-of-the-art health centres, and an education programme with emphasis on peace and non-violence. The City of Peace will have homes, and in each home two foster-parents will look after ten orphaned children. Betty considers John, Andrew and Joanne Maguire, the children who died on Finaghy Road, as angels who transformed her life. They sacrificed their own lives so that many others might live. It is no wonder then that she dedicated her life to the cause of children.

She is a global citizen and acts as a member of a global family. In 2012, Betty conveyed to me her deep grief over the sad demise of Nirbhaya, a twenty-three-year-old physiotherapy intern, after she had been brutally assaulted and gang-raped by six men and been thrown out of a moving bus in Delhi, on 16 December 2012. The incident shocked the nation. Indians came together in one overwhelming wave and protested for justice in New Delhi. Betty wrote to me:

> Dear Supriya,
>   I am enraged by the inhuman, savage killing of the twenty-three-year-old medical student. That a woman, giver of life, could be subjected to such brutality is beyond comprehension.

And today we learn of a second attack on a woman. Indeed the government of India must act, and act very quickly, to create policies to protect and give women the respect they deserve. Please print or forward this message to do the most good, and know that I stand shoulder-to-shoulder with the women of India and will help in any way I can.

God bless you, Supriya

Love and peace,
Betty Williams

Betty feels that world peace is 'everybody's business', no matter what one does or where one lives. On 20 February 2014, she said admonishingly in a peace forum at the UN headquarters, 'We could sit all day and glorify it [peace], but it's not a thing that should be glorified. It's a thing that should be done in reality, every single day of our lives.' She says that change has to start from the grass roots and that a culture of peace should be imbibed in our houses, schools, workplaces and local communities, which alone can make change lasting and rewarding. For her part, she has crusaded against war, arms trade and the nuclear arms race. In 1992, she met President Bill Clinton and Vice President Al Gore of the US and prevailed upon them to help end the horrors in Myanmar and East Timor. She also highlights the importance of women in pushing for social change. She says, 'Start with the women and follow them, because when you give women a voice great things happen.'

MAIREAD MAGUIRE

Leading Dove of Ireland

'If Christ lived in America, would he … support nuclear
weapons, or a nuclear war that could annihilate millions of our
sisters and brothers in the world?'

Mairead Maguire was born on 27 January 1944 in Belfast, in Northern Ireland. They were seven siblings – two brothers and five sisters. Mairead was the second child to her parents. Her mother was a homemaker and her father, a window washer. She was brought up in a Catholic ghetto on Falls Road, the birthplace of the IRA. She attended St Vincent's Catholic Primary School, but had to abandon her school when she was just fourteen years old as her father could not afford her education. Determined to somehow continue with her studies, she worked as a babysitter in a Catholic community centre and earned enough money to eventually pursue a one-year secretarial course at a commercial college.

Later she got a job as a bookkeeper in a factory in Belfast. She was sixteen years old at the time. She quit the job and joined a beer brewery as a secretarial assistant when she was twenty-one years old, where she earned handsomely and could buy a car. Later her family shifted to a new home in Andersonstown, which, though was not a ghetto, was also a poor neighbourhood like Falls Road.

She has a sweet demeanour, and an aura of culture and courtliness, and is therefore revered by many as a saint. She told me very innocently that her parents were 'wonderful'. Her main interests in childhood were seeing mountains, swimming and reading books. Very early in life, she had developed a habit of buying books, which sometimes remained unread for long. Above all, people skills were her forte. Each day, she would write one letter to her friends to remain in touch with them.

Other than the ennobling influence of her parents, she was shaped by the influence of the Legion of Mary, a Catholic organization committed – in Mairead's own words – 'to the betterment of each individual and the propagation of the fundamental tenets of Christianity'. Mairead devoted most of her time to the Legion, in which she took care of handicapped children. While being with Legion, Mairead visited Thailand to attend a conference of the World Council of Churches, and to Russia to help with the production of a film about Catholics who live in Russia. She was later called upon to supervise a small chapter of the organization, wherein she took upon herself most challenging tasks. Mairead says:

> In the beginning, only half-dozen adolescents belonged to my group. Later I had as many as 150. We did some absolutely fantastic work in Andersonstown during the Troubles in 1969. We arranged to get children and young people away from the 'hot' areas so as to keep them from getting involved in the disturbances ... We asked for funds to build a meeting hall. When the hall was built, another girl and I organized Andersonstown's first nursery school. Then we set up a recreation centre for the numerous handicapped children in the area.

Mairead was never politically conscious. She could not discern that the Catholics were being subjected to social, economic and educational deprivation by English Protestants. Others of her age joined the IRA's path of armed rebellion or became their sympathizers. However, true to her salt, she visited Catholic prisoners and urged them to change their ways, telling them that Christianity is a religion of peace. The prisoners retorted that they could only counter the British army's violence with violence. She was told the story of two sons whose father was an IRA sympathizer. The two sons had been apolitical and had remained aloof of the political turmoil in Ireland. But, later, when the British soldiers attacked their house and threw their parents down the steps, the two boys realized that the British army had to be countered by military force.

Once, Mairead herself was manhandled by British soldiers when she intervened in an army raid that was being conducted in a highly demeaning and objectionable manner. In another incident, the British army threw tear gas shells at a funeral Mairead was attending, forcing everyone present at the gathering to flee from the church. Mairead suffered the worst in 1976, after the Troubles had erupted, when her niece Joanne was killed by a car driven by an IRA fugitive. Gun culture seemed all-pervasive in Andersonstown as well. Several buildings had bullet holes, and many had been burnt down. Throwing stones at British barricades was all too common a scene. Mairead recalls:

> For a long time, it was a sort of national sport to throw stones at the British troops, and, I'm sorry to say, our children were champions at that sport. Andersonstown is one of those communities built in such haste by the Unionist government after the war in the west of Belfast. It was designed simply to house Catholics and nothing more. There is nothing. No stores, no cinemas, no playgrounds, no meeting halls. Once there, you're more or less stranded.

During the tear gas shelling at the funeral, a furious Mairead thought of joining the IRA. She later recalled, 'I remember thinking, "How can we get even for this kind of violence, for this unprovoked attack? By joining the IRA?" I asked myself the question in all seriousness.'

But Mairead stuck to her pacifist principles. She simply refused to see any difference between Catholics and Protestants, or other differences based on political, ethnic and social hues. She attributes her pacifism to her faith. She said, 'You can't be much of a believer if you can imagine Christ resorting to violence in response to that kind of provocation, and I knew that I did not believe in violence.'

After the Peace People split in 1980, Mairead put past recriminations behind, and started spreading the message of the Peace People with renewed vigour. More peace groups were formed. She advocated welfare reforms and demanded social justice. She undertook several other activities, such as encouraging young people to work for peace, and holding youth camps and peace campaigns in other countries. Mairead was successful in rebuilding the trust that earlier had been lost to their movement. Mairead rightly says, 'If we seek the truth in love and stand by that truth no matter what the cost, it will lead us to trust one another.' She also emphasizes the need of developing personal relationships in peacemaking operations, 'We must take time out for each other – time to listen, to be sensitive, to forgive and to show compassion towards each other.'

A year after the Troubles erupted in 1968, the British army was deployed for community policing – in Falls Road and other places where Catholics lived. The army was initially welcomed warmly, with each Catholic house warmly treating them to tea. Thus, the British army was stationed on Falls Road, where, until the 1960s, there had been no police station. The people felt that the army would deter sectarian clashes that had been roiling Northern Ireland during the time. However, people's expectations soon soured as British soldiers began searching several thousand homes under the pretext of eliminating threats to national security and suppressing the growth of the IRA. But the more repressively the army policed the streets, the more the IRA's ranks swelled. Incidents of sectarian violence mushroomed all over Northern Ireland, causing widespread devastation in its wake.

In the aftermath of this vast devastation, Mairead raised fundamental questions regarding the Christian faith. She asked, 'If Christ lived in Belfast, would he carry a gun and kill others for any cause? If Christ lived in America, would he prepare for, maintain or support nuclear weapons, or a nuclear war that could annihilate millions of our sisters and brothers in the world? Why are the best minds planning mass destruction instead of feeding the starving?' She also questioned the Christian leadership on its role in the ongoing crisis. Of them, she asked:

'If Jesus's non-violence is not being taught in our seminaries and has never been taught, if our educators have not been taught about non-violence, how can people make informed choices between allegedly justified violence or Jesus's non-violence? If there is to be any hope for Christianity and humanity's survival, must not non-violence be taught at every level of society?'

In an open letter addressed to the IRA, in December 1993, in the *Irish News*, she wrote:

[...] In the past twenty-five years, more than thirty-two hundred people have been killed leaving behind unimaginable suffering and pain for their families. You and your comrades in the IRA take responsibility for your part in causing this bloodshed. All of you in your time will want to say 'sorry'. And so will others, who for their reasons have inflicted so much pain on their fellow human being here.

You and your comrades are not strangers to suffering. In the days ahead as you choose between the peace framework or the 'armed struggle', Bobby Sands and many others who have died will be in your thoughts. You will want to remain faithful to the sacrifice for a free and united Ireland. That's only human. But change is also part of being human. As John Henry Newman says, 'In a higher world, it is otherwise, but here below, to live is to change and to be perfect is to have changed often.'

In the republican movement, you are now faced with the need to change radically, to move away from the 'armed struggle' and into a non-violent alternative. Your right to your political aspirations and national identity has been acknowledged. The way of active non-violence is in tune with your Christian roots and heritage. You know that in your heart. As a child, you learnt to pray, 'Help me to live like Jesus'. Jesus with a machine gun does not come off as an authentic figure! It is time now for a new vision and a fresh wisdom.

[…] I believe in and work for a non-violent, demilitarized, Northern Irish society, and I hope our friends in the south of Ireland will begin also to work for a demilitarized non-violent Ireland …

The last hope for the redemption of mankind, Mairead suggests, lies in the hands of women. She remembers that, when the Troubles started in Northern Ireland, it was the women who called for compassion and collaboration. She applauds the mothers of Northern Ireland who passed on values of pacifism to their children during the tumultuous times of the Troubles and saved their country. A mother's success, Mairead holds, is the success of mankind, and a mother's failure is the failure of mankind. Mairead herself exemplifies the role of a mother. In a letter Mairead wrote to her son Luke, she embodies the wishes of every woman. It reads:

Dear Luke,

Today you picked a little yellow rosebud from the garden and carried it into the house to give it to me. Your little baby face beamed up at me as you gave me the rosebud. What joy that moment held for me! What joy knowing how deeply I love you! As I went to put the rosebud in water, I realized it had no stem, and that without water, it would never grow from a rosebud into a beautiful full rose, but that soon, all too soon, it would die.

I felt sad for a moment at this thought, and as I watched you toddle across the room, I wondered how I might help you – my little rosebud – grow and blossom into manhood. What can I teach you? What can I say to you that will help you to grow up in this thorny world, and yet know peace, joy and happiness – which, dear Luke, are the greatest treasures anyone can possess?

Always know, Luke, that you are deeply loved. You are loved by Daddy and me, and your brothers and sisters. But as you grow up and begin to ask questions for yourself, you will know that men and women have a need in their hearts for something more, something deeper than that found even in the very best of human love.

As you walk along a beach at night and listen to the waves lapping gently on the shore, or look up into a night sky at millions of stars, know too that the One Who created all this created it for you because He loves you. You are the part of this beautiful creation and you are beautiful, special and unique in this Universe. Love and believe in yourself, because only then can you love and believe in others.

Luke, do not be afraid to love others unselfishly. Yes, many times you will get your fingers pricked on the thorns of disappointment or rejection, but many more times you will pluck the rose of love and receive great happiness and joy from its sweet scent and colour. Don't be afraid to risk loving and remember that as the little rosebud needed the water to live, so much more you and I and all the people of the world need to love and be loved. Know that love is the greatest gift you personally can give to another fellow traveller along the thorny path of life.

As you grow up in the Christian tradition, struggle each day to be more Christ-like. Pray to be more loving, compassionate, courageous, gentle and peaceful. Try to see Christ in everyone, especially the suffering Christ, and serve and help to remove causes of that suffering where you can. Remember it is a dead faith that has only words. Acts of love and compassion for the spiritually and materially poorest of the poor is where true faith blossoms.

With ever so gentle steps, walk side by side with all the travellers on this thorny path of life. They will differ from you in colour, creed – there are many paths to God – culture and politics, but above all remember that your fellow travellers have the same needs as you. Our common humanity is far more important than any religious or political ideologies. Treat every man and woman justly and gently as you would have them treat you.

In your life, Luke, pray to be a just man. Your life is precious and sacred, Luke, and your first right as a human being is your right to your life. So as you would ask natural justice of your fellow travellers in respecting your right to life, you too must give justice and must respect every person's right to life. This means, my little son, that you must never kill another human being.

It will not be easy for you to refuse to kill. Sadly, we live in a world where those who refuse to kill and choose to live non-violent lives are looked upon as naive or as cowards. Yes, it will take all of your courage to walk unarmed and refuse to hate and kill, in a world which insists that you must have enemies and be prepared to kill them before they kill you.

Stand tall and strong, armed only with love, dear Luke, and refuse to hate, refuse to have enemies, refuse to let fear master your life. Only love can bring down the barriers of hate and enmity between men and nations. Hate and weapons only fuel the fear and bring closer the day of war.

Let no man plant in your heart the false seed of pride in any country's flag, a seed that produces the flower of narrow nationalism which grows so wildly, trampling and killing all life around it. Remember always, Luke, people are more important than countries.

I will not give one hair of your precious head for any country – you are more important than any country. And if I feel this passionate love for you, and for my other children – Mark, Joanne, Marie-Louise and John – I too feel passionately for the little children who today die of starvation in Ethiopia, for the little children in Moscow and the little children in New York who are told they must be enemies and may end up someday killing each other – in the name of a flag.

Remember, Luke, you have no country. The world is your country. You have not only two brothers and two sisters but millions of brothers and sisters.

Pray also for the gift of wisdom. It is a wise person who soon comes to know that the human family's real enemies are injustice, war, starvation and poverty. But wise people also know that it is only by people becoming different and thinking in new ways that these things will change.

When human life is held as so sacred that no one can kill, justice will reign in people's heart and in all lands. Wars will no more. Justice will mean that no one has too much, while some have nothing. Greed and selfishness will turn into feeding the hungry and removing all poverty. It is possible, Luke, to change to this kind of world. You just have to refuse to accept the old ways of thinking and doing things and begin to think and act in a way more in tune with magnificent goodness in humanity. All people know today that killing and starvation are wrong. It is just that not enough are prepared to change themselves and to work and making things different.

And now, my little son, before you fall asleep, let me say the most important thing of all to you. Be happy, be joyous, live every minute of this beautiful gift of life. When suffering comes into your life, and sadly I cannot, much as I would love to, protect you from all suffering, and when you come through the winter of your life, remember that summer will return, the sun will shine again, and the road will be covered in beautiful, very beautiful, yellow roses of love.

God bless you and keep you, my little Luke.

Mummy

I shared this letter with Malala Yousafzai and her father, Ziauddin Yousafzai, and he thanked me. He wrote to me, 'Mairead's letter teems with love and humanity. She is so true, natural and genuine.' He said that it reminded him of Malala's mother's response when a person asked her about the prizes and accolades showered on Malala, 'I will not take the whole word in return for even one eyelash of Malala.'

Mairead travels around the world and is acquainted with various streams of people's struggles to attain peace and justice. During her journeys, she pays obeisance to individuals who have been in the forefront of such struggles. In 1994, she met Ken Saro-Wiwa at a peace conference in Holland. There, she learnt of the struggle of the Ogonis of Nigeria, whom Ken had led in a protest against the usurpation of their lands and homes by Shell Oil, the world's largest petroleum company. Later Ken and eight others from the Ogoni community were implicated in a fabricated criminal case and executed.

Her pilgrimages as a peace activist also took her to Auschwitz in 1988, where Zyklon B and hydrogen cyanide (HCN) gas were used to snuff out lives of millions of men, women and children. When she stood on the ground that had witnessed one of the most horrific brutalities in history, she cried out, 'Oh God, forgive us for what we do to one another!' She holds that Hitler had gone mad when he decided to exterminate Europe's Jews, but is also deeply dismayed to note that he could do so only due to the silence of the multitude towards his nefarious designs, and the pervasive anti-Semitism of Polish and European Christians. As a Christian, Mairead assumes responsibility for all wrongs committed by Christians. Auschwitz, she notes, is a monument to the dark side of human nature and is a constant reminder of the evil mankind is capable of. The abominable sight of Auschwitz did not make Mairead sullen and defeated, however, and only reinvigorated her faith in non-violence and her will to eliminate strife in the world. In October 1990, she visited Japan, which, in her opinion, is the worst manifestation of the immorality of war. She is ashamed that American Christians dropped atomic bombs on Hiroshima and Nagasaki in August 1945. She repents and asks the Japanese people's forgiveness for the inhuman cruelty perpetrated upon them.

In February 1998, she visited the seventy-four-year-old Philip Berrigan in Petersburg Federal Prison, who had been serving a two-year prison sentence for organizing anti-war protests on

Ash Wednesday 1997. In the jail, she pledged her solidarity with Berrigan and refused to leave him, in protest against the US and Britain's bombing of Iraq. She was arrested and taken to court, but the prosecutors in the case prayed for dismissal and the judge complied.

She holds the United States and European countries responsible for supplying weapons of mass destruction in the world. While their riches increase, the poor people upon whom these weapons are unleashed suffer excruciatingly and endlessly. Entire communities and nations are morphed, incapacitated and disabled, leaving behind only misery and helplessness for their future generations. The small conflicts that can be resolved easily and amicably flare up due to the easy availability of guns. She got a first-hand account of this geopolitical set-up when she visited Rwanda during the civil war of 1990–94. She said, 'Don't send us any guns. The place is awash with guns. But, in the refugee camps, our children need food, and we do not have enough money to buy ourselves food. Yet a child with a few cents can buy a weapon.' In recent times, she has also been a vocal critic of the UK's Nuclear Trident programme, which has taken away one hundred billion pounds that could have been used effectively to save children dying of malnutrition and lack of medical care in Third World countries.

In March 1999, she petitioned US president Bill Clinton to end the bombing of Iraq and to allow for UN sanctions to be lifted. She remarked, 'I have seen children dying with their mothers next to them and not being able to do anything.' She sat on a forty-day liquid fast outside the White House, along with members of Pax Christi USA and Christian Church leaders, to protest Iraq's impending invasion. In February 2006, after the Iraq war, she demanded that George Bush 'should be made accountable for illegally taking the world to war and for war crimes against humanity'. She tells me that America has tremendous responsibility to give real leadership to the world on issues of human rights, international laws and conflict resolution, and that she is greatly distressed and disappointed that the US is playing a role contrary to what is expected of it as a world leader.

She informs me that she looks upon religious leaders of all faiths to clearly declare armaments as immoral, and that no government should amass arms. She has high hopes for Pope Francis, whom she says is a man of peace, a man who loves the poor and a man who does not believe in discrimination among people. According to her, standing armies cannot be justified in the name of self-defence. There are more efficient and viable means to ensure security and peace than by spending trillions on armaments. She argues that if the world at large decides to annihilate all weapons, and resolves not to manufacture further weapons, it will instantly eliminate all perceptions of threats to security.

She also rejects the argument that human beings are anatomically and instinctively made towards aggression and violence. She asserts that the same species which has the biological make-up for war also has the biological make-up for peace. It is a matter of choice: choice which emerges out of sublime thoughts is peace, and the choice which emerges out of chaotic thoughts is war. Each one of us has the responsibility for the choice one makes.

๛

I ask her if she also finds her soul growing as philosopher Carl Jung says, 'Go into your grief for there your soul will grow?' I also suggest that the flurry with which she undertakes peacemaking efforts in various parts of the world seem to emanate from her empathy for the hapless, especially women and children, who bear the brunt of wars like in Iraq and Palestine – her grief seemingly bound to theirs.

Mairead says in reply that every single person experiences suffering; it brings our empathy and compassion, as well as joy. But we must not get stuck in suffering. We have ... we must become survivors, to see that other people don't suffer.

According to Mairead, the path of peace forks into two. One leads to the depths of one's inner self, and the other leads outward to our fellow human beings. If we do not inwardly cleanse ourselves of selfishness, greed and hate, it will generate cruelty and violence and further lead to homicide and war. Our inner journey will reveal to us that we are an integral part of the universe, and that when we hate or do violence to others, we, in fact, do violence to ourselves.

David Lynch, a celebrated follower of Maharishi Mahesh Yogi, lays much emphasis upon Transcendental Meditation (TM), a form of asceticism that takes us to higher planes of consciousness, beyond dualities of violence and non-violence, love and hatred, life and death, sorrow and happiness. Hindu theology ordains, of all the righteous paths, the path of non-violence as the most righteous: *Ahimsa parmo dharma*. The fourteenth-century Hindu saint Tulsi Das says, '*Daya dharam ka mool hai*' Compassion is the ground for the righteous path. Mairead cherishes precisely the same principles, as she hopes that the Christian Church – and leaders of other faiths – will adopt a theology of non-violence as their operative mantra.

She wants a just order in the world where there is no violence, no fear, no exploitation and no deprivation. Maguire hopes that her dream will be materialized before she passes into eternity. She says, 'I have a dream – of a time when human life is held as so sacred that no one can kill, when justice will reign in every heart and in every land. Wars will cease and no one will have too much while others have nothing.' Mairead's message is to awaken, act and tirelessly work for a non-violent world. She beckons to all of us to join her struggle to make her dream come true.

JANE ADDAMS

PRIESTESS OF PEACE

'If the meanest man in the republic is deprived of his rights,
every man in the republic is deprived of his rights.'

In history, it is rare for a woman to have waged a crusade – opposing one's own country and braving public condemnation – as did Jane Addams. She was part of the vanguard of peace activists who successfully campaigned to stop the US from entering World War I. Fortunately for Jane, her voice was heard and appreciated in her lifetime, as she became the second woman and first American to receive the Nobel Peace Prize in 1931. She shared the honours with Nicholas Murray Butler, a renowned academician and former president of Columbia University.

Jane is widely acknowledged as the first woman philosopher in the history of the United States, and her essays on peace and ethics are canonical texts in peace studies. A pioneer of social reform, Jane is also famous for having founded the Social Settlement Movement in Chicago.

But that, however, is the Jane Addams we remember now. There was a time when this highly successful woman felt utterly beaten by the circumstances of her life.

She was born in Cedarville, Illinois, on 6 September 1860. Her father, John Huy Addams, and mother, Sarah Weber Addams, married on 18 July 1844. Jane was the youngest in her family and one of the most fortunate ones, as she survived the tragedy that befell four of her eight siblings who died in their infancy.

Her mother too would leave her before her time, in 1863, in a tragic accident. Her mother had gone out to midwife a neighbour and had fallen on the way from the top of a hill. She herself had been seven months pregnant at the time and breathed her last while delivering a stillborn baby. It was a huge loss for young Jane – losing her mother at the tender age of just two-and-a-half. Her mother's death, however, was only one among the many ordeals in her tempestuous childhood.

When she was four years old, she contracted pulmonary tuberculosis, which caused a curvature in her spine. Jane was beautiful with attractive grey eyes, but her crooked spine made her feel ugly. She would squirm in shame when her father dressed in his best or if he accompanied her somewhere. Jane remained beset with health problems throughout her life.

In 1868, when Jane was only eight years old and still reeling from the loss of her mother, her father, John, remarried. Thus Anna Haldeman walked into Jane's life as if intruding on her grief. The only solace Jane had was the love and care of her older sister Mary, who acted as a mother to her. Anna Haldeman was a widow before her marriage to John, and had decided to marry owing mainly to financial insecurities and to ensure a comfortable life for her sons: Harry, twenty; and George, seven. She had a charming personality and was generally perceived as a cultured citizen of Cedarville town. She had tried to raise Jane's reckoning too to her own, and one day had bought Jane a new Sunday coat. Jane describes the coat in her memoir, as 'gorgeous beyond anything I had ever worn before'. But when her father learnt about her new coat, he advised her not to wear it, as he felt that it would make other girls at Sunday school feel bad. Jane was obedient and wore the old coat as per her father's wish. As a grown-up, however, she would indulge her taste for the finer things in life.

Jane's father was an agricultural businessman and possessed large business holdings – livestock and flour, timber and woollen mills. Her father was also a founding member of the Illinois Republican Party and was a friend of Abraham Lincoln whose presidential candidacy he supported in 1860. A man of his means, John was but austere and regarded highly the values of self-discipline and modesty. Jane would recollect in *Twenty Years at Hull House* that her father had been the one to '[draw] her into the moral concerns of life'.

After her mother's death, John was the most dominant influence on Jane's life. Being the youngest child, she was his favourite. He adored and pampered her so much that other members of Jane's large family complained he had spoilt her. In fact, Jane recalls how even though she confessed all her sins to her father she rarely received admonition. In her adolescence, she started exhibiting impatience in her relationship with her stepmother and her schoolteacher C.W. Moore, with whom she picked many rows over trivialities. Though directly responsible for Jane's development in this manner, her father was the one who helped her realize the need to control her anger too. Jane shared an intense, bitter-sweet relationship with her father, and in her memoir describes their bond using lines from Elizabeth Barrett Browning's poem 'Aurora Leigh': 'He wrapped me in his large man's doublet/ careless did it fit or no.'

At the age of seven, Jane had her first sight of poverty, or as her first impression of it were, of squalor. One of her father's mills from where he ran his businesses stood adjacent to a poor neighbourhood, and in one of her visits she observed that the streets were not 'as bewilderingly attractive' as the others she had seen. Jane asked her father why people lived in such 'horrid little houses'. After her father's casual answer, she decided that when she was grown-up she would have a large house. And since then Jane felt a feeling of responsibility in herself, as if she were a warder of the world whose actions could make the world a better place. She would fantasize about being among the poor, helping and curing them, as a doctor would a patient; she would be inspired by Dickens's novels, with its theme of the underdog winning in the face of adversity, armed only with righteousness and courage.

Besides her father, Jane looked to two columnists for inspiration – Robert Owen and John Brown. They both featured regularly in a long series of articles in a magazine – *Atlantic Monthly* – her stepmother subscribed to. Robert Owen was a cotton industrialist and had founded a cooperative movement in Great Britain and the United States. The gains of the cooperative society, including profit, were shared equally among all its labourers. His vision was to make mankind happy and not let only a few individuals profit from competitive capitalism. He wrote, 'The happiness of self, clearly understood, can only be attained by a direct and conscious service to the community.' He tested his ideas in New Harmony, Indiana, wherein he attempted to found a classless, utopian community. It worked well for three years – between 1824 and 1827 – but it soon failed and he lost all his wealth.

John Brown was not any less stubborn in practising his ideas of social reform. He was an abolitionist and instrumental in a guerrilla attack on pro-slavery forces in Kansas in 1856. He instigated an armed slave insurrection after he along with twenty other men seized the federal arsenal at Harper's Ferry, Virginia. Brown and his men's mission was to supply the weapons they had looted from the federal arsenal to the slaves, whom they expected to initiate an uprising against their masters. However, Brown's mission failed, and he was captured and promptly executed by the US Marines.

Jane was not very moved by the radical tenets of these men, but she was greatly inspired by their devotion to their social vision, which in the 1870s had captured the imagination of many in England and the United States. About John Brown's doctrine of 'direct action', she confided in a friend, 'I always had a secret sympathy for Brown's impatience and his determination that something should happen.' In her later life, she would successfully combine John Brown's political method of direct action and the communitarianism of Robert Owen's cooperative movement.

Another of Jane's literary heroes was Thomas Carlyle, whose work *On Heroes, Hero Worship and the Heroic in History* provided much intellectual ballast to her mind. Louisa May Alcott's *Little Women*, which portrays the contrasting ambitions of a mother and her daughters, was another literary work that similarly provoked her imagination. In the book, the mother, Marmee, is a devoted, selfless and an ideal housekeeper. The tomboyish daughter Jo, however, dreams of becoming a writer and of penning something so spectacular that her fame would be immortalized. Being fiercely independent and opinionated, and whose ambitions and goals were far in advance of the expectations of women at the time, Jane identified herself with Jo. Jane was also influenced by Ralph Waldo Emerson, especially by his essay *Man the Reformers*, which sowed seeds of a future career in social reform within Jane. In his essay, Emerson describes the reformer as 'a brave and upright man' who brings 'institutions of society to account'.

In 1887, Jane joined Rockford Seminary, a women's college in Illinois. She had wanted to study at another women's college, in Massachusetts, called Smith's College, but her father had denied her permission. She was to study along with her sisters at Rockford Seminary in Illinois. Her father's peremptory dismissal of her wishes deeply hurt Jane, but she complied uncomplainingly. A seemingly simple and trivial matter, this episode, however, was typical of many father–daughter relationships of Jane's day. In a world where women had yet to win franchise, the father wielded undue control over his daughter's life. Jane remembers her father gratefully for the freedom she enjoyed as a girl child, but it is clear that she was not above her father's word.

A further source of resentment for young Jane was the evangelical character of Rockford Seminary. In *Twenty Years*, she recounts the concerted pressure from members of the faculty to convert her into a missionary. She was 'unspeakably embarrassed' when any teacher would come to see her in her room to proselytize their ideas. However, her time at Rockford only strengthened her resolve to remain true to her conscience. As she would write in her memoir, she now was sure that 'individual conviction was the best moral training'.

In 1881, she graduated from Rockford Seminary, Illinois. Her father died of appendicitis in August of the same year. On the day of his funeral, a huge crowd arrived to pay their respects. The pastor of the Cedarville Presbyterian Church gave the funeral sermon, stressing on her father's qualities of being civic-minded and morally upright. He said, 'The world was his field, of humanity he thought, for humanity he acted. The guiding principle of his life was love of right and hatred of evil.' According to her brother-in-law Reverend John Linn, '[Jane's] heart and life were wrapped up with her father's.' Indeed, Jane derived tremendous pride from her father's being. At the time of her father's death, Jane wrote, 'My own vivid recollection of John H. Addams is the fact that he was a man of purest and sternest integrity and that bad men feared him.' After her father's death, Jane was burdened with the great responsibility of carrying on her father's legacy, and she feared she would get lost in the shadow of her father's memory. Here again, Jane's brother-in-law Linn would comfort her: 'He did not desire you to live for him, but for the world, for humanity, for yourself and for Christ.' But it was to take a long time for Jane to beat the gloom of her father's death and emerge, in her own right, as a leading reformist and an ethicist.

But for the time being, Jane came into possession a large share of John Addams's immense wealth. Her inheritance comprised a nearly 100-hectare farm in Cedarville, 24 hectares of timberland, 32 hectares of arable land in Dakota territory and some shares of a bank in Chicago. However, her new economic independence was of no personal importance to her as she could not find any immediate use of the wealth she now possessed. Besides, any use of the new riches had to be exercised with tact, as she clearly did not want to invite charges of ingratitude or impropriety during a period of grief for her family.

After a month and a half, she and her family shifted to Philadelphia, where Jane rented lodgings with her stepsister Alice

Haldeman and her stepbrother Harry Haldeman. There, Harry joined a postgraduate surgery programme at the University of Pennsylvania while Jane enrolled in a medical programme at the Woman's Medical College, where she took courses in anatomy, physiology and dissection. But she had to abandon her studies midway after being increasingly pained from the spinal problems that had plagued her since childhood. She would undergo a surgery conducted by her own stepbrother Harry in 1882, after which she suffered an excruciating year walking with a back brace. She would also reel from a severe bout of depression. In 1887 the family returned to Cedarville.

In the intervening five years – between her leaving her postgraduate studies and returning to Cedarville – she travelled to London with her friend and former classmate at Rockford Seminary Ellen Starr. There she visited Tonybee Hall, a settlement house founded by Samuel and Henrietta Barnett in 1884. It was envisioned as an educational and recreational facility that would provide, in addition to classes on various subjects, vocational training to the poor. Jane was fascinated by the settlement house and describes it as 'a community of university men who live there, have their recreation clubs and society all among the poor, yet [live] in the same style in which they would live in their own circle. It is free of "professional doing-good", so unaffectedly sincere and so productive of good results in its classes and libraries that it seems perfectly ideal.'

Back in the US, she mooted with Ellen Starr the idea of starting a settlement house in Chicago. They decided to experiment with the idea and together founded Hull House in Chicago, Illinois, in 1905. It was the first settlement house in the United States. The house was named after Charles Hull who had built it in 1856; Addams paid for the repair and renovation it needed. When the Hull House received publicity, donations started pouring in, with several wealthy women donating regularly to the house and filling its coffers. Also, the owners of the house allowed its use without rent. Addams and Starr were the first two inmates of the house; the number later grew to twenty-five women.

The Hull House ran on two main principles: teach by example and practise egalitarian social relations. This helped the dilution of class divisions and catalyse the evolution of a society mutually beneficial for all. All twenty-five occupants of Hull House were intellectual giants, most prominent of whom was Florence Kelley, who distinguished herself as a renowned social reformer of her times and was instrumental in changing the dynamic of the resident community. Before long, Jane Addams's Hull House became a hotbed of ideas and action.

The Hull House was visited by around 2,000 people each week. It provided a range of facilities, including a night school for adults, clubs for children, an art gallery, a gym, a girls' club, a bathhouse, a music school, a drama group, a library, a debate room and an employment bureau. There were kindergarten classes in the morning, club meetings for children in the afternoon and classes for adults in the evening and at night. The first facility in the Hull House was an art gallery. Later a public kitchen, a coffee house, a gymnasium, a swimming pool and a cooperative boarding club for girls were all intermittently added. Gradually the house became a thirteen-building complex that housed a playground and a summer camp. It proved to be a unique experiment in community living.

In its running, Jane cherished individual freedom. She wanted the inmates of the house to develop their own vocation rather than key into one created by the industrialized education system. In this regard, what endeared most to Jane was the art programme. She said, 'Art is the key to unlock the diversity of the city, through collective interaction, mutual self-discovery, recreation and imagination.' For her, art meant thinking beyond received ideas and stimulating the diversity of cultural interaction in society. She said, 'A society must be based on a continual rewriting of cultural identities through variation and multiculturalism.'

Besides being the mistress of the Hull House, Addams served as the chairperson of Chicago's Board of Education Committee. Later, she became the president of the National Conference of Social Work and was instrumental in establishing the National Federation of Settlements, steering it as its top woman for more than two decades. In the Hull House neighbourhood in Chicago, she conducted regular investigations on midwifery, narcotics consumption, milk supply and sanitation. In 1895, she was appointed the garbage inspector of her ward after she launched a campaign against corruption and mismanagement by the ward council members. Earning a meagre annual salary of a thousand dollars, the garbage inspector of nineteenth ward was the only paid job she even held in her life.

In 1896, she travelled to Russia with her companion Mary Rozet Smith and met Leo Tolstoy at his residence. In her earlier years as a student at Rockford Seminary she had been much enamoured of his writings and had written many reviews praising his books. However, her interaction with him was not to be a cosy chat by the fireplace. When he first met her he commented on her coat – '[There] is enough stuff on one arm to make a frock for a girl' – hinting at Jane's material conditions that alienated her from whom she served. Tolstoy was by now a radical Christian who believed in working shoulder to shoulder with the oppressed, and had left everything to take up the plough and work as a common peasant. He added: 'Do you think you will help the people more by adding yourself to the crowded city than you would by tilling your own soil?' Her encounter with Tolstoy greatly influenced her, and she began devoting two hours a day to preparing bread in the Hull House bakery. She also came under the influence of John Ruskin, who like Tolstoy also valued labour as a means of self-realization.

Jane's reform work was well received by Chicago's citizens, but, as one learns from history, public opinion can be very fickle. Jane would learn this in the latter half of her life, after she controversially opposed World War I. Though her transition to a pacifist was effected much earlier – in 1898, when she joined the Anti-Imperialist League in opposition to US annexation of the Philippines – she wouldn't emerge as a prominent peace activist until the outbreak of World War I. In 1915, she delivered a speech at the Carnegie Hall condemning the war in Europe. She said the soldiers had been intoxicated with drinks before being sent on to fight. In the wake of her criticism of the war, she was fiercely attacked in the press. The *New York Times* caricatured her words in one of its articles, saying 'all nations make their soldiers practically drunk [so they may be brought before the bayonet of each other]'. One renowned war correspondent Richard Harding David called her 'a complacent and self-satisfied woman'. Another New York paper branded her 'a silly, vain, impertinent old maid ... who is now meddling with matters far beyond her capacity'. *The Louisville Courier* journal called her a 'foolish, garrulous woman'. She was also expelled from the Daughters of the American Revolution, a prominent humanitarian organization she was part of at the time.

After Woodrow Wilson plunged the US into war on 6 April 1917, Jane arrayed many civil society members against the conflict. It led Edgar Hoover, the then FBI director, to call her 'the most dangerous woman in America'. Even those who had been supporters of her strong pacifist convictions now condemned her belligerent opposition to US foreign policy.

However, she remained unruffled even in the face of the most scathing public vitriol. She had learnt very early on that 'there is nothing as dangerous as being good to people, as opposed to being good *with* people'. The former is the quality of a sycophant, whose words lack truth and spine, while the latter is cooperation with sincerity and self-sacrifice. She would impart this difference to those around her with an uncanny knack for speaking in a calm, confident voice, with clarity and conviction. An exemplifying instance of this is the Women's Peace Congress held in The Hague under her leadership, in 1915, to develop a strategy to stop the US from entering World War I. At the congress, Jane inspired the creation of the International Committee of Women for Permanent Peace (ICWPP), later renamed Women's International League for Peace and Freedom (WILPF), and initiated formal actions to mitigate the ongoing conflict and prevent future wars. She later toured Europe's warring nations, meeting prominent public persons there, and even met President Wilson to bring an end to the conflict. The operative principles of WILPF were in accordance with her observations in *Newer Ideals of Peace*, a theoretical inquiry into notions of peace and its ethical implications, in which she conceives the concept 'positive peace' – a condition of peace more than just 'an absence of conflict'. She says, 'True peace is not merely the absence of war, it is the presence of justice.'

Jane felt that war hampered the progress of human civilization, encouraged political repression and even reversed man's cultural achievements. A visionary of a rare gene, Jane asks in *Peace and Bread in Time of War*, 'What after all has maintained the human race on this old globe despite all calamities of nature and all the tragic failings of mankind if not faith in new possibilities and courage to advocate them?'

She served WILPF as its first president till 1929.

Jane's public reckoning was such that there were hardly any issues of her time that did not engage her. In 1911, she took on the vice-presidency of the National American Women's Suffrage Association. She made several public speeches on women suffrage, and her speeches were widely distributed in the form of pamphlets. Women's suffrage had never been an issue of importance in America till then, but it was a contentious issue in the forthcoming presidential election in 1912. Jane's popularity had risen to such an extent that in 1912 Theodore Roosevelt, coming out in support of suffragettes, asked her to second his presidential nomination as a candidate of the Progressive Party. Roosevelt lost the election, but his campaign in alliance with the suffragist movement placed women's franchise as an issue of importance in the American political arena. The road they had lain would finally lead to 19 August 1920, when the US adopted the nineteenth amendment to its constitution and gave women the right to vote.

The scope and span of her work touched many other socio-political issues, too. For instance, in 1921, when white slavery was being widely debated, she published *A New Conscience and Ancient Evil*, a book on prostitution and the profession's evils. Her enlightened study of the subject received wide public attention as most of her work had throughout her life. In the book, she expresses her deep aguish at reports of sex trafficking in cities – of the allurements the city designedly placed around many young girls to draw them into a life of evil. She calls for urgent eradication – through all means necessary – of prostitution and the sexual trappings of city life through the concerted efforts of city officials, policemen, judges, attorneys, employers, trade unionists, physicians, teachers, clergymen and journalists. In her unsparing effort to help the girl child, she also founded the Juvenile Protective Association of Chicago, which conducted regular studies on child abuse, prostitution and child labour to chart their impact on child development. Its investigations took it to Chicago's dance halls, theatres, amusement parks, lake-excursion boats, department stores, factories, offices, hotels and restaurants.

On 10 December 1931, Jane became the first American woman to win the prestigious Nobel Peace Prize, with Halvdan Koht, member of the Nobel Committee, elaborating in his presentation speech the committee's reasons for choosing Jane Addams: 'Little by little, through ... patient self-sacrifice and quiet ardour ... she won an eminent place in the love and esteem of her people ... Since millions of men and women look up to her, she can give a new strength to that ideal among the American people.' Indeed it inspired many Americans, some of whom are of no lesser pedigree than Emily Greene Balch and Barack Obama, who are Nobel Peace Prize winners themselves. In fact, Emily Greene Balch wrote in 1951: 'Miss Addams shines, so respectful of everyone's views, so eager to understand, sympathize, so patient of anarchy and even ego, yet always there, strong, wise and in the lead.' Barack Obama also takes inspiration from Jane, in his celebrated book *Of Thee I Sing: A Letter to My Daughters*, in which he wishes his daughters would learn from Jane Addams.

She was truly an inspired soul, the length and breadth of which is hard to capture in words. A stand-out feature of her life was the scarce contrast between her ideal and personal world. Her eclectic interest in human affairs was in perfect tune with her own moral philosophy. As she exhorts in *Democracy and Social Ethics*, every person has to seek out and confront diverse experiences and perspectives.

On 21 May 1935, Jane died from cancer. The Chicago City Council described her as 'the greatest woman who ever lived'. A feature title in *Current Literature* anointed her 'The Only Saint America Has Produced'. In a more realistic vein, the *New York Times* obituary christened her 'a priestess of understanding among neighbours and peace among nations'.

EMILY GREENE BALCH

INDEFATIGABLE ACTIVIST

'We have a long, long way to go. So let us hasten along the road.
The road of human tenderness and generosity.'

In the year 1946, in a world still traumatized by the horrors of World War II, Emily Greene Balch emerged triumphant, as she became the first Quaker and third woman to receive the Nobel Peace Prize. She was chosen for her credentials as the dean and the leading light of the American peace movement. Peace, after all, was beginning to be held in high esteem in a war-weary world. Even though World War II officially came to an end in December 1945, it did so among troubling signs. Stalin had called Churchill 'a firebrand'; the United States had exploded a 20-kiloton nuclear bomb in Bikini Atoll; around 200,000 Hindus and Muslims had killed each other in India; and the war between the Vietminh and France had intensified in South East Asia.

Though Emily had risen to great prominence, she was not a Byzantine deity peering down on the world from a golden dome. She was a woman of humble origins, and that humility allowed her to walk among us in the darkest of nights. She was born on 8 January 1867 in Jamaica Plain, a suburb of Boston, the second daughter of Francis Vergnies Balch and Ellen Maria Noyes Balch. Her parents were first cousins and had known each other since childhood. By the time they were married and had six children their love for each other had grown to great heights. Emily loved the way her parents adored each other.

Her parents were the centre of all of Emily's activities. Emily's mother had a passion for languages which she passed on to Emily with great diligence. No surprises then that as a grown-up Emily was proficient in Latin, German and French. On the other hand, her father, Francis, was Emily's constant test and standard, and she inherited many of his scholarly traits. His story is an incredible tale of resilience and determination. As a child, he was constantly beset with illness, until the age of thirteen during which he remained under the care of a nurse. However, he was determined to bounce back from his setbacks, and cultivated a deep passion for books. On

9 April 1861, Francis became a member of Massachusetts Bar. His career as an attorney was a roaring success. Soon, his development was noticed by Senator Charles Sumner, who appointed him as his clerk. The bill for the reform of the civil services introduced by Sumner was drafted by Francis. By the time he married Ellen and Emily was born, he had had many achievements to his name and risen in social station. Francis is also said to have had a pleasing personality; 'he broke the Golden Rule only by exceeding it'. Emily described her father as 'a combination of Abraham Lincoln, Santa Claus and Jesus'.

On 18 June 1876, when she was only ten years old, she attended, along with her father, the ordaining of Charles Fletcher Dole as a church minister. Emily grew up in a Unitarian household, and she and her family regularly visited the First Church of Jamaica Plain. There, Dole urged her to dedicate her life 'to the service of goodness'. Young Emily was so entranced by the minister's call that she instantly made up her mind not to marry and place fully her life at the altar of humanitarian service. She gave her word to Dole with an air of solemnity with which nuns usually take their vows.

Dole first arrived in Jamaica Plain in April 1876 to preach at Jamaica Plain's First Church. Social progress and individual responsibility were the core of Dole's teachings, and he believed religion must 'be inclusive of all kinds and conditions of men, an open basis of our common spiritual humanity'. Emily described him as 'the chief of all influences that have played upon [her] life'.

In her late adolescence, Emily transitioned from a young girl to a strong woman, characterized by an unquenchable thirst for knowledge. She had begun reading books when she was only nine years old. She attended elementary school in the vicinity of her home in Jamaica Plain, run by one Ms Walker, and at the age of thirteen, started attending a private school called Miss

Ireland's School. There she befriended Helen Cheever – daughter of a Boston physician – who would provide her much-needed emotional support in her later life, and especially at a time when her mother had fallen sick with Bright's disease, lately called 'chronic nephritis'. Her mother would succumb to the disease on 14 September 1884 when Emily was seventeen.

After her mother's death Emily slumped to depression and loneliness. With a leaden heart, she wrote, '[My mother's affection] was the only passionate love I have ever felt.' Her father, however, was no less caring. To lift her out of her grief he send her on a tour of Europe, starting in April 1885. Later, rejuvenated from her travels abroad, she decided to pursue a degree at Bryn Mawr College, Philadelphia, in August 1886.

Emily was one of the first graduates of Bryn Mawr, in the spring of 1889. For her new year's resolution that year, she had written in her diary, 'I hope I shall not get lost in study, or pursue it for pleasure beyond its best measure for my purpose, unknown to me as yet.' Nonetheless she excelled in academics, and Dean Thomas would term her the 'the most civilized girl of the college'. Bryn Mawr College also awarded her, in April 1889, a European fellowship for 1890–91 to study economics in Paris.

In the summer of 1892, Emily had a life-altering experience. At the School of Applied Ethics in Plymouth, Massachusetts, she attended a lecture by Jane Addams. Jane, the celebrated founder of Hull House, played a significant role in shaping American society in the modern age. Emily was so inspired by the idea of Hull House that in the fall of 1892 she started working to found Denison House, in Boston, named after Edward Denison, an English philanthropist. On 27 December 1892, Denison House opened its doors, and, much like Hull House in Chicago, it was the first of its kind in its city. Besides offering recreational facilities such as a sports club, a gymnasium, a library and a health clinic, the settlement house catered mainly to the educational needs of the poor. In order to strengthen the labour movement in the late nineteenth century, special classes on trade unionism were also organized. Several notable women worked in the settlement house, including labour leader Mary Kenney O'Sullivan and pioneering aviator Amelia Earhart. The chief objective of the house was fostering cohesion among the poor, the privileged and educated workers, and it reflected Emily's life philosophy of intercultural cooperation. Emily was the head worker at Denison House, but did not live there and resided in her family home.

While in Paris, Emily studied France's social welfare policies and published her observations, in 1893, in *Public Assistance of the Poor in France*. In the book she traces the character of 'charitableness' to the ecclesiastical feature of ancient and medieval France, when the Church played a prominent role in government. Her study drew her to peruse Church archives and to conclude that charity is an essential Christian virtue, underlining in the book the role of bishops and priests in ancient and medieval France. The Church hierarchy, she observed, were bound by a moral duty to the poor so strong that it had the power of law. She finds in her surveys that most contemporary government charitable institutions in France, though run voluntarily, was based on this moral law or more accurately a feeling of 'public debt'. Her observations are set against her own experiences of living in Paris, as well as social institutions of similar structure and purpose in countries such as Britain and the United States. The book had important insights into the foundation of modern government and heralded her emergence as a sociologist and economist of renown. Her researching for writing her book also bettered her proficiency in French.

In 1896, she was offered a lectureership at Wellesley College by Katharine Coman, who headed the Department of Economics in Wellesley College and was her associate when Emily founded

Denison House. At the time she was concerned about her continued dependence on her father and was faced with a daunting decision – whether to pursue academics any further or seek employment.

Eventually she decided to set aside her academic pursuits and develop her strong passion for teaching, which she regarded as a privileged profession. She had once remarked that she was ready to 'pay for the privilege'. It was a decision of expediency that happily consumed the next twenty years of her life. In 1913, she rose to the rank of professor of economics and sociology. She was a charismatic teacher who could spur the minds of her students on the path of independent inquiry and judgement. According to one of her students,

> Miss Emily was an utterly unpretentious woman, spare of figure, unmindful of clothes and fripperies. Besides her learning, which was broad and deep, she had a wide personal acquaintance with civic and humanitarian leaders of Europe and America. Professor Emily would frequently overlook some of the mechanical details of teaching, but her teaching was all the better for her excursions into the buzzing centres beyond the placid college walls.

She was also known among her students and peers for being highly forgetful. Often she forgot to return examination papers or to inform the students about her absence from college. Once, she even travelled to Wellesley railway station wearing an overcoat with only a slip underneath. Some in the family attributed it to her forgetfulness and some to her scant regard for such 'trivialities' as dressing up.

In the second year of her teaching career at Wellesley, she was bereaved by the sudden death of her father, in February

1898. She was crestfallen but refused to be morose. Her father's death changed her prayers to God. Henceforth, she prayed for God's assistance in being 'not slothful, duty loving, serviceable, considerate, generous and loving in thought and speech of others'. She invariably would add to the prayer, at the end – 'as he was'.

After her father's death, she undertook many social responsibilities. Emily founded the National Women's Trade Union League in 1903, in which she was joined by several women who were devoted to the cause of social justice. The league addressed child labour, minimum wages and social insurance. She was a member of two municipal boards and, in 1908, served as a member of the Massachusetts Commission on Industrial Education. She also served as a member of the State Commission on Immigration. A woman of genuine empathy, she participated in various campaigns for racial justice, abolition of child labour, labour welfare, wage reform and women's suffrage. She also came into public reckoning as a relentless peace activist, participating in the World Peace Conferences held in 1899 and 1907 at The Hague.

Her exploits as a social activist notwithstanding, Emily had one foot firmly in the academia, and produced many scholarly works of repute. In 1910, she authored *Our Slavic Fellow Citizens*, a demographic analysis of the Slavic population in the US. According to her, the US is a nation of immigrants, and until 1840 most of the immigrants in the US were English and Scottish, and most of them professed Protestant beliefs. Today, in a world charged with xenophobia and anti-immigrant sentiment, this study, though largely forgotten, is a document of great relevance. In her earlier writings, she had focussed on sociology and economics. She penned *Outline of Economics* (1899), a precise, thirty-one-page summary written for her students of various problems and concepts in economics. In *Women at The Hague* (1915), she discusses the various proceedings of the peace congresses at The Hague and highlights the role of women in the preservation of world peace. In *Approaches to the Great Settlement* (1918), she compiles and discusses many proposals for peace. When Nazism haunted Germany in the 1930s, Emily wrote *Refugees as Assets*, urging the US government to allow victims of Nazi persecution to immigrate to the United States.

In the early weeks of World War I, Emily could not comprehend the gravity of the war. It was the summer of 1914, and she was vacationing with her friend and fellow scholar Katharine Coman in Maine. Shortly after her vacation, Coman was bedridden with cancer, and Emily, oblivious of the war, was engrossed in taking care of her friend. It was only after her friend's demise in January 1915 that Emily became aware of the war. At first, she did not find herself on the same page as other Americans, who were condemning Germany. Though she was apprehensive of German militarism and despised the country's chauvinistic nationalism, she continued to hold faith in Germany's potential. As a true peace activist, she remained neutral towards all warring nations.

During this time there were several peace organizations in the US; nonetheless Emily Greene Balch and other peace activists collaborated to form the Woman's Peace Party (WPP) in 1915. This was in response to a few leading suffragists' approaching Jane Addams and American suffrage leader Carrie Chapman Catt to lead a women's movement for bringing an end to the ongoing war. The formation meeting was held in January 1915 in Washington DC with Jane Addams as the chairperson. Emily joined WPP in the spring of 1915 following Jane Addams's invitation to WPP's meeting in The Hague: 'We feel that American women, having more freedom than those of most other countries, should especially respond to such a call issued by European women, at this critical moment in world affairs.'

Jane Addams valued Emily tremendously. She wrote to Emily, 'I am especially anxious that we should have delegates conversant with the racial and national situations, and I know of none who would meet these requirements better than you.' On 13 April 1915, Emily sought leave from Wellesley College and boarded a ship. She sailed from New York to Rotterdam along with forty-one other delegates from the United States. The meetings at The Hague were held between 28 April and 1 May 1915 and resulted in twenty resolutions being adopted and the formation of a transnational union of women peace advocates. It was named the International Committee of Women for Permanent Peace (ICWPP). The resolutions passed at the meetings were described by Emily as 'the best peace platform that has yet been drawn up'. The resolutions focused on charting peacemaking operations through regular mediation.

In the meeting Emily was selected as one of the envoys of the ICWPP. This turned the page to a new chapter in her life, with her embarking on a new career as a messenger of peace. Her first venture as an envoy was to Denmark, where Emily met Danish prime minister Carl Theodor Zahle, who assured his support for WPP's cause and with whom Emily had highly engaging talks. She then headed for Norway where she met King Haakon VII and the prime minister of Norway, who evinced a keen interest in WPP's plan for negotiated peace. Her subsequent jaunts were to Sweden and Russia, before returning to the United States. Her journeys as an envoy instilled in her a feeling of purpose and a hope that such delegations held promise for peace; she desired for Americans to be leaders in similar peacemaking missions. She wrote, 'Money and workers are needed, and America, unstricken by war, must do more than its share. Its fair share, even, is a large one.'

After her return from The Hague, Emily's political profile grew immensely. She met President Woodrow Wilson, upon whom she tried to impress the need for a conference of neutral nations. However, when later she met President Wilson's Secretary of State, Robert Lansing, he was lukewarm to WPP's proposals despite Emily's inspired presentation of the need for world peace. The idea of the US holding a conference of neutral nations thus never materialized.

But Emily would not give up. In the fall of 1916, she attempted again to mobilize public opinion against the World War. In *New Republic* she tried to clarify common misconceptions about the mediation conference of neutral nations she had mooted with Woodrow Wilson. She held that wars are fought for territorial expansion and because of greed. She also appealed to the international community to ameliorate the lot of the colonized rather than to exploit them.

However, around this time, the US itself was contemplating war. The number of public voices in favour of militarization had increased and 'pro-preparedness' rallies were being organized throughout the country. One of the prominent faces of the movement was ex-president Theodore Roosevelt, who was of the opinion that the US should increase its military units in anticipation of a conflict. There was palpable fear and paranoia everywhere, and the position of neutrality the US had proclaimed was hard to maintain in the face of such developments. With the political atmosphere thus on war's edge, the US was waiting only for a nudge to plunge into the bloodshed; and in early 1917, that would come in the form of the most innocuous of things – a telegram.

In January 1917, British intelligence intercepted a telegram from the German foreign secretary, Arthur Zimmerman, to the German ambassador to Mexico, Heinrich von Eckardt, proposing a possible Germany–Mexico alliance in the event of America's entering the war. The Zimmerman telegram sparked widespread outrage among Americans and provided ammunition to pro-war jingoists who had till then been largely sidelined in popular discourse. Politicians, highly perceptive as they are, saw the spike in pro-war rhetoric and stoked further the siege mentality that had gripped the masses. Woodrow Wilson – who had come to power with the campaign slogan 'He kept us out of war' – also turned towards the pro-war tide for political gain, and his administration passed several laws criminalizing peace activists.

In response, Emily joined hands, in early 1917, with the Emergency Peace Federation (EPF) – a group formed to oppose President Woodrow Wilson's decision to enter the war. They called for a referendum to decide whether the US should interfere in the conflict. The EPF's call for a referendum received full-throated support from the American Union against Militarism (AUAM) and the Woman's Peace Party. *Four Lights*, a radical progressive journal and the official newsletter of WPP, ran many articles in support of the EPF and Emily's campaign. Emily also lobbied for creating a war reparations fund.

She also wrote to the president of Wellesley College, as a devout Christian, that America should follow 'the way of Jesus'; the American political economy then, Emily lamented, was far from being in harmony with the teachings of Christianity. She also lampooned Congressmen for their demagoguery. She deeply regretted that even when the consensus among Americans was opposed to the war, the Congress backed the Wilson administration to join the conflict. In a letter to Congressman Isaac Sherwood of Ohio, dated March 1917 in the Congressional Record, Emily castigates Congressmen: 'They had voted against their own judgment, against their own conscience and against what they have reason to believe to be the will of their constituents.'

Her remonstrations, however, were in vain. The US was spiralling into the war and formally entered it in April 1917, despite the forceful resistance of peace groups in the US, including eminent and well-meaning individuals. Emily and Jane Addams had met President Wilson in March 1917 to persuade him against America's entering the war, but they were unsuccessful.

Europe was absorbed in its own avarice and scramble for new colonies and had blinded itself to the dangers of war. Part of the reason was the perception that the potential destruction would not be 'total' in its proportions and it was tempting to wage war, if only to expand one's borders at the cost of a few lives. America, under Woodrow Wilson – who ironically won the Nobel Peace Prize two years later – had, however, ostensibly different reasons, mainly the Zimmerman telegram. In short, World War I was the unadulterated expression of man's base nature – greed and mistrust. Later wars would forever be changed by this event; thereon, wars would be couched in sophisticated doctrines of national interest or security, as with the idea of a 'master race' by Nazi Germany.

The United States' entry into World War I made Emily more aggressive, and her political identity underwent a paradigm shift from a liberal centrist to a confirmed radical. During this radical transformation, she faced stiff opposition from her family, and, in particular, from her younger sister Marion. Although it was difficult to stand against the escalating public pressure to back the war, she remained firm in her belief of the futility of war. Eventually she would emerge, along with Jane Addams, as the face of anti-war sentiment in the US.

World War I finally came to an end on 11 November 1918, when the Triple Alliance agreed an armistice with the Triple

Entente. After the war, the International Committee of Women for Permanent Peace (ICWPP) decided to meet again, in Zurich. The meeting was attended by twenty-two women from the United States besides Jane Addams and Emily. Emily was the convenor of the meeting, and in consultation with other members, she finalized the committee panel, devised a programme for discussions and laid down the rules of order. On 12 May 1919, Jane Addams opened the congress. She congratulated the participants for raising their voices against war in the last four years. Their voices had rocked the corridors of power and now their mission was writing the covenants of peace. In the congress at Zurich, the women also changed the name of their organization to the Women's International League for Peace and Freedom (WILPF).

While in Zurich, she received word from Wellesley College that her tenure at the College would not be renewed. Though it shocked others, it came as no surprise to Emily. It was inevitable that her opposition to militant nationalism would bring her into conflict with American jingoists. Rather than ruing the loss of her job, she, in a sense, celebrated the occasion with other women at Zurich by joining them for a cigarette. Nonetheless she conveyed her displeasure to Wellesley College president Pendleton that by not reappointing her they had deprived her of a pension – even after having twenty-one years of service. She later issued a note of regret on her pacifist positions and assured the board of Wellesley College that she would not influence her students or dampen their patriotism. Her colleagues also vouched for her reinstatement, highlighting her accomplishments as an esteemed academic and teacher. Their entreaties, however, failed to move the board members, and Emily was dismissed thanklessly. Later Emily was rehabilitated by her friend and fellow peace campaigner Oswald Garrison Villard, who appointed her as the editor of his publication, *The Nation*, a leading liberal news magazine.

This was a period of immense personal growth and change for Emily. She would leave Unitarianism and become a Quaker, a member of the Society of Friends, in 1921. The Society of Friends had a long tradition of selfless service and pacifism, which also constituted her first impulse. The Quakers are Christians who do not abide by any scripture and believe in the simplicity of daily life and worship. They feel Christ works directly on the soul. On becoming a Quaker, she said,

> Religion seems to me one of the most interesting things in life, one of the most puzzling, thrilling and richest fields of human thought and speculation. Religious experience and thought need also a light, a day and sunshine, and a companionable sharing with others of which, it seems to me, there is generally too little. The Quaker worship gives opportunities for this sort of sharing without profanation.

Emily was also distressed over an uncertain future at the time; anticipating a pension, she had not saved towards retirement. Fortunately, her friend Helen Cheever came to her rescue and bestowed upon Emily an annual sum almost equal to the amount of her due pension. This support, however, was short-lived, as Cheever suspended the largesse on learning that Emily was giving away a substantial portion of the amount. Nonetheless, Cheever continued to interject in Emily's life quite closely. Moreover, it seems Cheever made known her affection for Emily in more ways than just financial support. Cheever had suggested setting up a common household with Emily, which was not taboo in those days in American society. Such arrangements were called 'Boston Marriages'. Jane Addams too had a similar relationship with Mary Rozet Smith; and whether the relationship was sexual – it was never discussed in their circles. Emily never refused to be the recipient of Cheever's unremitting affection or pecuniary support, but she rejected Cheever's idea of a live-in relationship. In her later life, Emily would pen an unpublished write-up in which she wistfully notes the absence of a spouse in her life as an unattached woman.

In the meantime, Emily continued her work in the WILPF. In 1919, after the Zurich congress, she had been appointed the first international secretary-treasurer of the international headquarters of the WILPF in Geneva, Switzerland. She was fifty-two years old at this time. Jane Addams and Helen Cheever constantly asked after her and her new role in the WILPF, and with the support and encouragement of her friends, she was able to reorient and reinvent herself. The new challenge catapulted Emily sky-high. By 1922, Emily had astounding accomplishments to her credit: She had established a good rapport with the League of Nations, started new international publications, and built an institutional framework for relief campaigns for war-torn countries and for the progress of women's movements around the world. She also helped expand the WILPF and establish new branches.

In the fall of 1922, she fell sick, and shortly afterwards, it became clear that she could not stay in Geneva. She resigned from WILPF despite Jane Addams's advice to the contrary, asking her to function as a travelling secretary. Emily returned to the United States in late 1925, and she set up a home in Wellesley, but continued to work for WILPF. Emily participated in many projects of the League of Nations and governments and international commissions, regarding disarmament, internationalization of aviation and drug control. In 1926, WILPF called on Emily to investigate the living conditions in Haiti, then garrisoned by the US Marines. She formed a committee with Charlotte Atwood, Zonia Baber, Paul Douglas, Addie Hunton and Grace Watson and left for Haiti in February 1926. The committee's report written by

Emily significantly contributed to the ending of US occupation of Haiti.

The decade following 1930 proved to be a real nightmare for Emily. Besides the Great Depression, this period was marked by violent struggles and the rise of fascism in the world. It raised its head in Italy, Germany and Japan, pursuing vigorously their nationalist–militarist agendas. Emily remarked, 'It did not take a prophet to foresee what the rapid war preparations would lead to.' She vigorously supported alternatives to war and suggested that disputes should be settled through international arbitration rather than through war.

Emily would shoot her arrows wherever she discerned an attempt at war. She castigated the German people for Hitler's desperadoes; when World War II was at its most gruesome, she helped Japanese Americans interned in US detention camps; when dictator Francisco Franco overtook the republican government of Spain in April 1936, after the Spanish Civil War, Emily cautioned the Spanish that 'the victors would be likely to fall to fighting among themselves'. And when Japan attacked the Chinese province of Manchuria, she appealed to both the United States and the League of Nations to denounce Japan's colonial designs. She sought for the United States to condemn Japan and declare that Japan had violated international treaties. Emily wrote to President Hoover in January 1932 to forbid the selling of arms to Japan and declare loans to Japan to be contrary to public policy. She was pained when Hoover declined to do so.

She deeply regretted that the United States, being well aware of the dangers, could think of nothing better than to wash its hands and draw aside. Reciprocating her warm gesture towards the people of China, China's minister of health invited Emily to China as his personal guest. Emily humbly declined the invitation, owing to her being too old to undertake the journey.

Finally, even Wellesley College recognized Emily's contribution to the peace effort and invited her to deliver the Armistice Day address to its students in 1935, almost a decade and a half after she had been evicted from Wellesley.

~◎

As sharp as Emily's diagnosis of war and its causes were, she invariably developed solutions to it too. She relentlessly persuaded the United States to involve itself in peace negotiations. For four years, she remained a dedicated activist of the WILPF and looked after its international office in Geneva as its chief organizer. The import of her work is reflected in how several resolutions passed by the WILPF were later adopted by the League of Nations. She was an academic of note and a near-point of moral perfection, and thus, through her life work, exemplified the makings of a peace activist: intellectual curiosity and moral bearings. In a poem 'Letter of Love' addressed to the 'Dear People of China', after the Japanese invasion, she had written:

> Let us be patient with one another
> And even patient with ourselves.
> We have a long, long way to go
> So let us hasten along the road,
> The road of human tenderness and generosity,
> Groping, we may find one another's hand in the dark.

However, later in life, as she grew wiser, her views on peace and pacifism would similarly mature. She shifted her position from absolute pacifism to a moderate, pragmatic dovishness. For instance, when Nazism bared its fangs in the 1930s, Emily called for defending 'the fundamental human rights, sword in hand'. She admitted, 'I realize that my position is neither very definite nor very consistent. How can one be either when an irresistible force meets an unmovable obstacle in one's own mind?' Appreciating her pragmatism, Bertram Pickard, the Quaker representative in Geneva, told her, 'One of the most attractive things about your pacifism is that it combines the wisdom of the political serpent and the harmlessness of the Quaker dove.' Her judgement would, in time, be proved correct, when Nazi Germany tore through Europe, and institutionalized violence – through concentration camps and death squads – had become banal.

Perhaps even more striking was Emily's extraordinary foresight and remarkably clear judgement of the future age. She was among the few who realized the importance of technology. She observed, 'Technology gives us facilities that lessen the barriers of time and distance – the telegraph and cable, the telephone, radio and the rest.' The 'rest' which were still to come after Emily were LED TVs, mobile phones, emails, Twitter and Facebook. These technological advancements did greatly lessen the barriers of time and distance. As she rightly observed, 'Industrialization based on machinery already referred to as a characteristic of our age is but one aspect of the revolution that is being wrought by technology.'

When she received the Nobel Peace Prize in 1946, she was seventy-nine years old. Her health had been failing, but her spirits were soaring high. She was still an active part of WILPF and donated her share of the Nobel Peace Prize money to the organization. In her Nobel Lecture, she reminded us of the dangers of nationalism: 'Nationalism has proved excessively dangerous in its divisiveness and self-adulation. It has given us an anarchic world of powerful armed bodies, with traditions steeped in conquest and military glory, and of competing commercial peoples as ruthless in their economic self-seeking as in their wars.'

In the process, her body aged but her spirit remained the same. Emily's health had been deteriorating. She spent her last five years in Mr Vernon's Nursing Home in Cambridge, Massachusetts, where she was bedridden with pneumonia. She breathed her last on 9 January 1961. She was witness to two world wars and the tenures of eighteen American presidents, beginning with Andrew Johnson and ending with Dwight D. Eisenhower. Her legacy continues to live on, as we still survive the fallout from events of her time. Emily left behind a legacy of challenge to future generations. At the bidding of minister Dole, at the tender age of ten, she had vowed to live a life of service. She served humanity with all her heart, until all of her potential was exhausted by her death.

It is not hard to imagine her father's influence on Emily. In a world so rigidly patriarchal, when women had just been enfranchized, it is only natural that the father, or 'the man of the house', wields undue influence over a child's formation. The liberal father, thus, is a paradoxical figure, whose influence is simultaneously a problem and solution by itself.

BERTHA VON SUTTNER

THE FIRST WOMAN OF PEACE

'Universal sisterhood is necessary before universal
brotherhood is possible.'

The first woman to receive the Nobel Peace Prize was Baroness Bertha von Suttner, a Czech-Austrian pacifist, journalist and novelist. Born Bertha Felicitas Sophie on 9 June 1843, in Prague, Bohemia, she boasted a proud military heritage. She was the daughter of a distinguished Austrian lieutenant general. Bertha was the second woman to win a Nobel Prize – Marie Curie being the first, two years earlier in 1903 – and the first Austrian Nobel laureate.

Her mother, Sophie von Körner, was an astonishing fifty years her father's junior. When her father died, he was seventy-five years old. Bertha was born posthumously and was brought up by her mother and remained under the guardianship of Friedrich Zu Fürstenberg, a member of the Austrian court. Her elder brother, Arthur, was sent to a military boarding school at the age of six and had little contact with his family thereafter. Bertha's early years were rich with education, voracious reading and travel. She evinced a strong interest in music, particularly singing, and learnt several languages – English, German, Italian and French. But though she enjoyed these trappings of her social milieu, having been born into an aristocratic family, she was of the unlanded nobility: Financial worries would haunt her, and she would face hardship at various stages of her life. Her mother had no means of sustaining the family comfortably and squandered what money she had by gambling and poor management of the family's already depleted resources.

Bertha was a bewitching beauty with gorgeous eyes. By the time she entered her teens, she had turned away overtures from many a beaus. She was looking for someone matching her brilliance and mental wavelength. So, it was no surprise that she had to wait for quite long. When she was twenty-nine, she was mesmerized by Prince Adolf Wittgenstein. Bertha accepted his marriage proposal as they both were music lovers. Unfortunately, Prince Adolf died at sea before they could marry.

Bertha chose, in 1873, at the age of thirty, to seek employment as governess in the house of a wealthy Suttner family, who lived in Canova Street, Vienna. Even for the lower aristocracy, such an engagement would only have been dishonour. But Bertha threw herself wholeheartedly into her work, as she did with all her endeavours. She became the much-loved tutor and companion to the wealthy nobleman Karl von Suttner's four daughters, who were aged between fifteen and twenty. She also began an intense affair with the youngest son of Karl von Suttner, Baron Arthur Gundaccar von Suttner, a young man seven years her junior. The couple was engaged, and although Arthur's sisters were delighted by the prospect of Bertha becoming their sister-in-law, Arthur's family was scandalized and refused the couple permission to marry. Her age and unimpressive aristocratic pedigree, at the very least, were not to their liking.

In 1876, with her employer's encouragement – and upon being persuaded by her friends – Bertha responded to an advertisement in a Viennese newspaper from Alfred Nobel, the Swedish millionaire and inventor of dynamite. The advertisement read, 'A VERY WEALTHY, CULTURED, ELDERLY GENTLEMAN, LIVING IN PARIS, DESIRES TO FIND A LADY ALSO OF MATURE YEARS, FAMILIAR WITH LANGUAGES, AS SECRETARY AND MANAGER OF HIS HOUSEHOLD.'

Bertha's knowledge of languages was her forte, and, with her good breeding and intelligence, her selection was all but assured. But when Nobel met Bertha, he was immediately drawn to her; his interest even extended to romance. He was, after all, hardly elderly as the advertisement had claimed: at forty-two, he was in his early middle age, and the attractive, well-schooled Bertha mesmerized him. The pair engaged in lively debates each day in Nobel's Paris apartment, discussing people, art, life, time, eternity and, above all, how to end war and establish peace. These discussions continued for eight days. On the ninth day of her employment, Alfred travelled to Stockholm. After a couple of days, Bertha received two telegrams. One was from Alfred Nobel informing her of his expected return in a week's time. The other from the man she loved, Arthur Gundaccar von Suttner, declaring that he could not live without her. On account of the latter telegram, Bertha's stint as Nobel's secretary ended abruptly. She returned to Vienna for Arthur. The pair married in secrecy on 12 June 1876 and eloped to Mingrelia (in present-day Georgia).

The marriage was not received well by Suttner's family. Arthur was immediately disinherited and cast out of his family. The couple spent nine years in Caucasus, where they earned their living writing novels and translating books. They also taught languages and music; they were kindred spirits in their talents and ideological leanings. Arthur firmly supported his wife in her writing and her pacifism, and their time in Caucasus was of great importance to Bertha's development.

This period, 1876–85, was marked by political upheaval in the region and, indeed, throughout Europe. Bertha's husband published several reports from the Russo-Turkish War of 1877–78, and Bertha keenly read reports from the battle front and interviewed war-weary military personnel. She witnessed war's ruination of the human spirit, and this had a profound impact on her. Her conviction that peace was an essential prerequisite for human existence is underpinned by her observations of the Russo-Turkish War and the trauma it wrought on the people of the region.

During her time in Caucasus, Bertha started her journalistic career under the pseudonym B. Oulot, short for her nickname 'Boulotte', given to her by the Suttner family. She wrote short stories and essays on the lives of the Georgian people, which were published in several Austrian newspapers. She also wrote *Es Löwos*, a romantic account of her life with Arthur, and a few novels, the most notable of which was *Inventarium einer Seele* (Inventory of a Soul). Influenced by the writings of Darwin, Immanuel Kant, Henry Thomas Buckle, Herbert Spencer and Leo Tolstoy – and no doubt by her own observations of the depredation of war on the body politic – she expounded in this book, her first serious literary work, the idea of a progressive society characterized by peace.

With the passage of time, Arthur's family's disapproval of his marriage diminished, and in 1885, the couple was welcomed back to the von Suttner household at Harmannsdorf Castle. Meanwhile, Bertha continued her writing. She began to tread a different path, concentrating on peace and conflict studies as espoused by French philosopher Ernest Renan. In 1887, at the age of forty-four, she learnt about the International Arbitration and Peace Association, founded by Hodgson Pratt in 1880, after stumbling on the record of one of the association's meetings. It was a revelation for her. Bertha later wrote of her surprise upon her discovery of this dedicated organization for peace: 'What? Such a league existed? The idea of justice between nations, the struggle to do away with war had assumed life? The news electrified me.' Thus, her quest became clear to her, and she would dedicate her life to championing ideals that negated the very materialistic and aristocratic traditions that had pervaded her life until this time.

Bertha's literary talent would serve her and her ideals well. Her book *Das Maschinenzeitalter* (The Machine Age) attracted wide acclaim. It was published under the nom de plume 'Jemand' (Anyone), as Bertha felt that, in those rather sexist times, it would not be taken seriously if she published it under her own name. The book envisioned a society that would achieve progress through peace; and with astonishing prescience, Bertha foretold the results of exaggerated nationalism and advanced armaments.

She stepped into the limelight of the peace movement in 1889 with her pacifist novel *Die Waffen nieder!* (Lay Down Your Arms!). The title was provocative and offensive for those who cherished militaristic traditions, but its implicit denouncement of war was welcomed by the general public, who embraced the book as entertainment but understood its message nonetheless. The book was translated into twelve languages and published in an astonishing thirty-seven editions, and, through it, Bertha became a household name. *Die Waffen nieder!* influenced all sections of society; so much so that the Austrian finance minister Julian Dunajewski, in a debate about the military budget on 18 April 1891, remarked, 'There has recently appeared a book called *Die Waffen nieder!*. I can only advise the gentlemen to devote a few hours to the reading of this novel. Anyone who then still has a predilection for war, I can only pity.'

Numerous eminent intellectuals of the time were also impressed with the book. Tolstoy was much enamoured of Bertha von Suttner's novel and its pacifist themes. He expressed high hopes for the work in a letter to her, in which his admiration for Bertha is manifest:

> Madame,
>
>   I was just reading your novel *Die Waffen nieder!*, which Mr Bulgakof had sent me when I received your letter. I greatly appreciate your work, and the idea comes to me that the publication of your novel is a happy augury.
>
>   The abolition of slavery was preceded by the famous book of a woman Mrs Beecher Stowe; God grant that the abolition of war may follow upon your book. I am just about finishing a

treatise on this subject in which I discuss the only means which, in my opinion, can render wars impossible. Nevertheless, all efforts dictated by a sincere love for humanity will bear fruit, and the congress at Rome, I am certain, will contribute much, just as that at London last year did, to popularize the idea of the flagrant contradiction in which Europe finds itself – between the military status of the nations and the Christian and humanitarian principle which they profess.

Receive, madame, the assurance of my sentiments of genuine esteem and sympathy.

Leo Tolstoy
Signed 22 October 1891

Bertha's compelling narrative became one of the nineteenth century's most influential books, and after its publication, she never looked back as a woman of peace. Thereafter, the cause of peace became an overriding passion for her; she began to devote all her time, energy and writings to furthering peace.

Though Bertha had served Alfred Nobel as secretary for but a brief period, she remained in constant touch with him through regular correspondence until his death in 1896. He was among the many eminent admirers of her work, as was expressed in one of his rather intimate letters:

Dear Baroness and Friend,
I have just finished reading your admirable masterpiece. We are told that there are two thousand languages – 1999 too many

– but certainly there is not one in which your delightful work should not be translated, read and studied.

How long did it take you to write this marvel? You shall tell me when next time I have the honour and happiness of pressing your hand – that Amazonian hand which makes so valiantly war on war.

Nevertheless you make a mistake to cry 'Away with Weapons!', because you yourself make use of them, and because yours – the charm of your style and the grandeur of your ideas – carry and will carry much farther than the Lebels, the Nordenfelts, the De Banges and all other implements of hell …

Yours for ever and more than ever,
A. Nobel
Paris 1/4/1890

From a tireless but struggling author, Bertha transformed herself into a crusader for peace. Her first speech on the world stage was at the International Peace Congress in Rome, in 1891. In this year, she established the Austrian Peace Society and emerged as a dynamic leader of the male-dominated peace congresses. She was a founding member in 1892 and chairwoman of the *Deutsche Friedensgesellschaft* (German Peace Society). She organized international congresses and helped people form peace groups, swelling the ranks of their members. She toured, lecturing on peace, and also corresponded with people all over the world to promote its cause. Her rigorous intellect, forged in her childhood by her reading and natural inquisitiveness, would serve her well here. She also formed a Venetian peace group, attended her first international peace conference and inaugurated the fund for the establishment of the Bern Peace Bureau. From 1892 to 1899, her reputation grew internationally as the editor of the international pacifist journal *Die Waffen nieder*, named after her book.

Throughout her years at the forefront of the peace movement, Bertha wrote articles, pamphlets, reviews, letters and petitions in support of world peace. She organized peace meetings among influential people. It was almost as if she had regarded ending war in the world as her personal responsibility. Bertha was the only woman present at the first Hague Peace Conference held in 1899, which she was allowed to attend only as an observer. She nevertheless was the cynosure of the event. Bertha, who had been brought up in an aristocratic society, whose militaristic traditions imbued her early years, was now opposing these traditions with martial determination and vigour. She had not rejected her heritage wholesale, though, as she continually expressed faith in God and read the Bible daily for inspiration. And in every respect, she did not flout social convention. She remained a dignified, patrician lady, and it was only her endeavours, her ideas and her achievements that set her apart from others of her class.

In 1897, Bertha initiated a signature campaign demanding the establishment of an international court of justice and presented a petition to Emperor Franz Joseph I of Austria to this end. It would be nearly half a century before the International Court of Justice was established by a UN Charter in 1945, in the aftermath of the carnage of World War II. In 1899, she actively participated in the organization of the First Hague Convention, and was instrumental in establishing the Permanent Court of Arbitration (PCA). The PCA exists even today to settle contentious issues between nations peacefully.

Bertha von Suttner's remarkable life of achievement was set against a backdrop of personal challenges, which she bore with hallmark dignity. Her husband whom she lovingly called 'My Own' died in 1902 after a long illness, and saddled with the von

Suttner family's debts, Bertha was forced to sell Harmannsdorf Castle and return to Vienna. Although Bertha had fallen apart after the death of her husband, she decided to carry on the peace work they had undertaken together, to keep his soul's flight with hers. She restricted all her movements and focused only on peace missions, and vigorously undertook several speaking tours. In 1904, Bertha addressed the International Congress of Women in Berlin. She also travelled the United States following her attendance at the International Peace Congress of 1904 in Boston, lecturing extensively and mobilizing people for peace congresses. On this American visit, she met President Theodore Roosevelt for promoting world peace.

By 1905, when she was awarded the Nobel Peace Prize – at a fortuitous time financially – she had been widely viewed as sharing the leadership of the peace movement with the venerable Frédéric Passy, himself a Nobel Peace Prize laureate. In the following years, Bertha played a prominent role in the Anglo-German Friendship Committee, formed at the 1905 Peace Congress to further Anglo-German reconciliation. She warned all who would listen about the dangers of militarizing China and of using aviation, which was rapidly developing in those years, as a military instrument. She contributed lectures, articles and interviews to the International Club set up at the 1907 Hague Peace Conference to promote the movement's objectives. She also spoke at the 1908 Peace Congress in London.

Bertha ceaselessly asserted 'Europe is one'. She was convinced that uniting its countries was the only way to prevent the world catastrophe that loomed. Her last major effort – in 1912, when she was almost seventy – was a second lecture tour of the United States. There, the newspapers hailed her as 'Peace Bertha' and the 'Angel of Peace'. One of Bertha's more celebrated moments was at a speech in San Francisco on 4 July 1912, a few months after women had enjoyed suffrage in California for the first time. She told the audience, and the world at large, 'Ladies and gentlemen, voters of California, the one half of humanity that has never borne arms is today ready to blaze into this living palpable force – the principle of the brotherhood of man. Perhaps, the universal sisterhood is necessary before the universal brotherhood is possible.' Bertha understood that women must occupy centre stage of human affairs, and, given the social strictures of her time, was surprisingly bold in expressing such views. This is not simply because women comprise half of humanity. It is because woman is the creator of this human world, and a creator will always protect her creation.

In 1913, Baroness von Suttner was given the title 'Generalissimo of the Peace Movement' by Kaiser Franz Josef. This was to be one of her last accolades. In August of that year, Bertha spoke at the International Peace Congress – her final congress – at The Hague, where she was greatly honoured as the elder stateswoman of the peace movement. Her body had by now been wrecked by a malignant cancer, and her strength was failing. But with her characteristic unflagging spirit she continued actively preparing, as late as May in 1914, for the twenty-first Peace Congress, planned for Vienna in September. However, Bertha breathed her last on 21 June 1914. In accordance with her will, her remains were cremated at Gotha Cemetery and her ashes interred at the columbarium there.

She died just seven days before the assassination of Archduke Franz Ferdinand of Austria in Sarajevo, which ignited the world war she had railed against and struggled to avert. It was as if the charismatic, enlightened von Suttner – one of the world's great moral leaders – had managed to stave off war, and with her gone, the global powers were free to do their worst. The congress in Vienna was cancelled, and the war and its immediate aftermath stifled the peace movement and thwarted its plans for a monument to Bertha von Suttner.

Always something of an outsider, Bertha von Suttner's remarkable ability lay in influencing public opinion and world events while being away from the corridors of power. This underscores a peculiarity of women Nobel Peace laureates: They wield the weapon of empathy for their fellow human beings – an innate feminine quality. It is little wonder then that Bertha von Suttner inspired, in no small degree, Alfred Nobel's decision to institute the Nobel Peace Prize.

In another of his numerous letters to Bertha, he informed her of his intention to institute the Nobel Peace Prize:

Dear Friend,

May the new year prove prosperous to you and to the noble campaign which you are carrying on with so much power against human ignorance and ferocity.

I should like to dispose of a part of my fortune by founding a prize to be granted every five years – say six times, for if in thirty years they have not succeeded in reforming the present system they will infallibly relapse into barbarism.

The prize would be awarded to him or her who had caused Europe to make the longest strides towards ideas of general pacification.

I am not speaking to you of disarmament which can be achieved only very slowly; I am not even speaking to you of obligatory arbitration between nations. But this result ought to be reached soon and it can be attained – to wit, that all states shall with solidarity agree to turn against the first aggressor. Then wars will become impossible, and the result would be to force even the most quarrelsome state to have recourse to a tribunal or else remain tranquil. If the Triple Alliance, instead of comprising only three states, should enlist all states, the peace of the centuries would be assured.

Nobel also understood the potential for the horror of technological war to drive humanity towards peace. In a letter to Bertha, he expressed such thoughts, which now seem reminiscent of the doctrine of mutually assured destruction of the cold war years:

> Perhaps my factories will put an end to war even sooner than your [peace] congresses. On the day when two army corps will be able to annihilate each other in a second, all civilized nations will recoil with horror and disband their troops on knowing that total devastation will be in store for them if they engage themselves in war.

The world was astounded when Nobel's will was opened after his death on 10 December 1896 and learnt that he had instituted a prize for peace. Alfred Nobel stipulated that the most coveted humanitarian prize in the world be awarded 'to the person who shall have done the most or the best work for fraternity between nations, for the abolition or reduction of standing armies and for the holding and promotion of peace congresses'. But the news of Nobel's will was no surprise to Bertha. Upon signing his will on 27 November 1895, Alfred Nobel had himself informed her of his decision to institute the prize. Expressing her delight at the news, she had remarked, 'Whether I am around then or not does not matter; what we have given, you and I, is going to live on.' This statement evinces the magnanimity of Bertha's soul: Accolades and worldly rewards were of far less importance to her than her work to ensure world peace. It is appropriate then that the motivating figure behind Alfred Nobel's prize for peace herself became the first woman recipient of the prize, just nine years after Nobel's death.

Notwithstanding her friendship with Nobel, Bertha von Suttner was one of the earliest women in the modern era to rise in prominence on her merits, as it were. She was recognized in her time as a great leader and thinker and, at the very least, the equal of her male contemporaries. Her strong suit was unquestionably her proficiency in language. Her other advantages were her strong practical intelligence, the courage of her convictions and, perhaps above all, her charisma, of which she was herself very much conscious. She regretted the fading of her charisma late in her life, when she wrote in her diaries, 'I know I've lost my magnetism. My getting ugly, my getting weak must not be shown to the world.' Bertha von Suttner, though, was no airbrushed demagogue. Behind her regal bearing was a brilliant mind: a finely honed intellect trained on the events of her world for the benefit of humanity.

In any event, her popularity and influence in her time were astounding. In 1903, a Berlin newspaper poll showed Bertha von Suttner to be one of the five most famous women of the era. What she achieved was against the winds of the time. Bertha von Suttner is virtually without parallel in the contemporary world, for in her time, women had little place in decision making, leave alone international affairs. She inspired and led men and women of goodwill in the twilight of a period when all but a few women were confined to homemaking. It must be remembered too that the men she inspired included those of the eminence of Leo Tolstoy, who is revered across the globe for his sagacity and lofty ideas.

However schooled was her intellect and dazzling her presence, much of Bertha's ability to inspire her contemporaries of all walks of life may be ascribed to the strength of her beliefs. Her public life amply demonstrated that success can depend greatly on the power of personality, on the power of self-confidence. Bertha von

Suttner exemplifies how a life wedded to ideals and bolstered by conviction can be influential almost beyond imagination.

She always behaved as if a Geneva Convention had already existed. People could not resist her noble-heartedness. When opinions clashed and agreements seemed impossible, Bertha von Suttner would rise to her feet, and this alone – the dignity of her appearance, the seriousness of her features – would bring the calm that is the precondition to agreement.

Bertha von Suttner indelibly left her impression on the world. It could be argued that her mission for peace failed with the onset of World War I and the even greater conflagration of World War II. But Bertha was simply ahead of her time. She was a prototype feminist, in an era when the concept of feminism was nascent. She moved in the world of men as an equal, and was admired as such. She advocated the union of Europe, which was to occur nearly eight decades after her death. She helped plant the seed for the International Court of Justice. And she argued for women's dignity and equality with men with a directness and aplomb that is the envy of many later feminists. In 1894, she opined in one of her articles that biological differences should not be the basis for ethical differences. She observed, 'After all, the racecourse mare does the same task as the horse; the bitch in the hound pack hunts as the dog does. Man and woman are born equal and should have equal rights.'

My hope in writing this book is to inspire women to rise up, to come to the forefront of all human affairs and help eliminate weapons from the world. Our world will know peace only when its people regard others as part of one world family, in which each member instinctively reaches out to the others with love and respect. Thus, for me, Bertha von Suttner is the laureate whose life story most demonstrates the values of the Nobel Peace Prize, which is essential for making any meaningful progress towards abiding world peace.

ACKNOWLEDGEMENTS

The writing of a book is credited to the person who pens it, but I believe book writing is a collective effort. I simply would not have undertaken the writing of this book if my father had not told me in my childhood the inspiring stories of Mahatma Gandhi, Abraham Lincoln, Martin Luther King Jr, Mikhail Gorbachev, Aung San Suu Kyi and a host of other great personalities. I have also to thank Aung San Suu Kyi, whose encouragement was prime fuel for my imagination while writing this book. I still feel the warmth of her hug and her holding both my hands tightly in her own – a moment so long it seemed eternal.

I am deeply grateful to the former UN Secretary General Ban Ki-moon, His Holiness the Dalai Lama and Kailash Satyarthi for their support. I have been especially lucky to receive the time and affection of Rigoberta, Jody, Mairead, Betty, Ellen, Shirin, Malala, Tawakkol and Leymah. A special thanks to Malala's parents, Ziauddin Yousafzai and Tor Pekai. Ziauddin is one of the noblest men I have met. He calls me an 'alchemist', and that is food for my soul.

Mikhail Gorbachev, Juan Manuel Santos, Fatou Bensouda, Arianna Huffington and Cherie Blair deserve a special mention for their moral support.

My aim in writing *Battling Injustice* is to acquaint the young people of today with the noble art of peace activism and, if possible, move them to work for its hallowed objectives. However, my own source of inspiration have come from the work of two celebrities – Angelina Jolie and Sharon Stone. Angelina's travels around the globe providing solace and comfort to the needy, especially her efforts during the recent refugee crisis, is commendable. I am stymied to express the profound debt I owe to Sharon Stone, whose lifelong work as a human rights activist is the touchstone for my own.

I also owe my deepest gratitude to a French family in Switzerland: Christian Marc, his wife, Anne, and their three wonderful daughters, Clara, Julie and Karen. Without the support of Christian, this book would not have been possible. He was the rock that stood by me through thick and thin.

Lastly, a book is never complete without the work of its editors, and my book has been fortunate to enjoy the editorial attention of some of the best in business. James N. Powell was the first to edit the book. The real magic, however, was created by Carl A Harte. He combined countless hours of hard work with his immense talent to make this mammoth project possible.

I would also like to thank Debasri Rakshit, who gave me the opportunity to publish my book with one of the most prestigious names in book publishing. Shantanu Ray Chaudhuri's insights have been crucial in the making of this book. Joseph Antony, who burnt the midnight oil in editing and refining the writing, deserves the utmost thanks. My thanks also to Bonita Shimray, Shreya Punj, Gokul Kumar and Sameer Mahale of HarperCollins India.

I thank Florence Olara, Swarnjit Singh, Father George Plathottam, Father Ramesh Matta, Bhavna Pawar, my parents Tarsem Lal and Madhur Bhashini, my sister Ishanu, brother Jai Eesh for supporting me in this venture.